W9-BAO-222

After the Trade Is Made

Processing Securities Transactions

Second Edition

David M. Weiss

NEW YORK INSTITUTE OF FINANCE

NEW YORK • TORONTO • SYDNEY • TOKYO • SINGAPORE

Library of Congress Cataloging-in-Publication Data

Weiss, David M.
After the trade is made : processing securities transactions / David M. Weiss.—2nd ed.
p. cm.
Includes index.
ISBN 0-13-177601-0
1. Stock-exchange—United States. 2. Securities—United States. 3. Commodity exchanges—United States. I. Title.
HG4910.W365 1993 93-25716
332.64'273—dc20 CIP

Printed in the United States of America

10 9 8 7 6

This publication is designed to provide accurate and authoritative information in regard to the subject matter covered. It is sold with the understanding that the publisher is not engaged in rendering legal, accounting, or other professional service. If legal advice or other expert assistance is required, the services of a competent professional person should be sought.
—From the Declaration of Principles jointly adopted by a Committee of the American Bar Association and a Committee of Publishers and Associations

ISBN 0-13-177601-0

NEW YORK INSTITUTE OF FINANCE
Paramus, NJ 07652

A Simon & Schuster Company

On the World Wide Web at http://www.phdirect.com

Prentice-Hall International (UK) Limited, *London*
Prentice-Hall of Australia Pty. Limited, *Sydney*
Prentice-Hall Canada Inc., *Toronto*
Prentice-Hall Hispanoamericana, S.A., *Mexico*
Prentice-Hall of India Private Limited, *New Delhi*
Prentice-Hall of Japan, Inc., *Tokyo*
Simon & Schuster Asia Pte. Ltd., *Singapore*
Editora Prentice-Hall do Brasil, Ltda., *Rio de Janeiro*

To my world—
Marcia, Randi, and Craig.

To the securities industry—
which, by investing time and patience,
gave me the opportunity to acquire knowledge.
This book is the return on that cherished investment.

Contents

Preface, xi

PART I
THE MULTIFACETED SECURITIES INDUSTRY, 1

1
Underwritings: The Birth of a Security, 3

2
Other Types of Underwritings, 16

3
The Over-the-Counter (OTC) Market, 25

4
The Exchanges, 35

PART II
OPERATIONS: AN OVERVIEW, 49

5
Operations: A Comparison, 51

6
Order Room, 55

7
Purchase and Sales (P & S), 64

8
Margin, 73

9
Cashiering, 89

10
Stock Record, 96

11
Accounting: The Daily Cash Record, 101

12
Dividend, 109

13
Proxy, 117

14
New Accounts, 120

15
Compliance, 128

16
Electronic Data Processing (EDP), 133

17
The Role of Banks, 145

PART III
TYPES OF SECURITIES, 153

18
Corporate Securities, 155

19
Common Stock, 157

20
Preferred Stocks, 163

21
Corporate Bonds and Notes, 172

22
Rights and Warrants, 186

23
Municipal Bonds and Notes, 194

24
U.S. Treasury Bills, Notes, and Bonds, 208

25
Asset-Backed Securities, 213

26
Commercial Paper, 222

27

Banker's Acceptances (BAs), 226

28

Certificates of Deposit (CDs), 228

29

Mutual Funds, 230

30

Options, 235

31

Futures, 241

32

Swaps, 245

33

Currency, 251

PART IV

OPERATIONS PROCEDURES, 257

34

Order Room, 259

35

OTC and Exchange Facilities, 274

36

Purchase and Sales, 288

37

Margin, 330

38
Cashiering, 355

39
Accounting, 377

40
Stock Record, 388

41
Dividend, 397

42
Proxy, 403

43
New Accounts (Name and Address), 406

PART V
THE BANK-BROKERAGE FIRM RELATIONSHIP, 421

44
The Commercial Bank as a Source of Financing, 423

45
The Commerical Bank as Underwriter, 429

46
The Commercial Bank as Issuer of Commercial Loans and Paper, 431

47
The Commercial Bank's Role in International Trade, 436

48
The Commercial Bank and Cashiering Services, 438

49
The Commercial Bank as Dividend Disbursing Agent (DDA), 443

50
The Commercial Bank as Customer of the Brokerage Firm, 448

PART VI
Foreign Markets, 451

51
International Settlement, 453

Glossary, 464

Index, 490

Preface

The security industry is ever changing to suit the needs of its many participants. As new products are developed to better respond to participants' needs, so do the processes used to deliver these products. In turn, as the processes change, so does the industry.

Since the first edition of this book was published, other forces have also had a dramatic effect on the way we process transactions. First, we have seen a globalization of the market place. Fostered by such efforts as the Group of Thirty to standardize operations, a need arose for commonality in processing and settlement in cross-border transactions.

Second, technological improvements in the speed and ease of data dissemination enables participants to reduce trading market exposure through faster settlement cycles—at affordable costs.

The combination of these three factors—new products, globalization, and technological improvements—has changed the environment enough to require the updating of this book.

This new edition attempts to capture the salient developments. For example, the pages devoted to derivative products have been expanded. In addition, sections on the futures market have also been included. Each passing year seems to make the futures and securities markets more homogeneous. As with the futures, cross-border transactions are becoming more common. The book provides a look at some foreign markets, their methods of trading, and the settlement of securities.

Even with all its changes, the core of operations remains the same. Its functions still range from seeing to the accurate execution of customer orders, through their comparison and settlement, and ensuring that client accounts are operating within established requirements. Finally, the book explains the need for, and an understanding of, accurate recording of all such entries.

The industry is an interesting collage—highly regulated, yet highly flexible in its ability to adapt to new products and processes.

This book reviews the operational functions of a typical brokerage firm. It describes the relationships of operations departments within the firm, as well as with outside entities such as commercial banks, transfer agents, clearing corporations, and depositories. It also attempts to clarify the role of operations as a support to sales.

In short, the book explains what happens after a client enters the order with the firm's representatives. It shows how that order becomes part of a huge flow of data that the firm must control. Its purpose is to explain what happens *After the Trade Is Made.*

As with all such efforts, there must be a beginning. That beginning is how securities and other issues come to market. Pages are also devoted to explaining the various types of products that are offered.

My hope is that this book will not only inform you, but also heighten your appreciation of the many conscientious people who every day do their part in making this industry a success.

David M. Weiss

PART I

THE MULTIFACETED SECURITIES INDUSTRY

CHAPTER 1

Underwritings: The Birth of a Security

- Where do securities originate?
- How are they issued?
- Why are they issued?
- Which types of securities are issued?
- When do they come to the market?
- Who brings them to the market?

This chapter answers these questions by explaining the various forms of *underwriting,* which is the process by which securities are first brought to the market.

THE REASON FOR SECURITIES

Before you can understand underwriting, you must have a grasp of the private business sector of our economy. The United States of America is one of the top producers in the world. All of this country's products, which run the gamut of manufactured items, are turned out by companies that are owned not by the government, but by individuals. From the titan corporations to the smallest one-person firms, people—the "you and me" of this great country—are the owners.

There are three primary forms of business ownership:

1. The Proprietorship.
2. The Partnership.
3. The Corporation.

The Proprietorship (Sole or Individual Proprietorship)

The *proprietorship* is the simplest form of business. The only formal document needed to start this type of business is, sometimes, a license. One person owns the business and runs it—the owner/operator, or *proprietor*, who does not share the ownership or responsibilities. Responsibility may be delegated but not truly shared.

In this type of business, the proprietor risks his or her money in the enterprise, with the expectation of deriving income and of accumulating wealth. The proprietor is typically the only one to invest in the business. If anyone else invests in the business, the "investment" has to take the form of a loan, with the understanding that the principal will be paid back at some time in the future.

If the business prospers, the owner reaps all the rewards. Any others who loaned money to the business are paid back with interest, and their involvement in the enterprise ends there.

If the business fails, the loss can devastate the owner. At risk is not only the money invested in the business, but also the proprietor's home, car, furniture, and all other possessions of value. The result can very well be personal bankruptcy.

The Partnership

If the individual decides to share the responsibility of running the business, other individuals may be permitted to "buy into the business." This arrangement changes the form of business from a proprietorship to a *partnership*, a business form in which two or more persons own and/or operate the business. The partners must draw up and agree upon a formal *partnership agreement.* Profits earned by the partnership are distributed among all the partners in accordance with this agreement, as are losses. If and when losses become too great, then the creditors of the partnership may attempt to collect from all the partners collectively. As in the case of the proprietorship, creditors can claim the personal belongings of the partners to satisfy the obligation. If the losses are great enough, the partners could lose all their personal wealth.

Partners who share in management decisions are known as *general partners.* Occasionally, however, an individual wants to invest in a partnership but does not want to risk all of his or her assets. This individual can be designated in the agreement as a *limited partner.* Although limited partners may work for the partnership, they cannot have any voice in management or make a policy decision on behalf of the partnership.

Besides general and limited types of partners, there is the *silent partner,* an individual who wishes to invest in the partnership but does not want the involvement known. Usually this is strictly a monetary arrangement, and the individual does not take an active role in the partnership.

The Corporation

The proprietorship and the partnership face two problems:

First, *the ability to raise capital is directly related to the participating individuals.* Banks and other would-be lenders are cognizant of this shortcoming. In the case of the sole proprietorship, the money is lent to the individual, not to the business. So lenders must be concerned about such things as the death or illness of the individual. The same is basically true of the partnership: Money is lent to the partners, and the ability to repay the loan is that of the individual partners. Upon the demise of one of the partners, a new partnership must be formed. In the eyes of potential lenders, the new partnership could be far less able than the original one to repay the loan.

Secondly, *terminating the investment can be a very complicated procedure.* All loans attributed to the proprietor or partners must be repaid or assigned to another with the permission of the lender. To disengage from a proprietorship, the owner must find someone to buy the business. The price must be negotiated, and the selling process can take a long time. In a partnership, the partner who wants out may have to find a replacement upon whom the remaining partners can agree, if the partners are not able or willing to purchase the selling partner's portion.

A business form had to be created, under the law, to avoid these pitfalls. This need gave rise to a form of business called a *corporation.* Under the law, a corporation is a person. It can sue and be sued. It pays income taxes. Its existence continues, despite changes of ownership.

To own a part of a corporation, an individual simply buys the company's *stock* through a broker. The stock certificate represents not a loan to the corporation but rather an interest in the company's worth. As the worth of the company rises, so does the value of the stock; if it declines, so does the stock.

This form of ownership offers several benefits. For one, the life of the business is separate and apart from those of the owners, whose involvement is purely monetary. The business may "live on," even if one or more of its owners should die. Second, the risk of the owners is limited. Should the corporation fail, creditors may claim only the assets of the company itself, not the assets of the individual owners. All that the owners can lose is the amount they paid for the stock. The third advantage is that ownership may be easily transferred by the buying and selling of the corporation's stock.

A corporation's stock may be privately or publicly held. *Privately held corporations* are usually small firms that require limited capital or that are newly formed. Their stock is owned by a small number of people and is not traded regularly. Most major corporations, however, are owned by hundreds or thousands of people who do not work for the companies and who don't even know where the headquarters are located. These corporations, for obvious reasons, are said to be owned *publicly.* This, then, is where we can begin to explain the role of the stock market. In fact, without the corporate form of business, there could be no securities industry.

THE UNDERWRITING PROCEDURE

When a corporation first offers its stock for sale to the public, it is said to be *going public*. This is also known as an IPO—*initial public offering*. The process by which the stock is offered, or *issued*, is called an *underwriting*.

Choosing the Investment Banker

Before the underwriting process may begin, the issuing corporation must locate and choose an "investment banker," a name that is a little misleading. An *investment banker* is usually a brokerage firm, not a bank, that is in touch with the markets for the public's receptivity to the various types of securities.

The investment banker can advise the management of the issuing corporation as to which type of security should be issued:

1. If *common stock* is issued, the ownership of the corporation is shared by a great number of stockholders, and the former private owners will see their percentage of ownership diluted. (Common stock is generally what people mean when they say "stock.")
2. By issuing debt securities, or *bonds*, the corporation incurs the obligation of paying back not only the money borrowed at some time in the future, but also interest every year. If management is unable to meet the interest obligation, the bondholders, who are creditors (not owners), may foreclose on the company.
3. By issuing *preferred stock*, the corporation offers a form of ownership similar to common stock. Preferred stockholders do not have any vote for management or on key issues, but they do receive dividends before the common stockholders receive theirs.

Because the terms and the class of security are discussed between the issuing corporation and investment banker, this type of underwriting is referred to as a *negotiated underwriting*.

The Syndicate

Now the underwriting process itself may begin. The investment banker forms what is called the *syndicate* (or *underwriting group*), which is a group of brokerage firms that will guarantee, or underwrite, the sale of the new issue.

The first ordering of business for the group is to draw up a preliminary prospectus, known as a *red herring,* and a registration statement.

The *preliminary prospectus* is a booklet that contains information regarding the new issue, the issuing corporation, its management, as well as other important aspects of the corporation such as its products, subsidiaries, and the like. (See Figure 1-1.) The preliminary prospectus may be shown by brokerage firms to their customers, only at the request of the customer. Broker/dealers may accept from customers what are called *indications of interest,* which they will try to "fill" when and if the issue is actually offered.

The preliminary prospectus is actually a draft version of the final prospectus. It contains a legend, printed in red along the inside border of the cover, which is the red herring. This legend warns against the offering or selling of this unregistered security to the public.

Missing from this preliminary document are the offering price, the coupon or interest rate of debt instruments (sometimes), and, inside, the list of other underwriters participating in the offering. These facts are either unknown at the printing of the preliminary prospectus or subject to change by the final printing. The *final* prospectus contains all of this missing information. (See Figure 1-2).

Under the 1933 Truth in Security Act, all issues (as well as certain other forms of securities) of corporations involving interstate ownership must be registered with the Securities and Exchange Commission (SEC). The *registration statement* is the document by which the issue is registered. It contains the preliminary prospectus plus additional information that will be needed to register this offering.

The SEC reviews the subject matter in the registration statement to insure that proper disclosure standards are met. If the SEC is satisfied that all the facts are fairly represented, it allows the issue to be offered. If, on the other hand, it determines that the prospectus could be or is misleading, the SEC issues a stop order thereby delaying the pending offering. The SEC, however, does

FIGURE 1-1. *The preliminary prospectus.*

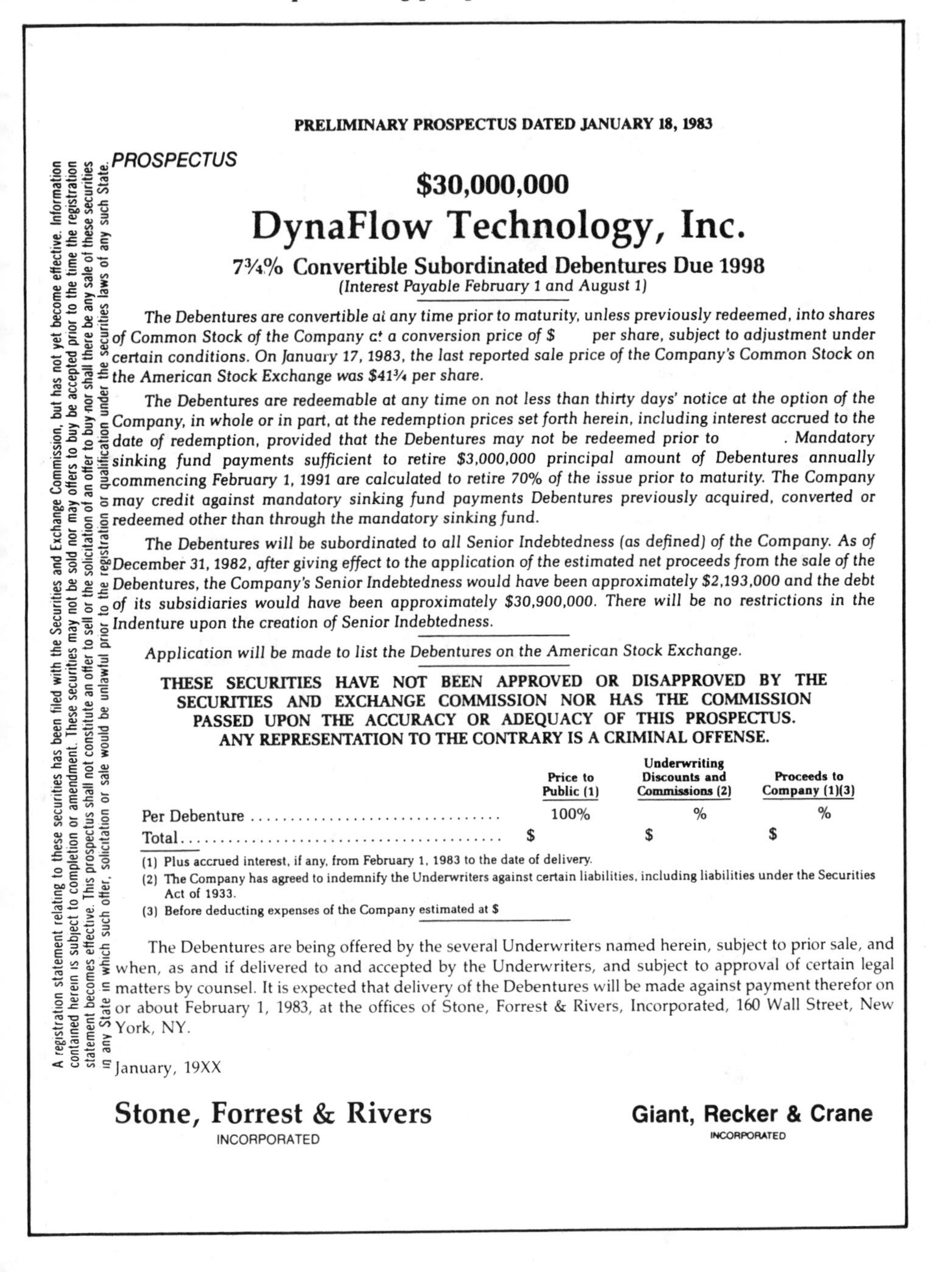

PRELIMINARY PROSPECTUS DATED JANUARY 18, 1983

A registration statement relating to these securities has been filed with the Securities and Exchange Commission, but has not yet become effective. Information contained herein is subject to completion or amendment. These securities may not be sold nor may offers to buy be accepted prior to the time the registration statement becomes effective. This prospectus shall not constitute an offer to sell or the solicitation of an offer to buy nor shall there be any sale of these securities in any State in which such offer, solicitation or sale would be unlawful prior to the registration or qualification under the securities laws of any such State.

PROSPECTUS

$30,000,000

DynaFlow Technology, Inc.

7¾% Convertible Subordinated Debentures Due 1998

(Interest Payable February 1 and August 1)

The Debentures are convertible at any time prior to maturity, unless previously redeemed, into shares of Common Stock of the Company at a conversion price of $ per share, subject to adjustment under certain conditions. On January 17, 1983, the last reported sale price of the Company's Common Stock on the American Stock Exchange was $41¾ per share.

The Debentures are redeemable at any time on not less than thirty days' notice at the option of the Company, in whole or in part, at the redemption prices set forth herein, including interest accrued to the date of redemption, provided that the Debentures may not be redeemed prior to . Mandatory sinking fund payments sufficient to retire $3,000,000 principal amount of Debentures annually commencing February 1, 1991 are calculated to retire 70% of the issue prior to maturity. The Company may credit against mandatory sinking fund payments Debentures previously acquired, converted or redeemed other than through the mandatory sinking fund.

The Debentures will be subordinated to all Senior Indebtedness (as defined) of the Company. As of December 31, 1982, after giving effect to the application of the estimated net proceeds from the sale of the Debentures, the Company's Senior Indebtedness would have been approximately $2,193,000 and the debt of its subsidiaries would have been approximately $30,900,000. There will be no restrictions in the Indenture upon the creation of Senior Indebtedness.

Application will be made to list the Debentures on the American Stock Exchange.

THESE SECURITIES HAVE NOT BEEN APPROVED OR DISAPPROVED BY THE SECURITIES AND EXCHANGE COMMISSION NOR HAS THE COMMISSION PASSED UPON THE ACCURACY OR ADEQUACY OF THIS PROSPECTUS. ANY REPRESENTATION TO THE CONTRARY IS A CRIMINAL OFFENSE.

	Price to Public (1)	Underwriting Discounts and Commissions (2)	Proceeds to Company (1)(3)
Per Debenture	100%	%	%
Total	$	$	$

(1) Plus accrued interest, if any, from February 1, 1983 to the date of delivery.
(2) The Company has agreed to indemnify the Underwriters against certain liabilities, including liabilities under the Securities Act of 1933.
(3) Before deducting expenses of the Company estimated at $

The Debentures are being offered by the several Underwriters named herein, subject to prior sale, and when, as and if delivered to and accepted by the Underwriters, and subject to approval of certain legal matters by counsel. It is expected that delivery of the Debentures will be made against payment therefor on or about February 1, 1983, at the offices of Stone, Forrest & Rivers, Incorporated, 160 Wall Street, New York, NY.

January, 19XX

Stone, Forrest & Rivers
INCORPORATED

Giant, Recker & Crane
INCORPORATED

FIGURE 1-2. *The final prospectus.*

PROSPECTUS

$75,000,000

DynaFlow Technology, Inc.

7¾% Convertible Subordinated Debentures Due 1998

(Interest Payable February 1 and August 1)

The Debentures are convertible at any time prior to maturity, unless previously redeemed, into shares of Common Stock of the Company at a conversion price of $46.43 per share, subject to adjustment under certain conditions. On January 26, 1983, the last reported sale price of the Company's Common Stock on the American Stock Exchange was $40⅜ per share.

The Debentures are redeemable at any time on not less than thirty days' notice at the option of the Company, in whole or in part, at the redemption prices set forth herein, including interest accrued to the date of redemption, provided that the Debentures may not be redeemed prior to February 1, 1985, unless prior to the mailing of the notice of redemption the price of the Company's Common Stock has been at least 150% of the conversion price for 30 successive trading days. Mandatory sinking fund payments sufficient to retire $7,500,000 principal amount of Debentures annually commencing February 1, 1991 are calculated to retire 70% of the issue prior to maturity. The Company may credit against mandatory sinking fund payments Debentures previously acquired, converted or redeemed other than through the mandatory sinking fund.

The Debentures will be subordinated to all Senior Indebtedness (as defined) of the Company. As of December 31, 1982, after giving effect to the application of the estimated net proceeds from the sale of the Debentures, the Company's Senior Indebtedness would have been approximately $2,193,000. There will be no restrictions in the Indenture upon the creation of Senior Indebtedness.

Application will be made to list the Debentures on the American Stock Exchange.

THESE SECURITIES HAVE NOT BEEN APPROVED OR DISAPPROVED BY THE SECURITIES AND EXCHANGE COMMISSION NOR HAS THE COMMISSION PASSED UPON THE ACCURACY OR ADEQUACY OF THIS PROSPECTUS. ANY REPRESENTATION TO THE CONTRARY IS A CRIMINAL OFFENSE.

	Price to Public (1)	Underwriting Discounts and Commissions (2)	Proceeds to Company (1)(3)
Per Debenture	100%	2.75%	97.25%
Total	$75,000,000	$2,062,500	$72,937,500

(1) Plus accrued interest, if any, from February 1, 1983 to the date of delivery.
(2) The Company has agreed to indemnify the Underwriters against certain liabilities, including liabilities under the Securities Act of 1933.
(3) Before deducting expenses of the Company estimated at $260,000.

The Debentures are being offered by the several Underwriters named herein, subject to prior sale, and when, as and if delivered to and accepted by the Underwriters, and subject to approval of certain legal matters by counsel. It is expected that delivery of the Debentures will be made against payment therefor on or about February 3, 1983, at the offices of **Stone, Forrest & Rivers**
160 Wall Street
New York, NY 10041

Stone, Forrest & Rivers
INCORPORATED

Giant, Recker & Crane

not guarantee either that the issue is free of fraud or that it will be profitable. The 1933 Act therefore provides that the SEC cannot be sued for any omission or misrepresentation of material fact, because its role is that of overseer, not participant. On the other hand, the issuing corporation, its board of directors, the investment banker, the members of the underwriting group, the independent accounting firm used by the corporation, and anyone else whose name appears in the prospectus may be held civilly liable.

The Cooling-Off Period

During the period that the SEC uses to review the registration statement, known as the *cooling-off period*, several things are getting done.

For one, the underwriting (or syndicate) manager completes the forming of the underwriting group. The underwriters participating in the group have to pay the corporation an agreed-upon sum for the underwriting. In turn, they hope to offer the securities to the public at a higher price, thereby earning a profit. If their judgment is incorrect, they will incur a loss. So the various underwriting firms review the preliminary prospectus to determine if they want to be part of the underwriting. Among the questions that must be answered are: Does the security being sold fit into the firm's marketing plans? Is it salable?

With the underwriting group formed, other firms are often invited to participate in the *selling group*. The firms in this group, although not part of the syndicate, help the syndicate to sell, or *distribute*, the issue. Since their risk is less than that of the underwriters, so is their profit.

At the same time, the underwriting manager is also busy having the new issue approved for sale in all the individual states. (A new issue may not be sold to residents of a state unless the state has approved the offering.) This process is known as *blue skying the issue*. As each state government approves the new issue, the issue is said to be "blue skied" in that state.

Finally, during the cooling-off-period, the officials of the corporation, the members of the underwriting group, and the other participants gather for a final meeting, known as the *Due*

Diligence meeting. At this meeting, the prospectus is reviewed for accuracy, and the terms of the underwriting are reaffirmed. Everything must be correct and in place, because this is the last time the participants will congregate to discuss this new offering.

Approximately twenty days after the registration statement is filed, the SEC either allows the issue to be offered or delays it. Assuming all goes well and the SEC allows the underwriting to proceed, the twentieth day becomes an *effective date*. It is the first date that the issue can be offered to the public.

Distributing the Security

Either on or soon after the effective date is the *public offering date,* which is the date on which sales actually begin. The selling group members begin to sell the security to their respective customers. (Some of these customers have read about the underwriting in the preliminary prospectus; others are informed by phone on the offering date as they discuss it with their stockbrokers.) The brokerage firms try to fill their customers' indications of interest. Usually, however, the requests are only partially filled, and some customers may not receive any at all, because the limited supply of the new issue is not equal to the demand of the customers.

If the demand for the new issue is greater than the supply, the distribution is called a *hot issue*. In the case of a hot issue, the price of the new issue in the aftermarket (or over-the-counter market) typically rises to a *premium* (a price higher than the offering price), and this increase neutralizes the supply-and-demand imbalance.

Stabilizing the Market

Some issues are not so hot. When the security is not selling as well as the underwriters, would like, it is referred to as a *weak issue*. In such a case, the manager places a syndicate bid for the security with an over-the-counter (OTC) market maker. (We will say more about OTC transactions and market makers later.) The *bid* is to buy the security at or slightly below the offering price of the issue; it cannot be higher.

What good does the bid do? Brokerage firm customers who buy the issue might be tempted to sell it right away—that is, *dump* or flip it—if they see that its price is dropping in the market. A rush to resell the issue right after the offering would just about kill the underwriters' chances of fully distributing the issue. On the other hand, if they see that there is a bid in the market at or only slightly below the offering price, they are more likely to hold onto the issue.

The syndicate bid may seem like a form of market manipulation, but it is permissible in these circumstances. The procedure is called *stabilizing the market.*

As an additional safeguard against the quick resale of the security, the National Association of Securities Dealers (NASD) has a rule that brokerage firms must distribute securities to customers according to their *investment habits.* They must avoid, in other words, selling the issue to speculators, who would trade the security within days, not holding onto them for investment purposes. If a syndicate member's customer does resell the security right after the offering date, the security is going to wind up with the syndicate manager, who is maintaining the bid. In that case, the manager can take back the selling concession on the security from the selling brokerage firm and eventually resell the security.

AN EXAMPLE OF A NEGOTIATED UNDERWRITING

To illustrate the negotiated underwriting process, let's create fictitious firms: A & Co. is the managing underwriting, B Securities, Inc. is one of the five members of the underwriting group. C&C Partnership is one of ten members of the selling group. The corporation issuing the new security is the XYZ Corporation.

The XYZ Corporation, a very successful company, now wishes to raise $8 million. Management calls their investment advisor A & Co. to discuss the pending offering. A & Co., after reviewing the corporation and the current market, advises the management of XYZ to issue one million shares of XYZ common stock. XYZ management agrees.

A preliminary prospectus is printed, and a registration statement is prepared and filed with the SEC. During the cooling-off period, A & Co. begins to form the underwriting group by sending copies of the preliminary prospectus to underwriters, including B securities, Inc. A & Co. assumes the responsibilities of syndicate manager. Other brokerage firms, including C&C Partnership, are invited to participate in selling or distributing the new issue.

The underwriting group and the manager meet with the issuing corporation at the Due Diligence meeting to discuss the prospectus. The price of the 1,000,000-share offering is set at $10 per share. The syndicate pays the corporation $8 per share and offers it to the public for $10. The $2 difference is known as the *spread*. This profit is divided among the underwriters and members of the selling group, according to a prearranged formula.

The members of the underwriting group also place some of the shares at the disposal of the selling group. In our example, the underwriting group has agreed to place half of the underwritten shares (500,000) into a *pot*. Shares in the pot are distributed among the selling group members. For each share sold by a selling group firm, the underwriting firm receives $.25. The selling group member gets $1.50.

1. A & Co. receives $.25 on every share of the issue for being the syndicate manager. It also underwrites 200,000 shares, half of which it passes on to members of a selling group; for each of these 200,000 shares, it gets an additional $.25. Finally, it sells the remaining 100,000 shares, with a *selling concession* per share of $1.50. A & Co.'s earnings are as follows:

Management fee ($.25 × 1,000,000 shares)	$250,000
Underwriting fee ($.25 × 200,000 shares)	50,000
Selling concession ($1.50 × 100,000 shares)	150,000
	$450,000

2. B Securities receives $.25 for every share in its portion of the issue that it underwrites. In this case, it underwrites 200,000 shares. It also receives the $1.50 selling concession for each share it sells; the firm sells 100,000 and gives 100,000 to C&C Partnership to sell.

Underwriting fee ($.25 × 200,000 shares)	$ 50,000
Selling concession ($1.50 × 100,000 shares)	150,000
	$200,000

3. C&C Partnership, a selling group member, sells (or distributes) 100,000 shares to its customers, getting $1.50 for each share sold. (Don't forget: The manager has taken out a quarter per share and the underwriter has taken a quarter per share.)

Selling concession ($1.50 × 100,000 shares) $150,000

Underwriting appears to be an easy way to earn money, but don't overlook certain facts. The XYZ Corporation received $8,000,000 from the underwriting group. The group's capital is at risk. The firms involved will not be repaid entirely until all the customers have paid for their purchases. In the interim, the firms must borrow money and pay interest on the loan. Also, if the issue cannot be sold at $10 per share, the participants will not earn the anticipated profits. As a matter of fact, they may very well incur a loss. Finally, the issue is ultimately sold to the customers of the underwriting firms. These customers represent a part of the brokerage firms' source of revenue, which permits the firms to stay in business. If this underwriting and possibly other underwritings prove to be bad investments, the firm will eventually lose its customers and the revenue they represent.

CHAPTER 2

Other Types of Underwritings

In the last chapter, we saw how a corporation issues securities to the public through a formal procedure known as a "negotiated underwriting." In this chapter, we will explain more about security issuance, not only by the corporation, but also by the various forms of government and their respective agencies.

THE ISSUANCE OF SECURITIES BY THE CORPORATION

The *private sector* (defined as those establishments that are owned by individuals) includes the sole proprietorship, the partnership, and the publicly or privately owned corporation. The corporate charter and bylaws contain all the rules that govern the individual corporation. The charter is issued by state, which is known as the *state of incorporation*. Some states are very strict, others very lenient, as to the flexibility allowed corporations under these charters.

Of the three forms of business, only the corporation is considered a legal "person" under law. As such, it raises money in two ways:

- It can issue (that is sell) shares of ownership of itself, known as "common" or "preferred" stock.
- It can incur debt (that is, take out loans) through the issuance of "bonds."

Because the corporation is able to issue these different types of securities—stocks and bonds—this form of business became a major part of the security industry.

Preemptive Right

A corporation may issue additional common stock as it sees fit. When it does so, of course, it increases the number of shares in circulation and decreases the percentage of ownership for each current shareholder. The reason: The percentage of ownership is directly related to the total number of shares the company has outstanding.

Example: Let's say that you own 10,000 shares of a corporation with 1,000,000 shares outstanding. You own 1% of the corporation. If the corporation decides to issue an additional 1,000,000 shares of common stock to raise more capital, you would wake up one morning to discover that you now own only .5% of the company (10,000 shares ÷ 2,000,000).

Some charters, therefore, contain a clause by which current common stockholders *must* be given the opportunity to maintain their percentage of ownership in the corporation before additional common stock can be issued to others. The privilege is known as *preemptive right.* Corporations whose charters contain this preemptive right must first offer the additional issue of common stock to current common stockholders before they can offer them to the public. Such a clause protects the common stockholder, as an owner in the corporation, by preventing dilution of ownership.

Under the preemptive right feature, a common stockholder receives one *right* for each share of common stock owned. Given these rights, the individual has the privilege to *subscribe to*—that is, purchase—the new security at the subscription price per share.

Example: You own 100 shares of stock. The corporation currently has 1,000,000 shares outstanding. Your percentage of ownership is .01% (100 ÷ 1,000,000). The management decides to issue an additional 100,000 shares. Because you own 100 shares, you receive 100 rights. To maintain your percentage of ownership, you need only 10 shares. In other words, you would purchase 10 more shares (110 ÷ 1,100,000 = .01% ownership). If you choose to subscribe, you submit all your 100 rights plus the money needed for the purchase of 10 additional shares.

Rights as Securities

During the period that the rights offering is effective, the existing common stock issue (those shares with rights) is referred to as *old,* and the forthcoming issue (those shares without rights) is called *new.* After the rights offer expires, *all* the common stock is the same. The old and new designations cease.

The reason for the distinction is that each share of old stock contains a right and is therefore worth more than the new. In other words, the right, because it is the only difference between the new and the old, embodies the additional value. Inasmuch as the rights usually have value, they can be bought and sold. They are therefore traded by the customers of brokerage firms.

Other Types of Underwritings

In addition to a negotiated underwriting, standby and best efforts agreements are two other ways for the corporation to successfully issue new securities. For either type of agreement, the formal registration statement and the remaining portions of the formal underwriting have already been satisfied. The underwriters are generally acting as sale conduits for the new issue.

Standby Underwriting. Occasionally, the management of the corporation is not certain that the new rights offering will be 100% successful. If it is not, then many rights may expire, due to a lack of interest in the subscription among current stockholders and the public. In such a situation, the company would not be able to raise the money it needs. To prevent this from happening, the corporation may ask an investment banker to enter into a "standby" underwriting.

In a *standby underwriting*, the investment banker "stands by," ready to acquire all available rights that are not used in subscription. The underwriter buys up all the rights not used by old shareholders and, with the rights and a check for the subscription cost, subscribes to whatever is left of the additional security. The underwriter then sells the new issue to the public. The selling of the new issue is called a *layoff*, or *laying off the new issue*.

Best Efforts Underwriting. In a *best efforts underwriting*, an underwriter agrees to participate in the issuance only for the amount that it can place (that is, sell). The underwriter is not responsible for the remainder. This type of underwriting is employed usually when most of the "deal" has been sold and the corporation needs assistance with placing the remaining portion. The underwriter attempts to sell the remaining issue; if it is unsuccessful, it incurs no obligation and may return the unsold portion.

All-or-None. In a best efforts underwriting, the corporation may demand an *all-or-none* feature, which simply states that the underwriter is responsible for the portion of the offering that it has agreed to sell. The underwriter must sell all of its portion or it may have none of it to sell.

While the best efforts and the all-or-none definitions may appear to contradict each other, they simply neutralize each other. An underwriter agreeing to a best efforts underwriting with an all-or-none feature estimates sales more conservatively: It *has* to sell the portion of the issue that it takes. As a result, the corporation knows almost immediately how successful the new issue is going to be—rather than discovering that its plan for additional capital are only partially filled due to the public's unwillingness to accept the new issue.

THE ISSUANCE OF SECURITIES BY MUNICIPALITIES

Because states, cities, and other local governments, generally referred to as *municipalities*, must raise money or funds for various purposes, they are constantly coming to market to raise money. Governments, however, cannot issue shares of stock (that is, share of ownership) because they already belong to the people. Instead, they must borrow money in return for which they issue not stocks but *notes and bonds*. The value of these bonds depends on the government's ability to pay back the loan with interest, which in turn depends on their ability to generate income through taxes, fees, tolls, and the like. Revenue generated through this taxing ability pays government workers' salaries and expenses, thereby keeping the municipality running. The revenue also pays the interest on bonds during the *term* (that is, the life or maturity) of the loan and eventually the *principal* (or the amount borrowed) at the end of the term.

Competitive Underwriting

To make certain that the municipality obtains the best possible terms for borrowing, it utilizes a form of agreement known as *competitive bidding* or *competitive underwriting*. In this procedure, a number of underwriting managers submit bids to the municipality. In a bond offering, the bid includes a price and interest for the issue for each of various maturities. The manager that submits the most favorable terms is awarded the underwriting; gaining the award is usually referred to as *winning the bid*. (Some corporations may, and do, use competitive bidding when issuing bonds.)

The Bidding Procedure. Once invited to submit a bid, the underwriting manager and the potential underwriters gather to discuss the terms of the issue, which may be bonds and/or notes. (The underwriters usually know which issue it's going to be.) The group prepares a bid based on current market conditions, the financial stability of the municipality, and other factors. Members of the group submit their thoughts. The manager reviews all the recommendations and then renders a collective bid. If the bid is accepted, the group wins the bid. The other competitive groups lose.

On occasion, a participating underwriting may choose to drop out of the underwriting, usually because the bid submitted by the manager and accepted by the issuer is too "rich" (that is, too high) for the member's clients to accept. Rather than risk being unable to sell the offering, the member drops out.

Comparison of Competitive and Negotiated Agreements

Both the negotiated and competitive forms of underwriting are formal. Both require the formation of a syndicate, formal registration with the Security Exchange Commission (except in the case of some types of municipal bonds, which are exempt from registration), due diligence meetings, and so on. Standby and best efforts agreements, when they are formed to assist in an issuance of securities, render many of these formal steps unnecessary.

ISSUANCE OF SECURITIES BY THE US GOVERNMENT

U.S. Treasury Securities

U.S. Government securities are actually U.S. Treasury obligations. They are issued under the direction of the Federal Reserve Board, which is responsible for implementing monetary policy and controlling the direction of our economy. (How the "Fed" does so is explained in a later chapter.)

The United States (or Fed) issues its securities differently from corporations or municipalities. Because of the usual heavy demand for government securities, very little sales effort is needed for a successful distribution. When the Fed issues Treasury bills, notes, or bonds, various *government dealers* bid for the issue. Usually, an individual dealer does not have the financial ability to absorb an entire issue. So the Federal Reserve begins by accepting the highest bid and descends through the multitude of bids until the supply of debt instruments being offered meets the demand, that is, until the entire issue is sold. At this level, the new issue is brought out. Dealers that bid a high enough price receive the issue; those that bid too low lose the opportunity to participate.

The public can also purchase Treasury bills, notes, and

bonds directly from the Fed. At the time of issuance, the public's bids are filled at the average issuance price bid by the dealers. The public bidders, however, do not participate with the dealers, and they therefore have no effect on the offering. Because the government dealers' bids are ranked in descending order, it is a *pure auction.* The public orders, however, are filled at a weighted average price; this is a *Dutch auction.*

Government Agency Obligations

Securities are also issued by agencies of the Federal government such as the Federal National Mortgage Association (FNMA, or "Fannie Mae"). These securities are sold at face values less a selling *concession* (or commission) to the dealers.

Example: A $100,000 obligation of the Federal Land Bank (FLB) with 1/4 of a point selling concession ($250) is sold to the dealer for $99,750 ($100,000 – $250). The dealer, in turn, sells it to the public for $100,000. The difference, or profit, is the selling concession (which enables the participating brokerage firms operating to pay salaries and keep their employees).

THE ISSUANCE OF SECURITIES BY MUTUAL FUNDS

A *mutual fund* is a pool of money used to achieve a specific investment goal. The public buys shares of the fund (a corporation), and the fund buys the desired securities. The public, through these fund shares, participates in all of the securities that the fund purchases.

Example: You want to purchase 100 shares of stock. You are interested in income-producing securities (securities that pay large dividends in relation to their selling price). Yet the amount of money that you have to invest is limited. You can purchase only 100 shares of Security A or 100 shares of Security B—or 100 shares of one of five hundred securities that look attractive! Yet you can invest in only 100 shares.

Let's say you pick a stock and invest all your money in it. If anything happens to adversely affect the company you selected, the income (dividend), or even your entire investment, may be severely reduced. If, on the other hand, you purchase 100 shares of a mutual fund, you automatically own a portion of every income security that the fund has in its portfolio. If the fund is large enough, it may include in its portfolio all 500 of the securities that you think are good income-producing (dividend-paying) securities.

Getting Funds Shares to the Market

Mutual funds come into existence in one of two ways:

1. In a *formal offering* type of underwriting, fund shares are offered through brokerage firms.
2. In a *direct solicitation,* the fund sells its shares directly to the public, through coupon ads in newspapers, magazines, and other periodicals. Interested parties subscribe through these coupons.

Family of Funds

A *family of funds* offers a variety of mutual funds, each having a different purpose or goal. When the shares of a new member of the family are brought to market, the owners of the other family members' shares are given an opportunity to acquire shares in the new fund. This offering to current family fund owners, plus coupon advertisements, constitute a direct solicitation approach to distribution.

THE ISSUANCE OF SECURITIES BY THE PUBLIC

Options and futures trade on exchanges. They are contractual agreements between buyers and sellers. A corporation, for example, may have options traded on its common stock, yet the corporation does not derive any revenue from the option trades. Futures are traded on U.S. Treasury bonds, yet the federal government does not derive funds. Those two issues are traded among public participants.

SUMMARY

New issues are brought to market to be sold, so that the issuer can raise needed capital. The public is given the chance to acquire these new issues. Once the issuer has received the proceeds of the sale, the price of the security may fluctuate, but the issuer does not participate in these fluctuations. The issue is "out," the issuer has been paid, and now the issues "trade" freely among members of the public in the marketplace. The price of each issue is determined by many factors, but they all boil down to one fundamental: supply and demand. The difference between supply and demand determines price movement for the security.

The arena for trading is the marketplace, which we discuss in the next two chapters.

CHAPTER 3

The Over-the-Counter (OTC) Market

Once security issues come to market, the public owns them. The public invests in issues expecting financial rewards. Investors expect to profit through price fluctuations or to augment their earnings by providing additional income (dividends or interest).

LIQUIDITY

While financial reward may be the motivation for investors, their reason for investing is *liquidity*, which is the relative ease with which an investor can convert the investment into cash. In securities investments, "liquidity" translates into the ability to buy or sell the security: The greater the liquidity, the easier it is to acquire or liquidate a position. Liquidity therefore allows the public to buy or sell securities *easily*. Members of the public are willing to invest because they know they can easily rid themselves of the investment. Usually all you have to do is call your stockbroker.

Liquidity arises from the interest of the public in the securities industry. All this interest focuses on where the issues are traded (that is, bought and sold)—the marketplace, which can be divided into two categories:

1. The *over-the-counter (OTC) market.*
2. The *exchanges.*

You may turn to either of those marketplaces to buy or sell an issue or just to obtain its current market price. We will explain the over-the-counter market in this chapter and exchanges in the next chapter.

NATURE OF THE OTC MARKET

The larger of the two markets is the over-the-counter market, which is actually a telephone network among brokers and dealers. A single place for trading issues does not exist. Instead, people called *market makers* specialize in trading particular issues with brokerage firms, which buy from and sell to them. The firms receive the orders from the public. In effect, the brokers turn to the market makers to fill orders in OTC securities, just as they would go to an exchange to fill an order for a security that is "listed" on the exchange. In either the OTC or exchange market, members of the public are the firms' customers (or clients).

National Association of Securities Dealers (NASD)

Most OTC broker dealers belong to the National Association of Security Dealers (NASD). This organization is one of several that serve as the industry's own self-policing and policy-making arms. The NASD has established—and continues to update—rules, regulations, and recommended procedures that its members follow in their daily activities.

There are three sections to the NASD rules:

1. *The Rules of Fair Practice* are concerned with broker-customer procedures.
2. The *Uniform Practice Code* establishes the procedures utilized in broker-broker or broker-dealer relationships.

3. The *Business Conduct Committee* administers to grievances.

Members of the NASD must adhere to these rules and regulations. If they don't, they may face fines, suspensions, or, even worse, loss of their memberships. Losing membership in the NASD is devastating, because the ousted firm or individual is *out of business* from that point. The reason: Under the rules, members of the NASD can conduct trading business *only* with other members.

The over-the-counter market therefore operates under the rules and procedures prescribed by its governing authority, the NASD. Members agree to the conditions of membership when they join the organization. The industry can be proud of its outstanding record for honesty and fair dealings.

MARKET MAKERS

Let's pick up a new issue right after it has been completely sold to the public. The firms that participated in the offering have all placed the issues with their customers, and the underwritten group, or syndicate, has closed.

A few firms have watched the issuance, and the public involvement in it, with great interest. They decide to become *market makers,* that is, they decide to buy the securities for their inventory and sell them for a profit. The market makers (also known as *dealers* or *traders*) are acting as *principals*; that is, they have committed their capital to the securities they are trading.

The Mark-Up

As principals, the dealers *mark up* the securities they trade with the public. Customers who purchase securities from a dealer who is acting as principal are not charged a commission; instead, they pay one price, which includes the mark-up. Brokerage firms charge commission only on "agency" transactions, in which they merely fill customers' orders. (Agency transactions are discussed later in the chapter.)

The trading price that a market maker offers must reflect the current market.

Example: A dealer purchases a security for inventory at $28 per share. Based on today's market, it is worth only $25 per share. If approached by a client, the dealer must sell it at today's prices and thereby incur a loss.

Under the rules of the NASD, the mark-up must be "fair." The amount of the mark-up on the current market price is determined by many factors. One factor is the issue's liquidity: The greater the liquidity, the smaller the mark-up should be; the more limited the liquidity, the higher the mark-up.

Example: A customer of a brokerage firm reads an article on XYZ Corporation. The brokerage firm's research department has reviewed XYZ and believes that, at its current price, it is an attractive buy. The customer discusses the security with the firm's stockbroker and decides to purchase 100 shares at the current market. The broker enters the order through the order room. As XYZ is traded in the over-the-counter market, the firm's over-the-counter department checks the various market makers and purchases 100 shares from the market maker who has the best current offer. A trade is consummated. The customer has purchased 100 shares; the market maker has sold it.

OTC QUOTATIONS

Each of the market makers (dealers) usually maintains markets for many different securities. They advertise their securities and the approximate prices in many interfirm publications that are available in the industry. Over-the-counter stocks are found in the *Pink Sheets,* while municipal bond issues and their prices can be found in a publication known as the *Blue List*. Quotations for other securities can be found in other, similar publications.

The computer age has greatly streamlined this geographically spread-out market. Because the markets are constantly changing, quotes (comprised of the bid price and offer price for particular securities) are valid for only a short period. By accessing large computers and electronic storage banks by means of cathode ray terminals (CRTs, or television-like equipment), dealers can enter their own current quotes or call out the up-to-the-minute quotes of other dealers—all within seconds. Firms that subscribe to the computer service can check current "markets" just by looking at their screens, or scopes. One such service is called National Association of Security Dealers Automated Quotation System (NASDAQ). (See Figure 3-1).

Types of Quotations

Operating within the rules of the NASD and/or the SEC over many years, market makers have developed a jargon or lingo of their own. When a trader renders a quote, it may be "firm," "subject," or "work-out."

A *firm quote* is one that the market maker is willing to trade at. The quote is valid for at least 100 shares of stock or five bonds. Any orders of a larger size may have to be negotiated between a stockbroker and the market maker.

FIGURE 3-1. *A NASDAQ quote.*

Subject (or *nominal*) *quotes* represent the price at which the trader believes the trade can be consummated. If the stockbroker expresses interest, the trader "checks out" or "firms up" the market. Actually, the trader verifies the market's *size*, which is the number of securities available, and then reports the firm quote to the inquiring stockbroker.

Work-out markets usually occur when a security is very inactive or when the size of the income order is large in comparison to the available market. The trader cannot know the price of execution for sure but is certain that the order can be executed. The trader then *shops* the order, that is, he or she makes inquiries of other market makers or other brokers who might have an interest in the security. Upon finding a possible execution, the trader confirms the price with the inquiring party and, if the price is agreeable, the trade is executed. Large orders are sometimes consummated in parts because they may be too large to be executed at one time.

Basis Pricing (Municipal and Government Securities)

Some municipal and government securities trade at a "basis." To understand the concept of basis pricing, you must understand *yields*, which is the percentage of return on investment. In the bond market, you will encounter three types of yield:

1. Nominal yield.
2. Current yield.
3. Yield to maturity.

Nominal Yield. This is the percentage of interest paid on the face value of the instrument.

Example: A $1,000 bond with an interest obligation of 7% has a nominal yield of 7% (.07 × $1,000). It pays $70 interest per year on each $1,000 bond.

Current Yield. Bonds pay interest based on the face value. The interest or coupon rate remains the same regardless of fluctuations in the market price of the bond. The investor is concerned with the return or the amount of interest received on the amount of money paid. Current yield tells the investor what that return is, given the price of the bond.

Example: The bond in our previous example is selling for 120, that is, the bond costs you $1,200 to acquire. It still pays only $70 in interest (7% on the face value of $1,000). Although, as the bond's owner, you receive $70, the return is based on a cost of $1,200. Your current yield is therefore only 5.83% ($70 ÷ $1,200).

Yield to Maturity. This type of yield takes into account the net dollar amount that an investor can expect if the bond is held to its maturity date.

Example: A $1,000 bond paying 7% interest will mature in thirty years. When you purchase it for $1,200, the bond has twenty years of life left. At the end of the 20 years (at maturity), the corporation is obligated to retire the debt for $1,000 (face value). If you paid $1,200 today for the bond, you will receive only $1,000 at maturity. It appears that you will lose $200.

Maybe not. Divide the $200 loss (or *amortize* it) over the twenty remaining years: $200 divided by 20 years equals $10 per year. You *are* losing $10 per year, which accumulates on this transaction. Yet the bond is going to pay you $70 per year in interest. So over 20 years, you actually earned an average of $60 per year for every year you own the bond. In dollars, this is your yield to maturity.

The formula for figuring the percentage of yield to maturity is complicated. A simpler one, known as the *rule of thumb*, is as follows:

$$\text{Yield to maturity} = \frac{\text{Interest rate} +/- \text{Amortized figure}}{(\text{Face value} + \text{Cost}) \div 2}$$

Example:

$$\text{Yield to maturity} = \frac{\$70 - \$10}{(\$1{,}000 + \$1{,}200) \div 2} = \frac{\$60}{\$1{,}100} = .0545$$

The yield to maturity (basis) is 5.45%.

Basis Price

Converting certain securities to and from their dollar prices to their yields to maturity or basis prices during the course of a busy trading day would be very cumbersome. Therefore, certain securities are traded on their yields to maturity, known as *basis prices*.

Example: A $1,000 bond with a 6% coupon, selling at 5.50 basis, costs more than $1,000. Conversely, a $1,000 bond with a 6% coupon, selling at a 6.50 basis, trades for less than $1,000.

If this is not clear, perhaps it will be when you understand the bid and offer system.

Bid and Offer System

The quotes for dollar-priced securities contain a *bid (purchase) price* and an *offer (sale) price*. On this type of quote, the bid is lower than the offer.

Example: The quote on ZAP is 45-1/2. The bid, or price, is 45, or $45; this is the highest price that someone is willing to buy the stock for, $45 per share. The offer is 45½, or $45.50; it is the lowest current price at which anyone is willing to offer the security for sale. Whenever the bid and offer are equal, a trade occurs.

Basis quotes confuse some people because the bid appears to be higher than the offer. But remember: The lower the yield, the higher the price; the higher the yield, the lower the price.

Example: A ZAP bond is a debt of ZAP Corporation with a 6% coupon expiring in 2005. It is referred to as "ZAP 6% FA95." The basis quote is 6.50-5.50. The "6.50" means that the highest price anyone will pay for the bond will yield 6.50% to maturity. The lowest price at which anyone will offer the bonds for sale will yield the new owner 5.50%. If you sell the bond at the bid (6.50), you actually receive *less than* $1,000. If you buy at the offer (5.50), you would pay *more than* $1,000. Either way the bond pays only 6% on $1,000.

MARKET MAKERS' INVENTORIES

Market makers usually make markets in many securities, and they *run an inventory* in each security that they have an interest in. Their inventories represent investments of their firms' capital. The firm's own money or capital is "tied up" or invested in these securities—the firms actually own the securities in their inventories. As a result, traders have to operate within the limits designated by the management of their firms. The market makers therefore keep abreast of current market happenings, all the while trying to determine how various conditions may affect their inventories. If, in their opinion, a condition will increase the price of their inventory, they acquire securities and *build up* their position. If, on the other hand, market makers feel the effect will be adverse, they may deplete their inventories completely. This talent for judging the future values of their inventories permits market makers to make a profit.

Normally, three or more different firms make markets in a given security, competing for orders from brokerage firms and buying or selling with these firms. Their quotes, usually for a minimum of 100 shares of stock or five bonds, generally reflect their interest in the security at a given moment.

Example: You are interested in acquiring 100 shares of XYZ, an over-the-counter security. Your stockbroker obtains the following quotes on the security from three market makers:

Market Maker	*Quote*
A	36-1/2
B	36 1/4-3/4
C	36 1/8-5/8

Reviewing these quotes, you see that market maker A is interested in selling stock; its offer is the lowest. Market maker B is interested in acquiring stock; its bid is the highest. Because you are interested in purchasing 100 shares, your brokerage firm trades with A.

As you probably can see by now, quotes change constantly as the market changes. Market makers must keep their quotes current and competitive if they want to stay in operation. As the market changes and as issues fluctuate in value, the traders change the compositions of their inventories. They may acquire more of this issue or reduce that issue. They may even *short* an issue, that is, sell a security they do not own with the hope of buying it at a later time at a lower price. By correctly managing their inventories, the market-making (or dealer) firms can make a handsome return on the capital they have invested in them. They are risking their capital at all times. The securities comprising the investors are at all times vulnerable to adverse news and contingent losses.

BROKERS AND DEALERS

A broker is not a dealer. The term "market maker," used throughout this book, can mean either "broker" or "dealer." When market makers actually buy for and sell from their own inventories, they are acting as *dealers*; they are acting as *principals*. If they just put buyers in contact with sellers or vice versa, but never own the inventory themselves, they are *brokers*; they are acting as *agents*.

Securities that are not traded over-the-counter are "listed" and traded on exchanges, which are discussed in the next chapter.

CHAPTER 4

The Exchanges

- Why should corporations have their securities listed on an exchange?
- Why are exchanges called "auction markets?"
- Who owns the exchanges?

These questions and many more are answered in this chapter.

TYPES OF EXCHANGES

When a security is traded on an exchange, it is said to be *listed* on the exchange. All stock exchanges have listing requirements, although they differ from one exchange to another. A corporation that seeks the listing of its common and preferred stocks must satisfy the exchange's listing requirements before it may even submit an application. Among the requirements are such items as:

- A minimum number of shares outstanding.
- A minimum number of shareholders.
- A wide geographic distribution of its securities.
- A history of earnings of a certain amount.

There are two *national stock exchanges*: The New York Stock Exchange (NYSE) and the American Stock Exchange (AMEX).

The requirements of the New York Stock Exchange are more stringent of the two. On this exchange you find the common stocks of major national and international corporations.

While the listing requirements of the American Stock Exchange are not quite as strict as those of the NYSE, the Amex-listed securities are nevertheless those of well known corporations. These companies, however, are usually younger or have smaller capitalization than those listed on the New York Stock Exchange.

For a long time, a security could be listed on only one of these two national exchanges, not both. If a security was listed on the NYSE, it could not be listed on the Amex—and vice versa. Nowadays the exchange rules covering this stipulation have come under review, and experiments in *dually listed securities* (those listed on Amex and NYSE) are underway.

Regional exchanges trade a few of the securities traded on the NYSE and the Amex, in addition to the securities of local corporations. These exchanges include the Boston Stock Exchange (BSE), the Midwest Stock Exchange (MSE), Pacific Stock Exchange (PSE), and Philadelphia Stock Exchange (PHLX).

In 1973 a new type of exchange was created in Chicago. It was the first *options exchange* and it was named the Chicago Board Options Exchange (CBOE). Following in the path of this pioneer are a number of stock exchanges that have added options to their product mix to offer more salable products to the public.

Commodity futures, or *commods*, are also traded on specific exchanges. The Chicago Board of Trade and the Mercantile Exchange are only two such exchanges. (Commods, as well as listed option and bond trading, are discussed later in the book.)

Each exchange operates in a slightly different fashion from the rest, to provide an auction market where the public's orders can be executed. The prices on the exchanges represent the highest bid for a purchase and the lowest offer for a sale of a given stock, option, commodity, or bond (some bonds are traded on exchanges).

THE NEW YORK STOCK EXCHANGE

Membership

Members of the New York Stock Exchange are said to own *seats* on the exchange. These seats allow the members access to the floor and the privilege of trading there. (See Figure 4-1).

Members of the New York Stock Exchange may be categorized as follows:

1. Commission house brokers.
2. Two-dollar brokers.
3. Specialists.
4. Registered traders.

Commission House Brokers. Commission house brokers are individuals who are employed by member firms and who execute orders for their firms' customers on the exchange floor. Orders to buy or sell stock originate in the branch offices, where the stockbrokers discuss securities with their clients and write the order tickets. Floor brokers receive these orders from the brokerage firm's order room or automated order routing system. The broker takes the order to the specified place on the exchange floor where the stock is traded and attempts to execute it there. If a trade can be consummated, the broker reports the execution to the order room, who, in turn, advises the stockbroker of the execution. The stockbroker then reports the transaction to the customer.

Two-Dollar Brokers. The prices of seats (memberships) fluctuate with the activity on the exchange: The busier the market, the more expensive the seats are. In busy markets, seats on the NYSE have sold for approximately $500,000; during slow markets, for approximately $70,000. In busy markets, firms cannot even acquire extra seats. In slow markets, they cannot sell them because the seat has lost so much in value. Because the seats for these brokers are generally expensive (and because the members must, of course, also receive a salary), the brokerage firm can therefore afford to have only a certain number of commission house brokers in its employ. Firms try to minimize these expenses

FIGURE 4-1. *The floor of the NYSE.*

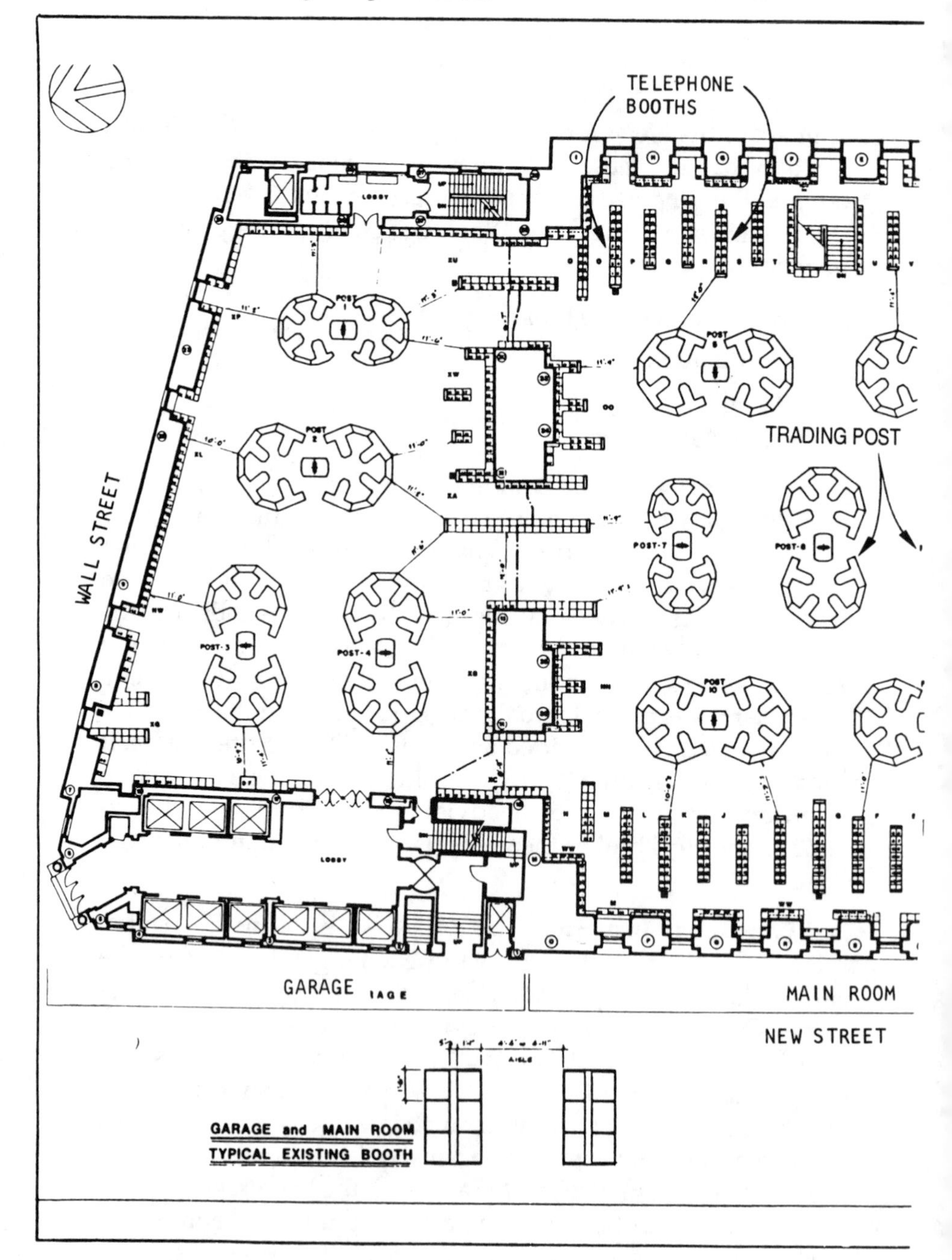

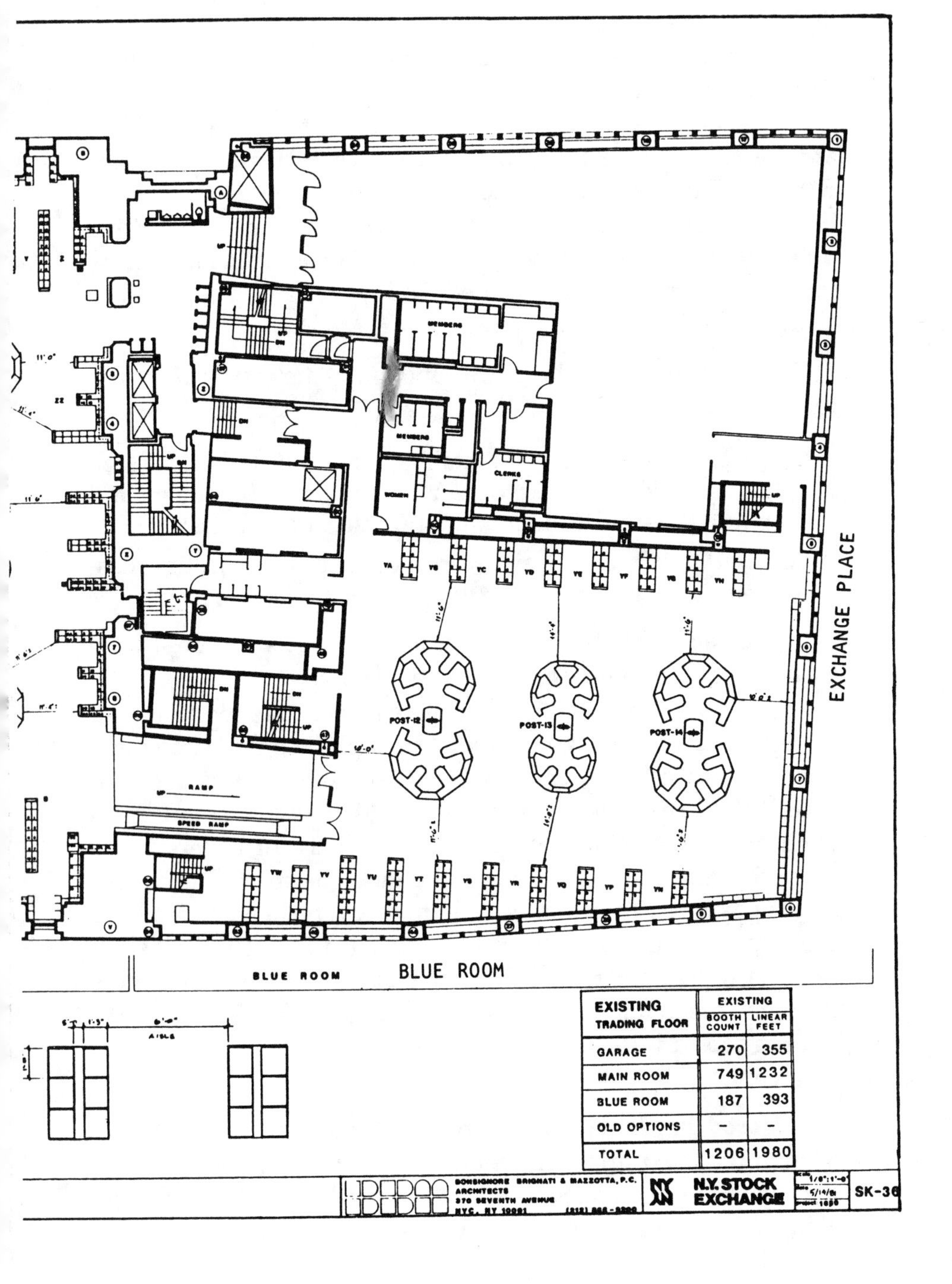

EXISTING TRADING FLOOR	EXISTING BOOTH COUNT	EXISTING LINEAR FEET
GARAGE	270	355
MAIN ROOM	749	1232
BLUE ROOM	187	393
OLD OPTIONS	–	–
TOTAL	1206	1980

by employing only enough commission house brokers to satisfy their basic needs.

What happens when the commission brokers cannot handle a peak load of orders?

Assisting the commission house brokers when they are busy are the *two-dollar brokers,* who either own or lease their seats. Either way, they act as freelance brokers, helping the commission house brokers by executing orders for the firm. The name "two-dollar broker" originated when this member actually received $2 for each 100-share trade executed. Today the rates charged have changed, but the name remains.

Specialists. On the NYSE and the Amex, *specialists* perform two functions:

1. *Making Markets*: They maintain a fair and orderly market in the securities assigned to their specialist unit by buying and selling the securities for "their own account and risk."
2. *Executing Orders*: They are responsible for executing customer orders entrusted to them by the brokerage firms.

Making Markets. Specialists are assigned securities by the exchange in which they are to *make markets.*

As market makers, specialists are responsible for maintaining a *fair and orderly market,* which is simply a logical succession of prices, *not* controlling the price of an issue. In this capacity, specialists are expected to buy or sell for their own accounts in an attempt to absorb any temporary imbalance of orders being entered. If the market becomes too erratic, the specialists call for a floor governor. They discuss the situation, and, if warranted, the exchange temporarily stops trading in this issue. This halt stays in effect until a fair market is reestablished. Depending on how well they facilitate trading in their assigned securities, they may be assigned additional securities or have securities removed from their control.

Executing Orders. The specialists receive *limit orders* (orders with a fixed price requirement) that are *away from,* or "off," the current market. These orders are posted in the *specialist book,* along with other orders already received. As the market fluctuates, the specialist executes the orders whose prices reflect the new market in the sequence received.

Example: XYZ is trading at 50. A client of a brokerage firm enters an order to buy 100 shares of XYZ at 46. The most the client is willing to pay is $46 per share. With the market currently trading at $50 per share, prospective sellers are unwilling to trade their securities at $46. The client with the buy order must wait until the market price falls to $46 before the order can be executed. The commission house broker who receives the order for that firm's customer does not hold the order until the market price falls (if it ever does). Instead, the order is turned over to a specialist who posts it in the book. Should the price of XYZ drop to $46., the specialist will try to execute it. If the specialist has already received other orders to buy XYZ at 46, those orders will be executed first.

The Registered Trader. Years ago, the primary occupation of registered traders was to trade for their own accounts in an attempt to make a profit. With the proliferation of rules and regulations, this privilege is now severely restricted. Today, *registered traders* either assist specialists as market makers or act as two-dollar brokers.

The Crowds on the Floor

The floor of the NYSE is divided into two parts: the telephone booths and the trading posts.

Along the periphery of the floor are *telephone booths*, where the member firms' floor employees work. Here is where the orders are taken from the firm's order room and assigned to the floor broker. A member firm may have positions at one or more of those booths.

Pages carry the orders to the appropriate *trading posts*. Each listed security is assigned to a particular post, which is the only place on the floor that the assigned security may be traded. For instance, XYZ common stock might be traded at, say, post 10. Specialists who are assigned to XYZ stand in front of the post. (All the securities assigned to a given specialist are traded at the same post.) Brokers who want to execute customer orders for XYZ or who are interested in trading XYZ come to this post. They make up what is known as the XYZ *crowd*. Specialists may also be members of the crowd, depending on whether they are holding public orders for the current market price or trying to balance supply or demand.

The Auction Market

To observing visitors, the people on the trading floor appear to be yelling at each other amid wholesale confusion. Actually, the brokers are shouting their respective bids and offers, while others yell out their acceptance, thereby creating the trades.

The special language of trading might also mislead observers. When brokers call out their orders, they use an abbreviated jargon that all members understand. For example, a broker bidding for a security calls "45¼ for 100"—meaning, "I am bidding $45.25 per share for 100 shares." A broker offering the security might call, "100 at 45¼." Or, "I am offering 100 shares for a sale at $45.25 per share." If a broker has a sell order that can be filled by one of the shouted bids, the broker calls out "Sold!" or "Sold 100!" A broker with a buy order that can be executed calls, "Take it!" or "Take 100!"

Priority, Precedence, and Parity

The brokers and specialists in the crowd on the NYSE execute orders according to a procedure known as *priority, precedence, and parity.*

Priority. One order and one order only can have *priority,* which is determined by the order's time of entry. The first member to call out the highest bid or lowest offer has priority on the floor. Sometimes the first bid or the offer is a mere fraction of a second sooner than the rest.

Example: The current quote on the floor for XYZ is 22-1/2. The highest price that anyone wants to pay for the security is $22.00 per share. The lowest price anyone wants to sell is 22.50 per share.

Each bid and offer rendered on the exchange floor must be for at least one *round lot,* or 100 shares. While the "quote" informs an interested party of the current market, it does not reveal the density or number of shares that the quote represents. The interested individual must request the size.

The response to "quote and size" will contain the highest bid, lowest offer, and the number of round lots for each price.

Example: A broker enters the crowd with an order to buy 100 shares. Upon requesting the quote and size, the broker is told, "22-1/2 3 by 5." This translates to, "Highest bid is $22.00 per share, lowest offer is $22.50 per share, 3 round lots (300 shares) bid at 22 and 5 round lots (500 shares) offered at $22.50." The broker bids 22¼ for 100. Another broker enters the crowd at that moment with an order to sell at 22¼. The broker calls "Sold." A trade is consummated.

What if you want to *sell* stock?

Example: Entering the crowd with an order to sell and requesting quote and size, a broker offers the security at 22¼. At that moment, another broker entering the crowd hears the offer and is willing to buy it. The broker calls, "Take it!" A trade is consummated.

Precedence. The order that can fill or best fill the quote takes *precedence.*

Example: With the quote and size 22-1/2 3×5, four brokers make offers. (the times are exaggerated for explanatory purposes. In reality, the offers are entered within seconds of each other.) All offers are at 22½.

- Broker A: 100 shares @ 10:15 a.m.
- Broker B: 100 shares @ 10:16 a.m.
- Broker C: 200 shares @ 10:17 a.m.
- Broker D: 100 shares @ 10:17 a.m.

If Broker X enters the crowd with a buy order for 100 shares *at the market* (that is, at the best possible offer), the trade is executed with Broker A, who has priority.

Let's say, however, that Broker X entered the crowd with an order to buy 300 shares. Then, Broker A and Broker C execute: Broker A, who has priority, sells 100 shares, and Broker C, who has precedence, sells 200 shares. After A's priority Broker C can "best fill the order" with the 200-share order.

If Broker X enters the crowd with a buy order of 200 shares, then A sells 100 shares and B the other 100 shares. A has priority, and B has a time advantage over C and D (even though B, C, and D can all fill the order).

Were Broker X to enter the crowd with an order for 400 shares, A executes because of priority, C executes because of precedence, and B executes before D because of time advantage.

Parity. When two brokers can both fill the order and both enter their intentions at the same time, there isn't any logical way of awarding the trade. This is parity. In this case, either the brokers agree to an equitable distribution, or they flip a coin and the winner takes the trade.

Example: The quote is 22-1/2, and the bids are:

Broker M: 100 shares, 10:14
Broker N: 100 shares, 10:15
Broker O: 100 shares, 10:15

If Broker Z enters the crowd with a sell market order for 100 shares, Broker M executes. If Broker Z enters the crowd with a sell market order for 200 shares, M executes 100 shares. Since Brokers N and O can fill or best fill the order and neither has a time advantage, they have parity. So Brokers N and O either agree to one of these two taking the 100 shares or toss a coin, and the winner of the toss executes 100 shares.

When an execution takes place, *the floor is cleared,* all remaining bids or offers at that price must be resubmitted. This procedure keeps quotes updated while reaffirming all orders.

The Specialist's Book

Specialists enter public orders, that are away from the market, in their books by price and in the order they are received.

Example: See Figure 4-2. If this specialist's book represents the highest bid and lowest offer of the crowd, the quote is 22 1/4-5/8. The highest bid is 22¼, the lowest offer, 22⅝. If these orders are the only shares comprising the quote, the size is 5 by 9. The largest order for a buy at 22¼ is for 500 shares (200 by Broker D and 300 by Broker E). The largest order for sale at 22⅝ is 900 shares (300 by Broker F and 600 by Broker G).

Specialists execute orders from their books by price on a first-in/first-out (FIFO) basis. The first order in is the first order out.

Example: If Broker Z enters the crowd with a 200-share buy order at the market, the specialist executes 200 of Broker F's 300-share order at 22⅝.

FIGURE 4-2. *A page in the specialist's book.*

BUY		SELL
BKR R - 100	22	
BKR L - 300 BKR A - 500	1/8	
BKR D - 200 BKR E - 300	1/4	
	3/8	
	1/2	
	5/8	BKR F - 300 BKR G - 600
	3/4	BKR B - 100 BKR M - 200
	7/8	BKR S - 400

The NYSE specialist's book is maintained on a CRT and referred to as *display book*. This electronic book sorts all orders coming to the specialist in time and price sequence; it also keeps track of executed orders, so that inquiries from member firms may be quickly researched.

Display book is part of a larger system, known as DOT (*designated order turnaround*). DOT orders are executed by the specialist either against other DOT orders (orders entered by member firms into the DOT system), or against brokers in the "crowd" or against the specialist's own position.

THE AMERICAN STOCK EXCHANGE (AMEX)

The Amex membership is basically like the NYSE's. On the floor are commission house brokers, two-dollar brokers, specialists, and traders. Their functions are very similar to those of their counterparts on the NYSE.

One notable difference from the NYSE is the way the member firms communicate with their employees. Conversations regarding security, shares, price, and the like are carried on through a system of hand signals. The individuals actually discuss quote, size, and other terms without speaking or writing a word.

The Amex trading floor also operates differently than the NYSE. Its procedure for awarding trades is known as *priority prorata*. Under this system, one broker may have priority, as on the NYSE. After priority, however, shares are allocated in round lots among the other participating brokers. Precedence and parity do not play a part in the Amex procedure.

Example: Three brokers enter bids for ABC at 26, as follows:

Broker A: 100 shares, 10:14

Broker B: 200 shares, 10:15

Broker C: 300 shares, 10:15

Broker X enters the crowd with a 400-share sell market order. Broker A executes a trade for 100 shares (priority). Broker B then buys 100 shares, and Broker C takes 200 shares. In other words, the remaining 300 shares are distributed "prorata."

CHICAGO BOARD OPTIONS EXCHANGE (CBOE)

The CBOE utilizes the priority prorata system of the Amex in the execution of its option trades. However, the CBOE utilizes a trading system that is unlike that of either the NYSE or Amex. Three types of principal members and employees of the CBOE execute orders:

- *Order book officials* (OBOs), who are employees of the exchange and who execute orders entrusted to them.
- *Market makers*, who are members and who make markets.
- *Brokers*, who are members and who execute off floor or public orders.

Order book officials have *to maintain a fair and orderly market* and do so by calling market makers to offset imbalances. On the CBOE, the order book officials can execute only the customer orders entrusted to them. Market makers buy and sell options for their own account and risk.

The CBOE assigns classes of options to order book officials in the same manner that the NYSE and the Amex assign stocks to their specialists. Assignments are based on the proficiency displayed by the individuals.

INSTITUTIONAL (BLOCK) SALE

Institutions (such as insurance companies, banks, or pension trusts) invest their funds in portfolios of securities. Professional managers try to maximize these portfolios' return or earnings (in terms of price appreciation, dividends, interest, and so on) by acquiring and liquidating securities. The institutions therefore trade their securities in *blocks* (that is, in large quantities). A block can be 10,000 shares, 100,000 shares, or millions of dollars worth of bonds.

At times, the normal exchange mechanisms may not be able to absorb such a quantity. (Don't forget: The exchanges deal in round lots of 100 shares and function for the benefit of the public.) So the institutional stockbroker may seek assistance either from special exchange procedures or from a "block trading" firm.

Block trading firms, specialize in expediting large quantity trades. They trade listed securities off (that is, away from) the exchange by finding large buyers for sellers and vice versa.

The next chapter begins our review of the typical organization of a brokerage firm. After an introduction to operations, we review the order room, its functions, the type of orders it receives, and its method of reporting.

PART II

OPERATIONS: AN OVERVIEW

CHAPTER 5

Operations: A Comparison

To better understand how a brokerage firm is organized and operated, just compare it with a manufacturing corporation, such as General Motors or Xerox. A manufacturing corporation is composed basically of three areas:

1. Marketing/sales.
2. Manufacturing/production.
3. Administration/support.

COMPONENTS OF A MANUFACTURING FIRM

Marketing/Sales

Marketing. The marketing people recommend the products to be sold, either to augment or to replace existing lines. To make their recommendations, they study the economic conditions that may affect the manufacturer's markets. They follow the public or market trends and make projections. They consider new product ideas or sales possibilities, and if the product is found to be salesworthy, they draw up cost and manufacturing specifications. Scrutinizing past products' performance, they may alter or even completely revise their design. Whatever the results of their studies, tests, and decisions, the marketing people are supposed to propose products that are salable and that will make a profit for the company.

Sales. The company's products have to be sold to the public. The greater the demand or the public's acceptance is, the easier the product is to sell. The less demand or less interest among the public, the more difficult it is to sell. The task of selling belongs to the company's salespersons and sales managers.

Selling strategy varies from one industry to another. Some products can best be sold by door-to-door canvassing—"Fuller brushman style." Other companies sell their products through stores, as food companies do in supermarkets. Still others offer their products for viewing at a specific location, such as automobile show rooms. Whatever its method, the company could not exist without sales.

Salespersons are usually compensated by means of a minimum salary plus a commission. The commission can be either a portion of the profit (or markup) or a percentage of the total commission generated by the firm. Salespersons who do not complete a single transaction do not get paid. Those who do not start producing sales have to be released from their employment sooner or later. The company has no choice.

Sales managers serve several purposes. They make certain that the members of the sales force have products to sell and that they understand the products. They also effectively and diligently sell the products themselves.

Manufacturing/Production

The manufacturing and production departments are where the products are made. Inventory is processed through a cycle of manufacturing steps, at the end of which is a finished product.

If the sales force brings the customers into the firm, the manufacturing division is said to keep them there. The product must live up to the fair expectations of the public, or all the sales techniques in the world are worthless. Customers expect a usable and reliable product. Shoddy workmanship or troublesome products only lead to fewer reorders. Unless customers are content with the product, the company is not likely to be selling to them on a continuing basis.

Administration/Support

This area consists of departments that assist, support, augment, and maintain sales and production. Here you find the personnel department, payroll department, and accounting and/or finance department. For example, some of these departments prepare the corporation's balance sheet and income statement, the two main financial reports utilized by all companies. Others prepare the invoices, bills, salaries, records, and other documents. Still others acquire and maintain equipment and furniture.

THE ORGANIZATION OF A BROKERAGE FIRM

A securities brokerage firm is very similar to a manufacturing company. Its "product" is the service it provides to its clients.

Like a manufacturing concern, a brokerage firm maintains a *marketing/sales function.* The marketing people determine which types of securities the public is interested in. They base their selections on economic conditions, projected economic growth patterns, current market conditions, and what the public (the firm's customers) are reading and talking about. If marketing personnel err in their judgment, the firm may miss the opportunity to service its clients. The result is obvious; it can lose customers.

Depending on the ability of the firm to adjust, from time to time it can alter its *product mix,* which is the combination of types of securities (such as common stocks, corporate bonds, municipal bonds, and so on) that the firm offers its customers. Generally firms try to adjust the mix of their products to suit their clientele.

After the marketing staff has selected the types of securities to offer, the stockbrokers contact the customers and sell the securities or ideas to their clients. In a brokerage firm, the stockbrokers are the salespersons. These professionals work with their firm's sales managers and marketing departments to offer the securities that best fill their customers' wants and needs: The stockbrokers work in offices known as *branches, sales branches,* or *board rooms*. From these offices, they contact their customers and discuss various security situations.

Once a stockbroker makes a sale, the "manufacturing" (that is, the processing) area comes into play. The employees in the processing area do the booking, posting, and completing of entries that culminate in rendering a trouble-free and satisfactory experience to the client. How a transaction is handled is most important because it shows customers that professionals are taking care of their accounts. If the trade is processed correctly and clients' instructions are all carried out, customers get the impression that their accounts are important and that their business is appreciated by the company. Clients are then willing to do more business with the firm. The service provided by the processing area is therefore an important part of the company's "product."

During this entire cycle, the people in the administrative area have also been at work. They "booked" the commission on the transaction to a revenue account, paid expenses, hired personnel, processed personal insurance claims, and so on.

As you can see, the brokerage firm's operation can be successful only if *everyone* performs his or her assignments diligently. Through everyone's conscientious participation, the company can continue to earn a profit and remain in business. The focal point for everyone's effort must remain always on the customers, their orders for purchases or sales, and their security accounts.

OPERATIONS: THE "MANUFACTURING" PHASE IN A BROKERAGE FIRM

In the next chapter, we will begin a short journey through the processing area, starting with the point from which orders emanate to the marketplaces: the order room. Not every detail will be covered. Instead, you should get a feel for how an order progresses through the system and how the departments and outside agencies work together. Figure 6-1 (page 54) is a flowchart of a typical operations organization. The heavily outlined boxes are departments within the firm, and the more lightly outlined boxes are agencies and companies outside the firm.

CHAPTER 6

Order Room

A brokerage firm may have one main order room, where all orders arrive from the sales locations. Or it may set up a number of order rooms, each taking orders for a particular security. Which type a firm has depends on the size of the firm and the degree of automation (that is, computer support). Large firms are likely to use decentralized order rooms, in which many functions are automated. Whether automated or not, however, each order room must perform certain functions and process certain types of orders.

WHERE ORDERS COME FROM

Orders are taken from clients by the sales staff. The stockbroker discusses an investment strategy or a particular security with the client. Once they decide on a course of action, the client gives an order to the stockbroker, who passes it on to the branch or main order room. The order room then routes the order to the point of execution. If a trade can be made, the order room reports the execution price to the branch so that the stockbroker may inform the client. A trade, or transaction, has been completed in accord-

FIGURE 6-1. *The order room.*

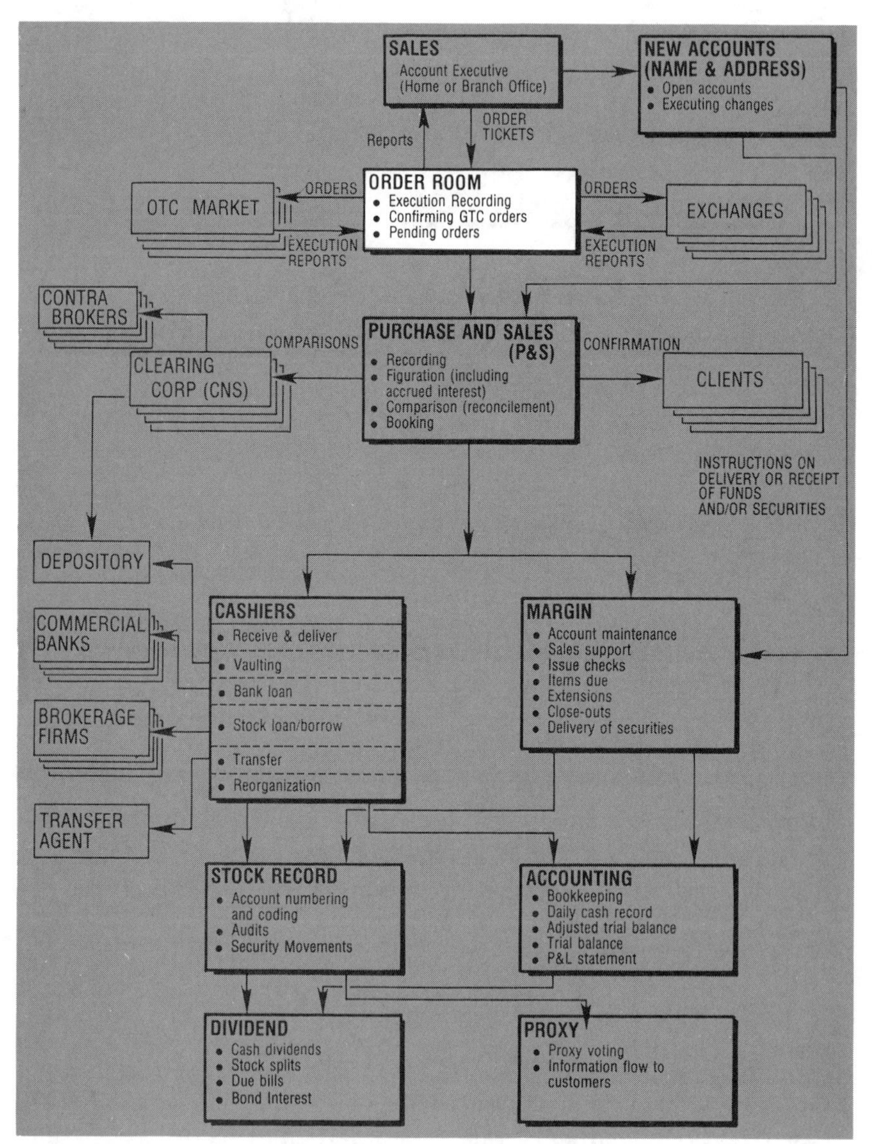

ance with the criteria set forth in the order and the circumstances of the current market. This procedure completes the order room's functions.

All the planning by marketing and sales people culminates in this first step in the "manufacturing" process of the brokerage firm. If their predictions, opinions, and valuations are correctly based on security research, economic indicators, and other factors, the customers have a very good possibility of attaining their goals. Yet these well thought out plans could go awry should changes occur in economic conditions, in the industry, between companies, or elsewhere. Such changes occur daily, and their effects on the marketplace may negate all plans. Against this uncertainty, the brokerage firm must be consistent in its operational service and trade processing.

BASIC ORDER INFORMATION

Every order that comes from a salesperson must contain certain basic information:

- Whether the order is to buy, sell long, or sell short.
- The quantity.
- A description of the security to be transacted.
- The customer's account number and usually the account name.
- Order type/price.

This information enables the people in the order room and at the place of execution to know which security is to be traded, what quantity is involved, and whether the client is acquiring (buying) or liquidating (selling) the security. The customer's name or account number is, of course, necessary for the later processing of the order, as well as for satisfying certain rules and regulations. (See Figure 6-2.)

TYPES OF ORDERS

In purchasing or selling securities, customers are attempting to attain goals—to buy or sell at a certain price, to lock in a profit and so on. To assist them, a myriad of different types of order instructions is at their disposal. Each type of order entails the use of additional information that custom-tailors it to the needs and wishes of the customer.

FIGURE 6-2. *A typical order form.*

B U Y

	STOCK EXCHANGES						BONDS												EXECUTED PRICE
	NYSE & ASE	NASDAQ	OVER THE CNTR	CHI'GO MID-WEST	PACIFIC COAST	BOSTON P-B-W	CORP-ORATE	MUNI-CIPAL	CONV-ERTIBLE	BLOCK DEPT	FINAN. SERV DEPT	SYNDI-CATE	MUTUAL FUNDS	SPECIAL HAND'NG	OTHER	ORDER NUMBER	OFFICE	
0	☐ NAX	☐ OTC	☐ OTN	☐ CMW	☐ PCX	☐ HEND	☐ BND	☐ BMUN	☐ CONV	☐ ID	☐ FND	☐ STIC	☐ CGE	☐ SHD				

1 ☐ POSS DUPE ☐ **BUY** ATTN:

2 QUANTITY | SYMBOL OR DESCRIPTION | SUFFIX* | PRICE OR MARKET | STOP ☐ STP | STOP LIMIT PRICE ______LMT | TYPE OF ORDER OTHER THAN LIMITED OR MARKET ☐ BAS ☐ OB ☐ WITH DISCRETION ☐ WOW ☐ CLO

3 ☐ AON ☐ N H ☐ DAY ☐ GTC ☐ OPG ☐ FOK ☐ OC | ☐ DNR ☐ CASH ☐ ND | PRINCIPAL TRANSACTION

4 ☐ POSS DUPE ☐ OR ☐ SW ☐ CXL ☐ BUY | ☐ INFORM CUSTOMER WE MAKE MARKET

5 QUANTITY | SYMBOL OR DESCRIPTION | SUFFIX* | PRICE OR MARKET | STOP ☐ STP | STOP LIMIT PRICE ______LMT | ☐ BAS ☐ OB ☐ WITH DISCRETION ☐ WOW ☐ CLO

6 LVS ☐ AON ☐ NH ☐ DAY ☐ GTC ☐ OPG ☐ FOK ☐ OC ☐ DNR ☐ CASH ☐ ND ☐ CHECK IF NEW ACCOUNT

7 OFFICE | ACCOUNT NUMBER | TYPE | TYPE OF ACCOUNT (0-COD, 1-CASH, 2-MARGIN, 3-SHORT, 4-SPEC. SUBSCRIPTION, 5-CONV. BOND, 6-SPEC. BOND) | SPLIT SHARES | DISCRETIONARY NYSE RULE 408 | EMPLOYEE | A.E. NO. | MGR'S. APPROVAL

8 CXL'S ONLY | REF | ORIG STATION | MESSAGE NO. | CUSTOMER NAME

9 COM ☐ A.E. OVERRIDE [R/ _ _ _] ☐ NEG. ¢ PER SH [M/90 _ _ _] ☐ NEG. DISC. [CD _ _ %] ☐ ST INS OVERRIDE [I/ _]

10 COM ☐ SPECIAL DESCRIPTIVE INST. [D/ _] ☐ D/UNSOL

11 COM

12 COM

13 CONFIRM LINE CFN LINE 2 & 5

SUFFIX CODES

CALLED	CL
CERTIFICATE	CT
CLASS OF	AB
SECURITY	ETC.
CONVERTIBLE	CV
FOREIGN	F
PREFERRED	PR
RIGHTS	RT
SPECIAL STAMPED	SP SD
WHEN DISTRIBUTED	WD
WHEN ISSUED	WI
WITH WARRANTS	WW
WITHOUT WARRANTS	XW
WARRANTS	WS

ORDER COPY

In addition to the basic information, traders or floor brokers on the exchange must know if there are any constraints on the price and method of order execution. Such constraints are governed by the rules and regulations of the exchanges and other associations.

Market Order

A *market order* is an order to execute at whatever the market price is when the broker enters the crowd. A *buy market order* accepts the current offer, and a *sell market order* accepts the bid.

Limit Order

A *limit order* places a limit on the price that the customer is willing to accept. A *buy limit order* establishes the highest price someone is willing to pay. The order can be executed at the limit price or lower. *Sell limit order* sets the lowest price someone is willing to accept. The order can be executed at the limit price or higher.

Stop Order

A *stop order* is a memorandum that becomes a market order when the price on the order ticket is reached or passed. A *buy stop order* is entered *above* the current market. A *sell stop order* is entered *below* it. Stop orders could be executed immediately if it weren't for the "stop" instruction.

Example: Mike Rafoen buys 100 shares of RAM at $55 per share. He does not have access to a "tape" or quote machine and therefore cannot watch the price movement of the security. Yet he wants to risk no more than $500 on this transaction. Mike could enter an order to "Sell 100 RAM at 50 *stop*." Because the market is now 55, Rafoen's order would be executed immediately if it were not for the stop instruction: With the word "stop," the market has to fall to 50 or below before this order can be executed.

Other Types of Orders

Other orders are entered for special purposes. Given our broad purpose in this text, let's take just a quick look at each:

1. *Stop Limit:* This is the same as stop order, but it becomes a limit order instead of a market order when the stop price is reached.
2. *Fill-or-Kill (FOK):* This order must be executed in its entirety immediately or it's cancelled.
3. *Immediate or Cancel (IOC):* Any part of the order may be executed immediately and the rest cancelled.
4. *All-or-None (AON):* Given time constraints, such as a day, *all* of the order must be filled or the client does not have to accept the execution.
5. *Spread Order:* Used in listed options and futures trading, a spread order contains the instruction to buy one product or issue and simultaneously sell the same with different terms. For example, "B" (buy) 1 call ZAP Apr 40, S (sell) 1 call ZAP Apr 45."
6. *Straddle Order:* Used in listed options, this is the simultaneous purchase or sale of a put and a call on the same underlying stock in the same series. For example, "B (buy) 1 call WIP Jul 60, B (buy) 1 put WIP Jul 60." Straddle Orders also apply to certain future transactions.
7. *Combination Order:* This order is similar to a straddle, but it uses a different series designation.
8. *One Cancels Other (OCO):* This order has two possible executions. The first one to get executed automatically cancels the other. Hence its name: one cancels other.

TASKS OF THE ORDER DEPARTMENT

Reconcilement

People in the order room match, or *reconcile,* the execution reports coming in from the trading area with the orders, to make certain that all of the customer's original criteria have been met. For each "match" the order department reports to the stockbroker, who in turn advises the client. Since this is the first step in the service (or "manufacturing") cycle, the customers' transactions *must* meet their specifications.

Confirming GTC Orders

GTC orders are *good-til-canceled;* that is, they stay "open" until they are executed or the customer cancels them.

The order department also confirms all open (GTC) orders with clients. That is, it advises clients that their orders have been entered on their behalf and that they are currently being handled. Should the customer change the order, the order department advises the client that the change has been noted. Most firms confirm open orders with their clients on the day they are entered, on the day the orders are cancelled, and on the day the order is three months old. Naturally, when the order is executed, the client receives a report of execution, which negates the need of an open order confirmation.

Organization of Pending Orders

The order room must keep track of orders until executed. The order has to be sent to the OTC or exchange market. When executed, the order comes back with an *execution report.* The order room staff have to match the report with the original order and then advise the account executive of the execution. The sales rep then advises the client of the execution. So the order department has to have a system for keeping track of pending orders.

Pending orders (that is, orders awaiting execution) have to be organized in a logical system. (See Figure 6-3.) Usually, orders are first grouped according to the security involved. For instance, all buy and sell orders for XYZ are put into one group, all orders for ABC in another, and so on for each security. Within each group, the buy orders are separated from the sell orders. Within the group of buy orders, the highest execution price is put on the top, with the other orders arranged in descending price order. In the sell orders group, the lowest sale price is put on top, with the

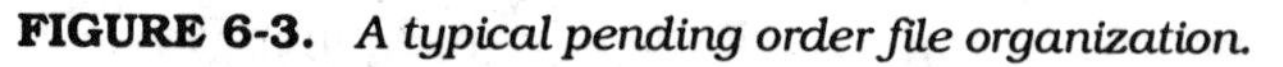

FIGURE 6-3. *A typical pending order file organization.*

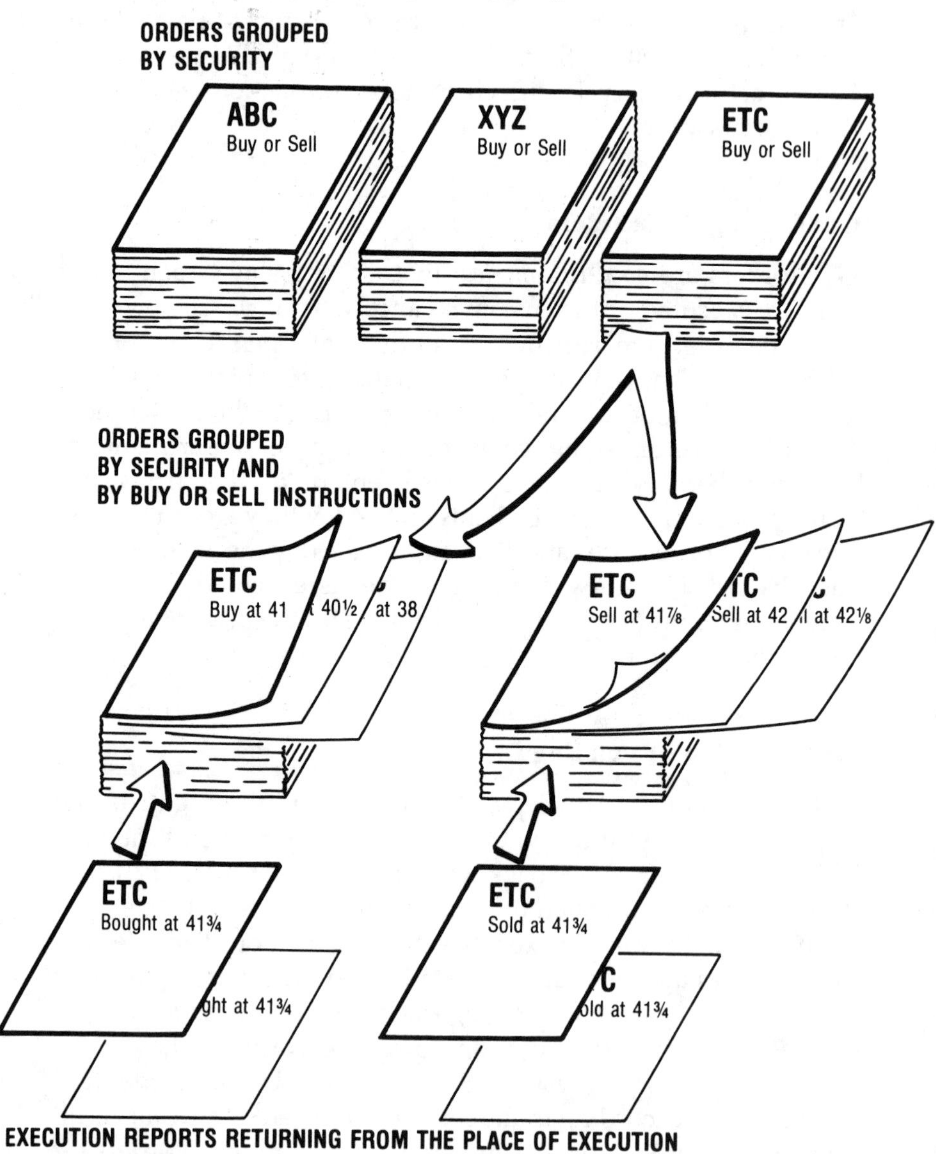

others arranged in ascending price order. With such a system, the people in the order room can easily locate the corresponding order ticket when an execution occurs.

The orders should therefore be executed on the floor in the same order as they are arranged in the order room. If they are executed in any other order, the order room is automatically alerted to a possible problem. The best possible prices, for either purchases or sales, are those on top of the groups. If other orders in the group are being executed before those on top, then something is wrong. Perhaps the order went astray on its way to the floor. Maybe the order was executed but the report did not reach the order room. Although the system does not necessarily identify the problem itself, it does act as a built-in troubleshooting procedure.

SUMMARY

In this chapter, we discussed the basic makeup of a brokerage firm and the first step in the service, or "manufacturing," process. All the work, planning, and effort performed by the marketing and sales area of the firm now begin to take shape in the processing cycle.

Order rooms are responsible for controlling, servicing, maintaining, and recording the execution of *all* orders directed to them. Every order represents a customer's attempt to conduct business with the firm. Every report of execution represents an agreement between buyer and seller that a transaction has, in fact, taken place.

The next step is the P&S function, which includes computing the amount of money involved in the trade, making certain that the opposing brokerage firm agrees with the terms of the transaction, and balancing customer and brokerage trades.

CHAPTER 7

Purchase and Sales (P&S)

Of all the departments in the operation cycle, the purchase and sales (P&S) department has probably changed the most over the years, generally due to automation both within the brokerage firm and within the industry. These changes have permitted many firms to process large volumes of transactions easily, efficiently, and at reduced cost.

Although a transaction occurs between two parties, or *principals*, they may not, and probably do not, know each other. Yet, through their trust and respect for the security industry, they verbally agree to enter into this transaction. The P&S function now comes into play.

The P&S department is responsible for basically four tasks:

1. Recording.
2. Figuration.
3. Comparison (reconcilement).
4. Confirmation and Booking.

RECORDING

To keep track of the huge number of trades each day, each transaction has to be coded. Each trade is assigned a CUSIP or in-

FIGURE 7-1. *P&S Department.*

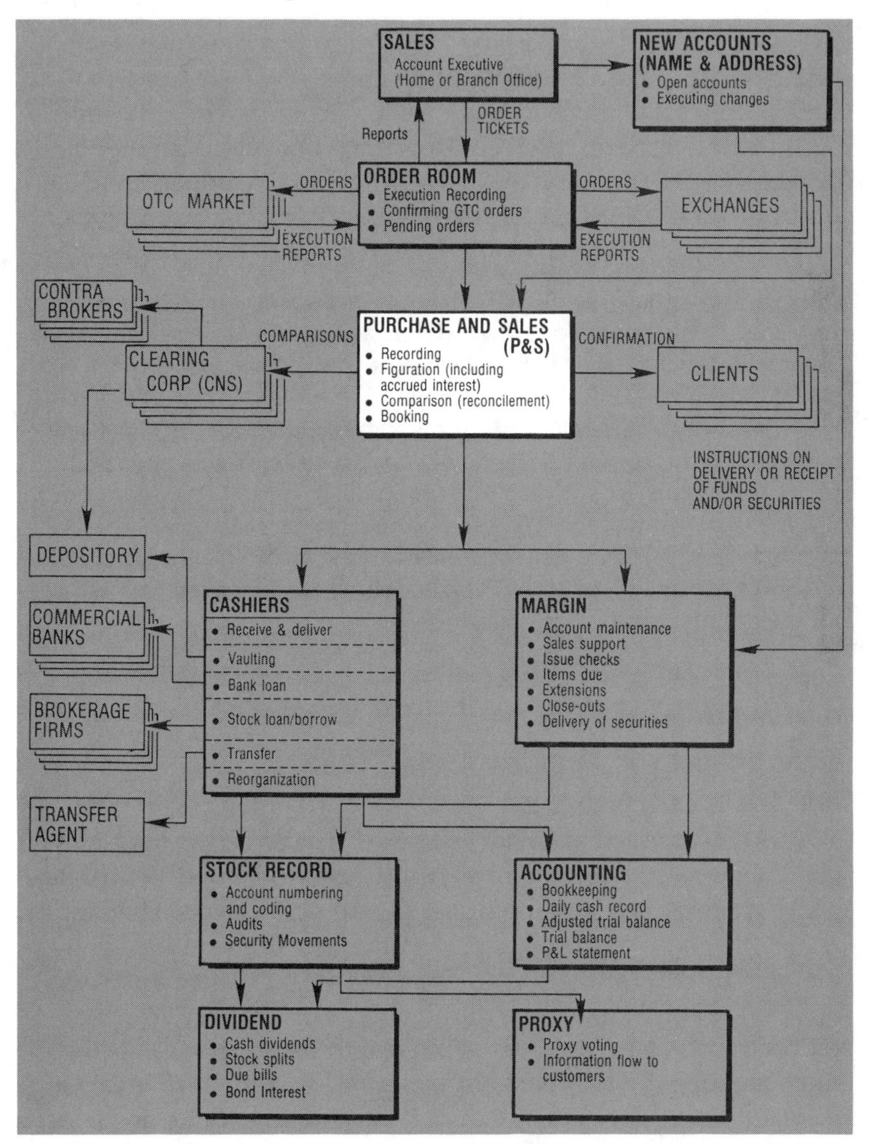

house number, which identifies the issuer, and issue. In addition, to handle the clearing of a great many trades, known as *tickets*, each is assigned a *code*, which designates the type of transaction, point of execution, and any other details needed for properly processing the ticket.

FIGURATION

Every trade that a brokerage firm processes must undergo a series of computations. How much money was involved in the transaction? How much does the selling firm receive? How much does the buying firm receive? How much does the customer pay or receive? These computations are known as *figuration.* In some firms, programmed computers perform these calculations. Other firms employ individuals to perform the calculations manually.

Example: Brokerage firm McGrath & Co. purchases securities for their customer from Stone, Forrest & Rivers, another brokerage firm, also operating on behalf of one of its customers. The transaction involves 100 shares of XYZ at 42.

Basically, McGrath & Co. pays Stone, Forrest & Rivers $4,200 and receives 100 shares of XYZ from them. McGrath's customer pays $4,200 plus commission (let's say it's $50) for a total cost of $4,250. Stone, Forrest & Rivers receives the 100 shares of XYZ from its customer; from the proceeds ($4,200), they deduct their commission ($50) plus taxes and fees (let's assume it's another $5). The selling customer receives $4,145 for the transaction.

Accrued Interest

The P&S department has to include, in its figuration, the computation of accrued interest.

If the transaction involves bonds instead of stock, interest has to be accrued and paid by the buyer to the seller. Corporate bonds, for example, pay interest at six-month intervals. Their representative banks or agents pay, to the bondholder, the full six months' interest at the time the interest is due. The owner who bought the bonds sometime during the six months between interest payments *owes* some of the interest to the seller, who owned the bonds for the first part of the period. This interest is said to have *accrued* to the owner, that is, it became due to the owner as the six months passed.

Keeping track of and collecting the accrued interest could be cumbersome for the seller of the bonds. So the buyer pays all the accrued interest due to the seller as of the day that the transaction settles. Then the new owner receives the full six months' payment when the interest is due and paid.

Example: XYZ 8% AO—2010 pays 8% interest, or $80 per $1,000 bond. Since the bond pays interest every April and October, the six-month interest is $40 per $1,000 bond. Owner A holds the bond for three months after an interest payment date and then sells it. Owner B, who acquires the bonds pays $20 (or half of the interest that would accrue in a six-month period) to the seller at the time of the transaction. Three months later, XYZ Corporation, the issuer, pays the new owner $40, representing a full six months' of interest. The new owner has received $40 but paid $20 accrued interest to the seller at the time of purchase. The remaining $20 ($40 – $20 = $20) represents the interest accrued to the new owner for the second three months.

When computing interest on corporate bonds, you assume that the year contains 360 days and that each month contains 30 days. The month of sale is counted in actual days.

Example: If XYZ bonds are acquired on settlement date of April 1 and sold on a settlement date of July 1, the owner receives all the interest accrued during the period.

April 1 to April 30	30 days
May 1 to May 31	30 days
June 1 to June 30	30 days
Total	90 days

The formula is:

$$\text{Accrued interest} = \frac{\text{Principal}}{1} \times \frac{\text{Interest}}{100} \times \frac{\text{Number of days}}{\text{Base number}}$$

The face amount of the XYZ bond is $1,000. The interest rate is 8%, the number of days owned is 90. The base number of days is 360. So:

$$\text{Accrued interest} = \frac{\$1{,}000}{1} \times \frac{8}{100} \times \frac{90 \text{ days}}{360 \text{ days}}$$

$$= \frac{\$1{,}000}{1} \times \frac{2}{25} \times \frac{1}{4}$$

$$= \frac{\$2{,}000}{100} = \$20$$

Interest calculations for different types of debt instruments (bonds, notes, bills, CDs, and the like) call for different bases. The P&S department has to make certain that accrued interest computations are figured using the correct formulas. Mistakes cause a multitude of problems, all resulting in poor service to the client and unnecessary expense to the firm. The variety of computations needed for processing trades is directly related to the brokerage firms' product mix: the more varied the product mix, the more varied the calculations. The firm's customer knows only that a transaction occurred and that the billing should be correct in all details.

COMPARISON (RECONCILEMENT) [NON-AUTOMATED ORDER SYSTEM]

Comparison is the process, handled by the P&S department, by which customers' trades are *balanced* (or *reconciled*) against the opposing brokerage firm's (or street-side) transactions. Each customer trade must agree to the penny with the contra broker's side and executing broker's side. In P&S, each trade is grouped on the *balance listing, or blotter,* with all other trades of the same origin.

From that point, trades are broken down, or separated into groups depending on the volume of transactions and/or the firm's processing systems. The firm may separate the trades into those executed on the NYSE, those executed on the Amex, those executed on the Midwest Stock Exchange, those on the Chicago Board Options exchange, and so on. They may be separated further into buy and sell order, types of security, and so on.

After the orders are properly coded, dated, and, where necessary, calculated, they are sent out for processing, usually to the EDP or computer center. The processing center sends computer output reports of certain trades to the clearing centers of listed exchanges and OTC market places for further processing there. For equities and certain debt instruments, this is done on the day after trade date, or trade date plus one (T+1).

On the morning of the next day (that is, on the trade date plus two), the P&S receives listings of all broker trades that were processed the day before but executed two days before. Upon receipt of this report, the P&S department begins another important operation. The task on this day is to *balance*, or pair off, each customer-side trade with its opposing and corresponding broker-side trade. Both sides must agree on quantity, security, execution price, and terms of settlement. All discrepancies should be corrected on the same day and adjustments processed so that they are reflected on the trade date plus three. Due to as-of trades (explained later) and other problems, any given day's trades are not balanced until trade date plus three, and the final *balance* or *settlement blotters* do not appear until trade date plus four.

The Manual Procedure

Balancing of trades has been simplified over the years.

At one time every trade had to be balanced and settlement made with the opposing broker.

Example: Customer Leitch puts in an order to buy 100 shares of XYZ at 42 through her brokerage firm, W. Rini & Co. The trade is consummated on the floor of the New York Stock Exchange, between a house broker representing W. Rini & Co. and one for another brokerage firm, Christiansen & Sons. W. Rini & Co.'s. P&S knows only that customer Leitch purchased 100 XYZ at 42 and that Christiansen & Sons sold it. Each firm sends a multicopy comparison to the other. Upon receiving and checking the comparison, each firm stamps one copy with the firm's name and sends the stamped copy back to the other firm. The selling firm delivers the certificates to the purchasing firm, in return for a check for the purchase amount.

The Clearing Facilities

Today, clearing organizations, such as the National Securities Clearing Corporation (NSCC), issue *contract sheets,* which are listings of the trade information from both buyer and seller firms. Trades on which both firms agree appear in the *compared* portion of the listing. Since these trades have been compared and agreed to, further comparison is unnecessary.

Trades to which the opposing brokers do not agree appear on the *uncompared,* part of the contract listing. Both firms check their trade tickets for mistakes, and the firm in error processes an adjustment notice. The adjusted trade then appears in the compared section the next day.

Example: After Leitch's purchase of 100 shares of XYZ at 42, one of the firms gives the clearing organization erroneous trade information. One firm submits a price of 4 1/8, not 42. This discrepancy appears on the uncompared listing, and the firm that made the error corrects it by adjustment. The next day, the corrected trade appears on the compared listing.

Although some trades are still compared by the manual method, each year this time-consuming and tedious process is edged out a little more as the clearing facilities expand. The comparison cycle will be explained in more detail later.

CUSTOMER CONFIRMATION

In addition to a verbal notice of execution from the stockbroker, the customer receives a written notification, known as the *customer's confirmation*, from the brokerage firm. The customer's confirmation may be manually typed or computer-generated Usually prepared the night the trade is processed, these confirmations are placed in the mail the next morning. At the same time, additional copies are sent to the stockbroker and to certain operating departments for information and record retention purposes.

The customer's confirmation contains the following information:

1. A description of the trade (bought or sold).
   - The quantity.
   - The security's name.
   - The execution price.
   - The settlement money.
   - The accrued interest (if applicable).
   - The commission (for an agency trade).
   - The SEC fee (for a listed equity sale), other fees, or handling charges.
2. The trade date.
3. The settlement date.
4. The place of execution.
5. The capacity in which the firm acted (agency, principal, or principal as market maker).
6. The customer's name and address.

FIGURE 7-2. *A typical confirmation.*

Stone,
Forrest
& Rivers

OFFICE ACCOUNT NO.	TYPE	A E	TRADE DATE	SETTLEMENT DATE	TRANS. NO.	CUSIP NO.	EXCH	ORIG.	S

YOU BOUGHT	YOU SOLD

PRICE

SECURITY DESCRIPTION

GROSS AMOUNT	
INTEREST	
COMMISSION	
STATE TAX	
SERVICE CHG.	
SEC/POST	
AMOUNT DUE *	
SYMBOL	

PLEASE RETURN SECOND COPY

WITH SECURITIES SOLD (IF IN YOUR POSSESSION) OR WITH AMOUNT DUE * (IF NOT ALREADY IN YOUR ACCOUNT).

BY SETTLEMENT DATE

IN THE ENCLOSED ENVELOPE

IN ACCORDANCE WITH YOUR INSTRUCTIONS WE ARE PLEASED TO CONFIRM THE ABOVE TRANSACTION FOR YOUR ACCOUNT AND RISK SUBJECT TO TERMS LISTED ON REVERSE SIDE.

7. The customer's account number to which the trade has been booked.
8. The type of account (cash or margin).
9. The stockbroker's ID number.

Some firms even include the customer settlement instruction and the business phone number of the customer's stockbroker. Some brokerage firms use simple confirmation forms, while others use fairly elaborate types, including a tear-off stub to be returned with the customer's check.

BOOKING

Once the trade has been processed and balanced, it must be entered on the firm's records, or *booked*. Part of the booking procedure is the recording of fees and commissions due to the firm. As always in operations, booking errors can cost the firm money to correct.

SUMMARY

For each transaction that takes place on a given day, in a given marketplace, with a given brokerage or dealer firm, and for a given customer, the P&S department must perform the initial processing, figuration, clearing, correcting, and preparation for settlement. All of this must be performed accurately.

CHAPTER 8

Margin

Member firms are subject to—and base many of their procedures on—the rules and regulations of the Securities and Exchange Commission, of the exchanges and of other self-regulatory associations. While some of these many directives govern firm-to-firm dealings, others affect the customer-to-firm relationships. Yet rarely are customers aware of all the rules and regulations that affect them. The brokerage firms must therefore act as "watchdogs" for their clients, maintaining their accounts in accordance with all applicable rules, if they are to conduct a violation-free business.

The majority of customer-firm rules are enforced by a department known as the *margin (or credit) department,* which monitors the current status of each customer's account. (See Figure 8-1.) The employees in this area review the firm's customer accounts to make certain that each one is operating within the framework of the rules and regulations applicable to a customer's purchasing and selling securities. They determine when the customer must pay for the securities purchased and how much must be paid. In the case of a sale, they determine when the securities must be delivered and how much of the proceeds the customer may withdraw.

FIGURE 8-1. *The magin departments.*

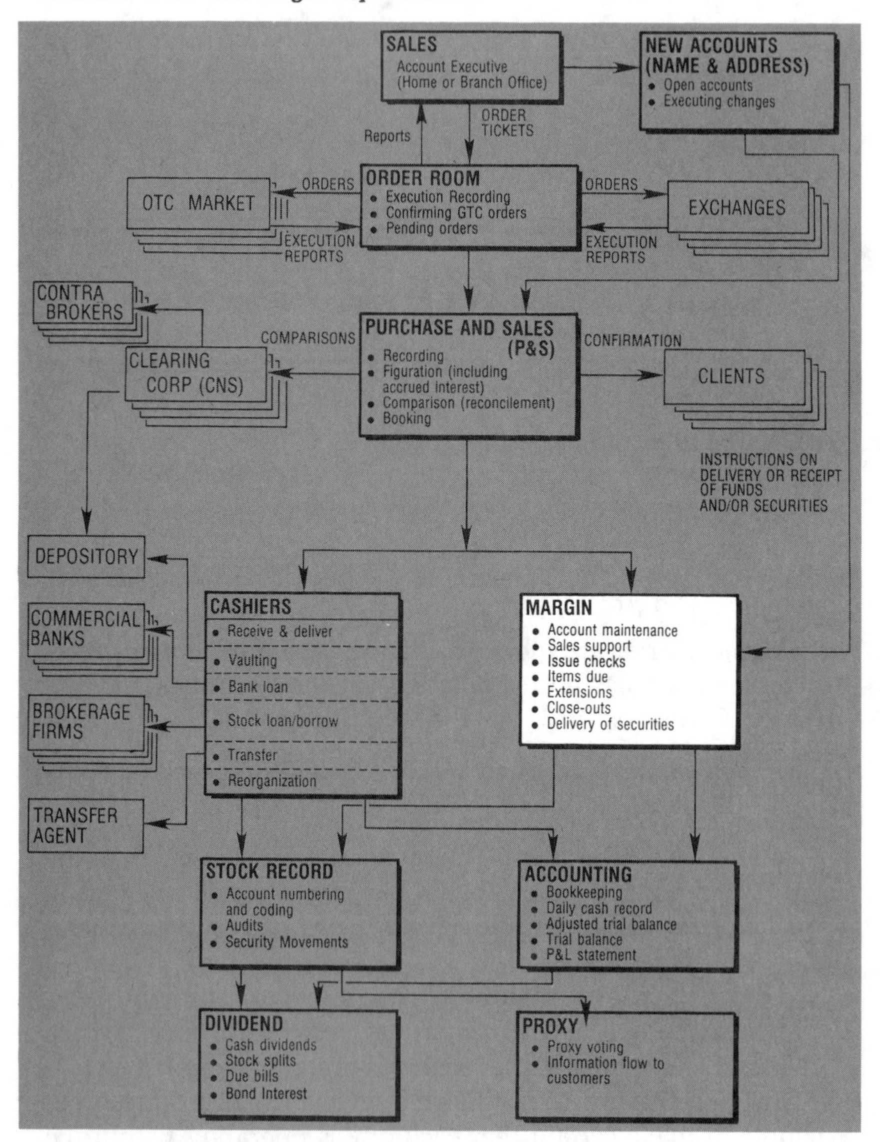

CASH VERSUS MARGIN PURCHASES

Customers may purchase securities in one of two ways.

1. In a *cash account purchase,* they must pay for the acquired securities in full.

2. In a *margin purchase,* the newly purchased securities are pledged as collateral to borrow part of the purchase money owed. The brokerage firm borrows the money from a bank and "reloans" it to the customer. The collateral for both loans (bank to firm and firm to client) is a portion of the purchased stock.

Not all securities may be purchased on margin. The security must meet certain criteria before it can be marginable. Generally, all securities listed on a national exchange are marginable, as are OTC securities that have been approved for margin by *The Federal Reserve Board*. The brokerage firm, however, has the final say in determining which securities it permits its customers to purchase on margin.

Not all customers may purchase on margin. A member firm can never permit a customer to margin an unapproved security, but it could prohibit a customer from margining an approved one.

Cash Account

When making a purchase in a cash account, the customer pays for securities in full. When making a sale, the client receives payment in full.

Example: A client of SF&R buys 100 shares of ZAP @ 42. The market value of the securities is therefore $4,200 (100 shares of ZAP times $42). (Ignore commission and other expenses.) The client pays for the purchase in full, and the equity in the account is therefore $4,200. If Zap rises to $60 per share, the market value becomes $6,000 (100 ZAP times $60), and the client's equity becomes $6,000.

In a margin account, however, the customer pays only part of the cost of purchase, and the brokerage firm lends the rest to the customer. Many securities are *marginable,* that is, the firm can lend the client money on them.

Trades purchased in a cash account must be paid for in full by the fifth business day after trade and no later than the seventh business day.

Margin Account

To understand margin, you must understand the terminology.

- *Loan value:* Securities have a market value. On certain securities, a client may borrow money against this market value, and, in such cases, this value is referred to as *loan value.*
- *Debit balance:* A client who borrows money from the brokerage firm establishes a loan, which, in a margin account, is known as the *debit balance.*
- *Equity:* This is either the difference between the debit balance and the market value or the sum of the market value and credit balance.
- *Margin Rate:* How much the firm can lend the customer is determined by the *margin rate,* which is the percentage of the market value that the customer has to pay. The margin rate is fixed by the Federal Reserve Board. Expressed as percentages, the margin rate and loan value always equals 100%.

Note: Federal Regulation "T," as supervised by the Securities and Exchange Commission, covers the lending of money by brokerage firms. The *amount* that a firm can lend is established by the *Federal Reserve Board.*

Example: A margin client of SF&R is interested in purchasing 100 shares of DUD, which is presently trading at $50. The client wants to invest the minimum amount permitted by Regulation T, as set by the Federal Reserve Board. At the time of purchase, the margin rate is 60%. The loan value is therefore 40%.

Margin rate % + Loan rate % = 100%
60% + Loan rate % = 100%
Loan rate % = 100% – 60%
Loan rate % = 40%

On the $5,000 purchase (100 shares at $50), the minimum the client has to pay is $3,000 (60% of $5,000). The client purchases the shares of DUD and pays $3,000, while the firm lends $2,000, which becomes the debit balance. As with *all* loans, the client pays interest on the outstanding principal.

Equity $ + Debit balance $ = Market value $
$3,000 + $2,000 = $5,000

The customer's $3,000 and the firm's loan of $2,000 go to pay for the purchase of DUD. There isn't any cash in the account, just a security position worth $5,000. Of that $5,000 in market value, $3,000 is the client's equity and $2,000 is the debit balance.

A LESSON IN MARGIN

Regulation T ("Reg T")

The backbone of all margin rules is a Federal Reserve Board regulation known as *Regulation T.* The Federal Reserve Board writes and changes Regulation T. The NYSE and NASD enforce it.

One of Reg T's provisions stipulates the percentage of margin (that is, the amount that the customer must put into the account), which is known as the *margin rate.* The rate is determined by the Federal Reserve Board.

Example: Given a margin rate of 50%, customer Fredrico must pay at least 50% of any purchase. If Fredrico purchases $10,000 value of stock, he must put $5,000 of his money into his account by the fifth business day. The brokerage firm lends the remaining $5,000, on which the customer pays a monthly interest charge.

The margin rate is therefore part of the system of controls that the FRB uses to regulate money and in turn the economy.

While Regulation T dictates the obligation of the customer at the time of trade, the exchanges and self-regulatory associations have instituted rules that not only augment Reg T, but also establish procedures to be followed after the initial transaction. Rules 431-432 of the New York Stock Exchange (NYSE) are two such rules. Among the areas covered by these rules are minimum equity requirements and minimum maintenance requirements.

To understand minimum equity requirements, you must be familiar with the jargon of the margin departments. We will explain:

1. Current market value.
2. Equity.
3. Debit balance.

4. Loan value.
5. Excess.
6. Buying power.
7. Minimum maintenance requirement.

Current Market Value, Equity, and Debit Balance

First of all, every account can be divided into three parts:

1. *Current market value,* which is the total of the current market values of all securities maintained in the account.
2. *Equity,* which is the amount, in either a dollar value or a percentage, of the total current value in the account that belongs to the customer, should the account be liquidated.
3. *Debit balance,* which is the amount of money loaned by the firm or owed by the customer. Or *credit balance,* which is the amount of money in the account belonging to the customer.

These three components are related by a mathematical formula:

Equity = Current market value – Debit balance

As the current market value fluctuates, so does the customer's equity. Not subject to market fluctuations is the debit balance, which is the amount loaned by the firm to the customer. Because the customer must repay this debt at a later time, it is therefore an obligation of the customer.

In a cash purchase (when the customer pays for the purchase in full), no debit balance is incurred, and the customer's equity always equals the current market value.

Example: Customer D. Dawn purchases 100 shares of XYZ at 15 for $1,500, paying in full. (For all examples disregard commission and fees.) The current market value is $1,500, and the customer's equity is $1,500.

Equity = Current market value – Debit balance
$1,500 = $1,500 – $0

If the stock appreciates in value to $2,000, the equity increases to $2,000. Should the stock decline in value to $1,000, the equity also declines to $1,000.

Brokerage firms are prohibited from lending money to customers if the equity in the account is less than $2,000. This $2,000 minimum is known as the *minimum equity requirement.*

Example: If customer Dawn wanted to purchase the security on margin, she could not, because the equity in the account is below $2,000 (the purchase was for $1,500). She must pay in full.

Loan Value

The complement of the margin requirement is known as the *loan value,* which is the amount that the customer may borrow on the security. Together the margin rate and loan value, both expressed as percentage, must total 100%. If the Federal Reserve Board (FRB) establishes a margin rate of 60%, then the loan value of the security is 40%. If the customer is required to pay 70%, then the loan value is 30%.

Example: A customer, Mr. Scott Chensoda, wishes to purchase 100 shares of XYZ at $60 per share. The purchase would cost a total of $6,000. Chensoda can pay any amount of cash that represents a percentage between the current margin rate and 100%. If the margin rate is 60%, the minimum he has to pay is $3,600 (.60 × $6,000). The loan value is 40% or $2,400 (.40 × $6,000). Chensoda deposits a check for $3,600 within five business days, and the firm lends the remainder.

Chensoda's $3,600 and his firm's $2,400 go to the selling brokerage firm. The customer who sold the stock then receives $6,000 and doesn't care how Chensoda pays for it.

Chensoda's account is shown as follows:

Long 100 shares XYZ @ 60	$6,000
Less debit balance	2,400
Customer equity	$3,600

XYZ appreciates in value to $10,000. Then:

Long 100 XYZ @ 100	$10,000
Less debit balance	2,400
Customer equity	$ 7,600

Chensoda borrowed only $2,400 and therefore only owes that sum to the brokerage firm.

With the value of account now at $10,000, the loan value has increased $4,000. Chensoda can borrow an additional $1,600 if he wishes. If he *borrows* this sum, then:

Long 100 XYZ @ 100	$10,000	
Less debit balance	4,000	(40%)
Customer equity	$ 6,000	(60%)

The account has returned to maximum loan value.

Excess and Buying Power

Anytime the loan value is greater than the debit balance in the account, the difference is *excess*, which can be used to calculate *buying power*.

Example: XYZ is still at 100, the debit balance is $2,400, and Chensoda does *not* borrow the $1,600. Chensoda wants to purchase stock ABC, which is selling for 25⅝ or $2,662.50. If the customer wants to buy more stock, how much additional money does he or she have to deposit to meet the margin requirement for the new purchase?

$2,662.50
× .60
$1,597.50

Does Chensoda have enough excess to make the purchase on margin? He does:

Current market value	$10,000
Loan value rate	× .40
Maximum loan value	$ 4,000
Debit balance	– 2,400
Excess	$ 1,600

The $1,600 *excess* can be used to purchase additional stock. The firm lends the difference. Alternatively, the customer may withdraw excess. The total of excess and any additional funds amount to *buying power,* which is the dollar amount worth of securities that can be purchased without depositing additional funds.

Example: Chensoda purchases 100 ABC at 26 5/8. Then:

Original debit balance	$ 2,400.00
Excess supplied to ABC purchase	1,600.00
Debit balance in ABC purchase	1,062.50
New debit balance	$ 5,062.50

100 XYZ @ 100	$10,000.00	
100 ABC @ 26 5/8	2,662.50	
Current market value	$12,662.50	
Less debit balance	5,062.50	(approx. 40%)
	$ 7,600.00	(approx. 60%)

Let's look at another example with a different angle.

Example: The margin rate is 50%; so the loan value has to be 50% also. A client buys 100 XYZ at 50 and deposits the entire amount. Then:

100 XYZ @ 50	$5,000
Less debit balance	0
Customer's equity	$5,000

After deciding to purchase another 100 shares at $50 for an additional $5,000, the customer asks, "What is my buying power?"

Current market value	$5,000
Loan value rate	× .50
Loan value	2,500
Less debit balance	0

$$\text{Buying power} = \frac{100\%\ \text{Market value}}{50\%\ \text{Equity}} \text{ or } \frac{10}{5} \times \$2{,}500 = \$5{,}000$$

The customer purchases the additional stock and the account reveals:

Current market value (200 XYZ @ 50)	$10,000
Less debit balance (50%)	5,000
Equity (50%)	$ 5,000

Had the customer purchased 200 shares originally with a 50% margin requirement (and a 50% loan value), the account would have been:

Current market value (200 XYZ @ 50)	$10,000
Less debit balance (50%)	5,000
Equity (50%)	$ 5,000

Which is exactly how the account wound up after the two purchases.

Minimum Maintenance Requirement

Unfortunately accounts don't always increase in value. Sometimes they decrease, creating an altogether different set of problems. How far may the value of an account fall before the brokerage firm must "call" for additional money? The exchange rules state that the call must go out when the equity in the account is less than 25% of the market value. Most firms have even stricter requirements.

Example: Customer Phil O'Dendrin purchases 200 shares of EFG at 60 for a total cost of $12,000. With the margin rate at 50%, the brokerage firm receives Phil's check for $6,000 and lends the rest to the customer. Then:

Current market value (200 EFG @ 60)	$12,000
Less debit balance	6,000
Equity	$ 6,000

If EFG falls in value to 20, the account is:

Current market value (200 EFG @ 20)	4,000
Less debit balance	6,000
Equity	($ 2,000)

There is a *deficit* in the account of $2,000.

In this case, the firm risks losing $2,000 should the customer be unable to pay back the $6,000 loan. To prevent this from happening, the minimum maintenance requirement rules are enforced. When the equity goes below one-third the debit balance, firms send "calls" to customers for additional money. In our example, because the debit balance in the account is $6,000, the equity can decrease to only $2,000 (a third of 6,000). If it drops below this figure, the firm issues a *maintenance call* for additional money, or equity, to be deposited by the customer. If the customer does not meet the needs of the call, the firm must liquidate enough securities to satisfy the requirement. With the equity at $2,000 and the debit balance at $6,000, the market value would be $8,000. $2,000 is 25% of $8,000 (8,000 × .25 = 2,000).

Restricted Accounts

An account may have no excess but not be on call. Such an account has a debit balance that is higher than the current loan value.

Example:

Current market value	$10,000
Less debit balance	6,000
Equity	$ 4,000

With a 50% loan value, the account is currently undermargined, but not enough to justify a maintenance call.

Regulation T refers to this type of account as *restricted.*

Should the customer decide to purchase additional stock, the brokerage firm requires margin only for the new purchase. It does not compel the customer to deposit sufficient funds to bring the entire account up to the margin requirement.

When a client *sells* a security from a restricted account, the client is entitled to withdraw 50% of the proceeds. Any excess in this account is recomputed using the full proceeds of sale. The customer may withdraw 50% of the proceeds of sale or all of the recomputed excess, whichever is higher.

Special Memorandum Account (SMA)

In a restricted account, keeping track of the monies that the customer could have withdrawn is impossible. After a sale settles, the security position disappears, and the proceeds from the sale are merged with the account balance. To keep track of these entries, the *special memorandum account* (SMA), is employed. The SMA is *only* a bookkeeping account. Of and by itself, it does not figure into margin calculations. It is a vehicle for recording entries that the customer could have used. Either margin employees or computer programs keep track of the entries booked into and out of SMA.

There is much more to margin. This basic presentation should, however, provide some insight into the workings of a margin account. The margin department employee has a much more detailed understanding of these regulations, and the department manager must be cognizant of all the rules and regulations, as well as their interpretations and applicability. If these regulations are not enforced, the firm can face possible loss through unnecessary exposure to risk or fine, in addition to suspension from the regulatory agencies.

THE ROLES OF THE MARGIN DEPARTMENT

Account Maintenance

The margin department ensures that all the customer accounts are operating in accordance with the regulations. It reviews accounts, continuously computing excess and/or buying power.

Sales Support

Any one of a thousand questions may be directed to the margin department in a day. Reliable, accurate responses to these questions are vital to the overall operation of the firm. To this department the stockbroker in particular turns for information when soliciting orders from clients. For example, the stockbroker may be discussing a possible transaction with a client, such as buying 100 shares of XYZ and selling or writing a call on the stock. The stockbroker has to know what effect this transaction will have on the account.

Clearance for Issuance of Checks

In most retail firms, the branches must wire a message to the margin department for an *OKTP.* This message asks the margin employee to verify that an amount of money being paid to the customer is *"OK to pay."* Before the branch can draw the check, it must get the margin department's approval. In some firms, this data is transmitted to the branch offices each morning, and the branches can pay the amount transmitted *without* approval.

Items Due

Due to the nature of the industry, the credit department staff spends a good part of their time informing branch offices of *items due,* which are pending or actual deficiencies in customer accounts. Included in items due wires are:

1. *Money due on T calls*—the sum owed by a customer on a transaction.
2. *Money due on house calls*—the sum that a customer owes to

satisfy an equity deficiency (that is, the equity is below the minimum maintenance).

3. *Stocks or bonds due to be delivered* by the client against a sale in the account.
4. Any other pending problem.

Someone at the branch, usually a stockbroker, has to contact the clients and advise them of the discrepancies. The client's obligation is then to satisfy the discrepancy.

Extensions

Occasionally clients enter into a security transaction and, due to circumstances beyond their control, cannot satisfy the obligation in seven business days. In such a case, the firm on instruction from the stockbroker and with the approval of the margin department, files a request for an *extension of time* with the appropriate self-regulatory organization—the NYSE, AMEX, PCE, PHLX, NASD, and so on. If the request is granted, the client has additional time to satisfy the commitment. A customer is generally permitted to have five extensions per year, on an industry-wide basis.

Close-Outs

If a request is turned down at any time, the firm has to take the appropriate action and *close out* the transaction. If the client has failed to pay for a purchased security, the security is liquidated. In closing an unsatisfied purchase, the brokerage firm is said to *sell out* the purchased security. If the client has failed to deliver a sold security, the firm closes out the commitment. In closing out an unsatisfied sale, the firm is said to *buy in*, that is, the firm buys the security elsewhere and delivers to the buying firm.

Because the problem arises with the customer, the closing transactions must be effected in the customer's account. Any profit or losses from these close-out transactions, due to fluctuations in the security price, belong to the customer. Naturally, customers are only too willing to take profits, but losses create problems for the brokerage firm. If the client does not honor the loss, the firm has to absorb it or go to court to collect.

Delivery of Securities

The customer's account reflects the firm's obligation to the customer and the customer's obligation to the firm. Once the obligation ceases to exist, it is no longer reflected in the account. The obligation can be for either money or securities.

For fully paid-for securities that remain in the firm's possession, the firm owes the securities to the customer and so has a custodian obligation. The margin department, therefore also includes the release of securities for delivery to clients. (Some customers request physical delivery of the securities.) These securities can be delivered only if the client has paid for them in full.

On sales, the client can owe the firm delivery of the securities sold. Once delivery is made, the firm owes the customer the proceeds. Purchases entail a monetary obligation on the part of the client. A client who purchases securities on margin owes the value of the loan to the firm.

Certain securities, known as *registered securities*, must be sent by the brokerage firm, or by a depository on instructions from the brokerage firm, to a transfer agent. The transfer agent reregisters the security in the customer's name and mails the new security to the brokerage firm for delivery to the customer. Once these securities are delivered to the customer, the security is no longer reflected in the customer's account.

The margin department keeps track of all these entries, making sure that accounts reflect the correct balances. And "correct" is the word. The margin department has the dual responsibility of protecting the firm's money *and* the customer's funds. The margin department must be aware at all times of *all* the rules affecting broker-customer relationships.

A TYPICAL DAY IN THE MARGIN DEPARTMENT

The margin function, like all operations procedures, is an ongoing process. Every business day customers enter into new commitments, and others settle transactions. Securities and funds are paid, received, or delivered, while other securities go into transfer and others return. Stock dividends and bond interest are credited or charged to customers' accounts. Legal papers are received. Sellouts and buy-ins are issued. T calls or house calls are sent. All the while, the markets are open for trading and securities' prices are fluctuating. With all this happening at once, accuracy is a must. The margin employee must be able to deal quickly with figures and understand the applicable rules.

The typical business day of a margin employee begins with the receipt of the daily work.

Depending on the degree of computer support, the daily work takes on different forms. Some firms receive a listing known as the *exception report*, which includes all the accounts containing problems needing the margin clerk's attention. The margin clerk does not have to review accounts that are functioning within requirements. In firms without a computer-generated exception listing, the margin clerk has to review each and every account. The clerk passes over accounts that do not need attention and sets aside those requiring action.

When the margin employee finishes this review, the work on the stack for attention begins. The daily margin functions include:

1. Computing excess.
2. Computing buying power.
3. Adjusting SMA.
4. Computing SMA excess.
5. Issuing T calls.
6. Creating item due notifications.
7. Filing for extensions.
8. Issuing delivery or transfer instructions.
9. Approving checks to clients.
10. Issuing house calls.
11. Preparing sell-out/buy-in notices.
12. Issuing sell-out/buy-in orders.
13. Answering stockbrokers' inquiries.
14. Making various entries and adjustments.

This work can be quickened with the help of EDP support (see Chapter 16). Because all margin transactions follow prescribed rules, they are well suited for execution by a computer program. The EDP equipment can perform calculations and make tests against the limits of the rules much more quickly than any margin employee in a manual procedure.

The amount of manual work left up to margin clerks therefore determines the number of accounts that they can monitor: the greater the automation support, the more accounts one clerk can handle.

Accounts are usually maintained in the order of their branch office account numbers. The size of the branch office or number of its active accounts determines the number of margin clerks monitoring the office. Very small offices may be grouped together, with one clerk monitoring the group.

SUMMARY

The work of the margin area is the last checkpoint before the customer gets involved. Erroneously processed trades can be caught here and the adjustment made before the customer gets the confirmation in the mail.

Even when the customer calls to report the mistake that slips through, however, the firm can still appear very professional by telling the client, "Yes, we have already corrected it. Sorry for any inconvenience." But a customer who cannot get erroneous data corrected can only lose confidence in the firm. And the firm will lose customers. Reduced to its most basic form, the point is that the customer's money is on the line.

CHAPTER 9

Cashiering

The *cashiering function* is responsible for moving all securities and funds within the firm. Included in this responsibility are the following tasks:

- Receiving and delivering.
- Vaulting.
- Hypothecation of security for margin accounts (bank loan).
- Borrowing and lending money and securities (stock loan).
- Security transfer.
- Keeping track of reorganizations among issuers.

These functions may be performed on the premises, through outside institutions, or through a depository.

Of all the departments in the production cycle, the cashiers function has been most affected by industry processing problems. Yet, as a group, the cashiers' departments of the many firms have responded with viable new systems.

FIGURE 9-1. *The cashiering department.*

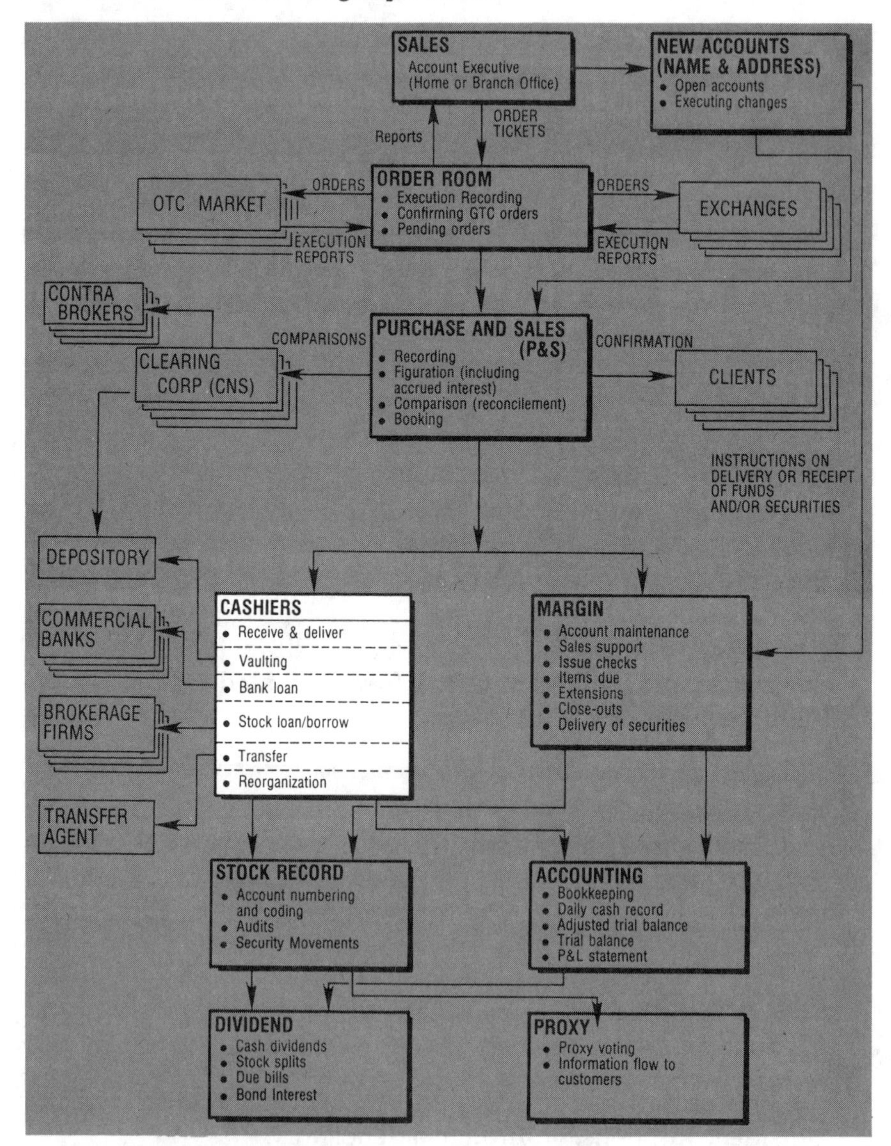

RECEIVE AND DELIVER

The cashier department's receive and deliver section must be fully informed of pending security movements. This section is responsible for expediting all deliveries and accepting all receipts, regardless of the type of settlement.

Good Deliverable Form

A major duty of the receive and deliver section is to make certain that the securities flowing through their area are in good deliverable form.

What is good deliverable form? Here are some typical problems:

- Securities received from a selling client may not be properly endorsed, and the firm then has to get the customers to complete a stock/bond power.
- Legal registered securities (such as corporation- or estate-registered securities) must be reregistered into a negotiable name (usually the firm's name, or street name) before they may be delivered to the purchasing firm.
- Coupon bonds are usually in *bearer form,* which means that they are not registered in anyone's name and are therefore fully negotiable at all times. Attached to these bonds are *coupons,* each of which represents an interest payment on the bond. If a coupon is missing, the holder of the instrument will not receive the interest payment due on that coupon. "Proof of ownership" also has to be attached, when a bearer bond is received from an individual customer.

The receive and deliver section must be constantly on watch for securities that are not in good deliverable form—sometimes referred to as *dirty stock.* If either a customer or another firm attempts to deliver dirty stock (undeliverable security), it is a *bad delivery.* In the case of a brokerage firm, the dirty stock has to be returned, or *bounced.* In the case of a customer, payment must be withheld.

The reason for either measure is that a bad delivery, if accepted, costs the firm money. Not only does the firm have to go to the expense of bringing the security up to good deliverable form, but it may not use that security until it is deliverable. If the firm pays the customer for the dirty stock, it actually loses the use of that money until the securities are deliverable. The firm might even have to borrow other securities for delivery elsewhere, thereby entailing the use of financing.

The receive and deliver employees are responsible for avoiding such unnecessary costs to the firm by not accepting securities.

VAULTING

At one time, security certificates were physically moved from one brokerage firm too another after a transaction. To facilitate such transfers, as well to expedite other types of processing (such as dividend control), the firm kept the customers' certificates on premises, along with its own.

Both the customers' and the firm's securities were kept on premises in a vault, called the "box." Securities belonging to customers were so recorded on the firm's records, so that the real owners, or *beneficial owners*, could always be identified.

The customers' certificates were, however, registered to the firm's name, that is, in *nominee name* (in name only). These securities could be delivered quickly by the firm. The beneficial owners were the customers. Yet, though registered, they were nonnegotiable and they remain so until a transaction caused the beneficial owner to change.

When the security was sold, it was pulled from the vault and prepared for delivery. On settlement date, the certificates were delivered to the purchasing firm.

As trading volume increased over the years, physical delivery became cumbersome and, in some cases almost impossible. Although physical delivery is still made in some cases, it is no longer the most common method.

Maintaining the "vault" (that is, keeping track of ownership) is one of the main functions of the cashiering area. Securities must be very carefully tracked and recorded because they represent ownership, by either the firm or its customers.

HYPOTHECATION (BANK LOAN)

When customers purchase securities in a cash account and leave them in the possession of the brokerage firm, the securities may not be used to secure bank loans. The securities belong to the customer.

Firms that maintain inventory positions (dealers) finance their positions by pledging their own securities at a bank.

Firms whose clients acquire stock on margin pledge a portion of the customer's security to finance the customer debit balance. As explained in Chapter 8, when customers purchase securities on margin, they pay for part of the purchase and the firm lends the rest to them. To lend money on a margin purchase, the firm pledges a portion of the customer's securities at a commercial bank and in doing so borrows the money.

The rules governing the amount of securities the firm can use are very strict. Securities that can be pledged in accordance with the rules is referred to as *free stock*. Stock that the firm cannot use is *segregated*, sometimes known as *seg securities*. If the firm pledges seg securities for a loan, it violates the seg requirements and is subject to fine, censure, or even suspension from the appropriate self-regulatory authority.

Brokerage firms naturally want to borrow money at the lowest rate possible. The employees in the cashiering area who arrange the financing at the best possible interest rates are *money managers;* they report to the firm's primary money manager, who may not work in cashiering and who is responsible for all the firm's financing. The money desk's role has a key effect on the firm's profitability. This department must take advantage of all money situations and constantly try to finance positions at the least possible cost.

Depending on the type of security involved in a transaction and its market, money managers attempt to borrow money from several sources:

1. Commercial banks.
2. Stock loan.
3. Repurchase agreements.

Commercial Banks

Brokerage firms maintain relationships with commercial banks, from whom they obtain collateralized and uncollateralized loans. *Collateral loans* necessitate the pledging of securities to secure them. So the banks charge lower rates of interest for this type of loan than for *uncollateralized loans*, for which no securities are pledged. The firms "shop" the loans, trying to obtain the best rate possible. The base rate, the usual minimum rate charged by banks for collateral loans, is known as the *broker's call rate.*

STOCK LOAN

Quite often a firm needs a particular security to complete a fail to deliver. So the firm borrows the security from another firm, using cash as collateral. The firm lending the security obtains funds, which reduce its financing costs. Arbitrage firms (firms that specialize in temporary differences in the marketplace) frequently need securities to cover short positions; these firms borrow securities and return them when the arbitrage is completed.

To obtain securities, the borrowing firm sometimes enlists the services of a *finder*, who locates loanable securities for a fee.

Repurchase Agreements (Repos)

In a *repurchase agreement (repos)*, a brokerage firm sells its inventories securities to a nonbank institution with the intention of repurchasing them at a later date. Government securities and commercial paper, for example, may be sold to organizations with funds available for a short period of time. These institutions might be unable to invest their money otherwise, either because of prohibitive regulations or their unwillingness to be exposed to market risk. They often do, therefore, enter into repos.

The money is, in effect, lent for a day or two, and usually for no longer than a week. The brokerage firm and lender agree on the terms and the interest rate at the time the trade is consummated. The firm's sell trade is processed as a same-day settlement, and the buy trade (or *buy-back*) is settled on the last day of the repo, as agreed upon. The difference between the two money amounts exchanged in the sell and buy transactions is the amount of interest charged on the money.

TRANSFER

The *transfer section* is assigned the task of sending registered securities to the *transfer agents* (that is, the banks that maintain the company's list of owners) to be reregistered in the new owners' names. As explained earlier, reregistration may be in either the beneficial owner's name or nominee name. Correct and timely registrations will remain important until all certificates are immobilized through the use of depositories.

Fortunately, most transfers are routine and require a minimum of paperwork. The certificates must be endorsed by the registered holder and authorized by a power of attorney, and then the appropriate stamps are affixed.

REORGANIZATION

The corporations whose securities are traded often "reorganize"—that is, they merge, one company buys out another, one sells another, and so on. The *reorganization* (or *reorg*) section of cashiering keeps track of these changes among issuers and makes the appropriate changes in customer accounts.

CHAPTER 10

Stock Record

Every brokerage firm maintains two records that make up the backbone of the organizations: the *stock record* and the *daily cash report*. (The names may vary from one firm to another.) These reports reflect each and every movement of securities and cash within the firm. In this chapter, we explain the stock record function.

During the day in a typical brokerage firm:

- Customers deliver securities to the branch offices, who in turn send the securities to a central office.
- The central office receives securities from all the branches, from other firms, through clearing corporations, from the transfer agent, from loan accounts, and from elsewhere.
- The central office delivers securities to their customers, to their branches, to depositories, to the transfer agent, and so on.

The firm must record all these movements and many others, on the stock record.

To properly record the movement of securities, the stock record must balance debits versus credits. That is, every debit entry must have an offsetting credit and vice versa. For example, when a security is received from a customer, the customer's ac-

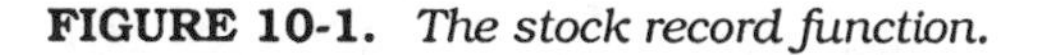

FIGURE 10-1. *The stock record function.*

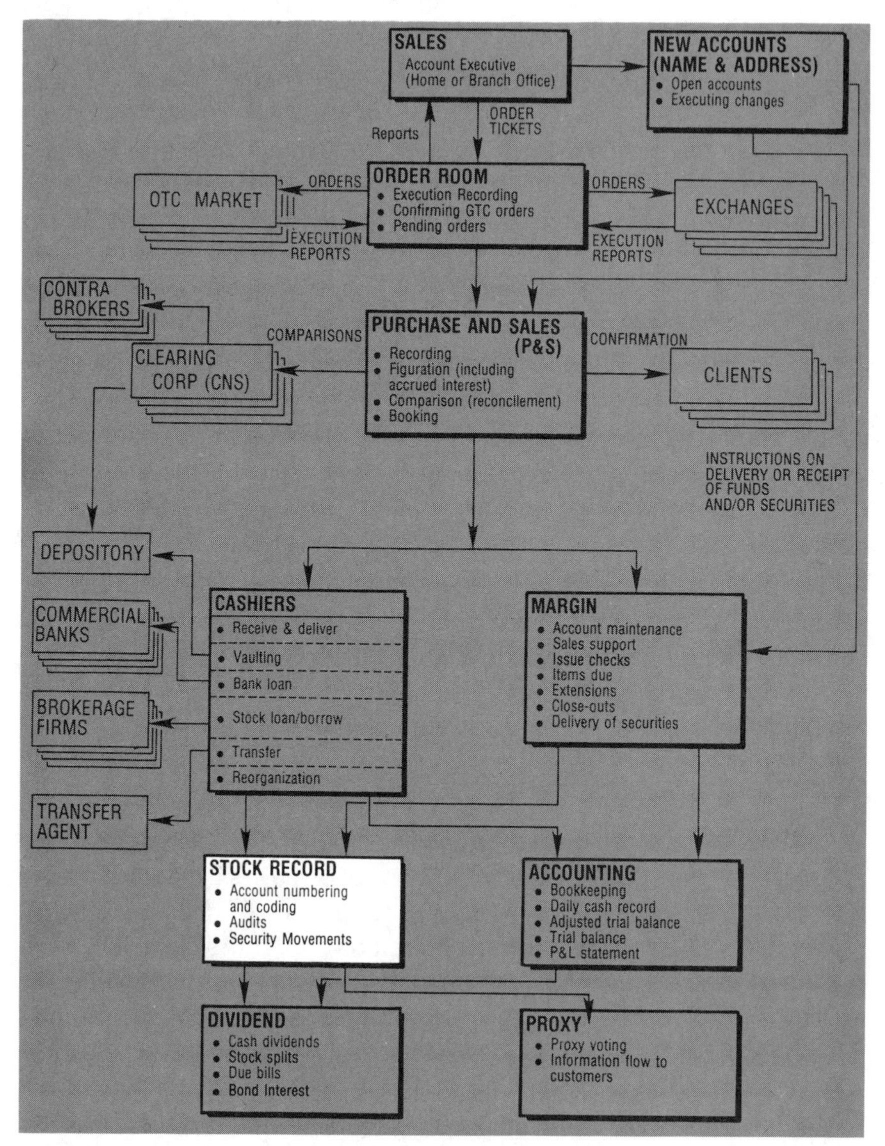

count is debited and the firm's box (or vault) account is credited. When the cashier sends the security to a central depository, corresponding debits and credits are entered on the box and depository accounts.

BREAKS

Each day the stock record department inspects the stock record take-off, looking for *breaks*, which occur when only one side of an entry is recorded. A debit might exist without a credit, or vice versa. For example, suppose ABC security is recorded as having been removed from the vault, but the record does not show when it was delivered. That's a "break." The stock record has to be balanced—that is, all breaks corrected—on a daily basis. The older the break, the more difficult it is to track down, and the more likely it becomes that it will create other breaks. So, in the event of a break, stock record employees must check copies of the original forms, phone entry-originating departments, and research the discrepancy right away.

ACCOUNT NUMBERING/CODING

Each firm has its own internal account numbering or coding system. An intelligent numbering system makes it relatively easy to resolve problems. *Wire houses*, for instance, usually identify their many branches with a key digit or two. If the branch is to be denoted by a two-letter code an intelligent approach is to code the branches by easily recognizable symbols, such as LA for the Los Angeles office, SF for the San Francisco location, and DC for the Washington, D.C. branch. If the firm uses a numerical system then the branches might be identified by numbered districts or zones. The number sequences for accounts in the western district could start with a 1; those in the midwest district could begin with a 2, and so on.

An intelligent numbering scheme enables the stock record department to easily read the stock record. To anyone outside the department, the record looks like a long series of numbers signifying nothing. But to stock record personnel, each entry is a sentence, and the sentences become paragraphs and the paragraphs become stories. Some of the stories tell the employee the probable solution to the problem.

Example: ZAP stock movement for yesterday is recorded as follows:

Account Number	*Debit*	*Credit*
DC10316	100	
DC09623	100	
LA04296	200	
SF90102		200
SF80602	200	
BDC0001		200
BSF0001	200	
BSF0001		200
9999999		200

The two-letter combinations (DC, LA, SF) designate the branch offices in which the accounts are located. The addition of a B (BDC, BLA, BSF) represents the box locations in those cities, and 9999999 is the break account. The 9999999 informs the employee that credits totaling two hundred shares are missing.

Can you figure out which entry is possibly missing?

All the stock received from DC office's accounts seems to be credited to the DC box or vault (BDC 0001). All the security movements affecting SF accounts seem to be offset by the BSF0001 account. But what happened to the LA security movement? The stock record employee would immediately look for an "in box" ticket for a BLA0001 account that wasn't processed.

Because many securities are similar, the BLA0001 ticket might have been erroneously processed as another security. If so, then that security position would have a debit break. The employee could correct both breaks at the same time.

Both breaks can and should be corrected as soon as possible.

THE AUDIT

The stock record department works in the shadow of one audit or another. Firms must audit their physical security positions quarterly. Once a year, an independent accounting firm performs a full audit, which includes all customer accounts, fail positions, and so on. In both kinds of audits, *all* the certificates are counted or verified in writing, and the results are compared to the stock record. Any discrepancy between the physical counts and the stock record position must be researched and explained.

Because the stock record is balanced daily, most errors are due to several commonplace circumstances:

- Both the original debit and credit entries were entered incorrectly.
- The wrong account was credited or debited the security.
- The wrong security was used to make delivery.

These types of errors are difficult to detect, because they do not create daily breaks. Even in these cases, however, an intelligent account numbering system may help. While scanning the record, an employee could spot improbable movements, check out possible errors and take corrective action.

SUMMARY

The stock record must be in balance at all times, not only because it is subject to frequent audit, but also—and more importantly—it is one of the firm's most valuable records.

In the next chapter, we look at another, equally valuable document, the daily cash record.

CHAPTER 11

Accounting: The Daily Cash Record

The brokerage firm is no different from any other company: It incurs expenses and takes in revenue. So, just as the stock record keeps track of security movement, the accounting department records, processes, and balances the movement of money within a brokerage firm. Such daily money movement involves not only the settlement of customer and broker transactions, but also the invoicing, paying, and recording of fees, salaries, operating expenses, and other money amounts. Without this function, the entire processing apparatus grinds to a halt.

The final step of the accounting process is the *daily cash record*. Produced each business day, this listing contains all the money movements that occurred in the firm on the previous business day.

ESTABLISHING ACCOUNTS

To accurately record the movement of money from one place to another, accounts are established, assigned numbers, and given descriptive ledger titles. Typical titles are the names of customer, business or street side names, and the firm's Revenue and Ex-

FIGURE 11-1. *The accounting department.*

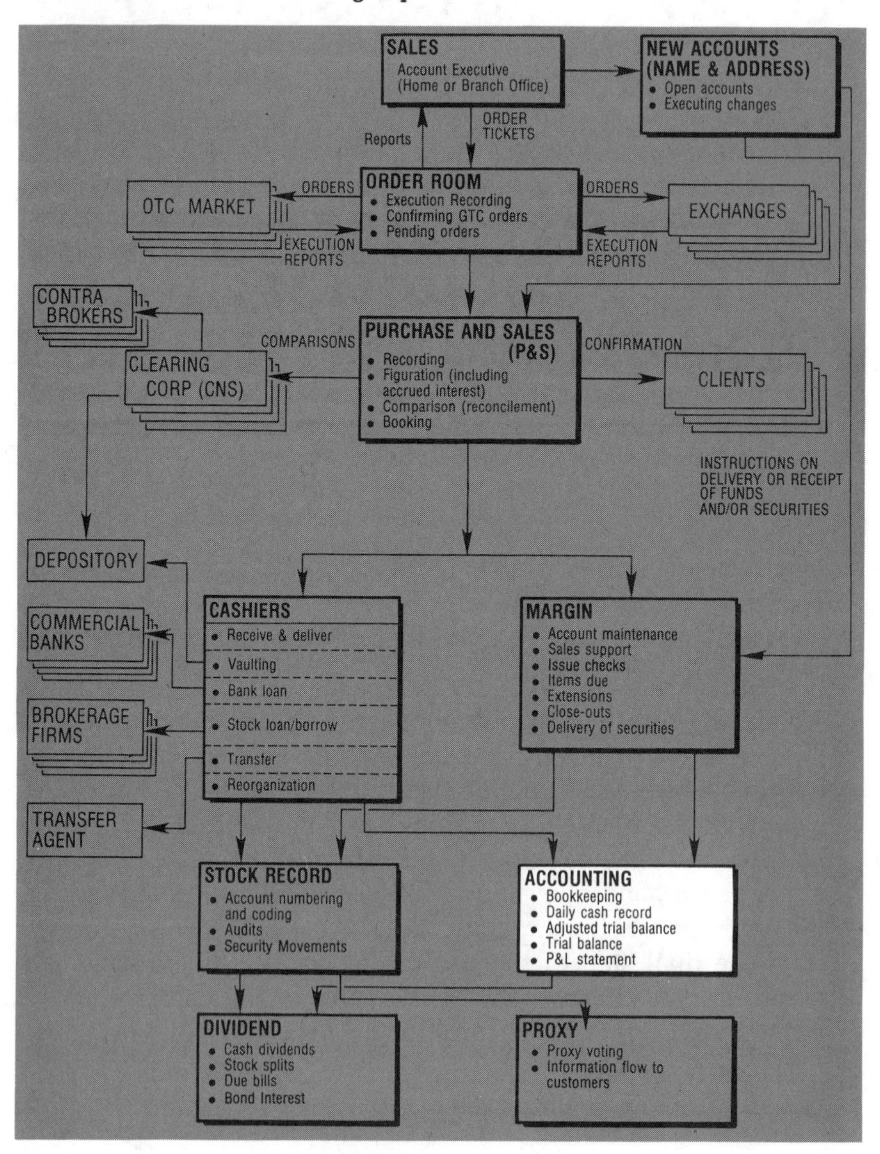

pense accounts. The systematic numbering of these accounts aids processing, research, and control. For example, the numbers assigned to customer ledger accounts are usually the same as those assigned to their security accounts. The use of the same number gives the firm more control of margin transactions and neatly keeps all the firm's obligations to a customer in one location. Account numbers are usually grouped for control purposes. As the customers' accounts make up the greatest percentage of a firm's accounts, their group is the largest.

DUAL-ENTRY BOOKKEEPING

Every movement of funds (checks, cash, and book entry memo items) must be properly recorded by means of dual entry bookkeeping procedures. Each movement will necessitate two entries, one a debit and the other a credit. So, like the stock record, the daily cash record (or listing) is processed strictly by account number order. Every debit entry must have a corresponding credit and vice versa. On any given day, the net result of all entries must be zero.

In addition to the obvious entries affecting customer accounts, such as payments for securities received and the like, many other money entries must routinely be processed. For example:

- Each margin account customer must be charged interest on the debit, or loan, portion of the account, usually once a month. So, if a firm maintains 100,000 active margin accounts, it has to process 100,000 debit entries (one for each account), plus one totalled credit entry to the firm's revenue account, representing the money sum of the debits.
- When a firm acts as a custodian for its customer's securities, it must credit each such account with any dividends or interest paid on the securities in the account—and at the appropriate time.
- Like any business, the brokerage firm pays its bills for rent, heat, power, light, stationery, processing forms, membership dues, selling and traveling expenses and, of course, salaries.

Most of the entries processed through the daily cash record

originate in other areas of the firm. Copies of each department's money-related forms are routed to the accounting department for use in reconciling this important document. The dividend department sends in dividend entries. P&S routes customer transaction net figures to accounting. Cashiering advises of checks paid to or received from customers or other firms. And these are but a few of the many entries every day.

THE USES OF THE DAILY CASH RECORD

The daily cash record serves as an *accounting journal*. Entries in it must be posted to individual *ledger* accounts by a method determined by the degree of computer support available. (Some firms make manual entries.) The ledgers are then reconciled to the journal to make certain that all entries have been posted properly. The debit and credit entries, as posted to the ledger, must also net out to zero, and their effect on the account must be reflected in the updated balances.

The Trial Balance

At lease once a month, the firm copies all its ledger account balances onto a document known as a *trial balance*. Because all entries posted from the journal to the ledger have been balanced and the ledger balances updated to reflect the impact of these entries, the trial balance should balance also. That is, the accounts with debit balances should equal all the accounts with credit balances. Through the trial balance, the firm checks to see that all entries have been posted from the daily journals to the ledger and that the balance in each account has been updated and carried forward. If the debits and credits do not equal each other, the accounting department personnel must find the source of the error and correct it.

The Adjusted Trial Balance

Once the trial balance is completed, additional entries are made for *accruals*, which are items incurred during a period but payable or receivable at another time. For instance, although taxes might be payable quarterly, the firm must accrue this month's tax liability against this month's income. In addition to accruals, end-of-month and other adjustments are entered in the appropriate accounts to more accurately reflect what took place over the past month. With these final entries, the accounting department now has what is called an *adjusted trial balance.*

All accounts in the adjusted trial balance are used to develop two primary business reports:

1. The profit and loss (P&L) statement.
2. The balance sheet.

The Profit and Loss (P&L) Statements

The accounts in the adjusted trial balance that reflect revenue (income) and expense become part of the *profit and loss statement.* A P&L statement therefore reports all revenue earned and all expenses incurred by the firm *over a period*. The report could cover a month, a quarter, half a year, or an entire year (fiscal or calendar). This document is also known as an *income statement* or *earnings report*.

The difference between the debit and credit totals taken from the adjusted trial balance and placed in the P&L statement is either a profit or loss for the firm. In other words, if credit accounts (income) exceed debit accounts (expense), the brokerage firm has made a profit. If the debit accounts (expense) exceed credit accounts (income), the firm has incurred a loss. The profit or loss must be journaled to the balance sheet.

The Balance Sheet

The accounts in the adjusted trial balance that describe the firm's assets, liabilities, and net worth become a part of the *balance sheet*.

1. *Assets* are items owned by or owed to the firm. The firm's assets are classified into current assets, fixed assets, and intangible assets.
2. Liabilities are divided into two categories: current liabilities

and long-term liabilities. A *liability* is any sum that the company owes.

3. *Net worth* is the value of the firm belonging to its owners.

Balance sheets therefore contain all the remaining debit and credit balances in the adjusted trial balance. Accounts transferred to the P&L statement are reflected in the profit or loss carried over from the P&L report. A profit is reflected as an addition to net worth, and a loss is entered as a subtraction or reduction from net worth. All other balance sheet entries—assets, liabilities, or net worth—are transferred directly from the trial balance.

The balance sheet is set up so that the total of assets equals the sum of total liabilities and net worth. The reason is that the balance sheet reflects, directly or indirectly, all the debit and credit entries on the trial balance, and those entries balance out to zero.

An Illustrative Case

Let's take an example of a mock trial balance, P&L statement, and balance sheets:

THE ADJUSTED TRIAL BALANCE

Cash (A)	$ 50,000	
Inventory (A)	150,000	
Furniture & fixtures (A)	75,000	
Commission (I)		$300,000
Salaries payable (L)		50,000
Salaries (E)	150,000	
Rent, power, & light (E)	125,000	
Interest income (I)		90,000
Interest expense (E)	80,000	
Net worth (N)		190,000
	$630,000	$630,000

A = Asset, L = Liability, N = Net worth, I = Income, E = Expense

To form the profit and loss statement, extract all income and expense accounts from the trial balance.

PROFIT & LOSS
FOR PERIOD ENDING
DECEMBER 31, 19XX

Commission (I)		$300,000
Interest income (I)		90,000
Salaries (E)	$150,000	
Rent, power, & light (E)	125,000	
Interest expense (E)	80,000	
	$355,000	$390,000

The difference between income and expense is $35,000 ($390,000 minus $355,000). Because income is greater than expense, the $35,000 represents a profit. The sum total of the entries in the P&L, a profit, can be labeled as one account called *net income*.

The balance sheet is composed of the remaining entries:

BALANCE SHEET
AS OF DECEMBER 31, 199X

Current Assets		*Liabilities*	
Cash (A)	$ 50,000	Salaries payable (L)	$ 50,000
Inventory (A)	150,000		
Fixed Assets		*Net Worth*	
Furniture & fixtures (A)	75,000	Net worth (N)	$190,000
	$275,000		$240,000

In this balance sheet, the total assets ($275,000) does *not* equal the sum of liabilities ($50,000) and net worth ($190,000). The difference of $35,000 ($275,000 minus $240,000) equals the profit of $35,000 reflected in the P&L.

The profit must be entered somewhere in the balance sheet so that it balances, presumably under either liabilities or net worth. By definition, a profit is not a liability (something the company owes). It must therefore belong under net worth, where, in fact, it is entered under the heading *Retained earnings*, as follows:

Current Assets		*Liabilities*	
Cash (A)	$ 50,000	Salaries payable	$ 50,000
Inventory	150,000		
Fixed Assets		*Net Worth*	
Furniture & fixtures (A)	75,000	Net worth	190,000
		Retained earnings	35,000
	$275,000		$275,000

This last entry is an adjusting entry that debits net income account in the P&L statement and credits net worth (that is, retained earnings) in the balance sheet.

OTHER REPORTS

Besides the usual reports, such as annual balance sheets and profit and loss statements, brokerage firms are required to file special reports with regulatory bodies, such as Focus or Joint Reg. These reports help to assure the protection of customer accounts and document the firm's liabilities. Readers who are interested in this phase of the business should consult the Securities and Exchange Commission's Rules 15c3-1 and 15c3-3.

SUMMARY

All money-related entries of the brokerage firm, and many more, pass through the daily cash record. The accounting staff must ensure that the entries are correctly recorded, and that each day's work balances out. Their work is reported in the daily cash record, which, like the daily stock record, is a primary record of the firm. The validity of the information in either document is essential to the well being and continued existence of the entity.

The accounting function keeps track of all money flows into, out of, and within the firm. It books entries into the appropriate accounts, produces key reports based on the account information, and closes out all entries, both actual and accrued, for the year-end reports.

CHAPTER 12

Dividend

Although some stocks pay dividends, no stocks pay interest. Bonds pay interest but never dividends. While the P& S department calculates accrued interest, the dividend staff has the task of figuring and properly crediting dividends. It also credits the interest paid on debt instruments. This chapter focuses on the area of operations known as the dividend/interest department.

WHERE DIVIDENDS COME FROM

A *dividend* is a distribution of cash or stock to stockholders by the issuing corporation. It is issued on a per-share basis to holders of record on a specific date. Stocks pay dividends when declared by the corporate board of directors, depending on the company's policy, its plans, and its current financial condition.

THE DIVIDEND CYCLE

The *dividend cycle* consists of three important dates, all of which are set by the corporation:

FIGURE 12-1. *The dividend department.*

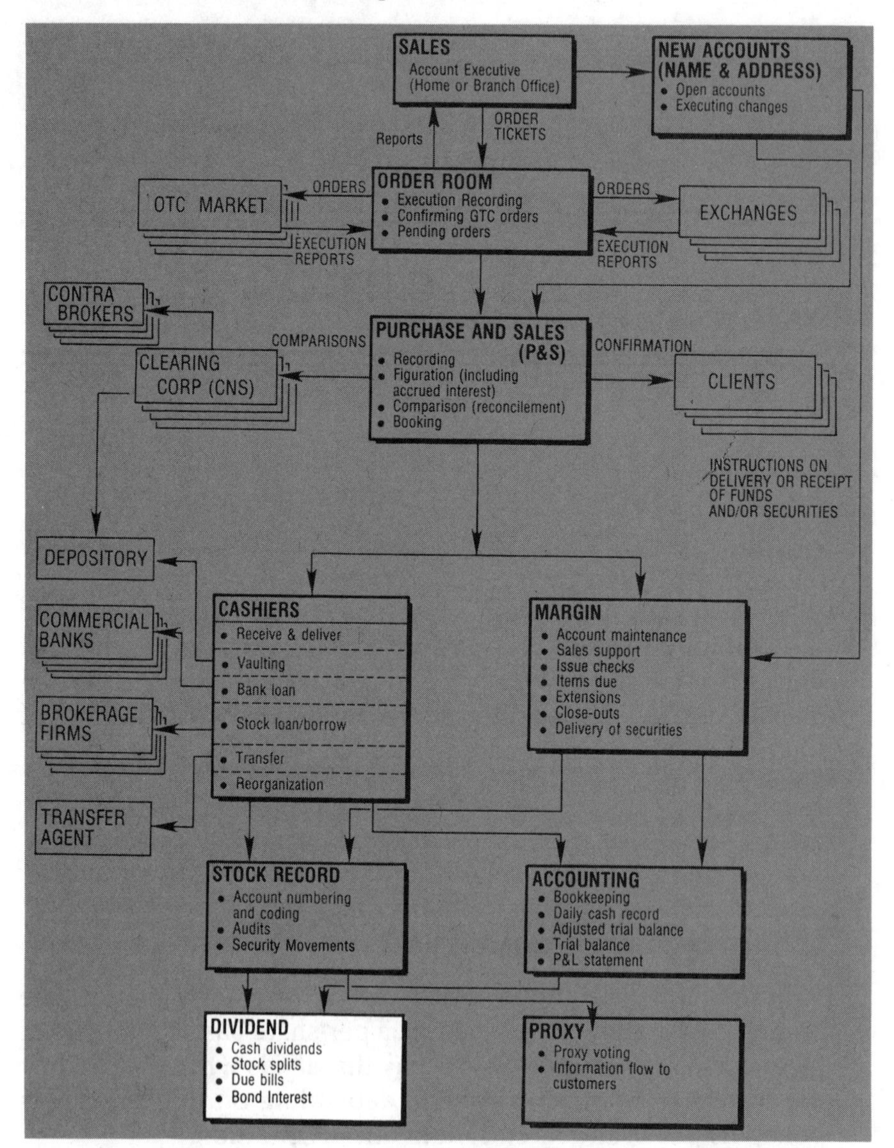

1. The *declaration date* is the date by which a corporation announces the dividend.
2. The dividend will be paid to stockholders who are registered owners on the night of the *record date*. (This date is used simply to identify the owners of record.)

3. The date of the actual dividend payment is the *payable date.*

Example: International Bushee declares a $.25-per-share dividend on April 1 (the declaration date), to be paid to holders of record on Friday, May 1 (the record date), for actual payment on June 1 (the payable date). To receive the dividend, you must be legal owner of the security on Friday evening, May 1. The last chance to buy the stock on a regular-way basis comes on the preceding Friday, April 24. If you purchased the security on that day, the transaction would settle on May 1, and you, not the seller, would be entitled to the dividend. If you purchased the security on Monday, April 27, you would not be entitled to the dividend because the transaction would settle Monday, May 4.

Cash Dividends: The Ex-Dividend Date

A fourth important date affects customers who buy and sell a security going through a dividend cycle. On the *ex-dividend date,* the market price of the security is reduced to reflect the amount of the dividend. For listed stocks, the exchange sets this date; in the OTC market, the NASD sets the date. For cash dividends, the ex-date is four business days before the record date.

Example: In the International Bushee dividend cycle, the ex-dividend date is Monday, April 27, four business days before the record date of Friday, May 1. On that day, to account for the "loss" of the $.25-per-share dividend, the market price of the security is reduced either by the amount of the dividend or by the next higher trading fraction. For a $.25 dividend, barring any other influences, the market price falls 1/4 of a point. If the security closes at $40 a share on the day before the ex-date (Friday, April 24), it opens for trading at 39 3/4 on the ex-date (Monday, April 27).

When the price of the security is reduced to reflect the dividend, the drop in value may trigger good-till-cancelled, buy limit, and sell stop orders. Because these orders are supposed to be executed only through the natural activity of the market, the prices marked on these orders are reduced by the amount of the dividend. A client may override this reduction by entering DNR *(do not reduce)* on the order.

Example: A GTC order entered to buy International Bushee at 39½ and marked "DNR" will not be reduced to 39¼ (1/4 of a point) on the morning of the ex-dividend date.

Stock Dividends

To preserve its cash, yet pay a dividend to its shareholders, a corporation may elect to pay a *stock dividend* which is paid as a percentage of outstanding stock.

Example: Given a 10% stock dividend, a shareholder receives one additional share for each 10 shares owned. The owner of 100 shares gets 10 shares, and so on.

Stock Splits

In a *stock split*, holders will receive one or more shares of additional issue for each share they now hold.

Example: A company's security is trading at $150 per share, when it announces a 3-for-1 split. The owner of one share receives two additional shares. The price of each new share is $50 ($150 ÷ 3).

As you can see from this example, stock splits are usually effected to adjust the trading price of a security, thereby making it more attractive to potential investors. A *reverse split* has an opposite effect on the market value. Yet, again, the effect of the split is to adjust the market price to more attractive investment levels.

Example: A security is trading at $2. In a 10-for-1 reverse split, the investor who has 10 shares will own the equivalent of one share worth $20.

Stock splits differ from cash dividends and stock dividends, which reflect an actual movement of corporate wealth to the stockholders. For both types of dividends, adjustments are made in the balance sheet's retained earnings account or to earning on the P&L to reflect the cost of the payout. Stock splits affect only the security's par value and number of shares outstanding. No assets leave the corporation, and so no change in retained earnings is necessary.

Example: The corporate records reveal 1,000,000 shares at $100 par value. Par value bears no relation to the stock's current market value. It is used for accounting purposes to establish a bookkeeping worth for the security. To arrive at this bookkeeping value, multiply the number of shares outstanding by the par value. So the total value of the shares is $100,000,000 (1,000,000 × $100). A 2-for-1 split increases the numbers of shares to 2,000,000, but then par value drops to $50—for a total value of $100,000,000.

DUTIES OF THE DIVIDEND DEPARTMENT

The employees of the dividend department are basically responsible for one thing: making certain that the rightful owner is paid the dividend. To discharge this duty, they have to keep careful records of all the firm's securities. Their task is therefore to reconcile the firm's record date positions with the physical securities on hand. In other words, they verify the record date positions on the stock record by counting all *street-side positions,* that is, all physical certificates of the firm, whether in the vault, in transfer, in fails to receive, in fails to deliver, in stock loan, and so on.

Outside agencies, usually banks or trust agencies, assist the dividend department in this task:

1. The number of shares outstanding are recorded and the position maintained by the *corporate registrar,* which is an agency selected by the issuing corporation to keep such records.
2. The *transfer agent* transfers securities from one name to another and maintains the name and address of the registered holders.
3. The actual payment of the dividends is made by the *dividend disbursing agent* (DDA).

Let's look at what the dividend department employees do with respect to the record, payable, and ex-dividend dates.

Record Date

The dividend department balances the stock record against the physical count of securities. It then takes and awards dividends (or not, depending on the circumstances), as follows:

1. Cash dividends on stock maintained by the firm in its

nominee name are credited to the beneficial owner. (Stock dividends are debited.)

2. Customers who have sold short which settled on or before the record date or who have maintained a short position in their accounts over the record date are charged the dividend, because they owe the dividend to the firm.
3. Dividends on securities held in position over record date by the firm, but registered in the name of the beneficial owner are not handled by the dividend department. The shareholder receives the dividend directly from the company's paying agent (DDA). If, however, the client sold the security before the record date, but the firm did not actually deliver these securities, the client is charged for the dividend, because he or she is not entitled to the dividend.
4. If a transaction occurs but does not settle in time for record date, or if the security is not re-registered in the new name by record date, the firm must claim the dividend, through the dividend department, in behalf of the owner.

Payable Date

On this date, the dividend department personnel rebalance the stock record. That is, the check received from the paying agent (the cash flow), the account being charged the dividend, and the account being credited the dividend must all equal one another. This rebalancing is necessary to correct any erroneous or last minute entries.

Ex-Dividend Date

Cash Dividend. The *ex-dividend date,* or *ex-date,* in the case of a *cash dividend* is four business days before record date. On the ex-dividend date, purchasers of a security are *not* entitled to a cash dividend because a transaction on that date settles on the business day after record date. Since a dividend is a payout of the corporate worth, the market price of the security is reduced before the opening of trading that day by the amount of dividend to the next highest fraction. For example, a dividend of $.18

means a reduction of 1/4-point, a $.10 dividend gives you an 1/8-point reduction, and so on.

Stock Splits or Stock Dividends over 25%. Like cash and smaller stock dividends, the owners of the security on record date are entitled to the large stock dividend. But, since stock is used for collateral against loans, a stock-split or dividend can temporarily leave such loans undercollateralized.

Example: XYZ is selling at $90 a share, and the corporation announces a three-for-one stock split. If the ex-date was set at four days before record date, the price of the security would fall to $30 per share on the ex-date. XYZ is going to "split" each $90 share into $30 shares, but the two additional shares for each old share is not paid until payable date. Any loans secured by XYZ stock are undercollateralized until the additional shares arrive.

To avoid this "collateral gap," the ex-date known in this situation as the Ex-Distribution Date, on splits and stock dividends over 25% is usually the day after payable date. The new shares are therefore available for collateral deposit when the value of the old securities falls in price. Securities undergoing a stock split or a large stock dividend cycle trade at full price through payable date. On the ex-date (the day after payable date), the value decreases.

Due Bills. In splits and stock dividends over 25% anyone who settles a purchase of the security between the record and payable dates would pay the full price but not actually receive the additional shares. During this period, purchasers must be protected.

A due bill provides this protection. A *due bill* is a promissory note that additional shares will be delivered on or shortly after payable date. It is basically an IOU, from seller to buyer, that goes into effect four business days before record date and "comes off" the day after payable. If a trade is settled after record date but before payable date, due bills must accompany the delivery. With the due bills in hand, the purchaser can buy the old stock at the old price and know that the additional shares will be delivered upon issuance.

The dividend staff keeps records on all due bills issued and received by the company.

INTEREST

Most debt instruments pay interest semiannually. The entire six-month interest is paid to holders of the security over record date. Usually, interest is paid to whoever is the record holder the night before payable date. (In the world of debt instruments, there is no declaration date or ex-date.) While the P&S personnel calculate accrued interest on bond transactions, the dividend/interest department credits and debits accounts with interest payments, when bonds are in position or so registered over the record date. The procedure for reconcilement is similar to that used in equities.

SUMMARY

The dividend/interest function ties all accounts affected by dividend or interest payments to the actual sum received from the paying agent. It includes debiting and crediting accounts, as well as claiming dividends and honoring such claims from other firms.

CHAPTER 13

Proxy

Customers of brokerage firms often leave their securities with the firm. In a cash account (that is, when a position is fully paid for), the firm acts merely as a custodian. In margin accounts, the security is the collateral for the loan to the client.

Securities may be registered in the client's name or in street name. If the securities are kept in the name of the client (the beneficial owner), all communications from the security's issuer are sent directly to the client. But the issuer does not know who the beneficial owner is of a security registered in street name. Any communication can be sent only to the nominee, who is then responsible for relaying the information to the beneficial owner.

In the brokerage firm, the proxy department handles this task.

Since stockholders are actually owners of the issuing corporation, they get to vote on certain matters that require a decision. To give shareholders the chance to vote, corporations issue proxy statements, or *proxies*, which enable the shareholders to vote for members of management (the board) and other key issues affecting the corporation. Proxies are printed forms that contain the number of shares being voted by the registered owner. For securities registered in the name of the beneficial

FIGURE 13-1 *The proxy department.*

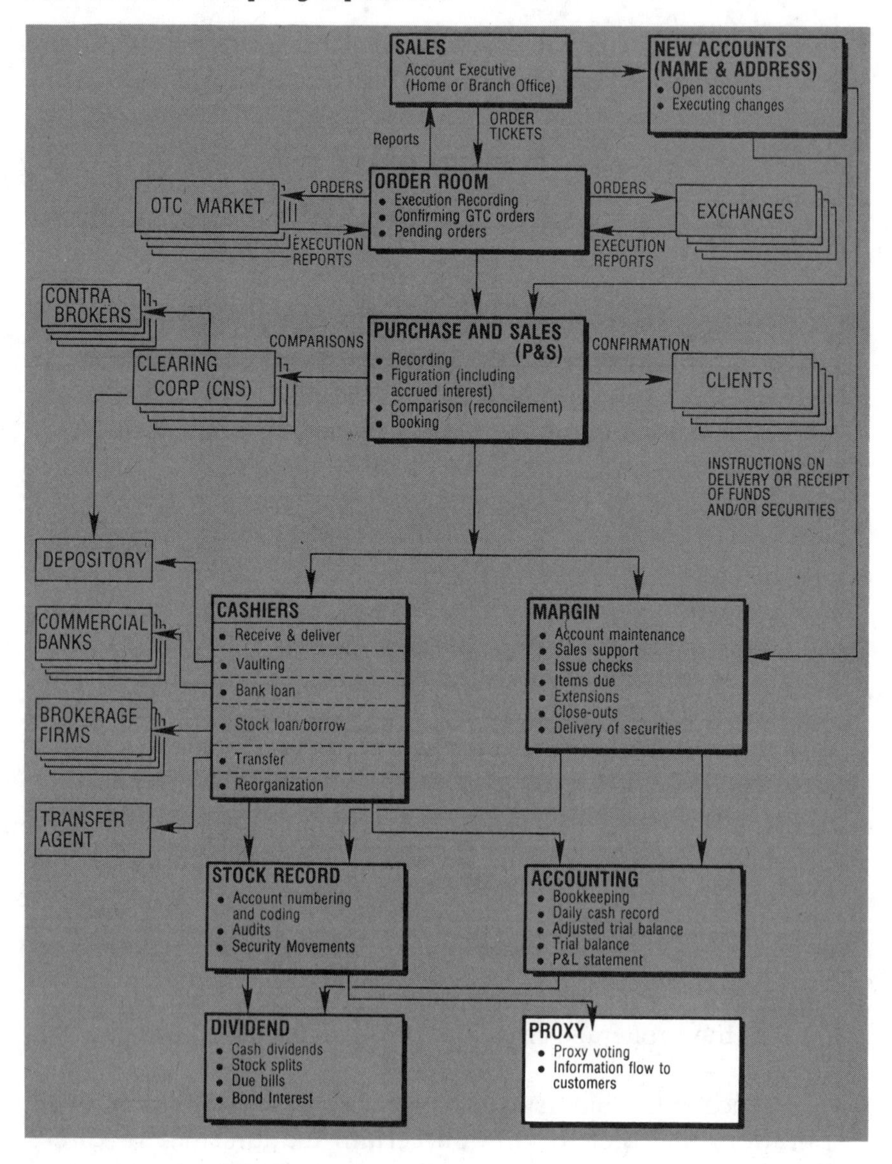

owners, proxies are sent directly to the shareholders, not to the brokerage firm.

Securities held in street name are a different matter. Because a brokerage firm holding shares for many clients is the only registered owner that the issuer knows, it gets one proxy containing all its customers' voting shares. Yet, as nominee owner, the brokerage firm cannot "vote" the proxy. Instead, it must obtain enough proxies from the issuer to send to the stockholders. The shareowners then vote the proxies and send them directly back to the firm, who in turn votes them on behalf of the beneficial owners.

Voting becomes especially important in the case of a *proxy fight,* in which two groups vie for control of the corporation. The shareholders must be allowed to choose between the factions. The proxy area transmits all proxy fight communiques to the owners.

The proxy function also includes obtaining from the issuer and distributing to the shareholders the yearly statements, audit reports, semiannual reports, and other documents. Whatever the corporation sends to its shareholders, the proxy area must obtain in sufficient numbers to supply each beneficial owner with a copy.

CHAPTER 14

New Accounts

If a firm must earn revenue to stay in business, then its revenue must equal its expenses. To prosper and expand, the firm must produce revenue in excess of its expenses. Where does a firm's revenue come from? From customers. Who are these customers? Where do they live? Where do they work? How can they be contacted? All this information and more is classified in the new accounts functions. Actually, the name of this area varies from one firm to another. It can be New Accounts, Names & Address, Customer Information, Client Data Department, or the like. Whatever its name, its responsibility is to properly document all the firm's customer accounts.

TYPES OF ACCOUNTS

The type of account that a customer opens determines the forms to be completed and filed.

Individual Cash Account

The simplest account to open is an *individual cash account,* which is an account in which only cash transactions may be executed

FIGURE 14-1.

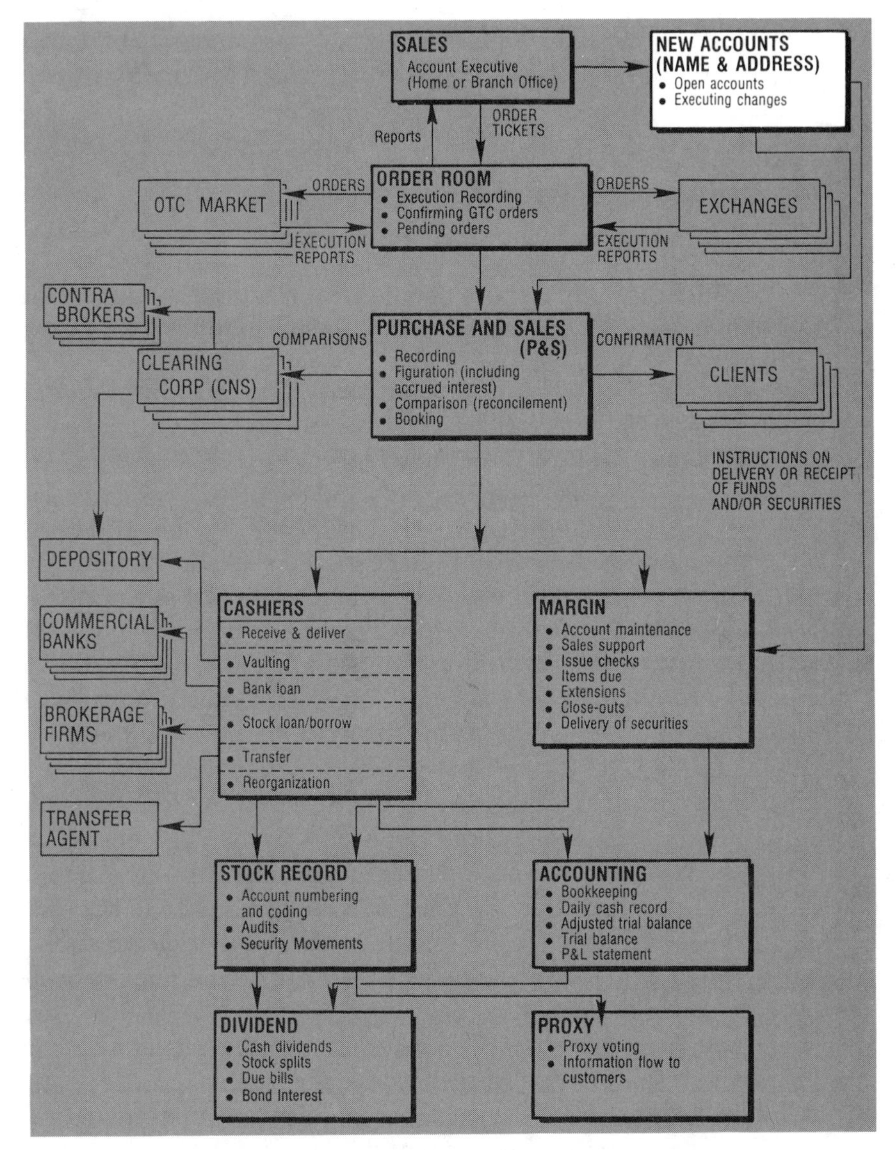

and which is in the name of one person. First the stockbroker or the customer fills out a *new account form,* which requests the following information:

1. Customer's full name

2. Customer's home address and telephone number.
3. Social Security number.
4. Occupation, place of employment, and business phone number.
5. Age or date of birth.
6. Spouse's name and place of employment.
7. Bank reference.

Some firms require more detailed information, as a matter of policy, even though such information is not mandatory by law. Such additional information might include:

8. Annual income and net worth.
9. Number of children and their ages.
10. Accounts at other brokerage firms.

The completed form is filed in the new accounts department.

Some firms microfilm or microfiche each and every document. *Microfilm* is a reel of documents photographed at a great reduction. *Microfiche* is a sheet of documents, also greatly reduced. On either reel or sheet, you can store vast numbers of documents in a very small area. Viewers enlarge the filmed images, as needed, very much as a projector would a regular movie film. Prints can also be made, at their original sizes, from the film.

To keep track of the daily flood of documents, firms use a coding system, which identifies the reel of microfilm or sheet of microfiche on which the document is located. This code appears on the customer's *master file*, which is a file (either electronic or manual) that lists all current accounts by number, name, and address, or some other way.

Some firms also require customers to sign *signature cards* (usually two sets). These cards become permanent records of the customer's signature. One set is maintained in the branch, and the other is sent to the new account department.

When both of these forms are completed, and when the age and other requirements are satisfied, the customer may do business with the firm. Since this is a cash account, all securities purchased must be paid for in full by the fifth business day, but no later than the seventh business day, after the day of the transaction. Any securities sold must be delivered in good deliverable form, by the fifth business day but no later than the tenth business day.

Margin Account

In a margin account, the customer actually borrows money from the brokerage firm to buy securities. The money borrowed is the loan, or margin, amount. (Margin is explained in greater detail later in the book.)

To open a margin account, the new account form and (sometimes) the signature cards must be filled out. In addition, the customer must sign two other forms:

1. The *margin agreement* sets forth the terms under which the firm will lend money to the customer, the rules by which the account must operate, when the firm has right to take action without the customer's permission, and the firm's right to charge interest on any *debit balance,* which is the amount of the loan.
2. The *lending agreement* gives the firm the privilege of lending the margined security to other firms or against other customers' short sales.

(Margin and lending of customer's securities are explained in Chapters 8 and 9.)

Joint Account

A *joint account* is an account in which two individuals, by legal agreement, may conduct transactions. It may be a cash or margin account. The two principal types are:

1. *Joint Tenants with Rights of Survivorship* (or *Tenant by the Entirety*). This type of account is usually established between husband and wife. By this agreement, upon the death of one principal, the entire account reverts to the survivor.
2. *Tenants in Common.* By this agreement, the death of one principal has no effect on the survivor's percentage of ownership in the account. The portion owned by the

deceased reverts to his or her estate. Under Tenants in Common, having the percentages of ownership on file is clearly important. In the absence of such a document, the account is automatically divided on a fifty-fifty basis.

The Dividend and Interest Compliance Act of 1983 mandates that customers must provide their Social Security number and must certify under penalty of perjury that their social security number is correct, as recorded by the broker, banks, or other payers of interest or dividends. Failure to satisfy this requirement will result in dividends and interest, being withheld at a rate of 20%.

Power of Attorney Accounts

Many times the account is managed not by the owner, but by someone else. For this individual to operate, the owner of the account must file a *power of attorney form*, of which there are two types:

1. The *limited power of attorney* permits the individual to enter buy and sell orders.
2. The *full power of attorney* permits the holder to deposit and withdraw securities and cash, in addition to buying and selling securities.

Generally, for accounts handled under power of attorney, the brokerage firm must have the following papers on file:

1. The usual papers for each owner.
2. A power of attorney (limited or full) from each owner.
3. A new account information form completed by the holder of the power of attorney.

Other Forms

Other forms may be needed, depending on the type of accounts being opened.

Before a corporation can purchase and sell securities, its charter must permit it to do so. Therefore, in addition to the usual papers connected with a corporate account, the brokerage firm must obtain a copy of the corporate customers' charter or bylaws.

Because a corporation is a legal entity, or person under law, the brokerage firm must know who is empowered to act on the corporation's behalf. A *corporate resolution,* signed by the appropriate officers of the corporation, authorizes one or more of the company's officers to transact business in the corporation's name and for its benefit.

For individuals acting in a fiduciary capacity, *trust agreements, custodial agreements,* and similar documents must be completed and signed by notaries (where applicable).

Customers trading options or future contracts have to sign a form stating that they understand the risks and/or conditions of such transactions. This form must be completed and on file for this kind of trading to be permitted in the account.

Community property states require forms only for persons domiciled within the states.

KEEPING TRACK OF IT ALL

Whatever forms are needed, the new accounts department must obtain, record, and file them for each and every account.

Keeping track of the paper work is relatively easy when the account first opens.

Example: A client who wants to open a margin account to trade common stocks and options must fill out the following forms:

1. New account form.
2. Signature cards (where mandatory).
3. Margin agreement.
4. Lending agreement.
5. Option agreement.

Until all these documents are received, the account cannot legally operate, and the brokerage firm must continue to request them from the client. Generally, customers are happy to satisfy the firm's requirements and establish a good relationship. If the forms are not submitted, however, the brokerage firm has no alternative but to forbid the client from entering into transactions. If the customer, after several requests, refuses to comply with the firm's policies, the account has to be closed. Without the proper documentation on file, the brokerage firm may be sued by the client, as well as censured, fined, or dismissed by the appropriate self-regulatory agency.

A most important part of customer service is opening a new account properly. All of the salesmanship, the firm's reputation, and advertising can amount to nothing if the account has consistently misspelled a name or sent confirmations to the wrong address. Think about it: *You* probably are annoyed when someone calls you by the wrong name or when your mail is sent to someone else. Would you not think, "How important can I be to them if they can't even get my name or address right?" You may expect the same reaction among customers of the brokerage firm.

Maintaining updated records is more of a problem.

Example: Customer Wilson opens a regular cash account, completing a new account form and signing two signature cards. He trades in the cash account for a year. Suddenly, after a discussion with the stockbroker, he enters into a margin transaction and soon after begins to trade options.

How does the new accounts department find out about this change in account status? In some firms, a computer program or routine monitors the status of each account. As an account's status changes, the computer automatically prints a notification and routes it to the new accounts section. Other firms use a manual method for checking a card index against the margin department's daily position reports. Still other firms utilize systems that combine manual and automated methods. No matter what the system, the brokerage firm must ensure that for every account, the proper papers are on file at all times.

Names and/or addresses on the accounts change quite often. People change their names when they get married or divorced (requiring address changes). They move from the city to the suburbs or vice versa. Instructions for such changes come either from the client or from the stockbroker. After a verification routine, the department enters the necessary instructions and the change is made. For good relations, the changes should be effected promptly and accurately.

SUMMARY

The tasks of the new accounts function—attentiveness to the account's status, the correct spelling of names and addresses, prompt and accurate changes—all serve to show customers that their business is valued and that they are very important.

With the account properly opened, the client is now ready to enter an order.

CHAPTER 15

Compliance

The securities industry is regulated at several levels. It is regulated by the federal government through the Securities and Exchange Commission, by the state regulatory agencies, and finally by the industry's self-regulatory organizations (SROs). The majority of the rules and regulations have been codified and primarily enforced by the principal exchanges, such as the New York Stock Exchange and the American Stock Exchange, or by the National Association of Security Dealers.

Ensuring the broker firm's conformance with these requirements is the compliance function. The firm's size and its production largely determine how many people work in this department.

REGISTRATION REQUIREMENTS

Stockbrokers are also known as *registered representatives* (or account executives) because they have to pass a written qualification examination to be registered as the sales representatives of the firm and, as such, conduct business with the public. Stockbrokers wishing to conduct business in NYSE securities must pass the registered representative exam. Those seeking to deal in over-the-counter securities have to be registered with the NASD. The compliance department employees make certain that brokers are correctly registered for the type of business they are conducting.

Sales representatives must also be registered in the states in which they conduct business. Some states require their own examinations, while others are satisfied with a formal registration with the NYSE, AMEX, and/or NASD, while still others maintain reciprocal agreements with other states. Whatever the requirements, stockbrokers must be approved before carrying on business in a state. Compliance sees to it that each state's requirements are met and that the stockbrokers abide by their rules.

CUSTOMER ACCOUNTS AND THE RESPONSIBILITIES OF THE STOCKBROKER

Through the stockbrokers, compliance monitors the firm's dealings with its customers. Members of the investing public are forever finding new ways to get rich in the stock market. Many of their ideas are well founded and ethical, but others are either illegal or improper. The stockbroker's role is to prevent customers from breaking the laws, whether intentionally or not, and to protect customers against the schemes of others. The compliance department reviews all reports of improprieties and takes appropriate action.

Perhaps the most important duty of registered representatives is to base their recommendations and actions on each customer's stated investment objective. This duty is so important that it is codified in what is known as the *know your customer* rule. To know the customer, the stockbrokers must have prospective clients state their investment objective in writing—growth, income, speculation, safety, or what-not. In addition, the stockbroker must also know such things as the types of accounts the client has with banks, business affiliations, and other financial facts.

Stockbrokers must then base all their actions in behalf of customers on the stated investment goal and other information.

For example, they must not jeopardize the life-long savings of an elderly investor by sinking them into a highly speculative futures program. Or they must be certain that investors who do insist on risky investments know the extent of the risk and have the disposable funds to cover losses.

Occasionally, despite the stockbroker's best effort, customers stray from their objectives. If they stray too far, the registered rep's duty is to advise the client and report the situation to the compliance department. Usually, customers must state in writing that they are aware of their variance from the stated objective and desire it.

Fiduciary and *quasi-fiduciary* accounts, such as custodian and trust accounts, are not allowed to stray too far. Since this account is administered by one person for the benefit of another, such as a child, they must follow what is called the *prudent man guidelines*. These guidelines generally dictate how a "prudent person" would invest. They are conservative rules of thumb, which usually call for investing in low-risk, highly rated vehicles.

COMPLIANCE RESPONSIBILITIES OF REGISTERED PRINCIPALS

Not all compliance's functions are administered directly. Obviously, compliance personnel cannot monitor every activity in the firm. So others in the firm act as a "first line of defense" against violations. Compliance therefore delegates some responsibility to registered personnel who are responsible for the supervision of the sales areas (branches). Managers of branches and divisions are responsible for supervising accounts. The NYSE requires the supervisor of each branch office to have passed the branch office manager's exam. The NASD requires certain individuals in specified geographical areas to be principal registered. To assist supervision personnel in their compliance roles, the firm must maintain a compliance manual that explains their responsibilities and procedures based on the various rules and regulations. Usually these personnel have to enforce daily, weekly, monthly, and quarterly routines, sometimes referred to as the firm's *procedures*.

The quarterly routines include reviewing customer accounts for excessive trading, for the type of investing, and for the verification of customer objectives. This routine is very important because it ensures that the accounts are in proper order and, by means of proper review, prevents problems from developing.

Example: Good-till-cancelled (GTC) limit orders remain in force until they are executed or cancelled by the customer. In other words, the pending order can be executed on any business day when the market price reaches the limit. The customer is notified that the order is in force at time of entry and again each quarter. Supervisory personnel are obliged to make certain that quarterly confirms are sent to customers and that the open orders are verified.

Other operational areas are empowered to enforce regulations. Two key areas are the margin and cashier's departments. The margin department routinely monitors accounts for their conformance with Regulation T and the exchange's minimum maintenance requirements. The cashier's department ensures that other firms operate within established intra-industry rules.

CUSTOMER COMPLAINTS

Like any business, a brokerage firm is not immune to customer complaints. Some complaints may be justified; others are not. Yet the compliance area must investigate each complaint and attempt to rectify the problem to the satisfaction of all concerned.

REPORTING

The various regulatory authorities send questionnaires to firms on many subjects, ranging from activity in a particular security to the transactions in a specific account. The compliance staff respond to such inquiries and return them to the requesting authorities. Some of these requests are simple. When a request calls for a long, detailed investigation, however, the compliance area usually enlists the support of other areas, usually the stock record, margin, or customer accounts.

SUMMARY

Compliance is by no means restricted to one department. It is the responsibility of every employee of the brokerage firm.

CHAPTER 16

Electronic Data Processing (EDP)

A vast majority of firms, regardless of their business, have either an in-house computer center or an outside service to process their daily, weekly, and monthly work. So it is with brokerage firms. The computer area is also referred to as *EDP,* which stands for electronic data processing, or just *DP,* data processing.

THE REPORTS PRODUCED

Whichever method it uses, the computer area or service produces the bulk of the brokerage firm's reports, statements, and listings. Among the many and varied reports coming out of the computer section are:

Daily

- Customer Trade Confirmations.
- P&S Trade Blotters.
- Cashier's Receive and Deliver Blotters.
- The Stock Record.
- Daily Cash Listing.

- Dividend Position Listing.
- Margin Status Reports.
- 'Seg' Reports.
- Inventory Positions.

Weekly

- Stock Record Balance Report.
- Mark to the Market Report.
- Various Activity (Trading) Reports.

As you can see, the bulk of the processing reports must be produced every business day. As the various sections of operations perform their assignments, the computer processing department must produce the necessary reports as and when they are needed.

Example: Trades executed on Monday, April 5, will settle Monday, April 12. For these trades, the computer has to produce:

- Trade listings for the P&S department on Tuesday, April 6.
- P&S balancing reports on Wednesday, April 7.
- P&S trade adjustment reports on Thursday April 8.
- Cashiering settlement blotters and margin "item due reports" on Friday April 9.
- Final settlement contracts and other documentation on the settlement day, April 12.
- Finally, the stock record and daily cash reports on Tuesday, April 13.

These are just some of the many reports produced. Bear in mind that, as each day passes, more trades are executed, other days' trades are balanced, others cleared, others settled, and on and on. In a typical brokerage firm, the workload is so heavy that the computer facility is *in-house,* that is the EDP equipment is on the firm's premises and used exclusively by the firm.

With so many reports to produce, it is little wonder that the computers are running day and night. In fact, most of the processing is performed during the evening hours. The computers are kept busy with other routines during the day.

The primary daytime function is the transmission of messages, orders, reports, and inquiries from one terminal (or location) to another. For example, a branch wires an order to the order room, and the order room relays it to the floor of an exchange. Some computer systems relay the order from the branch simultaneously to the order room and to the market for execution. Upon execution of the order, the employee on the exchange floor wires a report to the order room and to the branch. Meanwhile, in another branch, a stockholder might be wiring an inquiry to the margin department on the status of an account. The margin employee wires the branch office with the answer. Suddenly the research department wires *all* the branches of a new development. And so on. (The transmissions are called *wires* because the vast majority are sent over telephone lines (or "wires") from one location to another.)

These messages—and many others—flow into and out of the computer's processing unit in fractions of seconds, and each transmission must be processed right away.

By routing messages, orders, and reports during the day and producing major reports and listings during the evening, the EDP department serves a critical need for the firm. The computer service, in fact, has been called the heart of the operation. Its performance is vital to the entire firm. Yet, while its operation cannot go unnoticed, very few employees truly understand and appreciate it.

COMPUTER PROCESSING—THEN AND NOW

What is a computer? Is it a magical instrument? Can it see all, tell all, and know all? Will it replace humans in the work force? Will it someday master us? Or is it just a dumb mechanical thingamajig that goes haywire every now and then?

How does one department keep up with the work? They keep up because computers are getting better and faster all the time.

Breakthroughs in the computer technology and applications have affected the brokerage industry, as they have all other aspects of our daily lives. While computers are becoming more powerful and faster, they are also becoming less expensive and easier to use, thereby permitting more and more applications to be computerized or "automated." Automation in turn, has permitted the industry to process trading volumes that were unthinkable only a few years ago. Every day the industry relies a little more on computer technology, using "mainframes," and "minicomputers," and "micros" in varying degrees to process its work, develop statistical projections, store information, and perform difficult computations.

In the beginning there were *electronic accounting machines* (EAMs). By today's standards, EAMs were slow, unsophisticated, and noisy. Programming as such was nonexistent. Yet they chugged away all day, producing bookkeeping reports. confirmations, comparisons, and a few financial reports.

Eventually, EAMs were replaced by equipment that stored data, accepted programming, and worked electronically. In other words, the equipment had *memory*. These machines, called *electronic data processing* (EDP) equipment, grew in size and function to the mainframes we utilize today.

A Computer Is A System

A *computer system* consists of two main components: hardware and software. *Hardware* is the actual physical equipment, such as the central processing unit (CPU), the tape drive, the disc packs, printers, and all the other wires and boxes. The *software* is the logical set of instructions, or *programs*, that "tells" the computer how to process the firm's work.

Hardware

The computer's highly sophisticated and technical hardware is manufactured in a factory. The computer's "brain", (the central processing unit, sometimes referred to as the core) can be divided into three parts:

1. The *executive program*: Supplied by the computer manufacturer, this enables the computer to respond to other programs and is sometimes referred to as the computer's *logic.*
2. The *processing program*: A system might have one processing program to do a confirmation, another to make up a balancing report, and so on.

3. The *data*: This is the information that the processing programs need to produce their output, and it is entered into the the computer's system by the firm's employees. For example, the processing program that outputs a customer confirmation needs data on the security, quantity, price, and the like. This information is entered, say, by someone in the order room from the order ticket, which the salesperson filled out.

Software

Specialists in writing programs, called *programmers,* constantly update old programs or write new ones to ensure that the computer is being utilized to its fullest extent. Since each instruction by the programmer uses up "space" in the computer core, an efficient instruction is one that gets the greatest possible response while occupying as little core space as possible. The more concise the programmer makes the software, the more efficiently the whole computer system operates.

Computer Languages

Computers actually have their own languages. A *computer language* is a language that the computer can understand and that programmers use to write programs. The words of such a language have special meanings for the computer and effect specific responses. Certain words are even more restrictive and may be used only by the programmer under certain, very limited circumstances. Two popular computer languages are COBOL and Fortran. To the novice, COBOL seems very similar to the English language, but Fortran is more technical.

Usually programmers work with systems that have been in existence for a long time. The written work (or *coding*) in the programs for such systems can fill volumes. Programs run in interconnected cycles, called *routines*. Sometimes routines are made up of parts known as *subroutines*. Both routines and subroutines are run in series with the output of one serving as input for the next. For example, the P&S routine calculates the net money (that is, the amount of execution plus or minus commission, taxes, and fees), which is its output. This output is then posted to the customer's account in the margin routine.

The programs are so complex that a change in one part of a program can easily affect another part. In fact, a change in one part of any program can cause an unwanted change in another program in the routine. So, generally, any change in programming must be carefully designed to have *only* the desired effect on the routine and on any other routine. A mistake could *blow* the system, that is, bring the computer to an unwanted and puzzling halt.

When the system blows, programmers must be called in to determine what went wrong. Because most processing work is completed in the evening and early morning hours, programmers often get panic calls during these hours at home. If the situation cannot be rectified over the telephone, the programmer may have to come in to the processing center.

Types of Computer Systems

EDP systems can be very powerful and general-purpose, or less powerful and *dedicated* to a specific job. Basically, there are three types of computer systems:

1. Mainframes.
2. Minicomputers.
3. Microcomputers.

Mainframes. A *mainframe* is a computer that can, at one time, interface with many input or output devices, such as CRT terminals and tape drives. It has the capacity to process great volumes of work quickly and efficiently. During business hours, the mainframe routes and otherwise traffics messages for many firms. *Message switch* programs, resident in the central processing unit, enable the mainframe to route messages, orders, and reports from point *A* to point *B*.

Example: A customer of a firm's Omaha office gives instructions to buy 100 shares of ZAP at the market. The stockbroker writes the order and gives it to a teletypist who in turn enters the order in the branch's computer terminal. When the firm's main-office CPU polls the terminal in the Omaha branch, it picks up the order. (This is a little like a manual system in which the orders are put into a pickup box where someone from the main office would periodically collect them. Of course, this electronic "pickup" is *much* faster.)

Upon receipt of the order message in the CPU, a program prompts the computer to look up a "table" of security symbols to find where ZAP is traded. According to the firm's table, ZAP is traded on the New York Stock Exchange. The computer then checks the order size (100 shares). If it is for 1099 shares or less, the order is transmitted to the exchange's vital floor computer (designated order turnaround) (DOT), which is the exchange's order routing system.

All this—looking up the table, routing the order to the exchanges, transmission from the firm's computer—takes place in seconds. During the course of the day, the firm's mainframe does little else but do such routing over and over again.

In the evening, the mainframe becomes a "number cruncher," processing all the trades of the day, storing and updating data, and outputting the multitude of reports. All this is accomplished before the next day's business begins.

Minicomputers. Minicomputers are so similar to mainframes that the two kinds of computers are sometimes hard to distinguish. The prefix "mini," which refers to the number of input/output terminals the CPU can interface with, is therefore misleading. Many mini's have more capacity than some mainframes and definitely more capacity, or core, than the mainframes of a decade ago. Perhaps the real difference between mini's and mainframes is the volume of data that they can process.

Mini's are being used more and more to do special assignments and, as their capacity grows, to perform some or all of the functions once performed only by mainframes. For example, they often process trades settled on the same day as execution—the so-called *same-day settlers,* such as commercial paper trades. Firms whose mainframes are dedicated to the batch processing of equities transactions found that programming their mainframes to process same-day settlers is impossible or prohibitively expensive. Instead, they purchased or leased mini's to perform these functions. The mini is programmed to accept trades, perform the necessary price and interest calculations, produce confirmations, receive or delivery tickets, and, finally, balance the blotters—all within a few hours. It then stores the details of the trades, receives, and delivers on a magnetic file (mag), tape, or disc and feeds them into the firm's mainframe that evening.

Firms whose volume does not warrant the purchase of a mainframe have found the minicomputer to be a low-cost and efficient alternative. All the routines performed by the megabyte monster mainframes can be performed in smaller quantities by a mini.

Microcomputers. The newest entry into the field is the microcomputer, marketed as a home computer and lately finding acceptance in retail stores and business offices. Brokerage firms use micro's to perform in seconds many analytical tasks that were previously done by clerks who spent hours at a calculator. By being immediately available, micro's are more suitable to such tasks than larger computers because you have to wait for your "turn" in the computer's CPU and because changes in the mainframe's programming can be cumbersome. Changes in the micro's programming can be made relatively quickly and easily, usually by the actual user of the system.

Micro's are also used in the sales area to compute yields and yield equivalents between issues. Some micro's are programmed to give current yield to maturity, yield equivalent, and return after taxes, upon being fed the necessary input data. With such computations at their fingertips, brokers can discuss issues more intelligently with their clients.

In the highly technical computer industry, major breakthroughs happen all the time. Today's micro's have the processing power of yesterday's mini's, and the mini's in use now have the power of mainframes just a few years ago. As this industry continues to produce faster and more powerful hardware and programming, the lines of distinction among the three categories will be less and less clear.

THE IN-HOUSE COMPUTER FUNCTION AND THE DATA PROCESSING MANAGER

The data processing manager's responsibilities can be categorized into three principal areas:

1. *Production:* The data processing manager sees that the routines are run in proper sequence and at the proper times. Most important this person must have the day's work ready on time for distribution to employees in the various user departments, branches, or areas. The firm's daily, weekly, monthly, and yearly reports, statements, listings—all have to be produced on time and contain all the information they are supposed to have.
2. *Programming:* As rules, regulations, and the firm's product mix change, programs must be altered, rewritten, or written anew. The manager must make certain the changes are instituted at the scheduled times, that time is made available for computer testing, and that the programming staff is cognizant of the product being developed. The DP manager may not be in charge of both programming and production, depending on the firm and its management structure.
3. *Forward Planning:* The manager must keep abreast of all new developments in the computer industry, always planning for the growth of the brokerage firm, its products, and its reporting requirements. Most important, the manager must guarantee that the computer equipment will be used to earn a maximum return on the firm's investment in it.

THE SERVICE BUREAU

Some firms utilize *service bureaus,* which are companies that specialize in computer processing. They too have programs and routines to process the brokerage firm's daily, weekly, monthly, and yearly reports, statements, and listings.

Firm's that utilize service bureaus facilities are *customers* of the outside services. If the service is not of a good quality, the brokerage firms may contract with another service bureau to process their work. If enough brokerage firms leave a service bureau, the result is the same as when a brokerage firm's customers leave it. The service bureau goes out of business.

STEPS IN PROCESSING

Just as the computer operates by a logical program, the firm processes its daily work in a logical order. Although the routines may vary from firm to firm, the processing cycle follows this basic sequence:

1. *Data Entry:* All the trades must be entered into the computer system. The method of entry, or *input*, is determined by the system hardware and software. Input can be accomplished by means of keying onto keypunch machines or on a keyboard on a *CRT* terminal. Data can be captured and stored on punched cards, paper tape, magnetic tape, "floppy" diskettes, or disc packs.

2. *Figuration:* The trades are then passed through the figuration program, where the accrued interest on debt instruments is calculated, along with commission on agency transactions, fees, special charges, and other money amounts. After figuration, other routines come into play. For example, all agency commissions and the markups on principal transactions, both known as *sales credits*, are stored on a *pending tape*. Accumulated taxes and fees are stored for processing later on.

3. *P&S Listing:* The calculated trades are now sorted by the location of execution, and the P&S trade listings are prepared. The trades to be cleared through the various clearing facilities, such as NSCC, are prepared on cards or tape and delivered to the clearing service. As-of trades must be separated from the day's actual trades and placed on tapes. So the sorting goes.

4. *Customer Configurations:* Trade entries processed today are resorted from place of execution to account order. This resorted data is passed through the name and address program, which links the orders with the customers' names and addresses. Now the customers' confirmation or clients' invoices can be printed. Once printed, the confirmations are sent to the mail room for processing and mailing to the firm's clients.

5. *Balancing:* All of day's trades and trade corrections are stored on a pending tape, along with all previous days' trades that have not reached their settlement dates. The various balancing blotters, clearing blotters, and trade listings are drawn up.

6. *Margin Calculations:* Trades and corrections are merged with other entries being processed today. This other data (such as checks paid to customers, funds received from customers, securities received from and delivered to customers, brokers, and

depository entries) have previously been entered into the system via the keypunch machine or CRT terminal.

This merged data is then passed through the margin program. Entries affecting a customer's account are machine *posted* to that customer's account. The margin program then calculates how much money a customer owes the firm or may withdraw from each account, displaying the needs of the account on status sheets. Margin Department employees use these sheets to initiate *calls* for money, that is, they send the customer a notice requesting money. (We discuss this operation in greater detail in the chapter on the margin function.)

7. *Stock Records:* The computer is programmed to select trades that have settled, combine this information with all movement of securities, and print a daily stock record. The *stock record* is the brokerage firm's primary record depicting every security movement on a given day. To print the stock record, all applicable security data must be resorted into security order and then into account order. As each debit must have a credit, the stock record must balance. (This is explained when we review the stock record function in Chapter 10.)

8. *Cash Flow Summary:* Similarly, all cash movement, or *money entries,* must be sorted by account and printed on the daily cash summary. This document is another prime record of a brokerage firm because it captures every penny paid out from or received into each account of the firm.

The preceding routines are conducted during night time, on nonbusiness hours. The corresponding output—reports and the like—*must* be in the hands of users—the P&S department, the margin department, the cashier's department, and so on—first thing in the morning.

Whether done in the evening or during the day, all this work meets only the daily needs of the firm. Even while producing all these reports, EDP staff is responsible for a multitude of weekly, monthly, and yearly reports, many of which must be scheduled in and produced at the same time. Add to this workload the running time for the many *specials,* that is, unscheduled reports that different operation areas requested: You can appreciate tight scheduling that this area runs under.

But that's not all. Programmers need running time to test

and *debug* programs (that is, get the problems out of a new or revised program). Programs are continuously rewritten, tested, debugged, and tested again. The aim is to use the computer's capabilities to the fullest. Expansion of the computer's capability actually provides the impetus for the firm's growth. Over the years, computer capabilities have grown. So has the typical brokerage firm and so has the marketplace, each handling greater volume and introducing entirely new products and services to the public.

SUMMARY

Because so much information is concentrated in the EDP area, computers are not only the brain, but also the heart of the brokerage firm. It supervises the transmitting network by day and by night it processes data, calculates, and generates reports. Every message, wire, entry, and trade must pass through it. If the computer "goes down," the firm eventually has to stop also.

CHAPTER 17

The Role of Banks

We usually think of a bank as a place to cash our paychecks, take out loans, and keep our savings and checking accounts. A *commercial bank*, however, plays several important roles in the brokerage industry.

- It extends loans to brokerage firms to help it maintain security inventories and to extend margin loans to its clients.
- It plays a role in the underwriting of municipal bonds.
- It makes short-term credit available in the form of commercial loans and commercial paper.
- It facilitates international trade by creating banker's acceptances.
- It provides cashiering services in U.S. government securities.
- It acts as a custodian for institutions.

LOANS

Inventory Positions

Firms acting as dealers in the OTC market maintain inventory positions, and banks finance their inventory from day to day. Firms are involved with three types of positions:

1. Trading positions.
2. Settlement date positions.
3. Settled positions.

Trading Positions. These are securities that traders have positioned for the purpose of trading. A trading position does not mean that the physical security is in inventory. A trader can trade against a position that has not been settled or that has not yet been acquired. Traders move into and out of trading positions as the markets change.

Settlement Date Positions. These include securities:

- In vault.
- In bank loan.
- In fail to receive and fail to deliver.
- In customers' long and short positions.

Because these positions are monitored and balanced by the stock record department, trades in settlement date positions necessitate the debiting and crediting of all the appropriate accounts in given securities.

Settled Positions. These include:

- Physical inventory owned.
- Securities sold but not delivered.
- Securities bought and paid for, but not in good deliverable form.

The firm must finance settled positions through its cashier's area, which controls this portion of the inventory and sees to its financing.

Role of the Bank. Some of a firm's inventory financing is obtained from banks. Money managers of the firm poll the banks to determine which offers provide the most reasonable terms. With the security used as collateral, the inventory loan is set up as an *overnight*, so called because the inventory (the collateral) changes from day to day. The banks and brokerage houses work closely in "paying down" and reestablishing these loans daily. Generally, firms conduct business with more than one bank, and banks, of course, extend loans to more than one brokerage house. The ties are crucial to the well-being of the firm.

Margin Loans

When customers buy securities on margin, they put up part of the purchase price, called the *minimum margin requirement,* currently at 50%. The brokerage firm gives that money to the seller of the securities, along with the balance of the purchase price, which is actually the firm's money. The brokerage house has, in effect, loaned the money to the customer. The securities purchased in the transaction become collateral for the loan between client and firm.

But where does the brokerage house get the money? The answer is—from the banks.

When the firm borrows money from the bank, it must comply with federal law, specifically Regulation T. One of "Reg T's" requirements is that a firm may use up to 140% of a margin account's debit balance to secure financing.

Example: Customer Ms. Sulton buys $5,000 worth of securities (100 shares at $50) in a margin account. She deposits the minimum equity requirement of $2,500 (50%), and her firm puts up—lends her—the other $2,500. The firm pays the purchaser ($5,000) and takes delivery of the securities. Sulton's margin account is:

Minimum equity amount	$2,500
Debit balance	2,500
Market value	$5,000

The firm may now solicit bank financing using collateral in amounts up to 140% of Sulton's debit balance, or $3,500 (1.4 × $2,500).

The securities making up the difference between the market value of the securities and 140% of the debit balance have to be *segregated,* or kept separated from other securities.

Example: In sulton's account, $1,500 worth of the purchased securities have to be segregated. At $50 per share, that amounts to 30 shares ($1,500 divided by $50 per share). In effect, to borrow $2,500, the firm has put up the other $3,500 worth of collateral.

Firms must therefore "over-collateralize" its margin loans by 40%. Banks just won't lend a dollar for each dollar's worth of security. They must insist on excess collateral because they do not know the firm's customer activity or fluctuations in the security's price. The extra securities give them a "pad" against a quick drop in market value or other threats to the money loaned.

Segregated, or *seg*, securities are said to be *locked up in seg.* They cannot be used by the firm for loan purposes. Because they are customer-owned, these securities must be maintained in a good location, such as the firm's vault. These securities are registered in nominee name.

The banks rely on the firm to inform them of necessary adjustments as security positions change. Securities used for each such loan must therefore be verified daily. For an individual account, verifying positions and current market values is easy. On a firm-wide basis, however, the job is much more complex. Each business day, customers buy and sell securities, with each transaction altering the quantity of the securities that are loanable. At the same time, security prices fluctuate, thereby affecting the value of the pledged securities. So each day the cashier's area reviews all the new positions to determine and reconcile the loans held by the firm.

Should a particular issue drop sharply in value, or should the general market go into a decline, the bank loan can become undercollateralized. In such a case, the bank calls the firm either for additional securities or for the return of part of the loan. In turn, the firm's margin department is monitoring customers' positions and calls clients for more money as the value of their securities falls. If necessary the margin staff may liquidate positions in the account to cover the debit balance.

UNDERWRITINGS

Corporate Issues

Brokerage firms, known as *investment bankers,* either have underwriting facilities or specialize in underwriting.

Municipals

By assisting brokerage firms in the issuance of municipal debt instruments, banks play a critical role in enabling state and local governments to raise money. Municipal bonds, or *munis,* are brought to market through competitive underwriting. (See Chapter 2.) In this form of underwriting, the underwriting groups are formed first. Several different groups review the offering and submit bids to the issuing municipality. The group submitting the best bid wins the issue; the other groups lose. The winning group, comprised of banks and brokerage firms, offers the issue for sale to their customers and the public.

This form of underwriting is two-edged. It protects the public and ensures the most favorable terms available for the municipalities. If the bids are too low, the municipality simply does not accept them. If they are too high, the marketplace does not absorb (or buy) the issue.

COMMERCIAL LOANS AND PAPER

Banks serve corporations by offering short-term loans through commercial loans and the issuance of commercial paper.

Commercial Loans

These loans may be collateralized or uncollateralized in nature, depending on the borrowing corporation's need, its strength, its relationship with the bank, and the current economic climate.

On commercial loans, the bank charges a rate of interest that is based on the *prime lending rate,* or simply *prime rate.* Published in the daily newspapers, this rate reflects the rate at which banks will lend money to their financially strongest clients. The prime rate can vary from day to day, and the loan rate may vary from bank to bank. So, to obtain the lowest rates, corporations may borrow from one bank today and from another bank tomorrow.

Commercial Paper

Corporations also turn to other sources of short-term capital. Credit institutions, such as General Motors Acceptance Corporation (GMAC) and Ford Credit Corporation (FCC), have a constant need for short-term funds. To satisfy this need, corporations issue short-term "paper"—*commercial paper*—through banks to the banks' customers. On behalf of the customer, the bank polls a number of borrowing institutions and negotiates rate and time. Upon arriving at the best terms, the corporation instructs the bank to issue the "paper," which is placed in the account of the bank's client.

Commercial paper may be issued in "discount" or "plus interest" form. In *discount form,* the lender lends one amount (loan) and is paid back a higher amount (face). The difference between the loan and face amounts is the "interest" on the loan. In *plus interest* form, the lender receives, at the maturity date, the full principal plus all interest accrued during the life of the loan. This feature is also part of the negotiation. Operating in fiduciary capacity or under instruction from their customers, the bank invests the clients' funds in the corporation's commercial paper.

When banks assist a corporation in issuing paper, they are undercutting the need for their own commercial loans. Why should they compete with themselves in this way? Banks have customers with money to lend, and these customers are important to the bank. So the bank provides the service.

Commercial paper is traded as a security. Dealers in commercial paper are in continuous contact with issuing corporations. When a corporation has negotiated the terms of an issue, it instructs its commercial bank to issue the paper on its behalf for the acquiring dealer.

BANKER'S ACCEPTANCES

Bankers's acceptances are among the oldest forms of investment known. They are issued by banks involved in international trade to enable exporters to be paid for cargos before they are actually sold in the United States.

Example: A foreign corporation is shipping goods to an American importer, who will not pay for the cargo until it is received. The foreign corporation has incurred expenses in the manufacture of the goods and may not want to—or cannot—wait months for payment. In such a case, the foreign exporter takes the shipping documents—that is, the bill of lading and other evidence of the shipment—to a local bank. The bank sends the documents to a correspondent bank in America. Upon receipt of the documents, the U.S. bank accepts the bill of lading as collateral and pays the foreign bank. It then sells the acceptance to an investor. The buyer of the acceptance is, in effect, a lender and receives interest on the money loaned. The foreign exporter pays interest, which after a deduction for services rendered by the banks, goes to the owner of the banker's acceptance. The interest passes from the foreign exporter, through the foreign bank and U.S. bank, to the lender. In return for the interest, the foreign exporter has funds that would otherwise be tied up for months awaiting delivery.

The maturity of the acceptance should coincide with receipt of the goods. On that date, the United States importer, upon receipt of the cargo, pays the bank holding the bill of lading, and the bank retires the acceptance.

CASHIERING

Banks perform cashiering functions for some brokerage firms when the transactions involve "Fed" securities and the use of the "Fed" wire.

Fed funds is a term thrown around the industry to mean "same-day" money. Fed funds are transmitted among *member banks* (that is, banks that are members of the Federal Reserve System) through the use of the *Fed wire*. When this mechanism is used, the payor is charged and the payee is credited *on the same day*. Hence Fed funds are "same-day" money. The alternative is to settle trades with *clearing house funds*, a process that takes longer for the money to "clear." Clearing house funds clear very much as your own checks clear.

Firms that deal in government securities turn to banks for their cashiering function. There are several reasons for a brokerage firm's "farming out" their cashiering. For one thing, the settlement of trades in government securities requires large amounts of money, which the firms can get moved and cleared on the same day as they trade through the Fed wire. But brokerage firms don't have access to the Fed wire; banks do. So it pays firms to have banks handle cashiering of these transactions. Another reason is that the Fed maintains the ownership records of government securities on computer files, and it changes ownership by book entry. Letting a member bank handle the change of ownership therefore makes sense in this respect too.

In settling government trades, the cashier's area of the brokerage firm instructs the agent or clearing bank what to receive and what to deliver each day. The bank may also maintain the firm's vault position, perform transfer functions, and do related work. The bank, in effect, is an extension of the cashier's department.

Banks as Custodians

Banks also perform the function of custodians for the securities owned by institutions. In this capacity, they settle transactions, collect dividends and interest and ensure that the institution's account is maintained in proper order.

SUMMARY

Banks perform many key functions that augment the brokerage firm's service to the public and assist it in carrying out its daily routines. They also participate in the securities industry as the brokerage firm's customers or as their customers' agents. They buy and sell securities from inventory positions that they maintain for trusts and other institutions, as well as acting as custodians.

PART III

TYPES OF SECURITIES

A brokerage firm may offer many types of issues. In this section, the issues are grouped by categories, and each issue is then discussed separately. Bear in mind that entire texts have been written on most of these securities. This book merely highlights them for the purpose of explaining how they are handled in the operations areas.

CHAPTER 18

Corporate Securities

A corporation is a unique type of business enterprise in that the law recognizes it as a legal individual. As such, it can sue or be sued. Its shares of ownership can be easily transferred. It can amass large amounts of capital in its own name. Generally, its life, as defined by its charter, is perpetual.

The corporate charter describes what the corporation may or may not do. The charter is obtained from one of the fifty states, usually the corporation's home state. In some states, the charters are very strict, while in others they are very lenient. Some corporations therefore establish their home offices in states with lenient laws, to have as much flexibility as possible in conducting their business. The state that issues the charter becomes the corporation's *state of incorporation.*

One feature more than any other makes the corporation especially important to the securities industry. Shareholders, although owners, are liable only for the total amounts of their investment. This protection, which is known as limited liability, makes investment attractive. An individual can invest—that is, buy shares—in a corporation without fear of being sued and losing everything.

A corporation can issue two types of stock, *common* or *preferred,* either of which represents ownership in the company.

An investor who buys the corporation's stock owns a *share* of the company and is therefore known as a *shareholder*.

A corporation can also arrange long-term borrowing through the issuance of *bonds*. While stock is evidence of ownership, bonds are evidence of debt. A bondholder has loaned money to the corporation, not invested in it. As lenders, bondholders receive interest on their loan.

The next three chapters discuss the three principal types of corporate securities: common stock, preferred stock, and corporate bonds.

CHAPTER 19

Common Stock

Type: Ownership
Form: Registered
Denomination: Shares
Income payments: Dividend
Traded: Stock exchanges and OTC
Duration: Life of a corporation

The evidence of primary ownership in a corporation is its common stock. Each share of common stock represents one equal part of the entire ownership of the company.

Example: XYZ Corporation has 10,000 shares of common stock outstanding. Someone who owns one share owns 1/10,000 of the corporation, whereas an owner of 1,000 shares owns 1/10 of it (1,000 ÷ 10,000).

VOTING

Each share of common stock usually entitles its owner to one vote. An owner of 100 shares has 100 votes, an owner of 50 shares

FIGURE 19-1a. *A common stock certificate, front.*

FIGURE 19-1b. *A common stock certificate, back.*

W. R. GRACE & CO.

A statement of the designations, terms, limitations and relative rights and preferences of the shares of each class authorized to be issued, any variations in relative rights and preferences between the shares of any series of any class so far as said rights and preferences shall have been fixed and determined and the authority of the Board of Directors of the Company to fix and determine any relative rights and preferences of any subsequent series will be furnished to the holder hereof, without charge, upon request to the Secretary of the Company or to the Transfer Agent named on the face hereof.

The following abbreviations, when used in the inscription of ownership on the face of this certificate, shall be construed as though they were written out in full according to applicable laws or regulations:

JT TEN —As joint tenants, with right of survivorship, and not as tenants in common

TEN IN COM—As tenants in common

TEN BY ENT—As tenants by the entireties

Abbreviations in addition to those appearing above may be used.

For value received, ________ *hereby sell, assign and transfer unto*

PLEASE INSERT SOCIAL SECURITY OR OTHER IDENTIFYING NUMBER OF ASSIGNEE

[ ]

(PLEASE PRINT OR TYPEWRITE NAME AND ADDRESS OF ASSIGNEE)

________ *shares*

of the capital stock represented by the within Certificate, and do hereby irrevocably constitute and appoint

________ *Attorney*

to transfer the said stock on the books of the within named Company with full power of substitution in the premises.

Dated ________

NOTICE: The signature to this assignment must correspond with the name as written upon the face of the certificate in every particular, without alteration or enlargement or any change whatever.

has 50 votes. The more shares you own, the more votes you have, and the more control you have over the board of directors and, through them, the corporation. Common stockholders vote on key issues and on representation on the board of directors.

DIVIDENDS

Dividends may or may not be paid on shares of common stock. When dividends are paid depends on the policy and status of the corporation. Companies that are young and growing, or companies trying to conserve capital usually do not pay dividends to their common stockholders. When a corporation does pay a dividend, it may pay a cash or stock dividend.

Cash dividends are paid on a per-share basis. Some companies pay annually, while others pay semiannually or quarterly. Rarely are dividends paid more frequently than every quarter.

Stock dividends are paid as a percentage of the shares you own. For example, a 10% stock dividend means that, for every 100 shares you own, you receive 10 additional shares. Stock dividends are paid when a corporation has good earnings but wants to preserve its cash.

UNDERWRITING

Common stock may be publicly or privately owned. Usually small corporations are *privately owned.* These corporations are either "family owned" or closely held by a few principals. Because the shares of these companies are not easily bought or sold, they are not traded on any of the public markets. As a corporation grows in size, it needs capital. Once it outgrows the capital raised by the insiders, it must turn to the public.

New issues are brought to public market through underwriting, and the form of underwriting is negotiated.

The *public offering* of its securities takes place through a procedure known as *underwriting.* The corporation wishing to make a public offering seeks out an investment banker. The *investment banker,* usually a brokerage firm, forms an underwriting syndicate with other underwriters and begins the formal process of publicly issuing the securities.

Corporate underwritings are *negotiated.* In other words, the corporation usually turns to one investment banker whenever it needs long-term capital. The investment banker advises the corporation on market conditions, the corporation's position in the business environment, and the prospects of a successful issue. The investment banker and the corporation *negotiate* the type of security to bring to market.

TRADING OF COMMON STOCK

Once new issues of common stock are brought to market through an underwriting, they may trade in the over-the-counter market and/or on exchanges.

Common stocks usually first trade in the *over-the-counter (OTC) market.* In this marketplace, a brokerage firm *makes a market* in the security, that is, the firm stands ready to buy or sell the security against its inventory in the anticipation of making a profit. When the firm trades against its own inventory, it is considered a *dealer*. A dealer makes a profit by the spread between the securities it buys and sells.

The common stock of better known corporations are also traded on *stock exchanges,* which constitute an *auction market* where the highest bid and lowest offer have priority. Exchange-traded securities, known as *listed securities,* are traded between buyers and sellers through brokers, who charge commissions on listed transactions. Because brokers do not take ownership of the security, they make their profits through the commissions charged.

The unit of trading in common stock is usually 100 shares, which is called a *round lot*. Transactions for under 100 shares are known as *odd lots.* In a very few cases, the unit of trading is 10 shares.

Common stock is a *registered issue;* that is, the stock certificates are registered in the name of the owner. Securities may be owned by a brokerage firm's customers but registered in the name of either the firm or a bank. If they are registered in the customers's name, they are said to be registered, in the *beneficial owner's* (that is, the customer's) name. When they are registered in behalf of the beneficial owner, in the name of the firm or a bank (the nominee), they are said to be registered in *street name.* This form of registration, called *nominee registration,* makes the movement of securities easier.

To keep track of ownership, an issuing entity usually retains the services of one registrar, one or two transfer agents, and one dividend disbursing agent. The names and addresses of the registered holders are maintained by the *corporate transfer agent,* which is usually a bank or trust company. When common stock changes hands, the certificate is sent to its respective *transfer agent,* which cancels the old certificate and issues a new one in the name of the new owner. Dividends are disbursed to registered holders by the *dividend disbursing agent (DDA),* also a bank.

It is the function of the registrar to ensure that the quantity of an issue is properly maintained by the transfer agent. If a corporation is supposed to have 8,000,000 shares of common stock outstanding, it is the registrar's responsibility to see that all of the registrations on the transfer agent's books total 8,000,000 shares.

COMMON STOCK AS AN INVESTMENT VEHICLE

Because a corporation's liability is limited and because ownership can be easily transferred, common stock attracts many investors, who may be looking for income, for capital appreciation or for both. Stock-issuing corporations range from huge multimillion-dollar companies to fledging concerns offering their shares to the public for the first time. Some investments may be considered safe or conservative, while others are very risky or speculative. Whatever their investment goals, investors usually find something suitable in the common stock arena.

CHAPTER 20

Preferred Stock

Type: Ownership
Form: Registered
Denomination: Shares
Income payments: Dividend
Traded: Stock exchanges and OTC
Life: Varies with issue

Like common stock, preferred stock represents ownership in the corporation. Unlike common stock, however, preferred securities usually do not have voting privileges. This type of stock is called "preferred" because:

- Current dividends must be paid to preferred shareholders before they are paid to common stockholders.
- In case of liquidation, preferred owners receive the distribution of assets before common stock owners.

FIGURE 20-1a. *A preferred stock certificate, front.*

NOT MORE THAN 100,000 SHARES

W.R. Grace & Co.

INCORPORATED UNDER THE LAWS OF THE STATE OF CONNECTICUT

CLASS B PREFERRED STOCK

This Certifies that

SEE REVERSE FOR CERTAIN DEFINITIONS

CUSIP 383883 40 2

is the owner of

SHARES OF THE FULL-PAID AND NON-ASSESSABLE CLASS B PREFERRED STOCK OF THE PAR VALUE OF $100 EACH OF

W. R. Grace & Co., transferable on the books of the Company in person or by attorney upon surrender of this certificate properly endorsed. This certificate is not valid until countersigned by the Transfer Agent and registered by the Registrar.

Witness the facsimile seal of the Company and the facsimile signatures of its duly authorized officers.

Dated

REGISTERED: CHEMICAL BANK (NEW YORK) REGISTRAR

BY AUTHORIZED SIGNATURE

COUNTERSIGNED MARINE MIDLAND BANK TRANSFER AGENT

BY AUTHORIZED OFFICER

CHAIRMAN

SECRETARY

SPECIMEN 09 15 81

SPECIMEN 09 15 81

FIGURE 20-1b. *A preferred stock certificate, back.*

W. R. GRACE & CO.

A statement of the designations, terms, limitations and relative rights and preferences of the shares of each class authorized to be issued, any variations in relative rights and preferences between the shares of any series of any class so far as said rights and preferences shall have been fixed and determined and the authority of the Board of Directors of the Company to fix and determine any relative rights and preferences of any subsequent series will be furnished to the holder hereof without charge, upon request to the Secretary of the Company or to the Transfer Agent named on the face hereof.

The following abbreviations, when used in the inscription of ownership on the face of this certificate, shall be construed as though they were written out in full according to applicable laws or regulations:

JT TEN —As joint tenants, with right of survivorship, and not as tenants in common

TEN IN COM—As tenants in common

TEN BY ENT—As tenants by the entireties

Abbreviations in addition to those appearing above may be used.

For value received, ________ *hereby sell, assign and transfer unto*

____

(PLEASE PRINT OR TYPEWRITE NAME AND ADDRESS OF ASSIGNEE)

____

____

__________________________ *shares*

of the capital stock represented by the within Certificate, and do hereby irrevocably constitute and appoint

__________________________ *Attorney*

to transfer the said stock on the books of the within named Company with full power of substitution in the premises.

Dated ______________

____

NOTICE: The signature to this assignment must correspond with the name as written upon the face of the certificate in every particular, without alteration or enlargement or any change whatever.

DIVIDENDS

Preferred stocks are supposed to pay a fixed rate of dividend. The rate is expressed either as a dollar sum or as a percentage.

The *dollar rate* is the amount to be paid per share per year.

Example: A "$4.36 preferred" pays $4.36 per share per year.

The *percentage* is a percentage *not* of the selling price, but of the par value of a security, which is the value assigned to a stock for bookkeeping purposes. It has nothing to do with the market price or current value of a security.

Example: A "4% preferred" with a $100 par value is expected to pay $4 per share per year ($100 × .04). A dividend of 4% on a $50 par value is $2 per share per year ($50 × .04).

Because the rates of dividend are fixed, preferred stocks are usually included in a group of securities known as *fixed income securities*. Included in this group are corporate bonds, municipal bonds, and U.S. government obligations. The market price of preferred stock is therefore based on current yield rates for fixed income investments.

UNDERWRITING

Preferred securities are brought to market through an underwriting, which is usually *negotiated*. Once they decide on issuing a preferred security, corporate officials and the investment bankers discuss what features they must offer to make the preferred attractive to the public. Among the features discussed are:

- The dividend rate.
- Callable (noncallable).
- Convertible (nonconvertible).
- Cumulative.
- Participating.
- Adjustable rate.
- Putable.
- Self-liquidity.

Each of these features has an effect on the corporation's financial structure.

Dividend Rate

The dividend must be competitive not only with those of other issues from similar companies, but also with other fixed income securities. Yet, because the dividend draws earnings out of the company, it should not be "too high." Should the company fail to pay the dividend when it is due, it turns the preferred stockholder into just another common stockholder, neither of whom receives a dividend. Such a failure also broadcasts the company's financial difficulties to the world. To compete with the fixed income securities in a period of high interest rates, a preferred stock may have to pay an exceptionally high dividend rate.

Callable

During periods of uncertain interest rates, the corporation may be forced to issue a high yielding preferred. If the corporation and investment bankers believe that interest rates will fall in a few years, the corporation could raise capital at a lower dividend rate in the not-too-distant future. The problem is that, once issued, preferred stock has a lifetime that is as long as the corporation's.

In such cases, the corporation might make the new issue "callable." The *callable* feature permits the corporation to "call in," or retire, the issue at its option for a predetermined price. A preferred that does not contain the callable feature is referred to as *noncallable.*

The public sometimes shies away from a callable issue for fear that the corporation will call the issue quickly should rates fall. To assure investors of a return for a given period and yet retain the ability to call the issue, the corporation might offer a noncallable for, say, ten years, seven years, or five years. Thus stockholders are assured that the corporation will not retire the issue for a known period.

Convertible

If a corporation and its investment bankers believe that the price of the company's common stock is likely to rise over time, they may decide to offer a "convertible" preferred. The *convertible* feature allows preferred stockholders to convert their shares into common stock. When preferred shareholders actually convert their stock depends largely on the price of the common stocks. Convertibility is expressed in terms of the *conversion rate,* that is, how many shares of common stock can be had for each share of preferred. For example, if the rate is 4-for-1, then each share of preferred can be converted into four shares of common.

When the market price of the preferred stock is equal to that of the converted number of common stock, the two types of stock are said to be at *parity.*

Example: The preferred stock is convertible into four shares of common stock. The convertible preferred is currently selling at $100 per share, and the common stock is at $25 per share. We have parity—one preferred at $100 equals four common at $25 each.

As the preferred stock and common stock fluctuate in value, parity is possible whenever the price of the preferred stock and the conversion feature are equal. Once parity is reached, if the dividend of the converted shares is greater than the dividend on the preferred, the preferred shareholders normally convert.

Example: The preferred is paying $8 per share per year, while the common is paying $2.25 per share per year. If the two are trading at parity, the preferred holder should convert to the common and receive a larger dividend. So, while one share of preferred is yielding $8, the equivalent number of common shares pays $9 per year ($2.25 × 4 shares).

If the preferred is worth more than the value of the converted common, it is said to be *above parity.*

Example: A growth company's common stock is trading $20 per share. The corporation offers a preferred that is convertible into four shares of common. The dividends paid on this preferred causes its market price to rise to $100. The convertible feature is then computed to be worth $25 ($100 ÷ 4 common shares).

If the company continues to prosper, the value of the common stock normally increases. Once it crosses over parity, the common stock "pulls" the price of the preferred up with it, due to the work of *arbitrageurs*, who buy the preferred thereby forcing the preferred price upward. Then they convert it and sell the common stock.

Example: The preferred is trading at $96. If the common stock rises in value to $24.50, then arbitrageurs buy the preferred at 96 and convert to common, which is selling at 24½.

Cost of 100 preferred	$9,600
Sale of 400 common after conversion @ 24½	$9,800
Profit	$200

Eventually the demand for the preferred and the supply of common stock in the market neutralize each other, and the stocks go back to parity.

Cumulative

If the preferred is *noncumulative*, a "missed" (that is, not paid) dividend is lost forever. On *cumulative* preferreds, all dividends—both past and current—must be paid before the common stockholder can receive any dividend.

Example: You own one share of BAM Company preferred and one share of common. BAM pays all its earnings in dividends.

Noncumulative

Year	*1980*	*1981*	*1982*	*1983*
Earning	$3	0	$10	$20
$8 Preferred dividend	$3	0	$ 8	$ 8
Common stock	0	0	$ 2	$12

Cumulative

Year	*1980*	*1981*	*1982*	*1983*
Earning	$4	0	$10	$20
$8 Preferred dividend	$3	0	$10	$19
Common stock	0	0	0	$ 1

During the four-year period, the preferred shareholder is supposed to receive $8 per share per year. In 1980, the company earned $3, which was paid to the preferred holder. The next year the company earned nothing; so the noncumulative preferred shareholder lost a total of $13 in dividends ($8 – $3 = $5 + $8 = $13).

The cumulative shareholder, however, has the opportunity to recapture the lost dividend, should earnings improve. The preferred stockholder expected to receive $8 per year per share for a $32 total at the end of the four-year period. In the noncumulative example, the preferred owner received only $19, while the common shareowner received $14. The cumulative preferred holder eventually received $32, and the common shareowner received only $1.

Participating

Some companies have radical earning cycles. They can earn zero one year, suddenly earn a huge profit the next year, only to slide back to zero or worse in the third year. This type of company might offer a participating preferred, or the investment banker may strongly recommend it as an inducement in selling the security to the public. A *participating preferred* earns its set dividend, and then the common receives a set amount. Any additional earnings slated for payout as dividends are shared between the participating preferred and the common shareholders.

Adjustable Rate Preferred

A newer form of preferred is *adjustable rate preferred,* whose dividend rate is reset periodically. The rate is usually "pegged" to Treasury bonds or Treasury bond yields. Changing the dividend rate and updating the rate to reflect the current rates keeps the value of the issue close to its original issuance price.

Putable Preferred

Putable preferred stock usually has this feature included with adjustable rate preferred. It permits the share owners to "put" the shares back to the issuer and receive a predetermined price.

Self-Liquidating Preferred

A *self-liquidating preferred* will cease to exist at a specific time. The preferred shareholder will receive some of the issue, or cash, for the preferred shares.

SUMMARY

A preferred may be callable, convertible, cumulative, or participating, or it might have any combination of these features. Investors should know these features, to make intelligent investing decisions. Some features of preferred stock benefit the corporation and others benefit the shareholder. The corporation decides what to "give away" to assure a successful underwriting. All the while, the public is comparing issues and deciding which offer them the most attractive opportunity. Somewhere between what the corporation needs and what the public wants lies the compromise. It is here that the successful underwriting occurs.

People working in operations must know the different types of preferred stock to process them correctly and to thereby service the client efficiently.

CHAPTER 21

Corporate Bonds and Notes

Type: Debt
Form: Registered (usually)
Denomination: Terms established in indenture (usually $1,000)
Income payment: Interest
Traded: Stock exchanges or OTC
Duration: Varies, usually a 30-year maximum

Market conditions, the dilution of ownership, and a host of other reasons may lead a corporation to decide against issuing shares of stock to raise capital. Instead, because the corporation is a legal individual, it borrows money from the public sector in its own name.

- Corporations borrow long-term capital through debt instruments known as *bonds.*
- They borrow intermediate-term financing through *notes.*
- Short-term financing, referred to as *commercial loans,* is arranged through commercial banks. (Some corporations, especially finance corporations, issue a short-term instrument known as *commercial paper.*)

This chapter focuses on corporate bonds and notes. Bondholders and noteholders are creditors, or lenders, to the corporation. As such, they do not own the company or have any vote in corporate matters. They lend their money to the corporation, in return for interest payments as they become due and the repayment of their principal at the conclusion of the loan's term.

Corporate bonds and notes are brought to the public market through underwritings, which are usually negotiated but are sometimes competitive. (See Chapter 23, "Municipal Bonds and Notes," for an explanation of the competitive underwriting.) In the negotiated underwriting, corporate management and the underwriters meet and decide to issue bonds.

The bonds must be made attractive to the investment public, because corporate bonds and notes, by paying a fixed rate of interest, compete with other debt instruments for the investor's dollars. Yet the interest, as set, must be paid or the debt holders can foreclose on the corporation. So the set rate of interest must be high enough to compete with other debt instruments but not so high that the corporation cannot pay it.

How, then, does the corporation set the interest rate? One factor is the rate of return that the corporation can expect when it invests the borrowed funds.

Example: The issuing company wants to build a new factory. Based on their estimates, the factory will return 10% on money invested to build it. If the corporation must pay 8% on the money they are borrowing, the factory may be worth building. If they have to pay 11% interest, the factory may not.

Another term for using borrowed money to make money is *leverage*. The corporation knows that the income they earn fluctuates while the long-term financing is paid for at a fixed rate. They will therefore be "hedging" the borrowed funds against the possible income.

Hedging is a two-edged sword. On one side, the corporation can earn revenue on someone else's money. On the other side, if the interest cost is fixed, the corporation can lose money as a result of leverage.

Example: If the corporation can borrow money at 8% interest, it will earn 2% on the bondholders' money: 10% return less 8% cost of money

FIGURE 21-1a. *A bond certificate, front*

NUMBER

DOLLARS

W.R. Grace & Co.

REGISTERED

$12\frac{5}{8}\%$ NOTE DUE 1990

SEE REVERSE FOR CERTAIN DEFINITIONS

CUSIP 383883 AC 9

W. R. Grace & Co., a Connecticut corporation (hereinafter called the "Company," which term includes any successor corporation under the Indenture hereinafter referred to), for value received, hereby promises to pay to

$12\frac{5}{8}\%$ DUE 1990

$12\frac{5}{8}\%$ DUE 1990

, or registered assigns, the principal sum of

DOLLARS

on September 15, 1990, and to pay interest thereon from September 15, 1980 or from the most recent Interest Payment Date to which interest has been paid or duly provided for, semi-annually on March 15 and September 15 in each year, at the rate of $12\frac{5}{8}\%$ per annum, until the principal hereof is paid or is duly provided for. The interest so payable, and punctually paid or duly provided for, on any Interest Payment Date will, as provided in such Indenture, be paid to the Person in whose name this Note (or one or more Predecessor Notes, as defined in such Indenture) is registered at the close of business on the Regular Record Date for such interest which shall be the March 1 or September 1 (whether or not a Business Day), as the case may be, next preceding such Interest Payment Date. Any such interest not so punctually paid or duly provided for shall forthwith cease to be payable to the registered Holder on such Regular Record Date, and may be paid to the Person in whose name this Note (or one or more Predecessor Notes) is registered at the close of business on a Special Record Date for the payment of such Defaulted Interest to be fixed by the Trustee, notice whereof shall be given to Holders of Notes not less than 10 days prior to such Special Record Date, or may be paid at any time in any other lawful manner not inconsistent with the requirements of any securities exchange on which the Notes may be listed, and upon such notice as may be required by such exchange, all as more fully provided in such Indenture. Payment of the principal of and interest on this Note will be made at the office or agency of the Company maintained for that purpose in the Borough of Manhattan, The City of New York, in such coin or currency of the United States of America as at the time of payment is legal tender for payment of public and private debts; *provided, however,* that payment of interest may be made at the option of the Company by check mailed to the address of the Person entitled thereto as such address shall appear in the Note Register.

Reference is hereby made to the further provisions of this Note set forth on the reverse hereof, which further provisions shall for all purposes have the same effect as if set forth at this place.

Unless the certificate of authentication hereon has been executed by the Trustee referred to on the reverse hereof by manual signature, this Note shall not be entitled to any benefit under the Indenture or be valid or obligatory for any purpose.

In Witness Whereof, the Company has caused this instrument to be duly executed under its corporate seal.

W. R. Grace & Co.

DATED:

TRUSTEE'S CERTIFICATE OF AUTHENTICATION.

THIS IS ONE OF THE NOTES REFERRED TO IN THE WITHIN-MENTIONED INDENTURE.

BANKERS TRUST COMPANY, AS TRUSTEE

BY SPECIMEN

AUTHORIZED OFFICER

ATTEST:

SECRETARY

BY

J. Peter Grace

PRESIDENT

W. R. GRACE & CO. INCORPORATED 1899 LAWS OF CONNECTICUT

GRACE

FIGURE 21-1b. *A bond certificate, back.*

W. R. GRACE & CO.

12⅝% NOTE DUE 1990

This Note is one of a duly authorized issue of Notes of the Company nated as its 12⅝% Notes Due 1990 (herein called the "Notes"), limited pt as otherwise provided in the Indenture referred to below) in aggregate pal amount to $100,000,000, issued and to be issued under an indenture n called the "Indenture") dated as of September 15, 1980 between the any and Bankers Trust Company, Trustee (herein called the "Trustee", which includes any successor trustee under the Indenture), to which Indenture and dentures supplemental thereto reference is hereby made for a statement of the ctive rights thereunder of the Company, the Trustee and the Holders of the , and the terms upon which the Notes are, and are to be, authenticated elivered.

The Notes are subject to redemption, upon not less than 30 nor more than ys' notice by first-class mail, at any time on or after September 15, 1986, whole or from time to time in part, at the election of the Company, at a nption Price equal to 100% of their principal amount, together with accrued st to the Redemption Date (but interest instalments whose Stated Maturity or prior to the Redemption Date will be payable to the Holders of such Notes, or more Predecessor Notes, of record at the close of business on the relevant d Date referred to on the face hereof), all as provided in the Indenture.

In the event of redemption of this Note in part only, a new Note or Notes e unredeemed portion hereof shall be issued in the name of the Holder hereof the cancellation hereof.

If an Event of Default, as defined in the Indenture, shall occur and be con- g, the principal of all the Notes may be declared due and payable in the er and with the effect provided in the Indenture.

The Indenture permits, with certain exceptions as therein provided, the dment thereof and the modification of the rights and obligations of the ny and the rights of the Holders of the Notes under the Indenture at any time e Company and the Trustee with the consent of the Holders of 66⅔% in gate principal amount of the Notes at the time Outstanding, as defined in the ure. The Indenture also contains provisions permitting the Holders of ied percentages in aggregate principal amount of the Notes at the time Out- ng, as defined in the Indenture, on behalf of the Holders of all the Notes, to compliance by the Company with certain provisions of the Indenture and n past defaults under the Indenture and their consequences. Any such con- or waiver by the Holder of this Note shall be conclusive and binding upon Holder and upon all future Holders of this Note and of any Note issued upon ansfer hereof or in exchange herefor or in lieu hereof whether or not notation h consent or waiver is made upon this Note.

No reference herein to the Indenture and no provision of this Note or of the Indenture shall alter or impair the obligation of the Company, which is absolute and unconditional, to pay the principal of and interest on this Note at the times, places, and rate, and in the coin or currency, herein prescribed.

As provided in the Indenture and subject to certain limitations therein set forth, this Note is transferable on the Note Register of the Company, upon surrender of this Note for registration of transfer at the office or agency of the Company in the Borough of Manhattan, The City of New York, duly endorsed by, or accompanied by a written instrument of transfer in form satisfactory to the Company and the Note Registrar duly executed by, the Holder hereof or his attorney duly authorized in writing, and thereupon one or more new Notes, of authorized denominations and for the same aggregate principal amount, will be issued to the designated transferee or transferees.

The Notes are issuable only in registered form without coupons in denominations of $1,000 and any integral multiple thereof. As provided in the Indenture and subject to certain limitations therein set forth, Notes are exchangeable for a like aggregate principal amount of Notes of a different authorized denomination, as requested by the Holder surrendering the same.

No service charge shall be made for any such transfer or exchange, but the Company may require payment of a sum sufficient to cover any tax or other governmental charge payable in connection therewith.

The Company, the Trustee and any agent of the Company or the Trustee may treat the Person in whose name this Note is registered as the owner hereof for all purposes, whether or not this Note be overdue, and neither the Company, the Trustee nor any such agent shall be affected by notice to the contrary.

The Notes are hereby designated as Superior Indebtedness for the purposes of (a) the Indenture covering the Company's 4¼% Convertible Subordinate Debentures Due March 1, 1990 issued pursuant to the Indenture dated as of March 1, 1965 between the Company and Chemical Bank New York Trust Company, Trustee, within the meaning of, and as defined in, Section 3.01 of such Indenture and (b) the Indenture covering the Company's 6½% Convertible Subordinate Debentures Due 1996 issued pursuant to the Indenture dated as of November 15, 1971 between the Company and The Chase Manhattan Bank (National Association), Trustee, within the meaning of, and as defined in, Section 3.01 of such Indenture.

Terms used herein which are defined in the Indenture shall have the respective meanings assigned thereto in the Indenture.

ABBREVIATIONS

The following abbreviations, when used in the inscription on the face of this Note, shall be construed as though they were written out in full according to applicable laws or regulations:

TEN COM—as tenants in common
TEN ENT —as tenants by the entireties
JT TEN —as joint tenants with right of survivorship and not as tenants in common

UNIF GIFT MIN ACT—........ Custodian........
(Cust) (Minor)
under Uniform Gifts to Minors Act................
(State)

Additional abbreviations may also be used though not in the above list.

FOR VALUE RECEIVED, the undersigned hereby sells, assigns and transfers unto

ASE INSERT SOCIAL SECURITY OR OTHER IDENTIFYING NUMBER OF ASSIGNEE

PLEASE PRINT OR TYPEWRITE NAME AND ADDRESS OF ASSIGNEE

within Note of W. R. GRACE & CO. and does hereby irrevocably constitute and appoint

Attorney

ansfer the said Note on the books of the within-named Corporation, with full power of substitution in the premises.

ed

equals a 2% profit. On the other hand, if the return on the investment turns out to be only 7%, the corporation will lose 1% on the borrowed sum: 8% cost of money less 7% return equals 1% loss.

PAYMENT OF INTEREST

Interest is paid to bondholders usually on a semiannual basis. The periods are:

- January and July (J&J).
- February and August (F&A).
- March and September (M&S).
- April and October (A&O).
- May and November (M&N).
- June and December (J&D).

The actual payment date can be any day of the month, but it is the same day throughout the life of the instrument. For example, an F&A 15 pays interest on February 15 and August 15; an A&O (no date mentioned) pays April 1 and October 1. Because most bonds may pay interest on the first day of the interest month, the number "1" is often omitted; such bonds are referred to simply as "A&O," "M&N," and so on.

Corporate bonds are traded on national exchanges as well as over the counter. The typical bond transaction settles regular way, five business days after trade date.

Bonds trade at the market price plus accrued interest. When you buy a bond, you pay the agreed-upon price *plus* whatever interest has accrued to the former owner (the seller) of the bond. Let's look at the price of the bond first.

Pricing of a Corporate Bond

The quoted price of the bond represents a percentage of the face value, or par value.

Example: An XYZ bond is quoted 96-1/2. In other words, the bond is trading at 96% to 96½% of the par value. For a $1,000 par value bond, a seller with a market order receives $960 ($1,000 × .96). A buyer with a market order pays $965.00 ($1,000 × .965).

When the bond is trading at 100%, it is said to be trading at *par,* or par value. Bonds *over par* are said to be *at a premium,* whereas bonds trading *below par* are said to be selling *at a discount.*

The price at which a bond is trading has a direct impact on the investor's return, because interest is paid on the face amount of the bond, not on its market value. A bond pays the same dollar amount of interest regardless of its current market price. If the bond is trading at a discount, the investor's rate of return is higher than the stated interest rate on the bond, which is called the *coupon rate.*

Example: The $1,000 XYZ bond carries a coupon rate of 8%. If the bond is purchased at par, the owner receives an 8% return on the investment. Here's the interest calculation:

Face amount	$1,000
Coupon rate	8%
Interest period	1 year

$$\$1{,}000 \times \frac{8}{100} \times \frac{360}{360} = \$80$$

Bond price (par)	$1,000
Annual interest	$80

If a bond is trading below par, the rate of return is greater than the coupon rate.

Example: If the bond is trading at 80 (at a discount), the investor receives a return of 10% on the investment.

Bond price	$800
Annual interest	$ 80
Rate of return	10% (greater than the coupon rate)

If the bond is trading at a premium, the rate of return is less than the coupon rate.

Example: The XYZ bond is trading at a price of 120. The interest computation is as follows:

Bond price	$1,200
Annual interest	$ 80
Rate of return	.06667 or 6.67%

The rate of return can also be called *yield.* The formulas just demonstrated are used for *current yield.* In the fixed income security environment, many other formulas are used to calculate different yields, such as yield-to-maturity or yield-to-first sinking fund. We do not explore these formulas here.

Accrued Interest

The trade price, however, is only part of what you pay the seller. You must also pay any interest that has accrued to the seller since the last interest payment.

Interest is computed on a 360-day basis, with each half-year interest period comprising 180 days.

Example: An 8% bond pays $80 per year per $1,000 of face value, or $40 semiannually.

Interest continues to accrue to the bond's seller up to but not including settlement day, on which date the accrued interest is paid to the seller. The formula for calculating accrued interest is:

$$\text{Accrued interest} = \text{Face amount of bond} \times \text{Rate of interest} \times \frac{\text{Number of days bond is owned}}{360}$$

Example: On April 4, you purchase $1,000 XYZ 8% A&O 2005 @ 96, which settles on April 11. Because the bond pays interest on April 1 and October 1 (A&O), you owe the seller interest from April 1 through April 10. Counting the days from April 1, the first day of the interest period, up through but not including the settlement date of April 11, you get 10 days. You owe 10 days of interest. Let's calculate the accrued interest:

$$\text{Accrued interest} = \underset{\textit{Face Amount}}{\$1{,}000} \times \underset{\textit{Interest Rate}}{\frac{8}{100}} \times \underset{\textit{Days}}{\frac{10}{360}} = \$2.23$$

You pay the seller $960 (.96 × $1,000 face value) *plus* the accrued interest of $2.23.

On August 29, you sell the bonds at a price of 96 for settlement on September 5.

Now let's see the calculations on the sale of the bond. From April 11 through September 4, you accrue interest. Counting from April 11 through but not including the settlement date of September 5, you get 144 days, during which interest has accrued to you. You are entitled to 144 days of accrued interest.

	Days
April	20
May	30
June	30
July	30
August	30
September	4
Total	144

$$\text{Accrued interest} = \$1{,}000 \times \frac{8}{100} \times \frac{144}{360} = \$32.00$$

Because you paid $2.23 in accrued interest when you purchased the bond and you earned actual interest of $32, which equals the accrued interest for 144 days, the buyer of the bond must pay you a total of $34.23, which represents a total of 154 days.

On October 1, the corporation's agent pays $40 to the recorded holder of the bond. The purchaser of your bond has accumulated 26 days of accrued interest, for a sum of $5.77. The new owner, having paid you $34.23, ends up with the $5.77 difference.

Note that the corporation authorizes its agent to pay the entire six-month interest payment to the recorded holder. The parties who buy or sell bonds during the period simply settle the accrued interest among themselves.

Example:

First customer:	Receives accrued interest at time of sale	$ 2.23
You:	Pay at time of purchase	$ 2.23
	Receive at time of sale	$34.23
	Accrues to you	$32.00
Third customer:	Pays to you at time of purchase	$34.23
	Receives from corporation	$40.00
	Accrues to the new owner	$ 5.77
	Total	$40.00
	Total paid by company	$40.00

BOND PRICES AND INTEREST RATES

Many forces affect the trading price of a bond. Having a direct impact on the security's price are such influences as the economic outlook, the features of the bond, and the rating given by various service companies, to name but a few.

Perhaps interest rate fluctuations are the most conspicuous influence on income-bearing, or fixed dividend, securities:

- As interest rates rise, the trading prices of bonds in the marketplace fall.
- As interest rates fall, the prices of older bonds rise.

Example: Three years ago, a corporation received par for a bond carrying a 6% interest rate. Today the same company has to pay 10% before the public invests on a dollar-for-dollar (par) basis.

Today, if both bonds were offered to you at par, which would you purchase? You would naturally choose the 10% bond because it returns the high yield. Let's say, however, that you were offered the 6% bond for sale at 60 (or $600). The choice is not as simple, because both bonds now yield approximately 10%.

BOND RATINGS

Most fixed income issues are reviewed and rated by various rating services, of which the two best known are Standard & Poor's and Moody's. Such companies use many criteria to evaluate the financial strength of issuers. With easy access to these reports, the public may use these ratings in choosing the appropriate investment.

When the corporation and its investment banker negotiate the terms of the bond to be issued, the company's rating plays an important part. The higher the rating, the more willing the investing public is to purchase the security. On the other hand, the more willing investors are to buy the bond because of its rating, the less interest the issuer has to pay to attract investors.

INDENTURE

Other considerations enter into the negotiations. Bonds, like preferred stock, can contain features that make one more attractive than another. The terms of a corporate bond are found in the *indenture* (also known as the *deed of trust*), which is printed on the back of the certificates.

RETIRING BONDS

Like a preferred stock, a bond can be callable or convertible (into common stock, not preferred). Sometimes a corporation expects to retire an issue of bonds by buying them on the open market with money it earns. In such a case, the corporation sets up a *sinking fund,* that is, it periodically places money in a fund for the purpose of buying back the bonds.

A sinking fund differs from a callable feature, in that the callable price is predetermined and appears in the indenture. With the sinking fund, the corporation acquires the bonds *at the current market price.* Generally, a corporation is not permitted to acquire or purchase bonds if they are trading at a premium.

Bonds may be retired by three methods:

1. In a *redemption,* the bonds are retired and the bondholders are paid cash.
2. In a *conversion,* the bondholders exchange their bonds for shares of common stock.
3. In a *refunding,* the corporation retires one bond issue by issuing another.

BOND SECURITY

By buying bonds, members of the public are, in fact, risking their capital. Should the company default, what assurance do bondholders have of getting their money back? What security must the corporation pledge to ensure the public of the safety of the investment? Bond issues are commonly supported by mortgages, collateral, equipment, or just the good name of the company. (In the latter case, the bond is known as a "debenture.")

Mortgage Bonds

Mortgage Bonds are supported by a lien on the corporation's property, usually a plant or office building. The mortgage issue may be *open-ended,* which means that subsequent issues are equal in all respects to the original issue. In a *closed-end* mortgage issue, subsequent issues are junior to the original issue in any claims against the corporation. Each subsequent issue is junior to the previous one in the payment of interest and the coverage that supports the issue.

Collateral Trust

Collateral trust bonds are secured by the collateral of another corporation. A company secures the issue with stock it owns in another company. The strength of another company's securities supports the issue.

Equipment Trust

Equipment trust bonds are secured by a corporation's equipment, usually its rolling stock. This type of bond is common in the railroad, trucking, and airline industries. For example, an airline pledges its planes and other vehicles as security for the bond.

Debenture

The *debenture bond,* issued by only the strongest of companies, is secured by the good faith and name of the issuing company. Nothing tangible secures the issue, but the possibility of the company's defaulting on the issue is generally believed to be nil.

REGISTRATION

Corporate bond certificates are fully registered. Until the late 1950s or early 1960s, two other forms existed:

1. *Bearer certificates,* in which the holders are the assumed owners.
2. *Registered to principal* bonds had the actual owners' names or nominees names maintained by a corporate transfer agent.

Both forms necessitated the "clipping" of coupons to receive interest payments. As of July 1, 1983, no new bonds can be issued in coupon form.

The fully registered bond form has superseded these other

forms. For a *fully registered bond,* the name of the owner, or the nominee, is maintained by a registrar. The semiannual interest payments are mailed to the registered holders by the corporation's interest paying agent. This type of registration has made transfer of bonds much easier than in the past, and it safeguards against theft.

DEFAULT

When a company gets into financial trouble, it may turn to two different types of debt instruments: either a receiver's certificate or an income bond.

A *receiver's certificate* is a short-term note, issued by the *receiver*, that is, the person handling the company's bankruptcy proceedings. It is usually employed to enable the company to complete the production cycle. Bond owners purchase the receiver certificate, thereby giving the company additional cash, in anticipation of getting a better adjustment in the bankruptcy. For example, let's say a company fails at the beginning of a production cycle, with most of its capital tied up in inventory. If the company *liquidates*, that is, sells off all its assets, bond owners would receive only pennies on each dollar they invested in the company's bonds. If the bondholders advance funds by buying receiver's certificates, so that the company is able to finish the cycle, they may receive a higher rate on the dollar.

Income bonds are longer-term bonds issued by the company with an extremely high interest rate because they are extremely risky. When a company cannot pay interest on its outstanding debt, income bonds are issued on a pay-when-earned basis. The purchaser of these bonds is "trading" the possibility of receiving a very good return against losing part or all of the principal.

BOND FEATURES

Callable

As with preferred stocks, bonds may be callable. The callable feature exists not only in corporate issues, but also in municipal and government issues. Issuers have the ability to retire the issue before maturity, if they want to, under set conditions.

Convertible

Again as with preferred stocks, the bonds may be convertible into another issue at the desire of the bondholder. Usually, this convertible feature allows the bond to be converted into equity (stock), thereby reducing the corporate debt.

Adjustable Rate Bonds

The coupon rate on this type of bond is changed periodically. By changing the coupon rate to reflect current economic conditions, the bond's price behaves more like that of a short-term instrument.

Zero-Coupon Bonds

Zero-coupon bonds are discounted instruments offered below the face amount, paying par or face amount at maturity. The difference is the interest earned.

Example: A $10,000, 10-year bond is discounted at a rate of 6%. The formula would be:

$$\text{Present value} = \text{principal} \frac{1}{(1 + \text{rate})}^{\text{term}}$$

$$\text{Present value} = \$10{,}000 \frac{1}{(1 + .06)}^{10}$$

$$\text{Present value} = \$10{,}000 \frac{1}{1.79085}$$

$$\text{Present value} = 10{,}000 \times .5560189$$

$$\text{Present value} = \$5{,}560.19$$

If you were to purchase a $10,000 zero-coupon 10-year bond, discounted at an annual rate of 6%, you would pay $5,560.19 today. Ten years from now, you would receive $10,000. The difference would be in interest earned.

Sinking Fund

Some bonds have a feature known as a *sinking fund*, or *sinker*. Under this feature, the issuer may go into the open market and acquire (buy back) its debt out of earnings or retained earnings.

SUMMARY

Corporate bonds represent loans to, not ownership in, the company. When you buy a bond, you are buying the interest payments made, usually, twice a year. On settlement date, the buyer pays the purchase price (expressed as a percentage of the face value) and accrued interest. Bonds may be callable or convertible (usually to common stock). Bonds may be secured in various ways. In the event of default, bondholders might be offered either short-term receiver certificates or longer-term income bonds.

CHAPTER 22

Rights and Warrants

Type: Ownership
Form: Registered (usually)
Denomination: Rights-warrants
Income payment: None
Traded: Stock exchanges and OTC
Duration: Rights, short-term
Warrants, long-term

From time to time, a company may need to raise additional capital by issuing common stock. It may do so either through the usual underwriting methods or through the issuance of rights or warrants to current stockholders.

Rights and warrants are similar in that both permit their holders to subscribe to the new shares. They differ in that rights are generally short-term, whereas warrants have much longer lives. Also, a corporation may have several warrant issues outstanding at one time, but it may offer only one rights issue at a time.

RIGHTS

A *right, or subscription right,* is a privilege granted by a corporation to its stockholders to purchase new securities in proportion to the

FIGURE 22-1. A right.

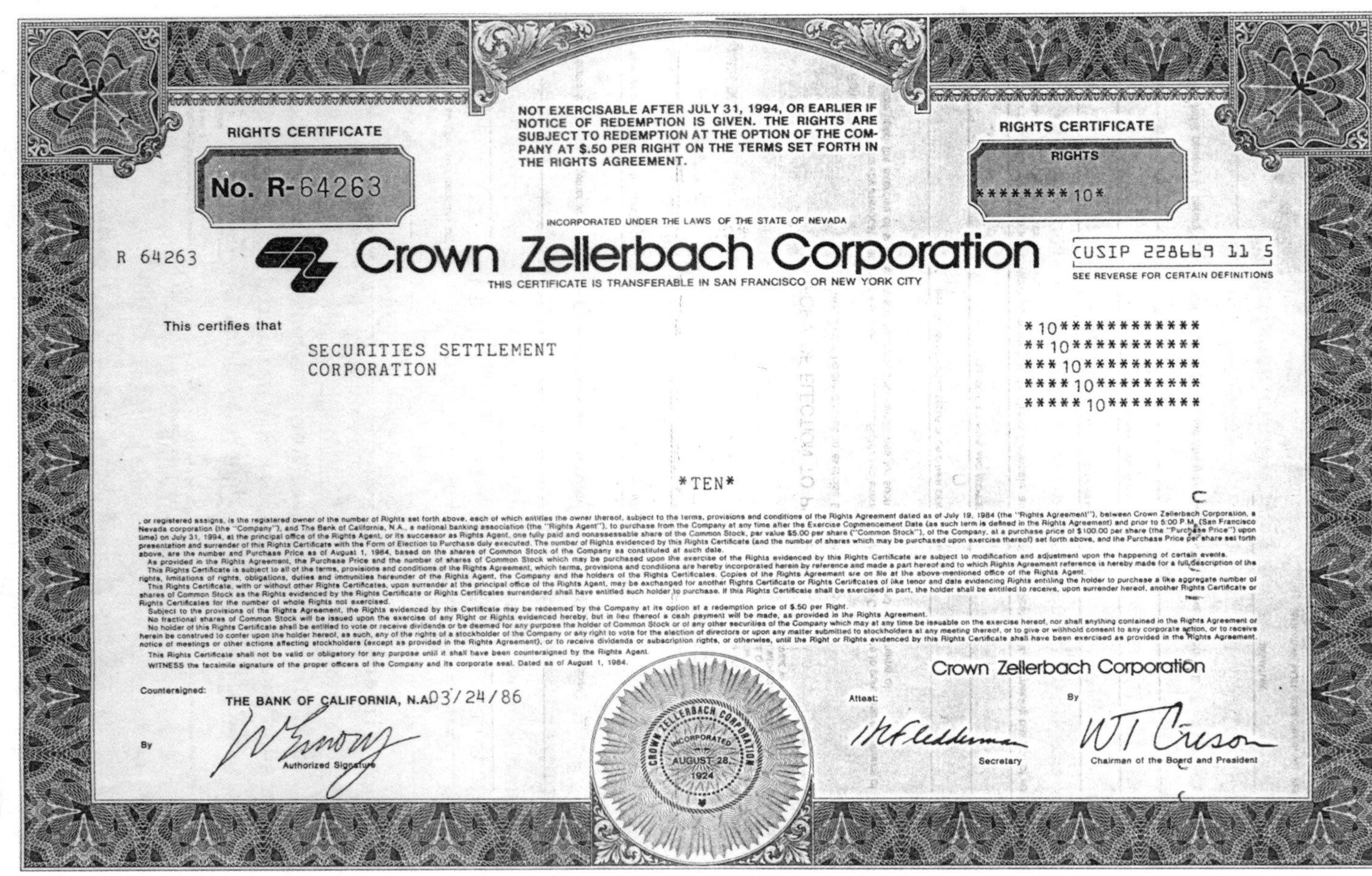

RIGHTS CERTIFICATE

No. R-64263

NOT EXERCISABLE AFTER JULY 31, 1994, OR EARLIER IF NOTICE OF REDEMPTION IS GIVEN. THE RIGHTS ARE SUBJECT TO REDEMPTION AT THE OPTION OF THE COMPANY AT $.50 PER RIGHT ON THE TERMS SET FORTH IN THE RIGHTS AGREEMENT.

RIGHTS CERTIFICATE

RIGHTS

********10*

INCORPORATED UNDER THE LAWS OF THE STATE OF NEVADA

R 64263

Crown Zellerbach Corporation

THIS CERTIFICATE IS TRANSFERABLE IN SAN FRANCISCO OR NEW YORK CITY

CUSIP 228669 11 5

SEE REVERSE FOR CERTAIN DEFINITIONS

This certifies that

SECURITIES SETTLEMENT
CORPORATION

*10************
10*********
10*******
****10*********
*****10********

TEN

, or registered assigns, is the registered owner of the number of Rights set forth above, each of which entitles the owner thereof, subject to the terms, provisions and conditions of the Rights Agreement dated as of July 19, 1984 (the "Rights Agreement"), between Crown Zellerbach Corporation, a Nevada corporation (the "Company"), and The Bank of California, N.A., a national banking association (the "Rights Agent"), to purchase from the Company at any time after the Exercise Commencement Date (as such term is defined in the Rights Agreement) and prior to 5:00 P.M. (San Francisco time) on July 31, 1994, at the principal office of the Rights Agent, or its successor as Rights Agent, one fully paid and nonassessable share of the Common Stock, par value $5.00 per share ("Common Stock"), of the Company, at a purchase price of $100.00 per share (the "Purchase Price") upon presentation and surrender of this Rights Certificate with the Form of Election to Purchase duly executed. The number of Rights evidenced by this Rights Certificate (and the number of shares which may be purchased upon exercise thereof) set forth above, and the Purchase Price per share set forth above, are the number and Purchase Price as of August 1, 1984, based on the shares of Common Stock of the Company as constituted at such date.

As provided in the Rights Agreement, the Purchase Price and the number of shares of Common Stock which may be purchased upon the exercise of the Rights evidenced by this Rights Certificate are subject to modification and adjustment upon the happening of certain events.

This Rights Certificate is subject to all of the terms, provisions and conditions of the Rights Agreement, which terms, provisions and conditions are hereby incorporated herein by reference and made a part hereof and to which Rights Agreement reference is hereby made for a full description of the rights, limitations of rights, obligations, duties and immunities hereunder of the Rights Agent, the Company and the holders of the Rights Certificates. Copies of the Rights Agreement are on file at the above-mentioned office of the Rights Agent.

This Rights Certificate, with or without other Rights Certificates, upon surrender at the principal office of the Rights Agent, may be exchanged for another Rights Certificate or Rights Certificates of like tenor and date evidencing Rights entitling the holder to purchase a like aggregate number of shares of Common Stock as the Rights evidenced by the Rights Certificate or Rights Certificates surrendered shall have entitled such holder to purchase. If this Rights Certificate shall be exercised in part, the holder shall be entitled to receive, upon surrender hereof, another Rights Certificate or Rights Certificates for the number of whole Rights not exercised.

Subject to the provisions of the Rights Agreement, the Rights evidenced by this Certificate may be redeemed by the Company at its option at a redemption price of $.50 per Right.

No fractional shares of Common Stock will be issued upon the exercise of any Right or Rights evidenced hereby, but in lieu thereof a cash payment will be made, as provided in the Rights Agreement.

No holder of this Rights Certificate shall be entitled to vote or receive dividends or be deemed for any purpose the holder of Common Stock or of any other securities of the Company which may at any time be issuable on the exercise hereof, nor shall anything contained in the Rights Agreement or herein be construed to confer upon the holder hereof, as such, any of the rights of a stockholder of the Company or any right to vote for the election of directors or upon any matter submitted to stockholders at any meeting thereof, or to give or withhold consent to any corporate action, or to receive notice of meetings or other actions affecting stockholders (except as provided in the Rights Agreement), or to receive dividends or subscription rights, or otherwise, until the Right or Rights evidenced by this Rights Certificate shall have been exercised as provided in the Rights Agreement.

This Rights Certificate shall not be valid or obligatory for any purpose until it shall have been countersigned by the Rights Agent.

WITNESS the facsimile signature of the proper officers of the Company and its corporate seal. Dated as of August 1, 1984.

Countersigned:

THE BANK OF CALIFORNIA, N.A. 03/24/86

By

Authorized Signature

Crown Zellerbach Corporation

Attest:

Secretary

By

Chairman of the Board and President

number of shares they own. Usually, rightholders are entitled to a purchase, or *subscription,* price that is lower than the stock's current market price.

Rights are offered because the *preemptive rights* clause in the charter or by-laws requires the corporation to offer new issues of common stock to its current common shareholders before offering it to anyone else. Shareholders must be given the chance to maintain their percentages of ownership. So the new shares must be issued to the stockholders in proportion to their percentage of ownership. The easiest way to meet this requirement is to issue one right per share of stock owned. For example, an owner of 100 shares of stock receives 100 rights.

Shareholders who want to subscribe use a number of the rights plus a dollar amount, which is the subscription price.

Example: Angelic Star Rockets, Inc. has 5,000,000 shares of common stock outstanding and wants to raise capital by issuing 1,000,000 additional shares. The common stock is trading at $80, and the subscription value is $60. Since 5,000,000 shares are outstanding, the company issues 5,000,000 rights—one for each share of stock. According to the terms of the right, a current stockholder, wishing to subscribe to a new share of stock, has to submit 5 rights and $60 to subscribe to the companies agent to receive one new share.

Shareholders who choose not to subscribe may sell their rights, because they have dollar value, called the "theoretical value." To calculate the *theoretical value* of a right, divide the difference between the subscription price and the market price by the number of rights required to purchase one new share:

$$\text{Theoretical value} = \frac{\text{Market price} - \text{Subscription price}}{\text{Number of rights for subscription}}$$

Example: The market price of Angelic common is $80, and the subscription price of the new stock is $60. If you need 5 rights to subscribe, the theoretical value of each right is calculated as follows:

$$\begin{aligned}\text{Theoretical value} &= \$80 - \frac{\$60}{\text{5 rights}} \\ &= \frac{\$20}{\text{5 rights}} = \$4.00/\text{right}\end{aligned}$$

Cum Rights

The value of the right is considered part of the stock owner's capital; if the right is discarded, the owner loses money. Some investors, who are not aware of this value, treat rights as junk mail and throw them away. They are throwing away money.

Before the new stock is actually issued, the shareholders of record know they are going to be issued the rights. So, before the new stock is offered to the public, the old stock is traded *cum rights;* that is, it trades with the theoretical value of one right added to its market price. (The word *cum* means "with" in Latin.)

To compute the actual value of the issue trading cum rights, add one right to the number of rights needed to subscribe, and divide that total into the difference between the market and subscription price. The additional right offsets the value included in the current market value of the old stock.

Example: The subscription price of Angelic is $60, and the market value of the common stock, cum rights, is $84. You need five rights to subscribe.

Value of common stock (cum rights)	$84.00
Subscription value	– 60.00
Difference	$24.00

Now add one right to the number needed to subscribe to offset the right included in the common stock's market value. Five plus one gives you six rights.

$24.00 ÷ 6 = $4.00 per right

ARBITRAGE

Arbitrageurs are professional traders who take advantage of price discrepancies in the same or similar issues, watch for price fluctuations, and try to make profits by trading between the rights and new issue.

Example: The Angelic rights are selling at 3³/₄, and the new stock is at $80 per share. An arbitrageur buys five rights and then applies the rights plus $60 toward one new share.

Purchase 5 × $3.75	$18.75	Sale of one share	$80.00
Plus subscription	60.00	Less *cost*	78.75
Total *cost*	$78.75	Profit	$ 1.25

In the real world, the arbitrageur naturally deals in more than one share, but one thousand shares at a $1.25 profit each is $1,250 profit—different story.

Note: Arbitrage situations should be left to the professionals.

WARRANTS

A *warrant*, attached to another security, entitles the holder to convert the security into common stock or some other instrument at a set price during a specified period of time. The price set in the warrant is higher than the current market value of the common stock.

Warrants are longer-term issues than rights. They generally come to the marketplace as part of a *unit*, which is comprised of two or more issues. For example, a corporation may issue a combination of bonds and warrants. The bonds are in regular form, and the warrants are used to make the offering more attractive. If the issuing company is growth-oriented, with a track record of accomplishing its goals, the warrants will attract investors. In such situations, warrants have not only conversion value, but also value as trading vehicles. Their prices increase as the price of the underlying security rises and approaches the warrant's conversion price.

Due to the length of time that warrants are outstanding, a corporation can have several different warrants outstanding at one time. The value of each issue is determined by the relationships among several factors: the conversion price, the time remaining in the warrant, and the value of its underlying stock.

THE "CERTIFICATE"

In the case of either a right or a warrant, the *certificate* itself is referred to as *a* right or *a* warrant. Actually, "a" right certificate could represent 100 rights, and "a" warrant certificate could rep-

FIGURE 22-2a. *A warrant, front.*

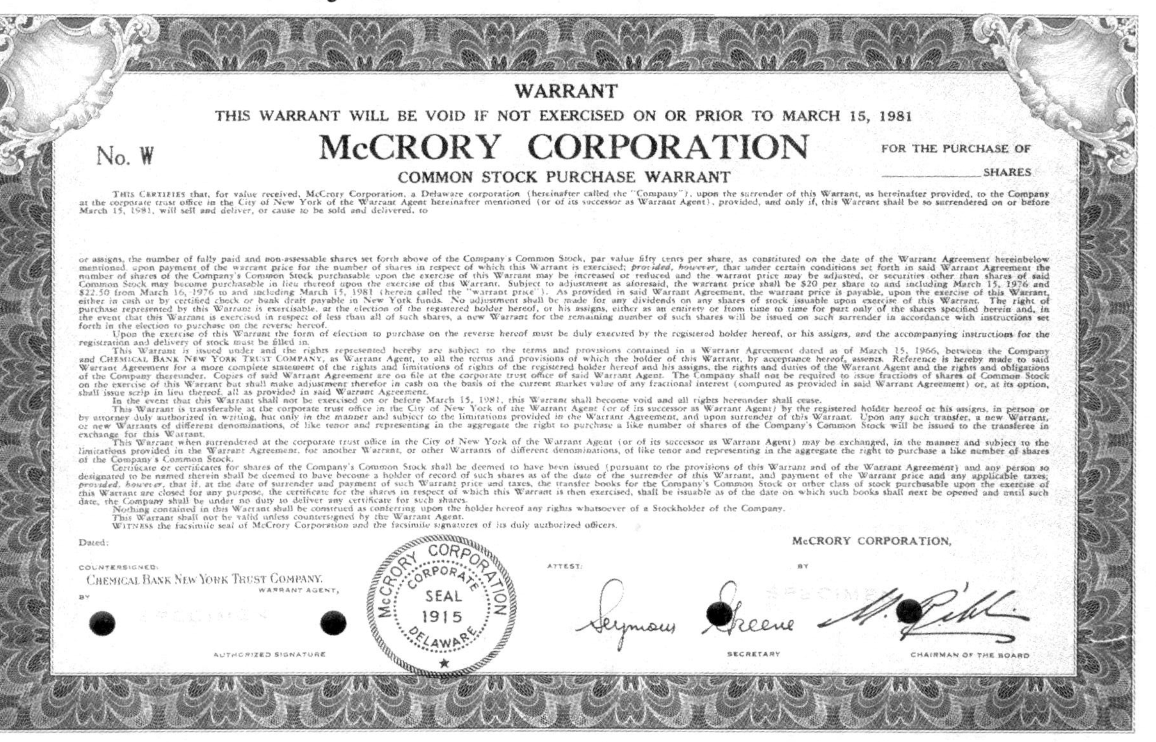

WARRANT

THIS WARRANT WILL BE VOID IF NOT EXERCISED ON OR PRIOR TO MARCH 15, 1981

No. W

McCRORY CORPORATION

COMMON STOCK PURCHASE WARRANT

FOR THE PURCHASE OF ______________ SHARES

THIS CERTIFIES that, for value received, McCrory Corporation, a Delaware corporation (hereinafter called the "Company"), upon the surrender of this Warrant, as hereinafter provided, to the Company at the corporate trust office in the City of New York of the Warrant Agent hereinafter mentioned (or of its successor as Warrant Agent), provided, and only if, this Warrant shall be so surrendered on or before March 15, 1981, will sell and deliver, or cause to be sold and delivered, to

or assigns, the number of fully paid and non-assessable shares set forth above of the Company's Common Stock, par value fifty cents per share, as constituted on the date of the Warrant Agreement hereinbelow mentioned, upon payment of the warrant price for the number of shares in respect of which this Warrant is exercised; *provided, however,* that under certain conditions set forth in said Warrant Agreement the number of shares of the Company's Common Stock purchasable upon the exercise of this Warrant may be increased or reduced and the warrant price may be adjusted, or securities other than shares of said Common Stock may become purchasable in lieu thereof upon the exercise of this Warrant. Subject to adjustment as aforesaid, the warrant price shall be $20 per share to and including March 15, 1976 and $22.50 from March 16, 1976 to and including March 15, 1981 (herein called the "warrant price"). As provided in said Warrant Agreement, the warrant price is payable, upon the exercise of this Warrant, either in cash or by certified check or bank draft payable in New York funds. No adjustment shall be made for any dividends on any shares of stock issuable upon exercise of this Warrant. The right of purchase represented by this Warrant is exercisable, at the election of the registered holder hereof, or his assigns, either as an entirety or from time to time for part only of the shares specified herein and, in the event that this Warrant is exercised in respect of less than all of such shares, a new Warrant for the remaining number of such shares will be issued on such surrender in accordance with instructions set forth in the election to purchase on the reverse hereof.

Upon the exercise of this Warrant the form of election to purchase on the reverse hereof must be duly executed by the registered holder hereof, or his assigns, and the accompanying instructions for the registration and delivery of stock must be filled in.

This Warrant is issued under and the rights represented hereby are subject to the terms and provisions contained in a Warrant Agreement dated as of March 15, 1966, between the Company and CHEMICAL BANK NEW YORK TRUST COMPANY, as Warrant Agent, to all the terms and provisions of which the holder of this Warrant, by acceptance hereof, assents. Reference is hereby made to said Warrant Agreement for a more complete statement of the rights and limitations of rights of the registered holder hereof and his assigns, the rights and duties of the Warrant Agent and the rights and obligations of the Company thereunder. Copies of said Warrant Agreement are on file at the corporate trust office of said Warrant Agent. The Company shall not be required to issue fractions of shares of Common Stock on the exercise of this Warrant but shall make adjustment therefor in cash on the basis of the current market value of any fractional interest (computed as provided in said Warrant Agreement) or, at its option, shall issue scrip in lieu thereof, all as provided in said Warrant Agreement.

In the event that this Warrant shall not be exercised on or before March 15, 1981, this Warrant shall become void and all rights hereunder shall cease.

This Warrant is transferable at the corporate trust office in the City of New York of the Warrant Agent (or of its successor as Warrant Agent) by the registered holder hereof or his assigns, in person or by attorney duly authorized in writing, but only in the manner and subject to the limitations provided in the Warrant Agreement, and upon surrender of this Warrant. Upon any such transfer, a new Warrant, or new Warrants of different denominations, of like tenor and representing in the aggregate the right to purchase a like number of shares of the Company's Common Stock will be issued to the transferee in exchange for this Warrant.

This Warrant when surrendered at the corporate trust office in the City of New York of the Warrant Agent (or of its successor as Warrant Agent) may be exchanged, in the manner and subject to the limitations provided in the Warrant Agreement, for another Warrant, or other Warrants of different denominations, of like tenor and representing in the aggregate the right to purchase a like number of shares of the Company's Common Stock.

Certificate or certificates for shares of the Company's Common Stock shall be deemed to have been issued (pursuant to the provisions of this Warrant and of the Warrant Agreement) and any person so designated to be named therein shall be deemed to have become a holder of record of such shares as of the date of the surrender of this Warrant, and payment of the Warrant price and any applicable taxes; *provided, however,* that if, at the date of surrender and payment of such Warrant price and taxes, the transfer books for the Company's Common Stock or other class of stock purchasable upon the exercise of this Warrant are closed for any purpose, the certificate for the shares in respect of which this Warrant is then exercised, shall be issuable as of the date on which such books shall next be opened and until such date, the Company shall be under no duty to deliver any certificate for such shares.

Nothing contained in this Warrant shall be construed as conferring upon the holder hereof any rights whatsoever of a Stockholder of the Company.

This Warrant shall not be valid unless countersigned by the Warrant Agent.

WITNESS the facsimile seal of McCrory Corporation and the facsimile signatures of its duly authorized officers.

Dated:

McCRORY CORPORATION,

COUNTERSIGNED:
CHEMICAL BANK NEW YORK TRUST COMPANY,
WARRANT AGENT,
BY

AUTHORIZED SIGNATURE

McCRORY CORPORATION CORPORATE SEAL 1915 DELAWARE

ATTEST:

Seymour Greene
SECRETARY

BY

CHAIRMAN OF THE BOARD

FIGURE 22-2b. *A warrant, back.*

ELECTION TO PURCHASE

(To be executed if owner desires to exercise the Warrant.)

TO MCCRORY CORPORATION:

The undersigned hereby irrevocably elects to exercise the right of purchase represented by the within Warrant for, and to purchase thereunder, ... shares of the stock provided for therein, and requests that certificates for such shares shall be issued in the name of ....

PLEASE INSERT SOCIAL SECURITY OR OTHER IDENTIFYING NUMBER

....

(Please print name and address)

....

and, if said number of shares shall not be all the shares purchasable thereunder, that a new Warrant for the unexercised portion of the within Warrant be registered in the name of ....

....

(Please print name and address)

....

Dated: ...., 19........

Signature: ....

NOTE: The above signature must correspond with the name as written upon the face of this Warrant or with the name of the person to whom this Warrant has been duly assigned in every particular, without alteration or enlargement or any change whatever, and if signed by an assignee, or if shares and/or Warrants are to be issued in a name other than that of the registered holder of the Warrant, the form of assignment hereon must be duly executed. If shares and/or Warrants are to be issued in a name other than that of the registered warrant holder, this election to purchase must be accompanied by appropriate documentary stamp taxes.

ASSIGNMENT

(To be executed if owner desires to transfer Warrant Certificate.)

FOR VALUE RECEIVED ....hereby sell, assign and transfer unto

....

....

the within Warrant, together with all right, title and interest therein, and do hereby irrevocably constitute and appoint

.... Attorney, to transfer said Warrant on the books of the within-named Corporation, with full power of substitution in the premises.

Dated: ...., 19........

....

(Signature)

NOTE: The above signature must correspond with the name as written upon the face of this W at in every particular, without alteration or enlargement or any change whatever. The signature to the Assignment must be guaranteed by a commercial bank or trust company having an office or correspondent in New York City or by a firm having membership in the New York Stock Exchange or in the American Stock Exchange Clearing Corporation.

Signature Guaranteed:

....

resent 100 warrants. This term causes confusion and is a constant cause of errors in the brokerage community.

Example: A company issues a unit comprised of a $1,000 bond with a warrant to purchase 10 shares of stock. When the parts of the unit are separated, the bond and the warrant sell separately. At that time, the warrant certificate represents 10 warrants—one per each share of stock.

Operations personnel should *always* make certain of whether the term means the right or warrant certificate *or* the quantity of rights or warrants represented there upon.

CHAPTER 23

Municipal Bonds and Notes

Type: Debt
Form: Bearer (usually)
Denomination: $1,000 minimum certificates
Income payment: Interest
Traded: Over-the-counter
Duration Set per issue

Municipal bonds, or *munis,* are debt instruments issued by state and local governments to raise capital to finance their projects and other needs. Income (that is, interest) earned on municipal securities is free from federal income tax. For a resident of the issuing municipality, interest from the bonds is also exempt from state and local income taxes.

THE COMPETITIVE UNDERWRITING

Just as a corporation is owned by its shareholders, the municipality is answerable to its taxpayers. New municipal issues are therefore brought to market through a competitive underwriting.

This method ensures that taxpayers are getting the best terms available. With several syndicates competing for the issue, there is no room for manipulation, collusion, or other illegal practices.

While corporate issues exclude the assistance of banks, municipalities work with banks and brokerage firms, which form syndicates to study the municipalities' needs.

In charge of each syndicate group is the *manager.* The manager organizes the group, prepares the prospectus (if required), and performs other assignments that are similar to their negotiated underwriting counterparts. When the group is formed, the upcoming underwriting is discussed. The participants each state what they believe would be a fair and competitive bid, which the manager uses in formulating the final bid. The participants meet and review the final bid, and it is submitted to the municipality.

Each group independently develops a proposal and submits it to the municipality. After all the groups have submitted their bids, the participants wait for the municipal's decision.

Officials of the municipality study all the proposals and select the one that best accommodates their goals. When they make a determination, they notify the winning syndicate. The bids of all the syndicates are available to members of the public if they desire the information.

Once the decision has been made, participants of the losing groups, if they are still interested in the issue, call the winning manager to see if they can participate in the distribution.

OFFERING OF MUNICIPAL BONDS

Generally when a new issue is brought to market, it is usually brought out in serial form. This type of issuance differs from corporate or federal offerings in that their issues come to market with one maturity date, such as $100,000,000 Starfire Power Corp. 8% JJ-2023. Municipals, while perhaps borrowing the same sum of financing, will issue its debt with several different maturities: for example, $100,000,000 Delmont county debt, $2,000,000 $6\frac{1}{2}$ FA=2003, 2,000,000 $6\frac{3}{8}$ FA-2004, 3,000,000 $6\frac{1}{2}$ FA-2005, and so on. This form of offering is known as a *serial.* Each issue is inde-

FIGURE 23-1a. *A municipal bond, front.*

E2438

No

UNITED STATES OF AMERICA
STATE OF CONNECTICUT
COUNTY OF NEW LONDON

CITY OF NORWICH

$5000

6.00%
GENERAL IMPROVEMENT BOND,
ISSUE OF 1970

DATED JULY 1, 1970

PRINCIPAL DUE JULY 1,

INTEREST PAYABLE
JULY 1 and JANUARY 1

SPECIMEN

PRINCIPAL AND INTEREST PAYABLE
AT THE PRINCIPAL OFFICE OF THE
HARTFORD NATIONAL BANK AND
TRUST COMPANY
IN THE CITY OF HARTFORD
STATE OF CONNECTICUT

SECURITY-COLUMBIAN BANKNOTE COMPANY

CERTIFICATE OF HARTFORD NATIONAL BANK AND TRUST COMPANY

The Hartford National Bank and Trust Company hereby certifies that this Bond is one of the issue of Bonds described in said Bond; that the signatures of the City officials and seal thereto affixed are genuine and that Messrs. Mudge Rose Guthrie & Alexander, attorneys at law, New York City, and Sabino P. Tamborra, Corporation Counsel of the City of Norwich, Connecticut, have rendered opinions approving the legality of such issue of Bonds, and that such opinions may be inspected at our principal office at any time.

Authorized Officer

The within Bond has been registered as to principal only, as follows:

DATE OF REGISTRATION	NAME OF REGISTERED HOLDER	SIGNATURE OF COMPTROLLER

FIGURE 23-1b. *A municipal bond, back.*

$5000 $5000

NUMBER

UNITED STATES OF AMERICA
STATE OF CONNECTICUT
COUNTY OF NEW LONDON

CITY OF NORWICH

GENERAL IMPROVEMENT BOND, ISSUE OF 1970

KNOW ALL MEN BY THESE PRESENTS that the **CITY OF NORWICH,** a municipal corporation organized and existing under and by virtue of the laws of the State of Connecticut, situated in the County of New London in said State, for value received hereby promises to pay to the bearer, or, if this Bond be registered, to the registered holder hereof, the principal sum of

FIVE THOUSAND DOLLARS ($5,000)

in lawful money of the United States of America, at the principal office of the Hartford National Bank and Trust Company, in the City of Hartford, State of Connecticut,

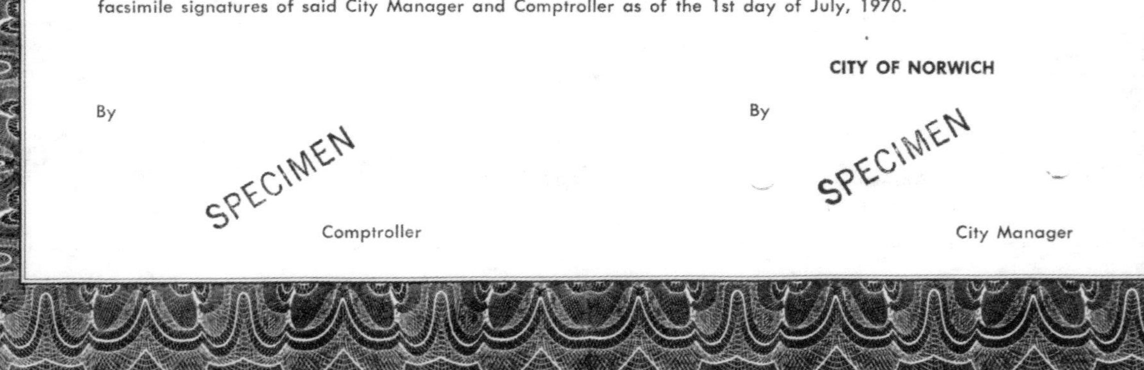

This Bond may be registered as to principal only by the holder in his name on the bond register of the City kept in the office of the Comptroller of said City, and such registration shall be noted hereon by said Comptroller. If so registered, this Bond may be transferred on said bond register by the registered owner in person or by attorney, upon presentation of this Bond to the Comptroller with a written instrument of transfer in a form approved by said Comptroller and executed by said registered owner. If this Bond be so registered, the principal shall thereafter be payable only to the person in whose name it is registered unless this Bond shall be discharged from registry by being registered as payable to bearer. Such registration shall not affect the negotiability of the coupons, which shall continue to pass by delivery.

This Bond is one of an authorized issue, the aggregate principal amount of which is $700,000, the Bonds of which are of like tenor, except as to number and date of maturity, and are issued pursuant to the Constitution and Statutes of the State of Connecticut, including the Charter of said City and other provisions of law applicable thereto, and a bond ordinance entitled: "AN ORDINANCE AUTHORIZING THE ISSUANCE OF $700,000 GENERAL IMPROVEMENT BONDS, ISSUE OF 1969, OF THE CITY OF NORWICH TO FINANCE THE COST OF THE CONSTRUCTING OF ACQUIRING VARIOUS CAPITAL IMPROVEMENTS FOR SAID CITY; PRESCRIBING THE FORM AND DETAILS THEREOF AND SECURITY THEREFOR; AND AUTHORIZING THE SALE THEREOF," duly enacted by the Council of said City on the 5th day of August, 1968, as amended, and approved by the qualified electors of said City at an election held in the City of Norwich on the 5th day of November, 1968.

It is hereby certified and recited that all acts, conditions and things required to exist or be done precedent to and in the issuance of this Bond by the Constitution and Statutes of the State of Connecticut, exist, have happened and have been performed; that provision has been made for the levy and collection of a direct annual tax upon all the taxable property within the City of Norwich sufficient to pay the interest on and principal of this Bond as the same become due; and that the total indebtedness of said City, including this Bond, does not exceed any constitutional, statutory or charter debt limitation or restriction.

The full faith and credit of the City of Norwich are hereby irrevocably pledged for the punctual payment of the principal of and interest on this Bond according to its terms.

IN WITNESS WHEREOF the **City of Norwich** has caused this Bond to be signed by its City Manager and Comptroller under its corporate seal and the interest coupons hereto attached to be authenticated with the facsimile signatures of said City Manager and Comptroller as of the 1st day of July, 1970.

CITY OF NORWICH

By SPECIMEN
Comptroller

By SPECIMEN
City Manager

FIGURE 23-2a. *Municipal bond coupons, front.*

COUPON No. 8 — $150.00

ON THE FIRST DAY OF JULY, 1974,

the **CITY OF NORWICH,** Connecticut,
will pay to bearer, at the principal office of the **Hartford National Bank and Trust Company,** in the City of Hartford and State of Connecticut, the sum of **One Hundred Fifty and No/100 Dollars ($150.00),** in lawful money of the United States of America being the semi-annual interest due that day on its General Improvement Bond, Issue of 1970, dated July 1, 1970, **NUMBER**

COMPTROLLER — CITY MANAGER

COUPON No. 7 — $150.00

ON THE FIRST DAY OF JANUARY, 1974,

the **CITY OF NORWICH,** Connecticut,
will pay to bearer, at the principal office of the **Hartford National Bank and Trust Company,** in the City of Hartford and State of Connecticut, the sum of **One Hundred Fifty and No/100 Dollars ($150.00),** in lawful money of the United States of America being the semi-annual interest due that day on its General Improvement Bond, Issue of 1970, dated July 1, 1970, **NUMBER**

COMPTROLLER — CITY MANAGER

COUPON No. 6 — $150.00

ON THE FIRST DAY OF JULY, 1973,

the **CITY OF NORWICH,** Connecticut,
will pay to bearer, at the principal office of the **Hartford National Bank and Trust Company,** in the City of Hartford and State of Connecticut, the sum of **One Hundred Fifty and No/100 Dollars ($150.00),** in lawful money of the United States of America being the semi-annual interest due that day on its General Improvement Bond, Issue of 1970, dated July 1, 1970, **NUMBER**

COMPTROLLER — CITY MANAGER

COUPON No. 5 — $150.00

ON THE FIRST DAY OF JANUARY, 1973,

the **CITY OF NORWICH,** Connecticut,
will pay to bearer, at the principal office of the **Hartford National Bank and Trust Company,** in the City of Hartford and State of Connecticut, the sum of **One Hundred Fifty and No/100 Dollars ($150.00),** in lawful money of the United States of America being the semi-annual interest due that day on its General Improvement Bond, Issue of 1970, dated July 1, 1970, **NUMBER**

COMPTROLLER — CITY MANAGER

COUPON No. 4 — $150.00

ON THE FIRST DAY OF JULY, 1972,

the **CITY OF NORWICH,** Connecticut,
will pay to bearer, at the principal office of the **Hartford National Bank and Trust Company,** in the City of Hartford and State of Connecticut, the sum of **One Hundred Fifty and No/100 Dollars ($150.00),** in lawful money of the United States of America being the semi-annual interest due that day on its General Improvement Bond, Issue of 1970, dated July 1, 1970, **NUMBER**

COMPTROLLER — CITY MANAGER

COUPON No. 3 — $150.00

ON THE FIRST DAY OF JANUARY, 1972,

the **CITY OF NORWICH,** Connecticut,
will pay to bearer, at the principal office of the **Hartford National Bank and Trust Company,** in the City of Hartford and State of Connecticut, the sum of **One Hundred Fifty and No/100 Dollars ($150.00),** in lawful money of the United States of America being the semi-annual interest due that day on its General Improvement Bond, Issue of 1970, dated July 1, 1970, **NUMBER**

COMPTROLLER — CITY MANAGER

COUPON No. 2 — $150.00

ON THE FIRST DAY OF JULY, 1971,

the **CITY OF NORWICH,** Connecticut,
will pay to bearer, at the principal office of the **Hartford National Bank and Trust Company,** in the City of Hartford and State of Connecticut, the sum of **One Hundred Fifty and No/100 Dollars ($150.00),** in lawful money of the United States of America being the semi-annual interest due that day on its General Improvement Bond, Issue of 1970, dated July 1, 1970, **NUMBER**

COMPTROLLER — CITY MANAGER

COUPON No. 1 — $150.00

ON THE FIRST DAY OF JANUARY, 1971,

the **CITY OF NORWICH,** Connecticut,
will pay to bearer, at the principal office of the **Hartford National Bank and Trust Company,** in the City of Hartford and State of Connecticut, the sum of **One Hundred Fifty and No/100 Dollars ($150.00),** in lawful money of the United States of America being the semi-annual interest due that day on its General Improvement Bond, Issue of 1970, dated July 1, 1970, **NUMBER**

COMPTROLLER — CITY MANAGER

FIGURE 23-2b. *Municipal bond coupons, back.*

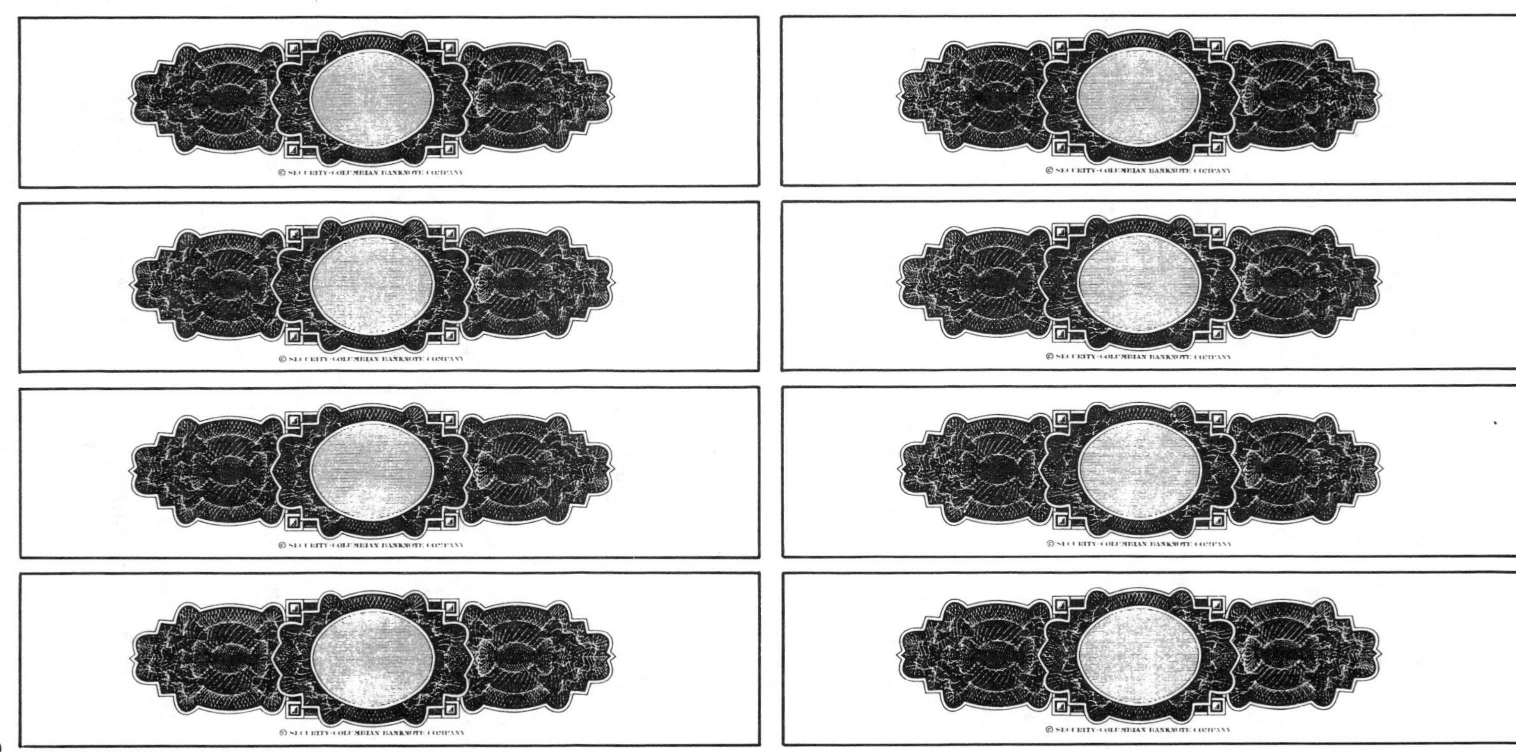

pendent and has its own unique "ID" or CUSIP number. Therefore, a municipal offering can have 10, 15, or more issues coming to market at the same time.

If the longer-term issues have substantially larger quantities than the other issues, the offering is said to contain a *balloon maturity*.

By having a serialized issue, the municipality can retire the issue part by part, rather than face an entire maturity requirement, as the Fed and corporations usually do. The serial form of offering results in the individual bond issue being relatively small in size.

THE EFFECT OF TAX RATES

Municipalities' debt instruments compete, in the over-the-counter market, for public funds with other fixed income securities. Investors choose from the many types of issues traded by determining which type of issue best suits their needs. Municipalities can issue their debt securities at interest rates lower than those for other debt securities for two reasons. For one thing, the interest and principal are paid from tax revenues, on which the municipality pays no interest. Second, the interest payments are not subject to federal taxation, making the tax-free yield especially attractive to investors in high income tax brackets.

Example: Investor DeVries in the 30% income tax bracket, realizes only 70 cents on each dollar she earns. She pays the difference to the government in the form of income tax. DeVries is considering buying either a 9½% corporate bond or a 7% municipal bond. Per $1,000 of face value, the corporate bond will pay $95 per year, whereas the municipal will pay $70. Tax on the corporate bond would be $28.50 (30% times $95.00). so that the net return to the investor is $66.50. Compare this with the tax-free $70 received from the municipal security. For DeVries, the municipal security is therefore the better of the two as an investment.

TRADING MUNICIPALS

At the time of the offering, brokerage firms buy the issue from underwriters for resale to their customers. Most of the trading in munis takes place at this time, because purchasers usually buy these securities for investment purposes, not for ongoing trading. Muni buyers generally buy these bonds, hold onto them, and look forward to the tax-free interest payments.

Typically, therefore, individual municipal issues are traded infrequently, or *thinly*. That is why they are more suitable for trading on the OTC market than on exchanges. That is also why they are *not* quoted on a dollar basis, as are corporate bonds, whose issues trade frequently throughout their lifetimes.

So, except for a few muni issues, it is difficult to acquire a municipal bond in the *secondary market*, that is, the OTC market, in which these securities are resold. Someone who invests municipal bonds in the OTC market selects from an inventory maintained by a municipal bond dealer.

BASIS PRICING

Suppose your stockbroker reads you a list of quotes for municipal bonds, as follows: Bond A 5% 2004 @ 94¾; Bond B 6⅛-2009 @ 95⅛; Bond C 5¾-2015 @ 93½, and so on. You might eventually say, "Hold up! Just tell me the return on my investment per bond." In other words, "What's my yield?" As a result, municipal bonds are quoted "at a basis" (that is, in terms of yield to maturity).

The computation of yield to maturity or base price is complex. But a "rule of thumb" formula gives you an approximate figure. The formula is:

$$\text{Yield to maturity} = \frac{\text{Annual interest amount} \begin{array}{c} + \\ - \end{array} \begin{array}{c} \text{Amortized premium } \textit{or} \\ \text{Amortized discount} \end{array}}{\left(\dfrac{\text{Face amount} + \text{Current value}}{2}\right)}$$

Example: Investor Morita purchases a $1,000 Russell County KY FA 8% 2011 @ 95 on trade date January 21, 1986. The bond matures in 25 years (2011 – 1986). The price of 95 translates into $950. At maturity, the bondholder receives $1,000 or $50 in capital gains ($1,000 – $950). You must amortize the $50 discount. $50 divided by 25 years equals $2 annual amortization. The 8% bond would pay $80 in interest payment per year. Therefore:

$$\text{Yield to maturity} = \frac{\$80 + \$2}{\frac{\$1{,}000 + \$950}{2}} = \frac{\$82}{\$975} = .841 = 8.41\%$$

The "rule of thumb" formula gives you the yield to maturity of 8.41%. Or you could say that the bond was purchased at an "8.41 basis."

Example: An Ebbets Stadium revenue bond 6% F&A 2003 is quoted "6.50-5.50 basis." The "6.50" part of the quote means "6½%." This is not the bid price; it is the percentage of the yield associated with the bid price (which is not reflected in the quote). The "5.50" means that, given the seller's offering price, the buyer will get a yield of 5½%.

What is the relationship between price and yield? Because the coupon rate is fixed, only price and yield can change. The rule is the *lower the price, the higher the yield.* Since a yield of 6½% is higher than the 6% coupon rate of Ebbet's municipals, it reflects a *discounted* price (a price lower than the face value of $1,000). The yield of 5½% reflects a *premium* price (one that is higher than the $1,000 face amount).

Let's look at this relationship from another point of view. Since lowering the price increases the yield, the bid in any quote is always lower than the offer. The bid is the price that a buyer is willing to pay; the buyer, naturally, bids as little as possible to get the greatest yield possible. The seller, on the other hand, has an offering price that is higher than the bid, because the seller wants the best sale price possible. If the bid and offer are equal, then the buyer and seller have an agreed-upon price and a transaction takes place.

Why does a discounted (below-par) price increase yield, or a premium (above-par) price reduce yield? The difference between the purchase price and face value has to be added to or subtracted from interest rates. At maturity, the bondholder is going to be paid the face value. If the holder paid less than the face value, then that difference is a kind of "bonus" payment and should be added to the interest amount. If the holder paid more, the extra amount is gone forever and has to be deducted from the overall or total interest payments.

Example: Investor Jurgens buys a $1,000 7% bond for $950. She holds it for 5 years to maturity, receiving $70 in interest each of those years ($1,000 × .70), for a total of $350 interest payments (5 times $70). Don't forget: The coupon rate does not change.) At the end of 5 years, however, she is paid back the face value of the bond, $1,000; that is $50 more than she paid. So, actually, the extra $50 ($1,000 – $950) is "like" an extra interest payment.)

The question is, to which year does it apply? The answer is that is applies to all 5 years. You have to *amortize*, or spread out, the $50 over 5 years.

To amortize the discount or premium amount, divide it by the number of years to maturity.

Example: To amortize $50 over 5 years, divide $50 by 5 years, for $10 a year.

A discount price therefore gives the buyer an increased dollar yield to maturity. And a premium price means a reduced dollar yield to maturity.

Quoting at a basis is also a convenient way to represent a dealer's inventory uniformly. Muni dealers trade with other dealers, with brokers, and with their own customers from their inventory positions. Given a customer's request, a firm shops among other dealers to locate an issue that suits the customer's needs. Quoting on basis puts all the quotes on a comparable basis and in a form that the customer can understand.

THE DEALER'S BROKER

In the secondary market, dealers occasionally have to acquire bonds that are difficult for them to resell. In such a case, a *dealer's broker* can assist the dealer. Through a system of computer terminals, the dealer's broker broadcasts available inventory to dealers across a nationwide network. Any user of the terminal network can locate a type of issue or a quantity that fills a customer's needs. This system enables dealers to find buyers of slow moving inventory.

The dealer's broker does not make markets (that is, take positions), but instead acts as an intermediary between prospective buying and selling firms. A dealer firm interested in buying or selling an issue expresses its interest to the dealer's broker, who in turn broadcasts the need through its computer network. Naturally, only the highest bid or lowest offer is shown per issue.

Firms wishing to transact business at these prices contact the dealer's broker, and trades are consummated. The actual buying and selling firm do not know each other, because the dealer's broker acts as intermediary between the two parties.

TYPES OF MUNICIPAL BONDS

Municipals may be categorized according to the type of security backing them.

General obligation bonds are secured by the full taxing power of the issuing state or local government. Money to pay interest and principal comes from general tax revenues.

A *limited tax* bond is backed by a particular tax, such as a state sales tax.

Revenue bonds are secured by the revenue from the project built by capital raised in the bond issue. For example, the proceeds of a bond issue might be used to build an energy plant. Revenue from the sale of energy then pays back the bondholders.

Industrial revenue bonds are issued for the development of industrial sites.

There are other types of bonds, and their backing naturally affects their marketability.

Municipals may also be categorized according to their time of maturity.

State and local authorities often issue short-term instruments in anticipation of an event. These instruments, known as *notes,* usually exist for six months or less. Notes issued in anticipation of taxes to be received are *tax anticipation notes (TANs).* Those issued in the expectation of future revenue are *revenue anticipation notes* (RANs). Those offered just before a new bond offering are called *bond anticipation notes* (BANs). Another form of short-term debt is the *project note*—(PN). The PN is used in the short-term financing of such projects as residences. PNs are eventually paid from financing received from bond issuance.

TANs, RANs, and BANs are usually discounted instruments. Holders receive no interest payments. Instead, buyers pay a price that is lower than (or discounted from) the full face value, which they are paid at maturity. The difference between the price paid at time of purchase and the sum received at maturity is the interest earned. (Discounted instruments are discussed in more detail in the next chapter on Treasury bills.)

SUMMARY

Municipal bonds represent an important part of the fixed income array of securities. Issued by state and local governments, they compete with other types of debt instruments at a unique advantage: their interest payments are exempt from federal taxation. Traded thinly in the OTC market, they are quoted at a basis.

CHAPTER 24

U.S. Treasury Bills, Notes, and Bonds

Type: Debt
Form: Book entry
Denomination: According to Instrument
Income payment: Interest
Traded: Over-the-counter (some listed)

A primary participant in the securities market place is the U.S. government, which acts as purchaser, seller, and issuer. Each of these roles represents a method by which the government carries out its monetary policy.

THE FED

The governmental arm for implementing monetary policy is the Federal Reserve Board or just *the Fed*. Through different procedures, the Fed can increase or decrease the amount of money in circulation, which in turn affects the availability of funds, interest rates, and the fixed income security segment of the market place.

Part of the FED's role is providing the financing for the

United States government through the issuance of three forms of securities:

1. Short-term instruments known as *U.S. Treasury bills (T bills).*
2. Intermediate financing called *U.S. Treasury Notes (T notes).*
3. Long-term financing in the form of *U.S. Treasury bonds (T bonds).*

All of these instruments are direct obligations of the United States government and, as such, are considered to be among the safest investment vehicles available.

AUCTION

The Fed brings these instruments to the market through an *auction.* U.S. government *primary dealers,* which are privately owned firms registered as dealers, bid for the issues.

Since no one dealer could possibly finance an entire issue, several dealers compete. Given the size of issue and the high degree of competition, the dealers fine-tune their bids, taking into account current market conditions, receptivity of the public to the new issue in the market place, and other factors. The dealers' bids are therefore very close to each other.

The Fed offers the new issue on a highest-bid-first basis. It sells as much to the dealer with the highest bid as the dealer will accept. Then it continues down the bids until supply equals demand, that is, until the issue is sold out.

Although only government dealers can compete in the auction market, the public can purchase U.S. Treasuries directly from the Fed by submitting requests. Their orders are filled at a weighted average price, formulated from the accepted dealers' bids. All eligible public orders are ranked at one price, making the public's participation a *Dutch auction.*

The dealers sell the acquired issue to their customers or to other brokerage firms. The bid submitted by the dealers for the issue must be in line with current market conditions, or else the dealer may have to take a loss when "trading them out." If the rates are not "in line," the dealer may not be able to sell the securities.

T BILLS

U.S. Treasury bills are short-term instruments, with the longest maturity of one year. Bills are discounted instruments. Discounted instruments usually do not have a coupon, or fixed, interest rate. Instead, the bills are bought at one dollar amount and you receive a higher amount (the face value) at maturity.The difference between the two dollar amounts is the *discount.* The rate of interest earned is "built into" the discount.

Example: You are interested in purchasing a 90-day T bill having a \$100,000 face or maturity value. To receive a yield of 8%, you pay a discounted price of (\$98,000). The difference between the purchase price (\$98,000) and the value received at maturity (\$100,000) is the interest earned.

The formula used to compute the purchase price on discount instruments is:

$$\text{Purchase price} = \text{Face amount} - \frac{\text{Number of days remaining}}{360} \times \frac{\text{Interest rate}}{100} \times \text{Face amount}$$

Example: Given the information from the previous example:

$$\begin{aligned}\text{Purchase price} &= \$100{,}000 - \frac{90}{360} \times \frac{8}{100} \times \frac{\$100{,}000}{1} \\ &= \$100{,}000 - \frac{1}{4} \times \frac{2}{25} \times \frac{\$100{,}000}{1} \\ &= \$100{,}000 - \$2{,}000 \\ &= \$\ 98{,}000\end{aligned}$$

You are sure of receiving 8% return only if you hold the instrument to maturity. From the time of purchase to the date of maturity, the instrument is subject to interest rate or market fluctuations. Should you have to sell the instrument before maturity, you may not receive the expected return.

T NOTES AND T BONDS

U.S. Treasury bonds and notes are longer-term instruments. Notes are issued for one to ten years. Bonds are issued with maturities ranging from 10 to 30 years. Bonds and notes have fixed, or coupon, interest rates and pay interest on a semiannual basis. The interest is computed on a 365-day basis, not 360 (as with bills and other instruments).

TREASURY STRIPS

The Treasury also issues long-term discounted Treasury instruments known as *strips.* These instruments do not pay interest periodically. Instead, they pay "face" at maturity. The difference between what is paid at the time of purchase and what is received at maturity represents the interest earned.

TRADING U.S. GOVERNMENT SECURITIES

Some Treasury instruments trade on the New York and American Stock Exchanges. The vast majority of the instruments trade in the over-the-counter market. As in the municipals' market, dealer's brokers assist brokerage firms in sales.

SETTLEMENT

In newer issues of U.S. Treasuries, transactions are settled through the Fed's *book entry system,* that is, delivery is effected through computer entry rather than physical delivery. The Fed maintains the nominee name and address, and debits or credits the appropriate accounts as transactions are made. This method of settlement is fairly new. As a result, many of the older instruments must still be settled through physical delivery.

SUMMARY

In the multimillion-dollar "government market," the spread between the bid and offer is small (or *tight*) on most issues. The dealers earn their income from the size of the trades. A sixteenth of a point mark-up on a $1,000,000 trade equals $625. While that sum may be appealing, remember that a 50-basis-point (or 1/2-point) drop in the market loses $5,000 for each $1,000,000 worth of securities in the dealer's inventory.

CHAPTER 25

Asset-Backed Securities

Type: Debt
Form: Registered
Denomination: $1,000,000 round lot
Income: Principal & Interest (usually monthly)
Principal: Paid down periodically (usually monthly)
Traded: Over-the-counter
Duration: 15- to 30-year issues (Others are available.)

A segment of the industry that has grown in leaps and bounds since first introduced in 1970 is the asset-backed securities sector. Originally called "mortgage-backed," the concept of pooling debt and then securitizing it has spread to other debit vehicles.

Initially, this type of issue took the form of a "pass-through." The first agency to offer this type of debt was the Government National Mortgage Association (GNMA). GNMA, as a part of Housing and Urban Development (HUD), is responsible for facilitating mortgages in new homes. The potential home buyers must qualify for VA- (Veterans Administration), FHA- (Federal Housing Authority), or FmHA- (Farmers Home Administration)

FIGURE 25-1. *A pass-through security.*

CERTIFICATE OF AUTHENTICATION
This note has been issued by the Federal National Mortgage Association.
FEDERAL RESERVE BANK OF NEW YORK
as Fiscal Agent

By ______________
AUTHORIZED SIGNATORY

FEDERAL NATIONAL MORTGAGE ASSOCIATION

$1,000,000. FOR VALUE RECEIVED No F

FEDERAL NATIONAL MORTGAGE ASSOCIATION
A CORPORATION CHARTERED BY THE CONGRESS OF THE UNITED STATES OF AMERICA,
will pay to BEARER on ______________, 19____
the sum of ONE MILLION ($1,000,000) DOLLARS at
FEDERAL RESERVE BANK OF NEW YORK

This note shall become valid only when the Certificate of Authentication on the margin shall have been signed by the Federal Reserve Bank of New York as Fiscal Agent.

______________, 19____.

ATTEST
SECRETARY

FEDERAL NATIONAL MORTGAGE ASSOCIATION INCORPORATED 1938

FEDERAL NATIONAL MORTGAGE ASSOCIATION
BY
CHAIRMAN

NOT AN OBLIGATION OF THE UNITED STATES

SECURITY-COLUMBIAN BANKNOTE COMPANY

insured or -guaranteed mortgages. As such, all mortgages in a GNMA pool carry some form of U.S. government backing.

ROLE OF THE MORTGAGE BANKER

The size of the GNMA pool is usually decided by a *mortgage banker.* It is the function of this individual, or entity, to obtain funds from "money-dense" areas of the country for use in "money-sparse" areas to facilitate the building of homes. The mortgage banker is usually not a bank at all, but some other corporate entity or division of an entity involved in real estate.

As an example of how the mortgage banker works, let's assume C. Long Construction Company is going to build a tract of 100 homes. Some of the potential home owners will qualify for VA, FHA, or FmHA loans; others will not. Those who do not qualify will obtain conventional mortgages, which will either be sold as whole loans or become part of some other entities, such as Freddie Mac or a bank-issued pool. Those who qualify under VA, FHA, FmHA will become part of a GNMA mortgage.

As the potential homeowners apply for their mortgages, some are forwarded to VA, FHA, or FmHA for approval. Those that have been approved become part of the GNMA pool. As long as the homeowners have not moved into their homes, the mortgages are said to be *approved,* but *not in force.*

During this period, the mortgage banker is exposed to losses due to interest rate changes. The mortgages that are approved but not in force are not paying any return. Mortgage bankers would want to sell the mortgages as soon as possible, since their purpose is not to take market risk, but to facilitate the development of homes through mortgages. Therefore, they take the pending pool of mortgages and solicit bids, from GNMA dealers. The dealers are buying a contract that will be delivered months from now and that is therefore known as a TBA *(to be announced).* What is to be announced is the unique pool number that GNMA will assign when the mortgages are actually in force.

TBAs/Forwards

TBAs trade along with another product known as a forward. Both of these are delayed delivery products requiring no settlement monies to change hands until settlement, which could be months from the time the trade is originally contracted for.

During the period that the TBA/forward is alive, it may be bought and sold, as well as sold and bought. The profit or loss from such trading is settled at the end of the contract's cycle.

Example: Abode Mortgage sells $5 million worth of 8% mortgages, retiring in 30 years, for a six-month delivery to Stone, Forrest & Rivers, a GNMA dealer. Stone can, and probably will , sell some or all of it to its clients and to other broker/dealers who are not GNMA dealers. These firms are acquiring the issue for their clients or for their own proprietary accounts. These contracts, in turn, can be brought and sold, sold and bought during the six-month period. As interest rates in the market place fluctuate, so does the value of the contracts.

At the end of the TBA/forwards term, when actual delivery is due, those who own the contract will receive the appropriate GNMA security and pay the called-for price. Those who are *short* the contract (those who sold the contract) will deliver the appropriate issue. Finally, those who are *flat,* (that is having bought and sold, or sold and bought) will settle the net profit or loss with their respective counterparties. (*Note:* It is within a broker/dealer's prerogative to secure funds covering part or all of their clients' losses prior to final settlement of the contract.)

As to the mortgage banker during this period, when the mortgages comprising the pool are in force, GNMA will assign a unique number. That number will represent that pool until all principal is paid down. At the assigning of the unique pool number, it is said to be *announced* (hence the prior name, "to be announced," or "TBA").

MODIFIED PASS-THROUGH

One form the asset-backed issue may take is that of pass-through, sometimes referred to as *modified pass-through.* The term *modified* refers to the interest paid on the mortgages being higher than the coupon carried on the pass-through itself. The difference, usually 50 basis points, is compensation for the mortgage banker. In the case of a GNMA, 44 basis points is compensation for the mortgage banker; .06 basis point goes to GNMA. So, for example, a pool of mortgages carrying 7% interest will produce a pass-through bearing 6½ interest.

As the debt holders in a pass-through make their periodic payments, the payments (both principal and interest) are passed through to the security owner. Unlike bonds, which pay their principal at the end of the loan, these instruments pay the amounts of the loan over their life; the principal "depletes" over time. It is this continuous cash flow that makes this product appealing.

Besides the normal pay-down of principal, the borrowers often prepay their loans. In case of mortgages, homeowners prepay their mortgages when they refinance their homes or move to other homes. As the mortgages in these pools are not substitutable, the old mortgage is paid off and the new mortgage becomes part of another pool, or it is sold as a whole loan.

The rate at which these prepayments take place affects the longevity of an instrument and therefore its pricing. Those instruments that tend to pay down slightly faster than others, tend to trade at a slight premium. When trading this type of pool, the unique number is specified, and the type of trade becomes a *known pool.* The only pool that can be delivered against this type of trade is that particular pool.

Another type of transaction is known as *guaranteed coupon.* Under this type of trade, the seller may deliver any pool(s) as long as the coupon rate(s) on the pool(s) agrees with the specified one.

Example: SF&R sells a guaranteed coupon 8% pool to another broker dealer. SF&R can deliver any 8% pool(s) to satisfy its obligation.

As outstanding pools are continuously paying down their principal, it is impossible to know the amount of principal outstanding at any particular time without the use of an official guide, referred to as the *factor tables.* The tables contain the original principal amount of the pool, the current outstanding principal, and the factor. By multiplying the factor by the original value, you obtain the current value. By dividing the current value by the factor, you arrive at the original value.

Since the factor tables provide this pool information for all pools, you can easily obtain current principal information on an existing pool. The particular factor becomes important when only part of a specific pool is in question.

Example: Against a $1,000,000 8% guaranteed coupon trade, SF&R receives from GRC one face amount $1,000,000 certificate and one $100,000 face amount certificate. (The securities always carry their original value.) It would appear that GRC "over-delivered" against the trade. However, upon checking, we find that the $1,000,000 certificate is from Pool #313131X, which has a factor of .912131843, and the $100,000 certificate is from Pool #246189X, which has a factor of .897431632. By multiplying the original by the factor, we find the current outstanding principal is $912,131.84 for the $1,000,000 certificate, and $89,743.16 for the $100,000. Together, they total $1,001,875.00, well within the acceptable delivery limits set by the Public Securities Association.

Note: Because the principal is constantly changing, it is virtually impossible to deliver exact contract amounts. Therefore, a tolerance level is set that accepts over- or under-delivery to a point. The level in the example was 2.499%, but the level is currently being phased in at 2.0% ± per million.

CMOs

Collateralized mortgage obligation (CMOs) are also a form of securitized pooled loans, but they differ from pass-throughs in that they are paid down differently. In a pass-through, all of the owners receive their proportionate amount of principal and prepayments from day one until the loans are paid off. CMO purchasers, however, receive payment of principal in predetermined time slots, called *tranches.* The owner of a tranche, or part of a tranche, will receive principal only when the tranches above have been paid off.

As an analogy, think of a pass-through as an elevator in a shaft and a CMO as a stack of automobile tires. As the elevator goes down the shaft, the amount of space remaining under the elevator decreases proportionally. If the elevator at its highest point was 200 feet above the ground, should it come down 10 feet, there would be only 190 feet left; the ten feet would be reduced universally. The same is true with a pass through. If the pass-through was $200,000 and paid down $10,000, there would be

$190,000 remaining; and the $10,000 would have been distributed to each of its owners.

On the other hand, the CMO is similar to the stack of tires. If we had interests in the middle tire, that tire would not be of concern until the tires above it were removed. If the tires were removed and used one at a time, the third tire wouldn't come into play until the first two were used up.

Similarly, if the stack of tires were a CMO and each tire a tranche, the owners of the third tranche would not receive principal until the first two tranches were paid off.

As with pass-throughs, CMO owners are subject to prepayments, and the owner of a certain tranche may start to receive principal payments earlier than expected, as the tranches above are paid down ahead of schedule.

The number of tranches in a CMO can range from five to any marketable number. Some of these tranches may pay interest; some may not. The tranches that do not pay interest are of the zero-coupon type and are therefore known as the *Z tranches*.

CMOs were first offered by Federal Home Loan Mortgage Corporation (FHLMC, or Freddie Mac). They initially appealed to those who wanted some control over their cash flows. It also made the instrument more appealing to different sectors of the market. For example, an investor looking to acquire an instrument for a few years would not invest in pass-through, since principal payments would continue for the life of the instrument. The same investor could, however, invest in the first tranche of a CMO because it would be paid off within that period.

Certain clients demand guarantees as to when they will begin to receive principal payments. If these guarantees cannot be given, they will buy some other instrument. To accommodate this need, the CMO packagers have developed a PAC, or *planned amortized certificate*. The PAC, if frozen from a particular tranche, will not start to receive principal until a specific time or criterion has been reached, regardless of what else is happening around it. It is possible that the owner of PAC could start receiving principal payments after the next tranche has been paid off.

As the tranches pay down sequentially, the shorter-term tranches usually carry a lower interest rate than do the longer-term versions. The loans in the pool, however, are at a fixed rate.

The difference between what is paid by the borrower and what is paid to the owner is known as the *residual.* The residual can vary from instrument to instrument, and is dependent on how long a period remains to the earlier tranches. The faster they pay down, the smaller the residual will be. These residuals are sometimes sold at a discount to the amount that is expected to accumulate.

REMIC

Real estate mortgage investment conduits *(REMICs)* are similar in structure to CMOs and are issued under certain tax rules. Because of the differences between the debits' interest rates and the different interest rates paid on the tranches, the residual varies from REMIC to REMIC.

STANDBYS AND CALLS

Standbys are the European form of put options. They give their owners the opportunity of putting (selling) a finite quantity of a specific issuer's pooled debt on a specific date for a specific price. If the owner of the standby doesn't want to sell on that date, the owner doesn't have to. For this opportunity, the owner pays a premium.

What makes standbys unique is that the product is usually booked as to what it does, not by its relationship to the principal party. The owner of the standby is booked as a sell trade, because the product allows the owner to "sell" the underlying pool. The person who sold the standby and receives the premium is booked as a buy or debit. This marks the only time the "seller" pays the "buyer" in a transaction.

Calls allow their owners to buy a specific quantity of a certain issuer's pools at a specific price on a specific day if they want to. If they don't, they let the call expire.

All parts of the standby and call are negotiable. This includes the exercise ability of the owner. Most standbys and calls are exercisable only at the end of their life; however, more liberal exercise privileges are possible.

Example: Stone, Forrest & Rivers own $100,000,000 GNMA 8% TBAs at an average price of 97. They are due for delivery in three months. The mortgage market appears to be getting soft, and SF&R is becoming concerned. Rather than reduce the position, SF&R's traders sell standbys for $20,000,000 GNMA 8% due in three months at a price of 97 for a premium of ½ point ($5,000 per million × 20 = $100,000). Since standbys settle next day, SF&R will pay $100,000 to who ever acquired the obligation via the standby. SF&R is comfortable with an "uncovered" position of $80,000,000 GNMAs. If the market doesn't improve, SF&R may sell more standbys. Three months from now, SF&R will make a decision to deliver the GNMAs against standbys and receive a price of 97, or let the standbys expire and lose the premium. They will let the standby expire if they can get higher prices in the market. The price of the 8% GNMAs at that time will determine the course of action.

SUMMARY

The concept of pooling debt is growing. There are pools comprising auto loans, credit cards, as well as boat loans and residential and commercial mortgages. For all we know, your mortgage, car loan, credit card balance, or other kind of loan may very well be part of this interesting sector of the market.

CHAPTER 26

Commercial Paper

Type:	Debt discount instrument or principal plus interest
Form:	Bearer
Denomination:	$25,000-$100,000 and larger
Income:	Interest
Traded:	Over-the-counter
Duration:	Usually 270 days

Corporations raise long-term capital by issuing stocks and bonds. They raise short-term money by taking out loans from commercial banks and by issuing commercial paper to the investing public.

Commercial paper is a debt instrument that is offered sometimes as a "discount instrument" and sometimes as "principal plus interest." In the case of a *discounted instrument.* no interest payments are made. Instead, the price paid to buy the instrument is lower than the face value, which is paid to the buyer at maturity. The difference between the price paid and the face value is the interest earned on the investment. For a *plus interest instrument,* the client pays the full face value to buy the paper and receives the face value plus the interest accrued at maturity.

Neither type of instrument has a fixed interest rate. Instead, the rate is negotiated at the time of purchase and the interest is calculated from face or full value. To receive the interest, the buyer must, for all practical purposes, hold the instrument until maturity. If the paper is sold during its life, its price is subject to market fluctuations. In the case of commercial paper, the secondary market is thin, almost nonexistent.

ISSUANCE

Commercial paper is sold through two conduits: by direct placement or through dealers. *Direct placement* takes place between a bank and its customers. On behalf of its clients, the bank contacts the issuing corporation and purchases the paper. The transaction is generally custom-tailored to the needs of the bank's clients. *Dealer-sold paper* is purchased by a commercial paper dealer in "bulk" and sold to its customers.

TRADING

Commercial paper trading lots are $1,000,000, but a minimum of $25,000 is possible depending on the marketplace. Maturities are 30, 60, 90, and seldom more than 270 days. Since commercial paper is as standardized as, say, Treasury securities or municipals, the terms of agreement—the minimum denomination, the length of maturities, and so on—can change as the needs of the corporation and lenders change.

SETTLEMENT

Transactions in commercial paper settle same day: If you buy today, you must pay today. Dealers must pay for commercial paper on the day of purchase. When dealers resell the paper to their customer, the new owners must pay on the day of purchase.

Usually both transactions—from corporation to dealer and from dealer to customer—occur on the same day. Control and accuracy are therefore mandatory due to the large sums of money involved and the limited time for settling all the daily transactions.

The normal method of payment is by Fed funds. Because of the transaction size, most settlement is effected between banks through the use of the *Fed wire*, a communications network among member banks of the Federal Reserve System. Funds received through this vehicle do not follow the usual overnight or several-day fund clearance cycle experienced with checks. Because a recipient of Fed funds can use the money when received as if it were cash, Fed funds are considered same-day funds.

HANDLING THE CERTIFICATES

The physical piece of commercial paper, the certificate, is issued by the commercial bank representing the corporation. The bank may purchase the paper for its own clients or issue it for purchase by other banks or dealers.

Because commercial paper is an investment instrument, the certificate is usually vaulted by a bank on behalf of the client, whether the paper is directly placed or dealer sold. The handling of the certificate can take several routes.

1. For the *issuing bank's client*, the certificate goes from the issuing department, to the customer service department, to the vault.
2. In a bank other than the issuing bank, it goes from the issuing bank, to the appropriate department of the customer's agent bank, to the vault.

So, if dealer-placed, the certificate is sent from the issuing bank to the dealer, to the agent banker of the dealer's customer, and finally to that bank's vault.

In every case, this handling occurs on trade date, which is settlement date.

FINANCING

If a dealer buys and resells paper on trade date, the paper does not have to be financed, because the issuing corporation is paid out of the proceeds of the resale. If the dealer does *not* resell the paper on the same day as purchase, the issuing corporation must still be paid. Financing is therefore needed.

Financing is arranged either through collateralized loans or repos.

For a *collateralized loan*, arranged between the dealer and a bank, the paper becomes the collateral. The lending bank advances the necessary funds upon receipt of paper from the dealer. The dealer has "line of credit" with various banking institutions and turns to these establishments for financing.

In a *repo* (or *repurchase agreement*), the borrower (dealer) obtains funds by "selling" the collateral to the lender with the agreement that it will be reacquired at a fixed price on a specific day. The difference between the sale price and the repurchase price is the interest to the lender. Repos are arranged with private individuals or with institutions that have funds available for investing but that do not want to expose it to financial or market risk. They therefore lend their funds for a short period, such as overnight or two days, in such an agreement.

In the case of a repo, the instrument actually isn't sold and repurchased, because ownership doesn't really change. The instrument is delivered to the lender in negotiable form and returned unaltered at the end of the commitment. Since most commercial paper is in bearer form, this fact is often overlooked.

MATURITY

At maturity, the client instructs its agent bank to surrender the paper to the issuing corporation, and the paper is paid off.

CHAPTER 27

Banker's Acceptances (BAs)

Type: Debt
Form: Bearer certificate
Denomination: $100,000
Income payment: Interest
Traded: Over-the-counter
Duration: 30-270 days

Banker's acceptances (BAs) are bills of exchange that are issued and guaranteed by a bank for payment within one to six months. The funds raised through their sale provide manufacturers and exporters with operating capital between the time of production or exporting and the time of payment by purchasers. In effect, the bank "accepts" evidence of the value of goods being either manufactured or exported. For that evidence, it issues its "acceptance" in the form of a cerificate, which can then be bought and sold as security.

USE IN IMPORTING

Suppose a U.S. importer wants to acquire goods from a foreign manufacturer. Because the goods must be produced and shipped, the foreign manufacturer wants to be assured of payment and does not want to wait until the goods are received in the United States. The importer goes to a U.S. bank, with which it has a business relationship, and applies for a letter of credit. The letter of credit is sent to a foreign bank representing the manufacturer. The letter, along with the merchandise invoice (that is, a bill of exchange), is returned to the importer's bank, which stamps "Accepted" on the invoice. The importer's bank pays the foreign manufacturer through the foreign bank, and the banker's acceptance is thus created.

The procedure can be reversed. A foreign importer can apply to an overseas bank for a letter of credit and an American manufacturer can be paid before delivery is actually taken. The "paper" is therefore dually gurarantееd by two parties; the accepting bank and the importing firm.

BAs can also be used by a domestic company to finance merchandise located in one foreign country and awaiting shipment to an importer in another foreign country.

TRADING

BAs are bearer instruments that are sold to investors as discounted instruments. (They are part of a security group known as *money market instruments.* Since the instrument is discounted, the difference between what investors pay for the BA and the face value they are paid at maturity is the interest earned.

Interest on BAs is computed on 360 days. Computations are therefore made following the procedures used for U.S. Treasury bills. Trades in BAs settle the same day.

The issuing bank can keep the BA or sell it. If it keeps the certificate, it has a loan on its books, between it and the importer. Any loan has an effect on the banks' *reserve requirements,* which is the percentage of their money that, by law, it may not lend out. By selling the BA, however, it applies the sales proceeds—the investor's money—to the loan, thereby freeing up bank funds for other loans.

If the bank sells the loan, it endorses it, thereby guaranteeing it and the loan becomes a banker's acceptance.

CHAPTER 28

Certificates of Deposit (CDs)

Type: Debt
Form: Bearer certificate
Denomination: $100,000 (in secondary market, $1,000,000 round lots)
Income payment: Interest
Traded: Over-the-counter
Duration: 14 days to one year

Certificates of deposit (CDs) are the last major instrument of the money market sector, which includes U.S. T Bills, commercial paper, and banker's acceptances. A *certificate of deposit* is a negotiable security issued by commercial banks against money deposited over a period of time. The value of CDs varies depending on the amount of deposit and maturity.

Included in the category of certificates of deposit are small issues that are not transferrable and therefore nonnegotiable. This form of CD, usually $10,000 in value and sometimes with a life of two years or more, is advertised by many banks to attract the retail investor. However, because these are not tradable, they are not part of the negotiable CD market.

TYPES OF CDs

There are actually four types of negotiable CDs:

1. *Domestic CDs* are issued by American banks to investors in the United States.
2. *Eurodollar CDs* are issued by American banks to investors abroad.
3. *Yankee CDs* are issued to investors in the United States by U.S. branches of foreign banks.
4. *Saving & loan institutions* also issue CDs.

TRADING

In the secondary market, where these instruments are resold, a round lot is $1,000,000. Issues of lesser amounts are therefore more difficult to sell because the liquidity of market may not always be present. In additon, although the maturities of most outstanding issues do not exceed six months, even longer-term issues are avaliable.

INTEREST

The interest on CDs is computed on a 360-day basis. The issue can be either plus interest or discounted. Investors prefer the discounted form because the yield can be understood easily, as in the case of T Bills. Trades in CDs settle on the same day as the trade.

CHAPTER 29

Mutual Funds

Type: Varies according to purpose
Form: Registered (when physically issued)
Income: Dividends, capital gains, interest
Traded: OTC, listed (closed-end), with fund (open-end)

A *mutual fund* is any pooling of money by contributors in an attempt to achieve a common goal. In a broad sense, this definition can include a joint venture with a one-time outcome, as well as a multimillion dollar managed company. Nevertheless, in the brokerage industry, the term "mutual fund" generally means only a managed company.

The purpose of the fund must be clearly set forth in its prospectus and charter, and it may not be changed without the approval of fund shareholders. The fund may be a growth fund, income fund, bond fund, common stock fund, and so on. Each type of fund attempts to acquire securities that best fill its goals, thereby benefitting its shareowners.

OPEN-AND CLOSED-END FUNDS

A fund may be "open-end" or "closed-end."

An *open-end fund,* makes a continuous offering of its shares to the public, and it stands ready to buy back (or redeem) its shares from fund owners who wish to liquidate.

Open-end funds can be purchased in several ways:

1. *Outright purchase:* The client invests a fixed sum of money.
2. *Letter of intent:* This is a thirteen-month commitment stating that the client will purchase x amount of the fund over the next thirteen months.
3. Voluntary plan: Clients are free to purchase shares at such times and in such amounts as they choose, as long as x number of dollars will be invested. In this plan, the clients are not penalized for failing to meet their objective.
4. *Contractual plan:* The client contracts to invest so much by a predetermined date. Many investors prefer this method because payments must be made at specific times. Under this plan, the purchasers are penalized if they do not meet their commitment.
5. *Rights of accumulation:* The sales charge reduces as investment increases over time.

A *closed-end-fund* issues its shares up to a predetermined number. Once all the shares are issued, the fund closes, and its shares are traded among the public. Individuals wishing to buy shares acquire them from shareholders who want to sell.

NET ASSET VALUE VERSUS MARKET VALUE

The price of a fund's shares is determined by the method used to buy and sell the shares. *Open-end-fund* shares, because they are sold to owners by the fund, trade at *net asset value* (NAV). The formula for NAV is as follows:

$$\text{Net asset value} = \frac{\text{Value of funds portfolio} + \text{Fund's cash awaiting investment} - \text{Expenses}}{\text{Number of shares outstanding}}$$

Because closed-end-fund shares trade among investors, their prices are determined by supply and demand. If there are more buyers than sellers, the price of the closed-end fund rises. If the reverse occurs, the price of the fund falls.

LOAD VERSUS NO-LOAD

Open-end funds can be "load" or "no-load." The *load* is the sales charge, which is expressed as a percentage of the purchase price.

Load Funds

Load funds, which charge a sales fee, or load, generally reduce the fee as the number of shares being purchased increases. The point at which the percentage of the fee drops is known as the *breakpoint.* Each fund establishes its own breakpoints, and the terms are explained in the fund's prospectus.

Example: Pyrrhic Mutual has the following schedule of breakpoints:

If the customer purchases:	*The load is:*
$9,999 or less	8%
$10,000-$24,999	7 1/2%
$25,000-$49,999	7%
$50,000-$74,999	6 1/2%

And so on.

Breakpoints are an important factor in choosing the method of investment in open-end funds:

1. The *outright purchase* qualifies for the sales charge applicable at the dollar amount of the purchase.
2. The *letter of intent and voluntary plan* carry a sales charge based on the total to be invested. The load is adjusted to the applicable higher rate if the investor fails to meet the objective.
3. In the *contractual plan,* the sales charge is based on the total amount contracted for. But a large percentage of the total sales charge is deducted from the deposits over the first few years of the contract's life.

Example: In one form of contractual plan, up to 64% of the total sales charge may be taken out of payments in the first four years, with no more than 20% taken in any one of those years.

4. Under *rights of accumulation,* the sales charge is reduced (but not retroactively) as each breakpoint is reached. Contributions are completely voluntary, and the rights continue for as long as the client owns the fund.

No-Load Funds

No-load funds can be purchased without paying a load, or sales charge. These funds are usually sold directly by the fund to the public. When interest rates become highly volatile, however, many brokerage firms offer money market funds to their customers. This type of fund is usually related to the customer's securities account; the firm moves cash between the securities account and the fund at no charge.

Quotes. No-load fund quotes are easily spotted in newspapers: First, their bid and offering prices are equal. Second, the initials *NL* (no-load) appear next to the quote.

For load funds, the offer is higher than the bid. The bid represents the net asset value, and the offer is the net asset value plus the maximum sales charge.

Closed-end funds, because their shares are not continuously offered, can be traded in the over-the-counter market or on a listed exchange. Their bid-and-offer quote follows the usual stock quotation practices.

BOND UNITS

Some brokerage firms "package," that is, accumulate, a series of bond portfolios. Each series is completed by purchasing bonds in the open market and pooling them in a central account. Then the firm sells what are known as *units* to the public. When one series is sold, a new series is formed and sold, and so on. Both corporate and or municipal bonds are used in these units.

Bond units differ from mutual funds. In a mutual bond fund, the fund managers buy and sell issues in their portfolios as the need arises. Once a bond series is formed, however, the bonds comprising the "trust" are not traded or changed.

MONEY MARKET FUNDS

Money market funds demonstrate how the securities industry adjusts to the needs of the public. With interest rates at a high level in the late seventies and early eighties, the public needed to invest in a short-term, high-yield vehicle. The minimum lot (or size) of, say, certificates of deposits or commercial paper was beyond the reach of most investors. Yet the high interest rates available at the time made it unwise to leave credit balances in brokerage firms where, uninvested, they earned little or no interest. So investors faced a problem: How rates of interest were available, but only for investments of larger amounts than they had in their securities accounts.

In response to this problem, money market funds were developed. Because the money is pooled, the funds can acquire short-term instruments in a quantity that pays high rates of interest. At the same time, operation systems were developed so that the brokerage firm can shift money between the customers' accounts and the fund. When a customer sells shares in the security account and does not want to reinvest it immediately, the credit balance can be moved to the fund account, where it earns a high rate of interest. When the client decides to invest in another security, the funds are transferred from the fund back to the security account.

SUMMARY

The mutual fund sector of our industry is ever changing to meet the public's needs. Demand changes from general funds through growth, to bond trust funds, to money market funds. Whatever the need, a fund is available to fill it.

CHAPTER 30

Options

Type: Options
Form: Book Entry (receipts on request)
Denomination: One
Income payment: None
Traded: Listed or OTC
Duration: By contract

Prior to 1973, a few options traded over-the-counter, but the public was generally not interested. In 1973, however, options came to the forefront as a trading vehicle when the Chicago Board Option Exchange (CBOE) offered listed option trading to the public for the first time. Options may be used by hedgers to protect against a loss in stock that they own. They may also be traded by speculators.

An *option* is a contract that entitles its owner to buy or sell a security (called the *underlying security*) at a certain price (the *strike price*) before a certain date, known as the *expiration date.* If the option owner decides to take advantage of the option, he or she is said to *exercise,* or *assign,* the option. The party who buys an option is the *owner* or *holder*. The holder pays a *premium* to the seller, or *writer,* of the option.

There are basically only two types of options: A *call* option gives the owner the privilege of *buying*. A *put* gives the owner the privilege of *selling*.

Example: The owner of an "XYZ Apr 50 call" has the privilege of buying 100 shares of XYZ at $50 per share between the time the option is purchased and the time the option expires (at *expiration date*, which in this case is April). The seller of the call is obligated to sell or deliver the underlying security (XYZ) should the owner of the option decide to make use of the call—that is, *exercise* it. While the owner (or holder) of the option has the privilege to exercise (that is, buy) the seller (or the writer) is obligated to perform (that is, sell). The owner has paid the writer a premium for this privilege.

Example: A put option on XYZ Apr 50 gives the holder the privilege of selling 100 shares at $50 until April, the expiration date. Should the holder exercise, the writer of the put must receive and pay for the securities.

LISTED VERSUS OTC OPTIONS

Since 1973, *listed options* have traded on option exchanges. "Traditional" or "conventional" options, however, have traded over-the-counter for decades, and they differ from the newer listed options in several aspects.

For OTC options:

1. The price is *negotiated* between the buyer and the seller.
2. The strike price is either the previous day's closing price of the underlying security or what can be negotiated between the contracted parties.
3. The number of days to expiration is not fixed; instead, it is determined at the time the option is written.

Because the strike prices and the days remaining to expiration vary so much, the secondary market for outstanding conventional options, is very limited. As a result, most of these options expire. Liquidity—a problem with this type of option—is the main reason that the public never actively participated in their trading.

In listed options, strike prices are set by the exchanges. The exchanges use a formula to establish strike prices. Generally:

- Equity (or stock) options with strike prices from $25 to $200 are issued in $5 variations; for strike prices below $25, options are issued in 2½-point multiples.
- Those with strike prices above $200 have $10 graduations.

The expiration dates are also uniform. Equity options are issued in 3-, 6-, and 9-month intervals with the near two months expiration dates being continuously offered. Recently, two-year options, known as *LEAPs*, have been offered on some of the more popular issues. The expiration date is set as the Saturday after the third Friday of the expiration month.

With such standardization in place, ready markets were established and listed trading began. Today, listed options are freely traded in a liquid market.

OTHER TYPES OF OPTIONS

In addition to equity options, investors may purchase options on T bills, T notes, T bonds, and indices. These options are intended to fill a need caused by the volatility of interest rates and of the marketplace in general. Like equity options, these newer forms may be used as hedging vehicles or for speculation.

As new forms of options are brought to market, they have different exercise and settlement routines. These routines generally follow the usual settlement cycle of the underlying securities.

U.S. Treasury Bills

U.S. Treasury bill options require the delivery of a three-month bill. Because three-month bills are issued on Thursdays, that day of the week becomes the delivery date for exercises. Any exercise from Wednesday of one week to Tuesday of the next week must be delivered on Thursday of the next week.

Six-month T bills are brought to market "in cycle" with three-month issues. So a six-month issue with three months of remaining life is the same as a newly issued three-month bill, and it can be used to satisfy an exercise. A one-year bill usually is not in the same cycle as a three-month bill, and therefore cannot be used to satisfy an option exercise.

U.S Treasury Notes and Bonds

Options are written on Treasury notes and bonds as they are on stocks. The option has a specific underlying issue of T bonds or notes. So the particular underlying bond or note must be delivered against exercise. On the exercise of a note or bond, delivery is due two business days after exercise.

Index Options

An *index option* is an option on a securities or other type of index. An *index* is a weighted average of the prices of the securities chosen to be in the index.

The index may be *share-weighted,* that is, all the common stocks are based on 100-share units. Or it may be *market-weighted,* that is, the number of shares outstanding or listed on an exchange is multiplied by the current market price. In both cases, a predetermined formula is applied to arrive at the index value.

Because the mathematical formula is applied against a large basket of stock, delivering an actual security against an exercise of an option is impossible. So, in the case of an index option exercise, cash is used for settlement, not securities. The difference between the exercise (or strike) price of the option and the closing index value is settled between the option owner and the option writer on the next business day.

All index options use the value of the given index and a multiplier of 100 to arrive at the underlying option value.

Example: An option on an index with a current value of 210.50 has an underlying value of $21,050 ($210.5 × 100).

Naturally, the premium of an index option cannot be multiplied by 100 shares, because there is no one underlying stock. Instead, an index option uses a multiplier that is applied to index factor.

Example: If an index option's multiplier is 100, and the premium is $2, the cost of the option is $200 ($2 × 100).

Foreign Currency Options

British pound, Japanese yen and other types of foreign currencies are traded against the dollars. Options on these forms of investment can sometimes offer better hedging than domestically placed interest instruments. They also can be used to offset dollar fluctuations by those involved in foreign trade.

SETTLEMENT

All exchange-traded options must be compared and settled on the next business day. Each of the option exchanges has a computer facility that performs the comparison function. For example, the Chicago Board Options Exchange has its own computer facility, and the Philadelphia Stock Exchange uses the Stock Clearing Corporation of Philadelphia.

Options not compared by the next business day must be returned to the exchange for reconcilement. This process is known as *reject option trade notice* (ROTN). The notice is sent to the exchange floor the morning after trade date, and the executing broker of the problem trade is responsible for rectifying any discrepancy.

Option Clearing Corporation (OCC)

Trades that are compared are sent to a central clearing facility for recording. This facility is known as *Option Clearing Corporation* (OCC). With this facility all member firms must settle the net cash differences from their daily activity and deposit the required position margin. This must be done on the morning after trade date.

All compared transactions in a listed option are recorded at OCC. So an investor can purchase an option series on one exchange and, if it is multiple traded, sell the same series on another exchange. The position nets to zero, because the trades are processed through the exchanges' computer facility to OCC.

Option Clearing Corporation guarantees performance on all compared trades processed through the clearing houses. Because all trades have been compared and the monies settled, the clearing corporation can stand between the original buyer and seller. Any holder (buyer) who exercises options does so against the OCC, which in turn assigns the exercise to a writer on a random basis.

EXPIRATION

Option positions that are not traded out or exercised eventually expire. Upon expiration, the buyer loses the premium paid, and the writer pockets the premium received.

SUMMARY

Investors and speculators use options or option combinations to implement many strategies. In the hands of a knowledgeable person, the option is a dynamic vehicle that can not only reduce risk, but also earn income or maximize profit.

CHAPTER 31

Futures

Type: Contract
Form: Book Entry
Denomination: One
Income: None
Traded: Exchange
Duration: By contract

A futures contract originally came about to solve an age-old problem: A farmer planted oats, wheat, or soybean—and waited six months for a crop. How could the farmer be assured of a profitable price when the crop is sold a half-year from planting? If the price is high, the farmer benefits. If it is low, then the buyer of the crop benefits.

Let's say a miller normally buys a farmer's wheat crop. In past years, the miller has either profited or lost depending on price fluctuations. Instead of taking chances on a high or low price, the miller and farmer agree on a mutually agreeable price at the time of planting. In so doing, they've arranged a futures contract.

This contract had a value: It assured a price. A third party who felt that the contract price was "too" low (that the actual price of the crop would be higher) might be tempted to buy the contract from the miller. Enter the *trader*. If the futures contract trader was right, he could buy the contract at one price, take delivery of the wheat, and then sell it at a higher price. Yet traders have no desire to take or make delivery of the actual wheat (commodity). All they want to do is deal in contracts to make profits. In the futures market, someone who buys a futures contract is said to take a *long position*. Someone who sells it takes a *short position*.

Thus *futures contracts* trading was born. And thus traders, with their willingness to buy and sell contracts, provide liquidity to the futures contracts market.

For many years, futures contracts were taken out only on commodities: wheat, soybeans, pork bellies, and the like. Then they extended to include oil or precious metals. Today, given the unpredictability of interest rates, they are taken out on debt instruments, such as Treasury securities, and on foreign currencies, such as South African krugerrands.

Nowadays, futures are traded on exchange floors by brokers and/or traders. *Brokers* execute orders for the benefit of others, that is, for the customers of firms. Traders execute transactions for their own accounts; they are speculators who own seats on the exchange.

SETTLEMENT

Futures trades must be settled by the next business day. On the trade date, member firms submit trade data to the clearing corporations of the exchanges for comparison. Trades that are not compared by trade date are returned to the floor of execution the next morning. These trades are known as *rejected trade notices (RTN)*, or *out trades*. Corrected trades are resubmitted to the clearing corporation as *as-of*. A newer concept employs the use of trading zones during the day. Trades occurring in one zone must be compared to a later zone.

MARGIN

Two types of margin are involved in futures contracts: margin from the brokerage firm to the clearing corporation and margin from the customer to the brokerage firm.

Clearing Corporation Margin Requirements

The margin required by clearing corporations varies. Some require margin on net positions, others require margin on broad. The amount of margin required is calculated on per-contract basis. The amount per contract is established by the exchange on which the future trades.

Brokerage Firm Margin Requirements

Customer margin is also computed on a per-contract basis. The amount required on each contract is determined by the exchange, but the firm may ask a higher sum.

Types of Margin

Two types of margin are charged on futures transactions:

1. *Standard margin* is the amount required per contract position.
2. *Variation margin* is an adjustment for market to market.

Market fluctuations affect the values of contracts in both long and short positions. In other words, buyers must equal sellers. Because all transactions in margin accounts are compared, there must be a long position (a buyer) for every short position (every seller). If the value of a long position changes, there must be a corresponding change in a short position, somewhere else in another account.

Keeping track of changes in value is important from the point of view of margin. Any adjustment affects the client's standard margin requirements. If credits to the account eventually exceed requirements, they create an *excess*, or profit. *Debits* reduce the amount of equity in the account and can eventually oblige the customer to deposit more money (or equity).

The brokerage firm adjusts the value of contract positions daily, carrying the adjustments through the clearing corporation. Internal adjustments are made by bookkeeping entries, while those netting through the clearing corporation are settled by check.

DELIVERY

Futures trade up to and in the last month of their contract life. During the last month, they cease being futures and become *spot,* or *cash, market contracts.* During this month, *delivery notices* are attached to many sales. During this month, traders must close out their positions or be responsible for receiving or delivering the underlying contract. After trading has ceased on the last day, accounts with long positions receive the contracted amount from the short position accounts. Deliveries must conform to the contract's specifications.

What happens if a trader still owns a contract when trading ceases? If a trader is long, say, a potato contract after trading ends, he or she does not have tons of spuds dumped all over the lawn. All that happens is that the trader *owns* the contents of the contract. Grain is stored in warehouses, U.S. Treasury bills are delivered against payment, and so on. In other words, the holder of a long position owns and must pay for the contract. In the case of commodities, such as wheat or pork bellies, the new owner must pay not only the contract costs, but also must pay any storage and spoilage costs.

DAILY TRADING LIMITS

Due to the relatively low margin necessary for futures trading, the exchanges set *daily trading limits* for various contracts. If the price of a future rises or falls the limit, trading ceases in the contract until it returns to the allowable limit or until the next day, when new limits are set. The stopping of trading permits member firms to obtain the necessary funds from their affected clients.

CHAPTER 32

Swaps

Type: Swaps (currency or interest rates)
Form: Negotiated contract
Denomination: Negotiated as part of contract
Income payment: Depends on contract terms
Traded: Negotiated, not actively traded
Duration: Part of contract

Swaps are a rather old concept with recent popularity. They are growing in popularity because they meet a need in international trading, with its proliferation of interest rate products.

Example 1. Marquis Corp. has long-term debt for financing, which goes to support short term loans that reflect current interest rates. Therefore, its profits or losses are tied to the current interest rate Marquis receives versus the fixed rate they must pay on their debt.

Lincoln Mortgage has the opposite problem. They finance some of their mortgages by short-term money market instruments. Their profits or losses are tied to the difference between the current interest rates paid on short-term money market instruments versus what they receive from the fixed-term mortgages.

Enter the first type of swap, an interest rate swap. Marquis would like to pair their short-term income against short-term debt; Lincoln Mortgage would like to finance their fixed-term mortgages with long-term debt.

To accomplish this, each company sets an amount of principal known as the *notional*, on which the swap is based. A *rate* must be negotiated between the two principals to the swap, and *broker* will handle these negotiations.

As the short rates on the loans made by Marquis are tied to some recognizable rate, such as the U.S. Treasury bill rate or the Federal fund rate, so are the funds that Marquis wants to obtain in swap. If the short-term money being borrowed by Lincoln Mortgage is at a rate that is attractive to Marquis, or if it can be swapped at such a rate, the first leg of the swap is "do-able." In the same manner, if the fixed long-term debt of Marquis can be "swapped" profitably to Lincoln Mortgage, the second leg of the swap will become attractive. The broker negotiates these terms.

As long as both companies maintain their ability to borrow money at the same level (that is, as long as their financial position does not weaken, causing them to pay a higher interest rate to borrow), the swap will be maintained. The financial strength of both companies depends on the ability of both companies to remain viable companies and to continue their financial composure. This includes their ability to borrow money at the best interest rates. The "best interest" rates at a moment in time may not be associated with the financing needs of the corporation. Swaps give the corporations another conduit to obtain the best possible terms.

The relationship between long-term and short-term rates changes as the perception of which way interest rates are heading changes. While short-term rates are *usually* lower than long-term rates, there are times when this is not true. In addition, the difference (or spread) between short- and long-term rates widens and narrows over time. Now add in the level of interest rates, and the decision of what and when to borrow becomes even more complex.

FIGURE 32.1. *Comparison of Marquis Corp.'s and Lincoln Mortgage's borrowing capabilities.*

	Borrowing Rate	
	Short-Term	*Long-Term*
Marquis Corp.	T bill + 8%	T bond + 4%
Lincoln Mortgage	T bill + 6%	T bond + 6%

The capital structure of a company is one of the main ingredients in determining the company's financial strength; through it, one can estimate the company's future. A company may not want to borrow "more" long-term funds, because of concern over the amount of debt the company may already be carrying. Therefore, it may borrow short-term funds, even though long-term funds may be more attractive as a borrowing vehicle. The company can now enter into swaps of short-term rates for long-term rates and get the desired offsets, without issuing the actual security.

As Marquis Corp.'s primary business is making short-term loans, its ability to finance these loans profitably depends on the debt market and its ability to "carry" loans of differing maturities. Lincoln Mortgage has a similar problem, but its concern focuses on long-term debt. If the long-term borrowing expense of Marquis exceeds the revenue generated from its short-term loans, or if the short-term borrowing of Lincoln Mortgage exceeds the income received from the mortgages, both firms would face losses. The use of swaps permits the two organizations to better pair off their expense and revenue streams.

FIGURE 32.2. *Comparison of Marquis Corp.'s and Lincoln Mortgage's borrowing capabilities.*

Corporation	*Primary Borrowing Rates*
Marquis Corp.	U.S. Treasury bond rate plus 4%
Lincoln Mortgage	U.S. Treasury bill rate plus 6%

By swapping, the two companies make the "swap" shown in Figure 32.3.

Figure 32.3. Swap arrangement between Marquis and Lincoln

	Borrowing at	*Lending at*
Marquis Corp.	T bill rate + 6%	T bill rate + 8%
Lincoln Mortgage	T bond rate + 4%	T bond rate + 6%

As long as both companies can maintain their financial position in the industry and continue to borrow money at favorable rates, the 2% spread between each company's borrowing and lending rates will keep the swap viable. As short-term interest rates change, Marquis Corp.'s borrowing and lending will parallel each other; and, as long-term rates change, Lincoln's borrowings and lending will also parallel each other. Both parties benefit.

Interest rate swaps can be:

- Fixed for floating rates.
- Floating for floating rates (different reset dates).
- Fixed for fixed rates (different payment date).
- Zeros vs. fixed rates (appreciation vs. payment).
- Zeros vs. floating rates (appreciation vs. payment).

Example 2. Swaps can also be conducted intercurrency. Stephans International Pte. is a French company. Vargus, Inc. is a U.S. corporation. Both companies conduct business in each other's country, and both need borrowings to expand their business. The problem both companies face is that, while they are well-known in their respective home countries, they are little known outside their borders.

Both companies can borrow the money needed to expand their foreign operations from their domestic or local bank at favorable rates. However, in doing so, they would be exposed to currency exchange rate risk. For example, Vargus borrows $500,000 from its local bank for use in France. At the time of the loan, one French franc is equal to 18½ cents, or $1 equals 5.40 French franc (F). Vargus converts the $500,000 into 2,700,000 French francs ($500,000 × 5.40 F = 2,700,000 F). A year later, Vargus wants to pay back the loan. At that time, one French franc is equal to 15¢, or $1 equals approximately 6.667 French francs. To pay $500,000, Vargus Corp. would need 3,333,333 F (3,333,334 F × 15¢ = $500,000). Besides interest, it has cost Vargus 633,333 F more than it borrowed. Of course, at the time the loan comes due, the rates could just as easily have moved in Vargus' favor. However, neither Vargus nor Stephans wants to take the exchange rate risk.

Enter the currency broker, with the swap shown in Figure

32.4. Assuming both companies are borrowing the equivalent amounts, the swap will occur.

FIGURE 32.4.

	U.S. Rate	*French Rate*
Stephans International Pte.	10%	7%
Vargus Corp.	7%	10%

Example: Vargus is borrowing from a U.S. bank at 7% U.S. funds, but paying 7% in French francs. Stephans is borrowing at 7% FF, but paying 7% U.S. funds. By doing the swap, both companies were able to borrow at the best rates in the countries in which they want to do business. This, plus the fact that neither company is exposed to exchange rate changes, makes the swap attractive. Both firms benefit from each other's good credit rating.

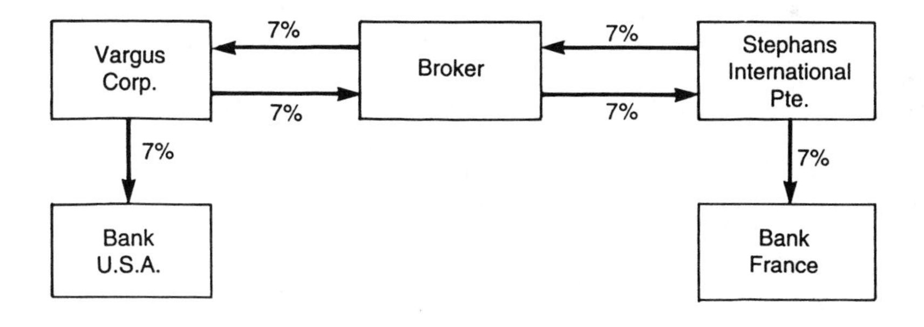

SUMMARY

There is growing concern as to the recording of swaps and other derivative products, since they are "off-balance-sheet" items—that is, no mention of the swap appears on the company's financial report. In the case of Vargus Corp., their records would show a loan that is really supporting Stephan's business; yet no mention is made of Stephan's loan, which is the loan really supporting Vargus' business. The same is true of the first example between Marquis and Lincoln Mortgage. What would happen if one of the participants to the swap fell into financial difficulty? Would the lender seek restitution from the other party, claiming that the obligation was actually theirs since they are benefitting from the loan? Would this leave the remaining participant with both obligations? Time will tell what actions regulators will take.

CHAPTER 33

Currency

Type:	Cash
Form:	Bearer
Denomination:	By issuing country or group of countries
Income payment:	None
Traded:	OTC (FX)
Duration:	Viable economy of issuing country or group of countries

The U.S. dollar (USD), the British pound sterling (GPB), the Canadian dollar (CD), the German Deutsche mark (DEM), the French franc (Ff), the Italian lira (IL), the Mexican peso (MP), the Japanese yen (JPX), the Swiss franc (SF), and the Spanish peseta (SP) are just a few of the 100-plus currencies traded on a daily basis and used for settlement of transactions on a world-wide basis. Based on the economies and monetary policies followed by their respective governments, the relationship of one currency to another is forever changing. Individuals involved with the exchanging of currency are involved in the foreign exchange (*FX*, or *forex market*).

Currency relationships are best described in terms of inflation. Under inflation, the dollar will buy less in the next period than in this period; in other words, the dollar can be described as "falling" against the product purchased. You need more dollars to buy the product later than you need today.

In the case of forex trading, the "other product" is another currency. But, instead of naming inflation as the reason that currency *x* cannot purchase as much of currency *y* as it used to, currency *x* is said to be "falling." As currency *x* is *falling* against currency *y*, currency *y* is, by definition, *rising* against currency *x*.

Example: Let's say it cost 2 British pounds to manufacture a widget in the United Kingdom and 4 U.S. dollars to manufacture the same widget in the United States. For simplicity, further assume that 1 British pound sterling is exchangeable for 2 U.S. dollars. (We will also assume that there isn't any transportation, charges, tariffs, taxes, or other charges, so that, before currency conversion, a widget costs the same to manufacture in England and America as well as to sell widgets in each owners' country.) If the dollar were to rise against the British pound, you would need fewer dollars to buy a British-made widget in America than you would need to buy an American-made widget. If the dollar should rise so that $1 equals £1, a British-produced widget would cost 2 U.S. dollars in the United States, where a U.S.-made widget would still cost $4. A U.S.-made widget in England would cost 4 British pounds, or double what a British-made widget costs.

Why? When 1 GBP equals 2 USD, a British-made widget costs 2 GBP and a U.S.-made widget cost 4 USD. As the British-U.S. exchange rate is 1 for 2, then a British-made (two-BPS) widget would cost 4 USD in American and a U.S.-made widget would cost 2 BPS in England. When the dollar is one for one with the pound (it buys more British pounds) the U.K.-made widget (2 GBP) would cost $2 in the United States, versus $4 for a U.S.-made one. Conversely, the price of a U.S.-made widget would cost 4 GBP in England versus 2 GBP for a British-made one.

Intercountry exchange rates do not affect the price of a product manufactured and sold within that country. Therefore a $4 widget manufactured and sold in the United States would cost $4 no matter what the exchange rate was. It would change its value only in another country as the exchange rate fluctuated.

Individuals or companies involved in international trade

must be concerned with currency fluctuations. As the rate changes, so does the opportunity for profit.

Example: An American investor wishes to purchase 1,000,000 DM (Deutsche-Mark) German government bonds, known as *Bundes* bonds, which are trading at 98 DM. Therefore, the U.S. investor must buy 980,000 DM to pay for the purchase. At the time of purchase, 1 DM equals .66 USD. Therefore, the U.S. investor must pay 646,800 USD for the 980,000 DM needed (980,000 DM × .66 = $646,800). Let's assume that, when the bonds mature and the German government pays the 1,000,000 DM owed, 1 DM equals .60 USD. The U.S. investor would receive 600,000 USD on conversion (1,000,000 DM × .60 = 600,000 USD) for a loss of 46,800 USD, even though the *Bundes* bond increased in value from 980,000 DM to 1,000,000 DM.

Let's observe this process on micro level.

German *Bundes* bonds have a three-business-day settlement cycle. The U.S. investor could buy the Deutsche marks on trade date, trade plus 1, or trade date plus 2 (settlement date). Let's assume at the time of the trade, 1 DM equals .66 USD; the next day 1 DM = .68 USD, and by settlement date 1 D.M. = .64 USD. On which day should the investor have bought Deutsche marks to best position the transaction for a profit? A look at the three days would point to best settlement date as the one that would require the least amount in U.S. dollars.

As of the writing of this chapter, the exchange rates for some of the major currencies are as follows:

	U.S. Dollars to . . .	*. . . to U.S. Dollars*
British pound sterling	1.51	.660
Canadian dollars	.77	1.287
French franc	.184	5.427
German deutsche mark	.625	1.599
Japanese yen	.008	124,45
Swiss franc	.694	1.441

For example, $1.51 will buy 1.00 British *pound* sterling, or .66 of a pound will buy 1.00 USD. Check your newspaper for the rates in force on the day you are reading this.

To offset the risk involved with currencies, hedgers can take advantage of options, futures and forwards. Option on currencies trade on the Phlx (Philadelphia Stock Exchange), or over the counter. Futures trade on IMM (International Monetary Market), part of the Chicago Mercantile Exchange (CME).

Options on currency are structured like equity options, with strike prices and expiration months. Unlike listed equity contracts, however, currency options have two expiration cycles during their expiration month: the Saturday before the third Wednesday and the last business day of the month. Exercise results in a two-business-day settlement.

Futures and forwards follow traditional product procedures. Future contracts, which trade on exchanges, have rigid contract specifications, whereas forwards are negotiable and trade OTC.

In dealing with FX trading and FX derivatives (i.e., forwards, futures, and options), participants must not only have arrangements with domestic banks but also with banks in the country of the foreign currency.

SUMMARY OF INVESTMENT PRODUCTS

Stock
Ownership of a corporation. The ownership is evidenced by shares. Two forms of ownership are common and preferred.

Corporate Bond or Note
Debt of a corporation. It usually carries a fixed rate of interest and is of long duration.

Commercial Paper
Short-term debt of a corporation.

Warrant & Right
Privileges issued by the corporation that gives the owner the opportunity to acquire stock under prescribed provisions.

Municipal Bond and Note
Long-term debt instrument (bond) or short-term instrument (note) issued by state or local governments.

U.S. Treasury Obligation
Debt issued by the federal government. Short-term instruments are known as bills; intermediate-term, notes; and long-term, bonds. There are other government securities known as agencies, which are also backed by the Fed.

Mortgage-Backed Security
Either GNMA (Government National Mortgage Association), Freddie Macs (Federal Home Loan Mortgage Corp.), or Federal National Mortgage Association (FNMA) represented by the modified pass-through form of issue.

Banker's Acceptance (BA)
Short-term debt issued by banks and used in international trade.

Certificates of Deposit (CD)
Short-term debt issued by banks.

Mutual Fund
Pooling of money to acquire a desired portfolio of securities or investment goal.

Option
A contract to trade an underlying security at a fixed price over a specified period of time.

Futures
Contract for settlement or delivery to occur sometime in the "future."

Swap
An exchange of currency for a fixed period of time or the exchange of interest payment terms for a stated period.

Currency
The buying and/or selling of currency from different countries to use for multiple purposes.

PART IV

OPERATIONS PROCEDURES

CHAPTER 34

Order Room

Orders enter the processing system from many sources and for many reasons. Perhaps an investor read an article about a company, a research report, or a technological breakthrough. Or maybe two people were simply discussing business in general. In some cases, especially in the commodity sector, the user of the product—such as a rancher and a beef packer, or a farmer and a miller—buy and sell in the futures marketplace.

Whatever a customer's reason for placing the order, the order itself does not generate revenue for a brokerage firm. Only its execution does.

"CHANGING OF THE GUARD" AT SF&R

It is 8:30 a.m. Employees of Stone, Forrest & Rivers are arriving for the day's work. The night shift personnel, whose routines are still uncompleted, are getting ready to turn over their work to the day shift.

The two areas still busy at this time are the computer center and the mail room. They have been processing the previous day's "work" for use by the rest of the staff today. Getting their work done on time is essential to the smooth running of the firm. For example, the sooner that customers' trade confirmations are produced and mailed, the less trouble the firm has collecting money and securities on settlement date. Also, the sooner that the margin department gets copies of the confirmation, the fewer problems the firm has with Reg T compliance.

The night processing staff have more to do, however, than confirmation. They must produce all the listings, reports, blotters, and other documentation that will be used in today's work. Each incoming operations employee gets a report of some sort and has some assignment or another to perform this day.

The *order room* at SF&R, like the order room in any firm, accepts orders and routes them for execution to either the appropriate exchange or market marker. The processing of an order begins after the stockbroker enters it for a client.

THE ORDER FORM

Because Stone, Forrest & Rivers is a multiproduct firm, it has an order form such as the one shown in Figure 34-1. *Note*:

- *Line 0:* contains destination codes and a place for the execution price.
- *Line 1:* Verifies that this is buy order. It also displays the name of the individual or department that should be called—the order needs special handling. The term "Poss Dupe" is checked when the order may be a duplicate of a previously entered one.
- *Line 2:* Describes the order—shares, symbol, price, and codes affecting odd lot and round lot special handling. For example, "BAS" means a basis price, which is a price at which an odd lot will be executed (between bid and offer), should no round lot transaction occur.
- *Line 3:* Includes such instructors as day order or good-til-cancelled (GTC).
- *Line 4-6:* Repeats the *type* of information appearing on Line 1-3. Used for *order* cancellation, and when the order is multiple-part copy type.
- *Line 7:* Provides the customer's account number and other customer-related information.

FIGURE 34-1. *SF&R's order form.*

B U Y

SUFFIX CODES

CALLED ... CL
CERTIFICATE ... CT
CLASS OF SECURITY ... AB ETC.
CONVERTIBLE ... CV
FOREIGN ... F
PREFERRED ... PR
RIGHTS ... RT
SPECIAL ... SP
STAMPED ... SD
WHEN DISTRIBUTED ... WD
WHEN ISSUED ... WI
WITH WARRANTS ... WW
WITHOUT WARRANTS ... XW
WARRANTS ... WS

0 — STOCK EXCHANGES: NYSE & ASE (NAX) | NASDAQ (OTC) | OVER THE CNTR (OTN) | CHI'GO MID-WEST (CMW) | PACIFIC COAST (PCX) | BOSTON P-B-W (HEND) — BONDS: CORP-ORATE (BND) | MUNI-CIPAL (BMUN) | CONV-ERTIBLE (CONV) — BLOCK DEPT (ID) | FINAN. SERV. DEPT. (FND) | SYNDI-CATE (STIC) | MUTUAL FUNDS (CGE) | SPECIAL HAND'NG (SHD) | OTHER | ORDER NUMBER | OFFICE | EXECUTED PRICE

1 — POSS DUPE | BUY | ATTN:

2 — QUANTITY | SYMBOL OR DESCRIPTION | SUFFIX* | PRICE OR MARKET | STOP (STP) | STOP LIMIT PRICE ______ LMT | TYPE OF ORDER OTHER THAN LIMITED OR MARKET: BAS, OB, WITH DISCRETION, WOW, CLO

3 — AON | N H | DAY | GTC | OPG | FOK | OC | DNR | CASH | ND | PRINCIPAL TRANSACTION

4 — POSS DUPE | OR | SW | CXL | BUY | INFORM CUSTOMER WE MAKE MARKET

5 — QUANTITY | SYMBOL OR DESCRIPTION | SUFFIX* | PRICE OR MARKET | STOP (STP) | STOP LIMIT PRICE ______ LMT | BAS, OB, WITH DISCRETION, WOW, CLO

6 — LVS | AON | NH | DAY | GTC | OPG | FOK | OC | DNR | CASH | ND | CHECK IF NEW ACCOUNT

7 — OFFICE | ACCOUNT NUMBER | TYPE | TYPE OF ACCOUNT (0-COD, 1-CASH, 2-MARGIN, 3-SHORT, 4-SPEC. SUBSCRIPTION, 5-CONV. BOND, 6-SPEC. BOND) | SPLIT SHARES | DISCRETIONARY NYSE RULE 405 | EMPLOYEE | A.E. NO. | MGR'S APPROVAL

8 — CXL'S ONLY | REF | ORIG STATION | MESSAGE NO. | CUSTOMER NAME

9 — COM | A.E. OVERRIDE [R/ _ _ _] | NEG. ¢ PER SH [M/90 _ _ _] | NEG. DISC. [CD _ _ %] | ST INS OVERRIDE [I/ _]

10 — COM | SPECIAL DESCRIPTIVE INST. [D/ _] | D/UNSOL

11 — COM

12 — COM

13 — CONFIRM LINE CFN LINE 2 & 5

ORDER COPY

The remaining portion of the order ticket deals with commission charges and other special instructions.

TYPES OF ORDERS

Market Orders

The most common type of order is the *market order,* which instructs the executing employee to accept the current market price, that is, the current bid and offer, or quote. If you are willing to *buy at the market,* you are willing to accept the lowest offer, whatever it is at that time. If you are willing to *sell at the market,* you are willing to accept the highest bid for your stock.

Example: The quote is 35-1/4. In other words, the highest bid is $35 per share ($35) for a 100-share order, and the lowest offer $35.25 per share (1/4) for a 100-share order. A client enters an order to purchase 100 shares "at the market." The trade is executed against the offer, and the customer pays $3,525 (100 shares × $35.25), plus any commission fees or

FIGURE 34-2. *A market order.*

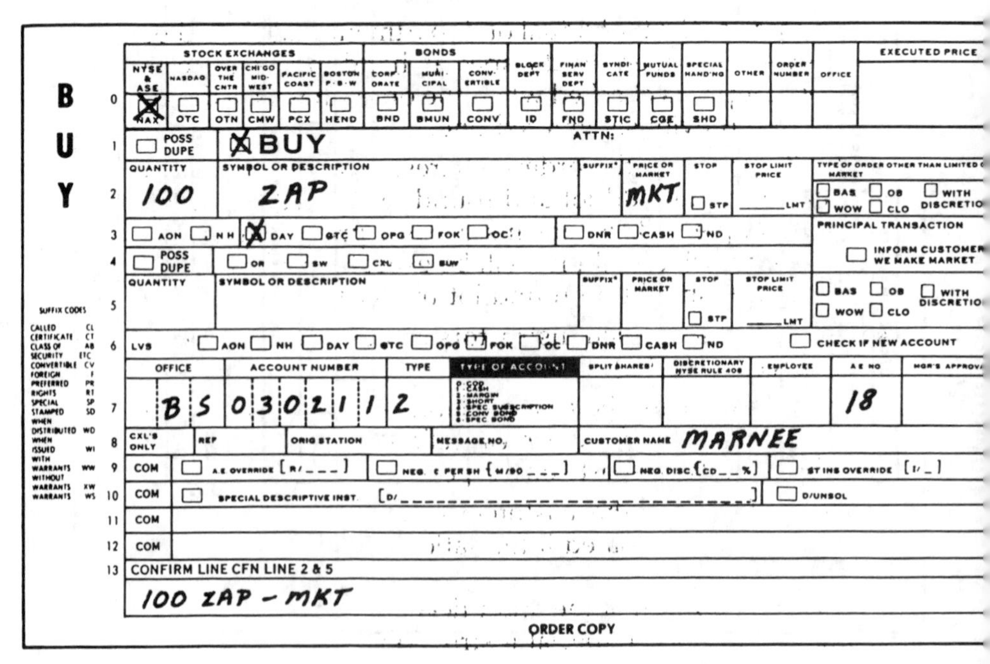

BUY

0 STOCK EXCHANGES: NYSE & ASE [X] NAX; NASDAQ OTC; OVER THE CNTR OTN; CHI GO MID-WEST CMW; PACIFIC COAST PCX; BOSTON P-B-W HEND — BONDS: CORPORATE BND; MUNICIPAL BMUN; CONVERTIBLE CONV — BLOCK DEPT ID; FINAN SERV DEPT FND; SYNDICATE STIC; MUTUAL FUNDS CGE; SPECIAL HAND'NG SHD; OTHER; ORDER NUMBER; OFFICE; EXECUTED PRICE

1 POSS DUPE — [X] BUY — ATTN:

2 QUANTITY 100 — SYMBOL OR DESCRIPTION ZAP — SUFFIX — PRICE OR MARKET MKT — STOP STP — STOP LIMIT PRICE ____ LMT — TYPE OF ORDER OTHER THAN LIMITED OR MARKET: BAS, OB, WITH DISCRETION, WOW, CLO

3 AON, NH, [X] DAY, GTC, OPG, FOK, OC — DNR, CASH, ND — PRINCIPAL TRANSACTION

4 POSS DUPE — OR, SW, CXL, BUY — INFORM CUSTOMER WE MAKE MARKET

5 QUANTITY — SYMBOL OR DESCRIPTION — SUFFIX — PRICE OR MARKET — STOP STP — STOP LIMIT PRICE ____ LMT — BAS, OB, WITH DISCRETION, WOW, CLO

SUFFIX CODES: CALLED CL; CERTIFICATE CT; CLASS OF AB; SECURITY ETC; CONVERTIBLE CV; FOREIGN F; PREFERRED PR; RIGHTS RT; SPECIAL SP; STAMPED SD; WHEN DISTRIBUTED WD; WHEN ISSUED WI; WITH WARRANTS WW; WITHOUT WARRANTS XW; WARRANTS WS

6 LVS — AON, NH, DAY, GTC, OPG, FOK, OC, DNR, CASH, ND — CHECK IF NEW ACCOUNT

7 OFFICE BS — ACCOUNT NUMBER 030211 — TYPE 1 2 — TYPE OF ACCOUNT: 0-COD, 1-CASH, 2-MARGIN, 3-SHORT, 4-SPEC SUBSCRIPTION, 5-CONV BOND, 6-SPEC BOND — SPLIT SHARES — DISCRETIONARY NYSE RULE 408 — EMPLOYEE — AE NO 18 — MGR'S APPROVAL

8 CXL'S ONLY — REF — ORIG STATION — MESSAGE NO. — CUSTOMER NAME MARNEE

9 COM — AE OVERRIDE [R/___] — NEG. ¢ PER SH [M/90___] — NEG DISC [CD__%] — ST INS OVERRIDE [I/_]

10 COM — SPECIAL DESCRIPTIVE INST [D/________] — D/UNSOL

11 COM

12 COM

13 CONFIRM LINE CFN LINE 2 & 5

100 ZAP – MKT

ORDER COPY

other expenses. A customer who wants to sell 100 shares receives $3,500 (100 shares × $35), less commissions, fees, taxes, and the like.

Limit Orders

Sometimes a customer is not willing to accept the current market price or is concerned that the market price may move disadvantageously before the order can be executed. For self-protection, the customer can enter a *limit order*, which places a limit on the price that the customer is willing to pay or receive. With a limit order, a customer acquiring securities can never pay more than the limit price on the order, and a customer selling securities can never receive less than the limit.

Example: Customer Dahl wants to purchase stock at $35 per share. The current quote is 34½—35 (34.50 bid, 35 offered). Dahl is not sure what the quote or market will be when the order arrives on the floor for execution; the market could move up from the time the stock is quoted to the time the order reaches the trading location. With a market order to buy, the customer would pay the higher price. To protect against paying this price, Dahl's broker enters a buy limit order, "Buy 100 XYZ

FIGURE 34-3. *A limit order.*

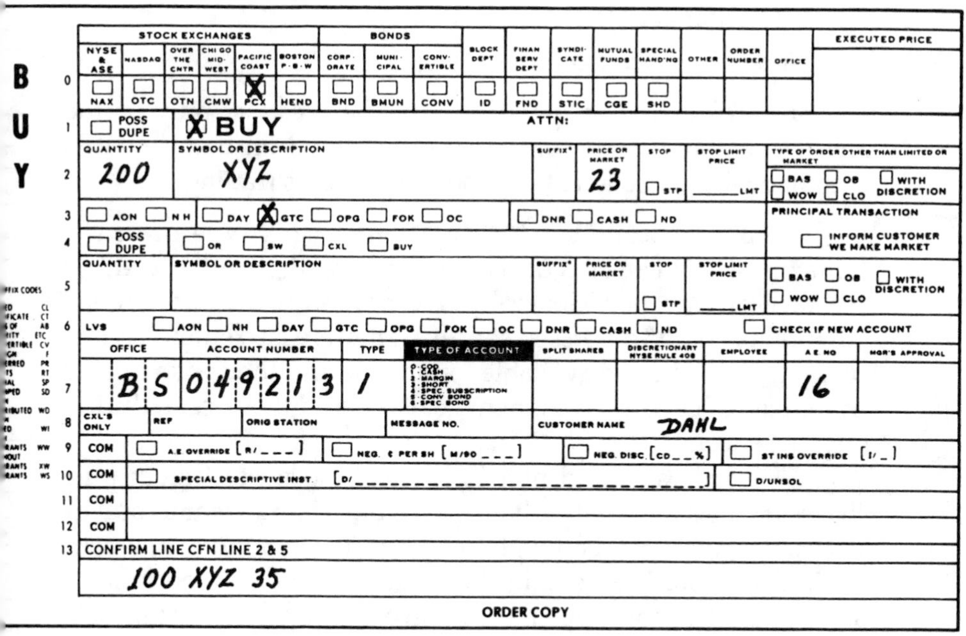

B U Y

0 — STOCK EXCHANGES: NYSE & ASE [ ] NAX | NASDAQ [ ] OTC | OVER THE CNTR [ ] OTN | CHI GO MID-WEST [ ] CMW | PACIFIC COAST [X] PCX | BOSTON P-B-W [ ] HEND — BONDS: CORPORATE [ ] BND | MUNICIPAL [ ] BMUN | CONVERTIBLE [ ] CONV — BLOCK DEPT [ ] ID | FINAN SERV DEPT [ ] FND | SYNDICATE [ ] STIC | MUTUAL FUNDS [ ] CGE | SPECIAL HAND'NG [ ] SHD | OTHER | ORDER NUMBER | OFFICE | EXECUTED PRICE

1 — [ ] POSS DUPE | [X] BUY | ATTN:

2 — QUANTITY: 200 | SYMBOL OR DESCRIPTION: XYZ | SUFFIX* | PRICE OR MARKET: 23 | STOP [ ] STP | STOP LIMIT PRICE ____ LMT | TYPE OF ORDER OTHER THAN LIMITED OR MARKET: [ ] BAS [ ] OB [ ] WITH DISCRETION [ ] WOW [ ] CLO

3 — [ ] AON [ ] N H | [ ] DAY [X] GTC [ ] OPG [ ] FOK [ ] OC | [ ] DNR [ ] CASH [ ] ND | PRINCIPAL TRANSACTION

4 — [ ] POSS DUPE | [ ] OR [ ] SW [ ] CXL [ ] BUY | [ ] INFORM CUSTOMER WE MAKE MARKET

5 — QUANTITY | SYMBOL OR DESCRIPTION | SUFFIX* | PRICE OR MARKET | STOP [ ] STP | STOP LIMIT PRICE ____ LMT | [ ] BAS [ ] OB [ ] WITH DISCRETION [ ] WOW [ ] CLO

6 — LVS [ ] AON [ ] NH [ ] DAY [ ] GTC [ ] OPG [ ] FOK [ ] OC [ ] DNR [ ] CASH [ ] ND | [ ] CHECK IF NEW ACCOUNT

7 — OFFICE: B S | ACCOUNT NUMBER: 0 4 9 2 1 3 | TYPE: 1 | TYPE OF ACCOUNT: 0-COD 1-CASH 2-MARGIN 3-SHORT 4-SPEC. SUBSCRIPTION 5-CONV BOND 6-SPEC. BOND | SPLIT SHARES | DISCRETIONARY NYSE RULE 408 | EMPLOYEE | A E NO: 16 | MGR'S APPROVAL

8 — CXL'S ONLY | REF | ORIG STATION | MESSAGE NO. | CUSTOMER NAME: DAHL

9 — COM [ ] A.E. OVERRIDE [R/ _ _ _] [ ] NEG. ¢ PER SH [M/90 _ _ _] [ ] NEG. DISC. [CD _ _ %] [ ] ST INS OVERRIDE [I/ _]

10 — COM [ ] SPECIAL DESCRIPTIVE INST. [D/ _] [ ] D/UNSOL

11 — COM

12 — COM

13 — CONFIRM LINE CFN LINE 2 & 5

100 XYZ 35

ORDER COPY

@ 35." If the market moves above the buy limit order's price, the order is not executed, thereby saving the customer from paying a higher price than intended.

What about sell orders? A customer can limit the sale price of the security.

Example: Customer Dahl wishes to sell 100 shares of XYZ for $50 per share. The current market is 50-1/4 (50 bid, $50.25 offered). If the current market doesn't decrease while the limit order is enroute to the trading location, Dahl is assured of execution. If the quote changes to, say, 49¾–50¼, the customer with a limit order would not receive an execution.

A limit order to sell at 50 negates a trade occurring at the lower price. With such an order, the customer's security cannot be sold for less than $50 per share. The order is held until the bid moves up and some other order comes along for a purchase of XYZ stock at 50. At that point, the trade is consummated.

Time Instructions

How long an order remains in force depends on the customer's instruction. There are basically two time instructions:

1. Day orders.
2. Good-till-cancelled orders.

Day Orders. The day order may be executed only on the day it is entered. If the order is not executed on that day, it is automatically cancelled at the end of that day's trading.

Good-Til Cancelled (GTC) Orders. This type of order, sometimes called an *open* order, remains effective until it is either executed or cancelled. Generally GTC orders are used as "protection orders" (to be discussed shortly). They are also entered when customers will not be available for a while and they wish to take advantage of certain investment goals, should they occur, during their absence.

GTC orders should not, as a rule, be used to trigger purchases or sales automatically in the future. If you want to buy or sell a stock, be concerned with today's prices and today's statistical information. If a security looks attractive based on today's prices, buy it. If now appears to be an opportune time to sell, sell.

Tomorrow's prices are tomorrow's prices, and tomorrow's statistical information may not have any bearing on your goals, your outlook, and your interest *today*. With a GTC order, you may acquire a security weeks or months from now, when it may not look as attractive as it does now. Remember, security prices are determined by supply and demand. A stock's price generally rises when the public believes it is an attractive purchase, and it falls when they believe it is overvalued.

Short Sales

A unique type of transaction permits you to make a profit from falling stock prices. This type of transaction is known as a *short sale*, in which you sell a security that you have borrowed (or that your firm has borrowed for you) and then buy it at a later date for return to the lender.

Example: Customers Smith and Jones maintain accounts with Morse and Russell, a brokerage firm. Smith owns 100 shares of XYZ, which has a current market value of $50 per share ($5,000). The stock is part of Smith's portfolio and is maintained in his margin account as a long-term investment. Jones does not own any shares of XYZ Corporation, but she is of the opinion that the price of the security will fall over the near term (the next few months). Her next step is to call her broker at Morse and Russell to discuss a short sale. After she has satisfied certain margin requirements and the firm has insured the availability of Smith's securities, she enters an order to sell 100 XYZ *short*. Upon execution, the Morse and Russell brokerage firm delivers Smith's stock to the purchasing brokerage firm, which pays Morse and Russell $5,000.

Three months later, XYZ is trading for $40 per share. Jones instructs her broker to buy 100 shares at the market. When the trade is settled, Morse and Russell take $4,000 from the $5,000 in Jones' account and pays for the purchase, and the firm returns the security to Smith. Because Jones originally sold the stock at 50 and purchased it three months later at 40, she makes a $1,000 profit, less commission, taxes, and fees.

That's not all there is to short selling, which will be discussed throughout the text. Just remember for now that, in a short sale, you sell someone else's stock and that it must be repurchased at some later date for return to the lender.

Stop Orders

Not all security acquisitions are profitable, and neither are all short sales.

Example: XYZ increases, instead of decreases, in value. In such a case, Jones would have to acquire the security at a price higher than $50, thereby sustaining a loss.

To protect against or to limit the loss, Smith could use a *stop order*, which is a memorandum order that becomes a market order when its price is reached or passed. This type of order is referred to as a "memorandum" because, without the word "stop" on it, it is executed as it is entered on the "in-the-money" side of the current market price. A "stop" order, on the other hand, becomes a market order when its price is reached or passed.

Example: Jones just sold short XYZ at 50, and the most she can afford to lose is $500. She enters a GTC order to buy 100 XYZ 55 *stop*.

FIGURE 34.4. *A stop order.*

B U Y

STOCK EXCHANGES: NYSE & ASE | NASDAQ | OVER THE CNTR | CHI GO MID-WEST | PACIFIC COAST | BOSTON P-B-W
BONDS: CORP-ORATE | MUNI-CIPAL | CONV-ERTIBLE
BLOCK DEPT | FINAN SERV DEPT | SYNDI-CATE | MUTUAL FUNDS | SPECIAL HAND'NG | OTHER | ORDER NUMBER | OFFICE | EXECUTED PRICE

0 [X] NAX | OTC | OTN | CMW | PCX | HEND | BND | BMUN | CONV | ID | FND | STIC | CGE | SHD

1 POSS DUPE | [X] BUY | ATTN:

2 QUANTITY 100 | SYMBOL OR DESCRIPTION XYZ | SUFFIX* | PRICE OR MARKET 50 | STOP [X] STP | STOP LIMIT PRICE ____ LMT | TYPE OF ORDER OTHER THAN LIMIT/MARKET: BAS, OB, WITH DISCRETION, WOW, CLO

3 AON | NH | DAY | [X] GTC | OPG | FOK | OC | DNR | CASH | ND | PRINCIPAL TRANSACTION

4 POSS DUPE | OR | SW | CXL | BUY | INFORM CUSTOMER WE MAKE MARKET

5 QUANTITY | SYMBOL OR DESCRIPTION | SUFFIX* | PRICE OR MARKET | STOP STP | STOP LIMIT PRICE ____ LMT | BAS, OB, WITH DISCRETION, WOW, CLO

6 LVS | AON | NH | DAY | GTC | OPG | FOK | OC | DNR | CASH | ND | CHECK IF NEW ACCOUNT

OFFICE | ACCOUNT NUMBER | TYPE | TYPE OF ACCOUNT | SPLIT SHARES | DISCRETIONARY NYSE RULE 408 | EMPLOYEE | AE NO | MGR'S APPROVAL

7 BS | 149381 | 1 | 0-COD, 1-CASH, 2-MARGIN, 3-SHORT, 4-SPEC SUBSCRIPTION, 5-CONV BOND, 6-SPEC BOND | | | | 06 |

8 CXL'S ONLY | REP | ORIG STATION | MESSAGE NO. | CUSTOMER NAME JONES

9 COM | A.E. OVERRIDE [R/___] | NEG. ¢ PER SH [M/90 _'__] | NEG. DISC [CD__%] | ST INS OVERRIDE [I/_]

10 COM | SPECIAL DESCRIPTIVE INST [D/________] | D/UNSOL

11 COM

12 COM

13 CONFIRM LINE CFN LINE 2 & 5

100 XYZ 50 STOP

ORDER COPY

SUFFIX CODES: CALLED CL; CERTIFICATE CT; CLASS OF SECURITY AB ETC; CONVERTIBLE CV; FOREIGN F; PREFERRED PR; RIGHTS RT; SPECIAL SP; STAMPED SD; WHEN DISTRIBUTED WD; WHEN ISSUED WI; WITH WARRANTS WW; WITHOUT WARRANTS XW; WARRANTS WS

If the word *stop* were not to appear on her order, she would be entering a limit order. With the current market price at 50, the limit order would be executed at 50 because 50 is on the in-the-money side of the 55 limit.

As a stop order, however, her instruction to buy 100 shares of XYZ at the market *when* the market reaches or goes through $55 per share. The order therefore remains a memorandum order until the stop price is reached or passes.

Should XYZ decline from the price Jones sold it at ($50), the stop order is never executed. If, on the other hand, the value of the stock increases from 50 to 55, the stop order is executed, thereby closing out the short transaction and curtailing the amount of loss.

Both *buy* stop and *sell* stop orders are used as valuable protective devices by sophisticated investors.

Stop Limit Order

Chartists, technical analysts, and certain other professionals use a type of stop order known as the "stop limit" order. Like the regular stop order, a *stop limit order* is a memorandum order but it becomes a limit order, instead of a market order, when its price is reached or passed. Whereas the stop order is a protective device, the stop limit order is more of a strategic tool.

Example: Jones has been following the movement of ABC for a long period. Beside noticing that ABC is a *volatile issue* (one whose price fluctuates considerably), Jones observes that, every time the security price has passed through $40 level, it appreciated to between $46 and $48 per share before falling. If ABC didn't "break 40," on the "upside," it tended to decline to about $30 per share. ABC is currently quoted at 38½-39½. While Jones believes ABC to be an attractive purchase, she must see if it appreciates through the $40 level before acquiring it.

She enters an order to "B (buy) 100 XYZ 40½ stop 41 limit." If the price increases to 40½ the order becomes a limit order ("B 100 XYZ 41"), and the broker attempts to execute it. Yet suppose that, after trading has closed today at 39½ some very good news concerning ABC is released. The stock may open tomorrow at 46, the price at which Jones wants to sell the stock. If she had entered a stop order at 40½ when the market price of ABC was 39½, she would be purchasing ABC today at the 46 range. But this is not what she wanted to do. By entering a stop limit ("B 100 XYZ 40½ stop 41 limit") with the current price higher than our limit price, no execution can take place.

Large Orders

Four types of instructions may be used on large orders. They concern themselves with the time of execution and the completion of the order. They are:

1. Immediate-or-cancel (IOC).
2. Fill-or-kill (FOK).
3. All-or-none (AON).
4. Not-held (NH).

Immediate-or-Cancel (IOC). This order instructs the broker to execute as many round lot shares as possible immediately upon receipt of the order and to cancel any remaining lots that are not executed.

Fill-or-Kill (FOK). The broker executes all of the order immediately or cancels it.

All-or-None (AON). Within the time limitation of the order (usually one day), the broker must execute the entire order ("all") or the client does not have to accept any of it "or none").

Not-Held (NH). This order informs the executing floor broker that the originator of the order is not holding the broker to the execution rules of the exchange pertaining to time and sales. Ordinarily, orders must be executed under the directive set forth by the exchange rules. But a floor broker with a not-held order may shield the size of the order from the crowd, and execute the order in piecemeal using his/her discretion.

The preceding types of orders make up the bulk of the orders handled by the order departments. Other types of orders will be discussed elsewhere in the book. For now, it is enough to see that each order belongs to a customer and that customers, through their market activity, produce the revenue that keeps a brokerage firm a going concern.

RESOLVING PROBLEM TRADES

Although the operations cycle starts in the order room, this department performs many other functions. Because the order room is the central point between order entry and trade execution, any problem between the two must be processed through this area. So one of the first functions in a day is the resolution of previous day's problem trades. For example, listed option transactions that could not be compared on trade date (the day before) are returned to the exchange floor of execution for reconcilement. At the exchange, the brokers involved with the problem transaction find the discrepancies and then resolve the differences. The resolved trade is then returned and processed through the trade stream on an as-of basis, that is, "as of" the actual trade date. Any transaction not entering the trade processing stream on its actual trade date is an as-of transaction. (The *as-of date* informs all parties of the day that the trade *should have* taken place.)

Some other problems are:

1. *Unentered Order:* Perhaps an order was supposed to be entered but, due to an employee's error, it was not. Such an order must be entered now, executed as soon as possible, and the price adjusted so that the client does not suffer any financial loss.
2. *Wrong Security:* An order was entered and executed for the wrong security. In this case, the erroneous trade must be *reversed* (or *traded out*) and the correct security traded. Price adjustments may be necessary.
3. *Unexecuted Order:* An order was entered and should have been executed, but, for whatever reasons, it was not.
4. *No Comparison:* A trade cannot be compared with the opposing broker. The order must be returned to the floor of execution or to the trading desk to be reconciled.
5. *Wrong Quantity:* An order was entered for the wrong quantity.

These and any other problems involving execution must be resolved through the order room. OTC transactions are returned to the traders; listed securities are returned to the floor of execution.

ADJUSTMENTS FOR DIVIDENDS

The order room also has to adjust good-til-cancelled (GTC) orders for stock with an upcoming dividend. A GTC order, once entered, is an open order until it is executed or until it is cancelled by the customer. Yet, when a corporation announces a dividend, the market value of its stock drops by the amount of the dividend on the ex-dividend date (four days before record date). Because of the "drop" in market price, the order department staff has to reduce pending buy limit, sell stop, and stop limit orders by the amount of the dividend. These orders should be triggered only by price movements due to supply and demand, not by price reactions to dividends.

Example: Downe DeTubes & Co. is going to pay a $.25-per-share dividend to holders of record Friday, May 5. The last time the stock may be purchased for dividend purposes is the previous Friday, April 28. Purchasers of the security on Monday, May 1, acquire the stock on the ex-dividend date. So the stock would open on Monday, May 1, at 1/4 of a point less than it closed at the previous Friday, April 28.

On Friday, April 28, the stock closes at $40 per share. A person buying the stock on that day pays $40 per share and receives $.25 per share dividend on the payable date, for a net cost of 39¾ or $39.75 per share. Because the stock price is reduced by the amount of the dividend on the ex-dividend date, the person purchasing the stock on Monday, May 1, pays 39¾ or $39.75 per share.

Any open GTC buy limit, sell stop, and sell stop limit orders for Downe DeTubes & Co. are adjusted by $.25. On an order to buy, the limit price is decreased by $.25; sell stop and stop limit sell orders are also decreased by $.25.

A client may override this automatic adjustment by entering the instruction *do not reduce* (DNR) in the case of a cash dividend or *do not increase* (DNI) in the case of a stock dividend. (See line 3 of the order form in Figure 34-1.) The order room must be very careful to treat these orders correctly.

NEW TRADES

As orders are entered during the day, one copy is filed and the other routed to the point of execution.

The filed orders are organized in such a way that they may be retrieved in the same order that they are executed. Buy market orders are grouped separately from sell market orders. In the buy group, the highest price follows the market orders, and other orders are filed in order of descending limit price. In the sell group, the lowest price follows the market order which is then followed by other orders in order of ascending prices.

The order room employees have to keep track of the orders as they are executed. As the marketplaces open for trading and orders begin to get executed, the reports of execution are relayed to the entering branch, and a copy of the trade is sent to P&S for further processing. As the prices of securities on various markets fluctuate, the order room makes certain that orders are being executed as they should be. For example, if the market price of a security falls below the price of a buy limit order, the order room must send an inquiry to the point of execution asking for a report.

Order entries, executions, and reports flow into and out of the order room during the trading day.

CLOSING ACTIVITIES

At the close of the market, last-minute requests for reports are made. After the market closes, the order department enters its close-out routines. Inquiries from branches are researched. Orders not entitled to a report get a *nothing done* (ND) response. Those that cannot be answered are held overnight for resolution the next business day.

Adds and Outs

On newly entered but unexecuted good-til-cancelled orders, commitment notices must be sent to the clients and their stockbrokers. GTC orders that are either executed or cancelled also call for the dissemination of notices. Newly entered GTC orders require *add* notices. Cancellations of former GTC orders are *outs*; the cancellation and the adds form contains the details of the order and the action taken. Hence this routine is known as *adds and outs*. Adds are "added" to the open order, or GTC, file; cancels and executions are deleted, or taken "out." Customers receive add or cancellation notices and, for executions, confirmations.

ODD-LOT ORDERS

The standard unit of trading is called a *round lot*. Orders for less than a round lot are known as an *odd lots*. (See Figure 34-5).

Example: Most stocks trade in 100-share round lots; so orders for one to 99 shares are odd lots. In GNMAs, $1,000,000 is a round lot; any lesser dollar amount is an odd lot. Five corporate bonds are a round lot; less is an odd lot, etc.

While round lots are readily traded as units, odd lots in listed securities have to be handled by a *specialist firm*. This type of firm among other key functions buys or sells round lots in the open market to offset inventory imbalances resulting from odd lot transactions. On the floor of either the NYSE or Amex, specialists maintain positions in their assigned securities. Against these positions, they execute odd lot orders entered by member firms on behalf of their clients. In the OTC marketplace, dealers perform this specialist function.

The order room monitors odd lot orders, making certain that orders are filled appropriately.

FIGURE 34-5. *An odd lot order.*

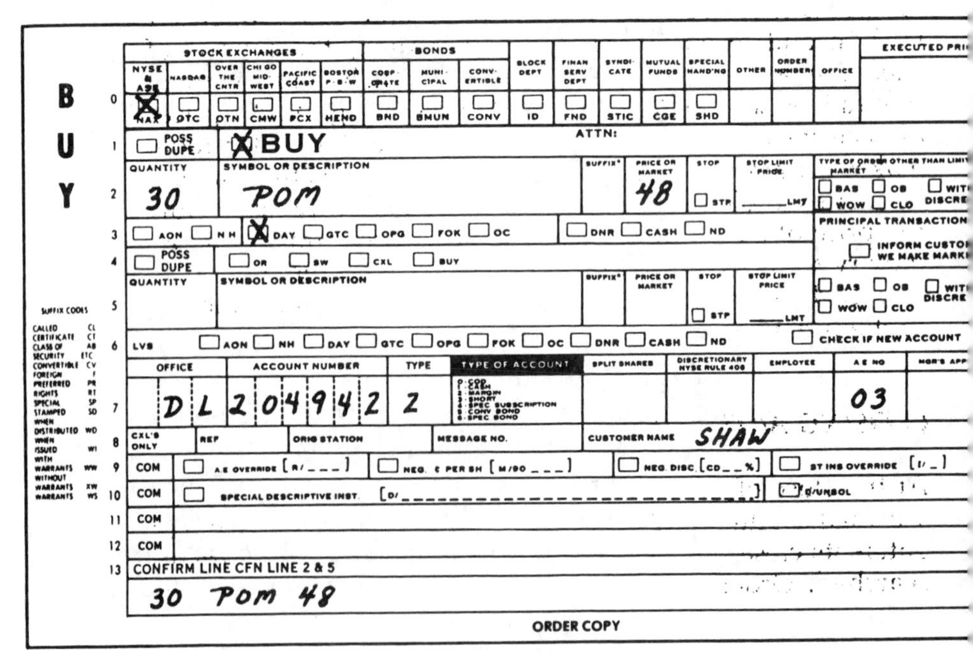

B U Y

0 STOCK EXCHANGES: NYSE & ASE (X) NAX; NASDAQ OTC; OVER THE CNTR OTN; CHI GO MID-WEST CMW; PACIFIC COAST PCX; BOSTON P-B-W HSNO — BONDS: CORP-ORATE BND; MUNI-CIPAL BMUN; CONV-ERTIBLE CONV — BLOCK DEPT ID; FINAN SERV DEPT FND; SYNDI-CATE STIC; MUTUAL FUNDS CGE; SPECIAL HAND'NG SHD; OTHER; ORDER NUMBER; OFFICE; EXECUTED PRI[CE]

1 POSS DUPE — (X) BUY — ATTN:

2 QUANTITY: 30 — SYMBOL OR DESCRIPTION: POM — SUFFIX — PRICE OR MARKET: 48 — STOP: STP — STOP LIMIT PRICE: LMT — TYPE OF ORDER OTHER THAN LIMIT MARKET: BAS, OB, WIT[H] DISCRE[TION], WOW, CLO

3 AON, NH, (X) DAY, GTC, OPG, FOK, OC — DNR, CASH, ND — PRINCIPAL TRANSACTION

4 POSS DUPE — OR, SW, CXL, BUY — INFORM CUSTO[MER] WE MAKE MARK[ET]

5 QUANTITY — SYMBOL OR DESCRIPTION — SUFFIX — PRICE OR MARKET — STOP: STP — STOP LIMIT PRICE: LMT — BAS, OB, WIT[H] DISCRE[TION], WOW, CLO

6 LVS — AON, NH, DAY, GTC, OPG, FOK, OC, DNR, CASH, ND — CHECK IF NEW ACCOUNT

7 OFFICE: DL — ACCOUNT NUMBER: 204942 — TYPE: 2 — TYPE OF ACCOUNT: 0: COD, 1: CASH, 2: MARGIN, 3: SHORT, 4: SPEC SUBSCRIPTION, 5: CONV BOND, 6: SPEC BOND — SPLIT SHARES — DISCRETIONARY NYSE RULE 408 — EMPLOYEE — AE NO: 03 — MGR'S APP

8 CXL'S ONLY — REF — ORIG STATION — MESSAGE NO. — CUSTOMER NAME: SHAW

9 COM — A.E. OVERRIDE [R/___] — NEG. ¢ PER SH [M/90 ___] — NEG. DISC [CD__%] — ST INS OVERRIDE [I/_]

10 COM — SPECIAL DESCRIPTIVE INST. [D/___] — D/UNSOL

11 COM

12 COM

13 CONFIRM LINE CFN LINE 2 & 5

30 POM 48

ORDER COPY

SUFFIX CODES: CALLED CL; CERTIFICATE CT; CLASS OF AB ETC; SECURITY; CONVERTIBLE CV; FOREIGN F; PREFERRED PR; RIGHTS RT; SPECIAL SP; STAMPED SD; WHEN DISTRIBUTED WD; WHEN ISSUED WI; WITH WARRANTS WW; WITHOUT WARRANTS XW; WARRANTS WS

SUMMARY

The order room accepts orders, routes them to the points of execution, and generally ensures that orders are handled properly.

The order room handles orders for both listed and over-the-counter securities. As orders flow from the branches, through the order room, and to the point of execution, reports of execution flow back to the branches and into operations for processing.

CHAPTER 35

OTC and Exchange Facilities

Orders must be executed within the framework of the regulations set by the prevailing authorities. In the OTC marketplace, trades must conform to the guidelines and rules of the National Association of Security Dealers (NASD). On the New York Stock Exchange, trades must comply with NYSE floor procedures. The Amex has its rules, etc. As such, rules and procedures are in place to ensure fair and equitable dealing between industry participants and to protect the public's interest. The regulatory authorities provide an important necessary, and ongoing type of control, not only of trading, but also of other aspects of processing.

Let's see how the order room interacts with first the OTC market and then with the exchanges.

THE OVER-THE-COUNTER MARKET

Many different securities trade in the OTC marketplace. These instruments include stocks, municipal bonds, U.S. Treasury and government obligations, commercial paper, banker's acceptances, GNMAs, Freddie Macs, and conventional options.

The OTC marketplace is flexible. It can adjust easily to the

FIGURE 35-1. *The order room in connection with the OTC and exchange markets.*

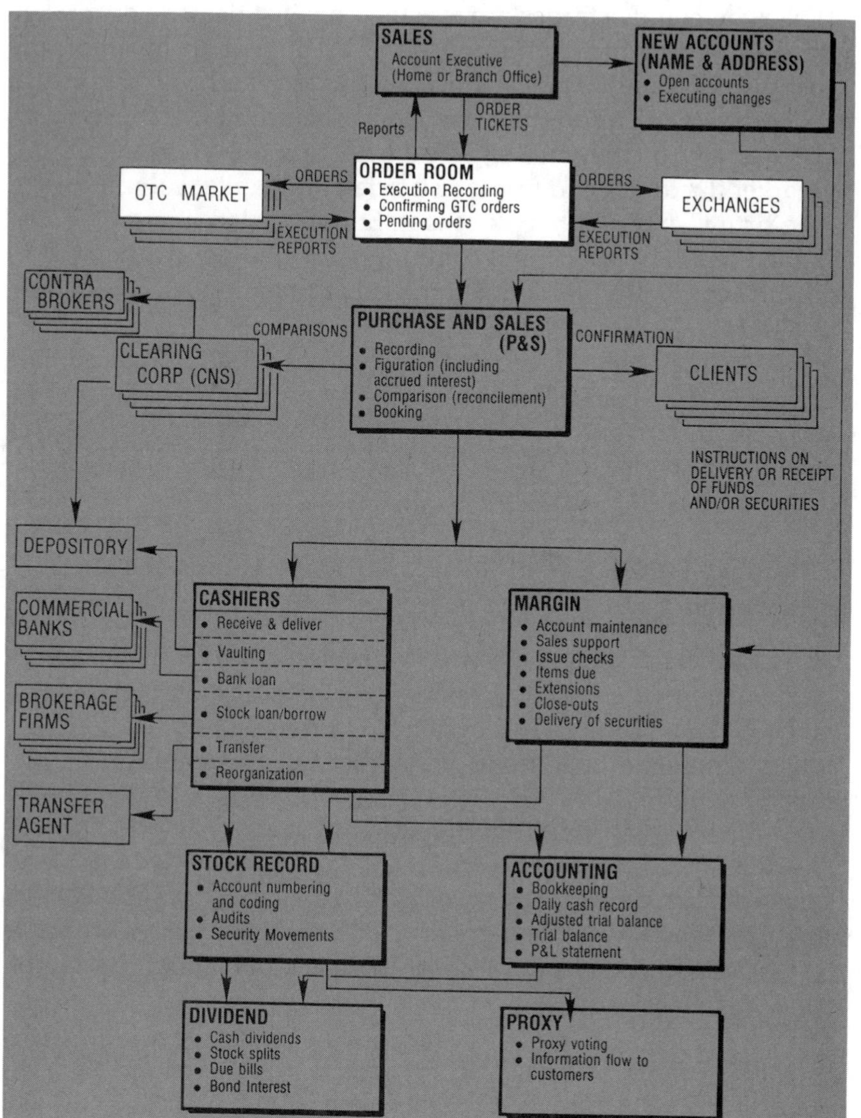

needs of any new type of issue or permit new issues of existing types to trade. In other words, the marketplace affords liquidity for investors and speculator/clients who wish to trade.

Inventory

Over-the-counter trades are executed against dealers, or market makers. These firms commit capital by buying an inventory in certain securities. Traders for these firms take positions in the chosen securities and trade against it. Their motive is the same as that of any other investor of capital—to make a profit. As the market fluctuates and prices rise or fall, the capital committed by the firm is exposed to risk of loss. Simply stated, there isn't any difference between capital committed for trading inventory and capital committed for any other kind of inventory. If you cannot sell it for a profit then you have a loss.

As in all other industries, inventory is usually financed. Because lenders charge interest on the money loaned and used to pay for the inventory, the financing represents an expense. As interest costs rise, the dealers' ability to earn profits diminishes.

National Association of Security Dealers Automated Quotation

OTC dealers display their inventoried securities on the National Association of Security Dealers Automated Quotation service (NASDAQ). Through this system of terminals, brokerage firms' sales offices trading desks, and other departments can access current quotes.

There are three NASDAQ levels:

Level I, Nominal Quote: Reveals the best highest bid and lowest offer made by dealers.

Level II, Dealer's Quote: Displays each quote and the dealer making the market.

Level III, Dealer's Entry: Permits dealers to change their quotes.

When an order is turned over to traders in the OTC marketplace, they check the dealers' quotes on the NASDAQ terminal.

Example: Stone, Forrest & Rivers makes markets in some but not all issues. One of the issues in which it acts as a dealer is Electra Century &

Co. Stone, Forrest & Rivers is one of three dealers that have selected this security. At this moment their quotes are:

	Bid	*Offer*
Stone, Forrest & Rivers	46 1/4	1/2
Kearney Securities	46 1/8	3/8
Medaglion, Inc.	46	3/8

The three quotes and the dealers making them appear on levels II and III of NASDAQ. On level I, you would see "46 1/4-3/8 but *not* the dealer's name. This level is used in SF&R's branch offices. Traders having orders to buy or sell Electra Century & Co. would quote the issue using level II or III. Apparently, SF&R is looking to buy and increase its inventory because it is making the highest *bid*. Any trader having an order to sell can contact Stone, Forrest & Rivers to negotiate a trade. A trader with an order to buy would contact either Kearney Securities or Medaglion, Inc.

Types of Quotes

In the OTC market, a negotiated market, dealers' quotes are either "firm" or "subject." *Firm quotes* are prices at which dealers must trade and which must represent at least one round lot. A *subject quote* is a bid or offer that is subject to verification with an interested party.

The OTC market is considered "negotiated" because quantities greater than a round lot may have to be negotiated.

Example: Kearney and Medaglion seem to be willing to sell Electra at prices lower than SF& R. Another firm, Russell, Rini & Morse, has a customer wanting to buy 1,000 shares at the market. The trader calls Kearney with the order and discovers that the firm will sell 1,000 shares as follows:

100 @ 46 3/8 (quote)
300 @ 46 1/2
300 @ 46 5/8
300 @ 46 3/4

Medaglion is willing to sell 1,000 shares as follows:

100 @ 46 3/8
500 @ 46 1/2
400 @ 46 5/8

Upon calling Stone, Forrest & Rivers, the trader from Russell is told "1,000 @ 46½." Russell's trader could buy 100 from Kearney @ 46⅜, 100 from Medaglion @ 46⅜, and the remaining 800 from Stone—but would buy all 1,000 from SF&R because they have the best price.

Dealers and brokers in the OTC market quote securities by means of *inside quotes,* which are not the prices the public would pay or receive. Instead, they are meant just for the execution of a trade between brokerage firms.

The reason for inside quotes is the OTC firms act as principals, or dealers; they buy and sell for their own accounts. Their customers are therefore really buying or selling from the dealer, not from the customer of another dealer. The brokerage firm does not execute a trade on behalf of the customer; it buys from or sells to the customer directly. The fact that the firm might have purchased the security only minutes before selling it to the customer does not matter. The customer has made a purchase and the seller is entitled to a profit.

In the OTC market, this profit is called the *mark-up*. No commission is charged, as in a listed security transaction. Instead, the markup is included in the total charge to the customer, called *first money*. Whereas in a listed stock transaction, a customer knows the commission, all the customer sees in an OTC trade is the total charge.

Example Russell, Rini & Morse trader purchases 1,000 shares, the firm adds, say, 1/8-point, or $12.50, mark-up per 100 shares as its profit. No commission is charged to Russell's client. The confirmation shows:

B/S	*Quantity*	*Price*	*First Money*	*Commission*	*Net Money*
Bought	1,000	46⅝	$46,625	0	$46,675

The same principle applies to a sale in the OTC market. When a customer wants to sell a security in the OTC market, the dealer charges a "mark-down." The dealer gets an inside quote, buys the security from the customer at one price, and sells it to a market maker at a higher price. The difference between the price the broker pays to the customer and what he/she gets from the market maker is the *mark-down.*

In effect, the OTC customer pays slightly more when buying and receives less when selling.

BONDS IN THE OTC MARKET

Municipal securities trade OTC because of their general *thinness* of issue, that is, the infrequency that a particular issue will trade. In most cases, most of the trading in a particular municipal bond occurs when it is first issued. After that, trading subsides, only to reappear sporadically during the issue's life.

Municipal bond traders therefore cannot make markets in a particular issue on an ongoing basis. They can, however, make markets in particular types of issues. An individual trader's inventory is composed of "pieces" of many different muni issues. Clients wanting to purchase municipal securities are concerned with tax exposure, bond rating (or safety), and yield. The particular issue is of secondary importance.

Example: A client of Stone, Forrest & Rivers' New York office is interested in acquiring municipal bonds. The client's broker, L. Christenson, discusses various possibilities with the client after obtaining the current list of inventory positions from SF&R's muni trading desk.

Christenson's client, who lives in New York State, is interested in debt instruments of that state. Christenson has informed the client of the tax consequences and the amount of risk the client should be willing take. They decide on bonds of an "A" rating or better (bonds are rated according to their financial strength), with 10 to 12 years to maturity. The client and account executive review the inventory list:

$10,000 New York Thruway: 8% F-A 2005 8.50 basis

$25,000 Buffalo High School District: 7 1/2 M&S 2005 8.90 basis

$15,000 New York State Housing Auth: 8 1/4 A&O 2007 8.60 basis

From this "menu," Christenson's client will select the desired muni.

Remember that, in a basis quote, the bid side is always higher than the offer. The quote of 8.50-8.25 on a muni could translate to a dollar quote of $91\frac{1}{2}$-$91\frac{3}{4}$. A few muni bonds trade actively and therefore sell at dollar prices. Quotes on these dollar resemble those on corporate bonds.

Dealer's Broker

A certain type of brokerage firm has as its customers the many dealers and brokers trading in the marketplace. This type of firm is called a *dealer's broker.* Firms inform a dealer's broker of what they are looking to sell or buy. The dealer's broker then communicates the request through a network to other participants.

Example: The SF&R municipal trading desk does not have any state of Oklahoma bonds in inventory, because SF&R does not have a branch in Oklahoma and its public is not interested in that state's issues. To accommodate a sudden request to buy or sell munis of Oklahoma, SF&R's trader could call either another firm that maintains a market in this security or a dealer's broker. The dealer's (or broker's) broker, with its extensive communication network, can give SF&R full view to the marketplace, and the responses will give SF&R and its client a better selection to choose from.

THE EXCHANGES

Exchanges make up the other part of the trading environment. Trading in this marketplace are listed options, many stocks, corporate bonds, some Treasury issues, commodities, and futures.

Stock Exchange

The NYSE and the Amex are the primary equity, or stock, exchanges. Both provide investors with a place to buy and sell national and international equity securities.

New York Stock Exchange (NYSE). Under NYSE rules, firms cannot own memberships (or seats); only individuals can. The seat-owning individuals are known as *members,* and firms that have members in their employ are known as *member firms.*

The New York Stock Exchange operates through four types of members:

1. *Specialists* are assigned securities by the NYSE. The specialists' function is twofold: to execute orders for the securities entrusted to them; and to maintain a fair and

orderly market by buying or selling for their own accounts and risk.

2. *Commission house brokers* execute orders entered by their employer-firms.
3. *Two-dollar brokers* execute orders that they receive from other member firms.
4. *Registered floor traders* execute orders in securities for their own accounts, and they are governed by a special set of rules enforced by the exchange.

The NYSE also operates a *bond room*. Brokers in this area are either commission house or two-dollar brokers. Specialists do not operate in the bond market.

American Stock Exchange (Amex). Amex operations are similar to those of the NYSE. The big difference, however, is how the firms' floor personnel communicate with their brokers. The system of hand signals used on the Amex is a language all its own and very interesting to observe.

Automation. Most exchanges are developing automated order entry and reporting. The NYSE has *Designated Order Turnaround (DOT)*. The Amex has *post-execution reporting (PERS)* and *Amex option switching system* (*AMOS*). PHLX has PACE, and so on. Each such system enables member firms not only to transmit orders (given certain quantity constraints) to the point of execution, but also to receive reports back.

Other Equity Exchanges. The Pacific Stock Exchange, Midwest Stock Exchange, Philadelphia Stock Exchange, and Boston Stock Exchange provide similar services. Besides listing some of the more popular giant corporations, these other exchanges provide places for the listing of smaller or locally known companies.

To assist member firms in obtaining the best price possible, many exchanges have joined together to establish an *intermarket trading system*. This concept ensures that a client receives the best price possible regardless of which exchange the order is entered on.

Through a telecommunications network, the quotes for securities traded on more than one exchange (that is, *multitraded securities)* are shown on terminal screens. Orders are routed from one exchange to the floor of the exchange having the best bid offer. The order is executed and reported back to the exchange of entry. From there, the report is returned to the submitting firm, which in turn reports the execution to the client or principal who originated the order.

Listed Options

Conventional (OTC) *options* were custom-tailored to fit the needs of clients, and their prices were negotiated with a *put and call dealer*. OTC options offered little liquidity to investors because there was no central point to trade and each option was unique.

Listed option trading began in April 1973. when the Chicago Board Option Exchange (CBOE) was born. The CBOE standardized option contracts with fixed terms, thus allowing the public to buy and sell the exact same instrument.

Example: A listed option notation is XYZ Jan 50. All the options issued in XYZ and expiring in January expire the same day. Anyone who is interested in XYZ at around $50 per share would trade this option. Conventional options on XYZ might read "XYZ Jan 12-48½" "XYZ Jan 15-49¼," "XYZ Jan 16-50½"—with differing expiration dates and strike prices.

Rotation. CBOE options are open for business the same time as the markets of the underlying stock. But, before a class of options starts trading for the day, the underlying security must open for trading.

Options open for trading by a method known as *rotation*, by which each series is called out in order and trading in any series cannot begin until it is called. Once all the issues are called, trading can be conducted in all issues at once.

The Floor. There are two types of members on the CBOE: floor brokers and market makers. In addition, an exchange employee, known as an *order book official (OBO)*, executes customers' limit orders maintained on the limit order book.

Executing Orders. All orders entering the floor must be marked as representing a client, firm, or market maker. Order book officials are permitted to execute only client orders. Floor brokers can execute customer or firm orders, and of course, market makers execute their own orders.

Because the CBOE operates for the public, the order book official's quote has priority at a given price, over that of a floor broker. This rule ensures that the market is attending to the public's interest.

The CBOE assigns option classes to order book officials and monitors their performance. OBOs receive customer orders for their assigned classes from member firms. The orders are usually limit orders that are "booked" by price and the time of receipt. As the market prices of the options fluctuate, the OBOs execute the orders from their books.

Every order going to the floor of the CBOE must contain at lest seven pieces of information.

1. Time and date entered.
2. Buy or sell.
3. Open or close.
4. Quantity.
5. Type, class, and series of option.
6. Customer, firm, market maker.
7. Firm name or designation.

Example:

May 11 85 10:42

Buy	5	Calls	XYZ	Oct 50
(B/S)	(quantity)	(type)	(class)	(series)

Open
(Open/Close)

James Collis
(Customer)

Stone, Forrest & River
(Firm)

Date and Time. These are particularly important because, on most orders, the firm and other participants are held accountable for executions or lack of them.

Open/close. This entry informs what effect this trade will have on the principal's position (that is, on the account entering the order). *Open* either establishes a new position or increases an existing position. *Close* either eliminates or decreases an existing position. For trading purposes, this entry is important because an open order cannot be entered under certain conditions. In operations, the information becomes important in balancing and reconcilement.

Buy or Sell/Type, Class, Series. "Buy 5 call XYZ Oct 50" gives the instructions to the executing broker. The absence of a premium price tells the executing broker that this is a market order.

Customer, Firm, Market Maker. Market makers are assigned the options that they trade by the CBOE. It is their responsibility to buy and sell for their account and risk, to maintain liquidity in the marketplace.

Floor brokers execute both customer and firm orders, and the order must be so designated. Some member firms, however, use the services of other member firms to get orders executed on the floor. In this case, although the submitting firm is a "customer" of the executing firm, the floor brokers of the executing firm treat the orders of the other firm as if they were their own. Nevertheless, these orders must identify the principal—that is, who entered the order. If entered by the submitting firm for its own trading account, the order must carry the designation "firm." If entered by the submitting firm's customer, the order is marked "customer."

Other Exchanges. After the CBOE, listed options are also traded on the Amex, PHLX, PSE, and NYSE.

Futures Exchanges

Originally, futures trading was linked to the trading of commodities, that is agricultural products and precious metals. In recent years, the concept has grown to include oil or petroleum, currencies, indexes, and certain U.S. government debt instruments.

Today, futures are traded on exchanges such as the COMEX,

Chicago Board of Trade (CBT), Chicago Mercantile, (CME), and, more recently, the New York Futures Exchange (NYFE). On these exchanges, trading varies from calm to very hectic depending on the current interest in the underlying commodity. On the exchange floor, brokers and traders execute orders for contracts for future deliveries. As the so-called *futures* contract nears the end of its life, the spot or cash trading begins. At the end of this cycle, delivery takes place.

Example: Leitch & Co. International, an SF&R client, settles its commitments in international trade in many currencies. Leitch & Co. has contracted with an English company to deliver its product three months from now.

At that time, Leitch is to make payment in English pound sterling. With the value of the U.S. dollar fluctuating daily against all other currencies, the dollar could "fall" against the pound sterling within the next three months. If so, then Leitch & Co. will have to pay more dollars to settle the bill, thereby making less profit or even incurring a loss. If the dollar rises, Leitch & Co. will pay fewer dollars.

If the company does not want to speculate or expose itself to such risk, it may enter an order through its SF&R account executive to buy a three-month future on the pound sterling. By so doing, it locks in the dollar cost of the pound sterling. Three months from now, Leitch & Co. will *buy* the pound sterling at the futures contract price and use the pound to pay for its purchase.

SOME TYPICAL EXECUTIONS

Throughout the day, the SF&R order and trading staff are busy executing customers' orders, making markets, trading with other firms, and performing other functions.

Because SF&R is a multiproduct firm, it may receive orders for and trade in:

- Common stock, both listed and OTC
- Preferred stock.
- Corporate bonds.
- Municipal bonds and notes.
- U.S. government obligations.
- GNMAs, Freddie Macs, FNMAs, and Sallie Maes.

- Mutual funds.
- Options.
- Futures.
- Commercial paper (CP).
- Certificates of deposits (CDs).
- Banker's acceptances (BAs).

Let's follow some of these transactions.

Example: An order is received from SF&R's Boston office to "B 5 call POP DD @ 6."

1. "B" stands for "buy."
2. The "5 call" notation means 5 call options.
3. The code "POP" indicates an option on 100 shares of POP, Inc. common stock. Since POP options are traded on the Amex, the order is directed there.
4. The first "D" stands for the month. Since "D" is the fourth letter of the alphabet, it translates in call options to the fourth month of the year: April.
5. The second "D" represents a multiple of five. Again, "D" is the fourth letter, so it means $4 \times 5 = 20$.
6. The number "6" represents the limit price on the order.

This customer is therefore buying 5 call options on 5×100 shares of POP Inc. expiring in April with a strike price of 20.

The limit on the order is 6, or $6 per share of the underlying POP common stock. The limit translates $3,000 ($6 \times 100 \times 5$). The customer has entered a limit order so that, if the current market is above 6, the order will not be executed. If, on the other hand, the current offer is at or below, it will be executed at the best price available.

Example: Another order is received from SF&R's Atlanta branch: "B 50 JOM Mkt."

1. "B" indicates a buy order.
2. The order is for "50" shares, which is an odd lot.

3. The notation JOM is the symbol for Jet Operation Management, Inc., whose stock is traded on the NYSE.

The order is routed through the exchanges APARS (automatic pricing and reporting system), and it will be executed on the next round lot sale.

Example: The SF&R muni trader receives a municipal bond order from St. Paul, Minnesota, to "SL 50, St. Paul HSD#4 9% FA 2003 at 9.40."

1. "SL" means "sell long."
2. The number "50" means "$50,000 worth" (50 × $1,000).
3. "St. Paul, HSD #4" is the issuer—the St Paul Minnesota High School District #4.
4. This bond pays 9% per year.
5. "FA" indicates the months of interest payments: Half is paid February (F), and the other half in August (A).
6. The bond matures in 2003.
7. The price of "at 9.40" is a basis price, the bond's yield to the buyer is 9.40% if held to maturity. (Because the coupon rate is 9%, this bond is being offered below its face value of $50,000.)

SUMMARY

All orders have been entered, executed, and reported to their clients. We now enter the next phase of processing, purchase and sales.

One last note: Most exchanges permit—and even welcome—visits by the public. Take advantage of their invitations and watch "floors" in operation. If a picture is worth a thousand words, then seeing these exchanges in operation is worth millions.

CHAPTER 36

Purchase and Sales

With the order entered, executed, and reported to the stockbroker and client, the trade must now go through a series of steps leading to its settlement, which is handled by purchase and sales (P&S). Because each type of issue has its own settlement cycle, the P&S functions must be completed within the instrument's time constraints.

P&S processing is comprised primarily of four functions:

1. Recording.
2. Figuration.
3. Comparison (reconcilement).
4. Confirmation and Booking.

RECORDING

For processing control, each trade being processed must be coded with a series of identification numbers, some of which become a part of the firm's master security file. Each time a trade occurs, the P&S department records it and assigns the appropriate ID numbers.

CUSIP

CUSIP is an interindustry security identification numbering system. A CUSIP number consists of nine characters: The first six digits identify the issuer, and the last three identify the issue. Some firms use CUSIP numbers for their in-house processing. Others, because of their computer program constraints or other reasons, use their own numbering systems for in-house processing, but they use "conversion" programs to communicate through computer interfaces with firms that use the CUSIP system.

Blotter Code

The place of execution must also be coded. This identifier, known as the *blotter code,* is important for reconcilement later in the P&S cycle.

Example: Bonneville, Inc. is traded on the Amex. SF&R's unique number for the common stock of Bonneville, Inc. as occurring on the Amex is A1. A round lot trade has taken place and is now being prepared for processing the security identifier, 084312441, is placed on the report ticket, along with the blotter code A1, to identify it as an Amex trade.

Trade Number

The trade receives a unique "trade" number too. These numbers start with the number one each day, and each trade is then counted sequentially.

FIGURATION

In figuration, the P&S department computes the contract money, the commission, taxes, fees, and all other related money amounts. The *net* is what the client has to pay or receives.

First money is simply the quantity of securities in the trade times the price of execution, without any deductions.

Example:
100 shares BIL @ 42 = $4,200 first money
$1,000 bond ZAP 7% FA 2005 @ 94 = $940 first money
1 call option XYZ Oct 40 @ 6 = $600 first money.

On agency transactions, the *commission* is added to first money in the case of buys and subtracted from it in the case of sells. The commission schedule is set by the management of Stone, Forrest & Rivers. The firm may decide to base it on the number of shares, on total money, or by some other value method. P&S follows the schedule in the computation of commissions.

The federal government *taxes* sell transactions, in the form of a 1 (.01) cent SEC fee for every $300 of first money or fraction thereof. The tax is applicable only to sales of securities on national securities exchanges.

Some firms, at their discretion, add an additional charge for *postage* and *handling*. These charges are not uniform from one firm to another.

Example: SF&R's P&S department has the following transactions to figure:

In an OTC transaction, a client bought 100 shares of Regal Corp. at 15, net from SF&R's inventory. See Figure 36-1.

Because this is a principal transaction, no commission is charged. The mark-up is in the price, or first money.

100 shares Regal Corp. @ 15 = First money	$1,500
Commission, taxes and fees	+ 0
Net money	$1,500

The client owes SF&R $1,500.

In a listed transaction, a client sold 100 shares of Bonneville, Inc. on the Amex @ 42. See Figure 36-2.

Because this is a listed equity sale, it is subject to commission and fees. The SF&R commission schedule calls for a computation of 1% of first money.

100 Bonneville, Inc. @ 42		$4,200.00
Less: Commission ($4,200 × .01)	$ 42.00	
Less: SEC fee	.14	
Total deductions		42.14
Net money		$4,157.86

The client selling the 100 shares receives $4,157.86 for the security.

FIGURE 36-1. *Confirmation of purchase.*

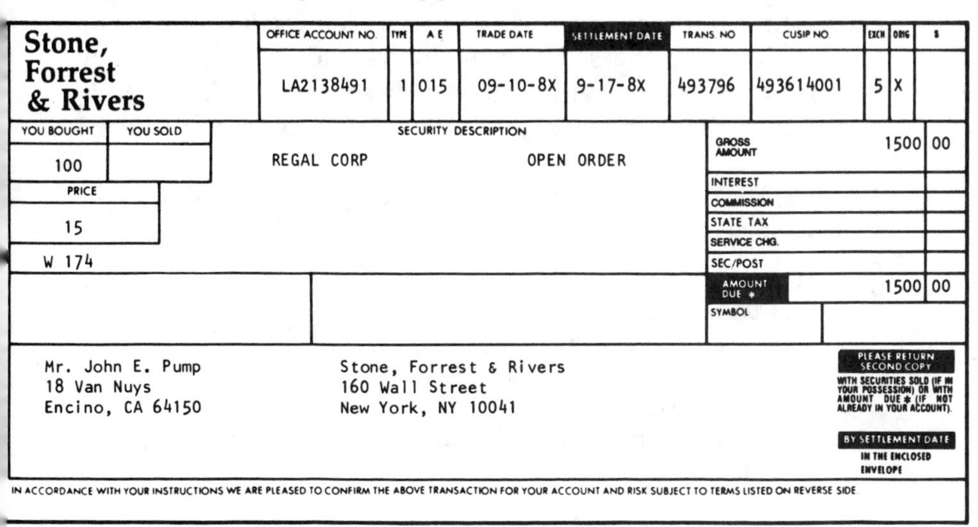

Stone, Forrest & Rivers

OFFICE ACCOUNT NO.	TYPE	A E	TRADE DATE	SETTLEMENT DATE	TRANS. NO.	CUSIP NO.	EXCH	ORIG	$
LA2138491	1	015	09-10-8X	9-17-8X	493796	493614001	5	X	

YOU BOUGHT	YOU SOLD	PRICE	SECURITY DESCRIPTION
100		15	REGAL CORP OPEN ORDER

W 174

GROSS AMOUNT	1500	00
INTEREST		
COMMISSION		
STATE TAX		
SERVICE CHG.		
SEC/POST		
AMOUNT DUE *	1500	00
SYMBOL		

Mr. John E. Pump
18 Van Nuys
Encino, CA 64150

Stone, Forrest & Rivers
160 Wall Street
New York, NY 10041

PLEASE RETURN SECOND COPY WITH SECURITIES SOLD (IF IN YOUR POSSESSION) OR WITH AMOUNT DUE * (IF NOT ALREADY IN YOUR ACCOUNT). BY SETTLEMENT DATE IN THE ENCLOSED ENVELOPE

IN ACCORDANCE WITH YOUR INSTRUCTIONS WE ARE PLEASED TO CONFIRM THE ABOVE TRANSACTION FOR YOUR ACCOUNT AND RISK SUBJECT TO TERMS LISTED ON REVERSE SIDE.

Corporate bonds pay interest every six months to the registered holder. In other words, anyone who owns the bond on the interest record date receives the full six months of interest. On any transaction occurring between the interest payment dates, the buyer and the seller must settle the interest accrued to the settlement date.

FIGURE 36-2. *Confirmation of sale.*

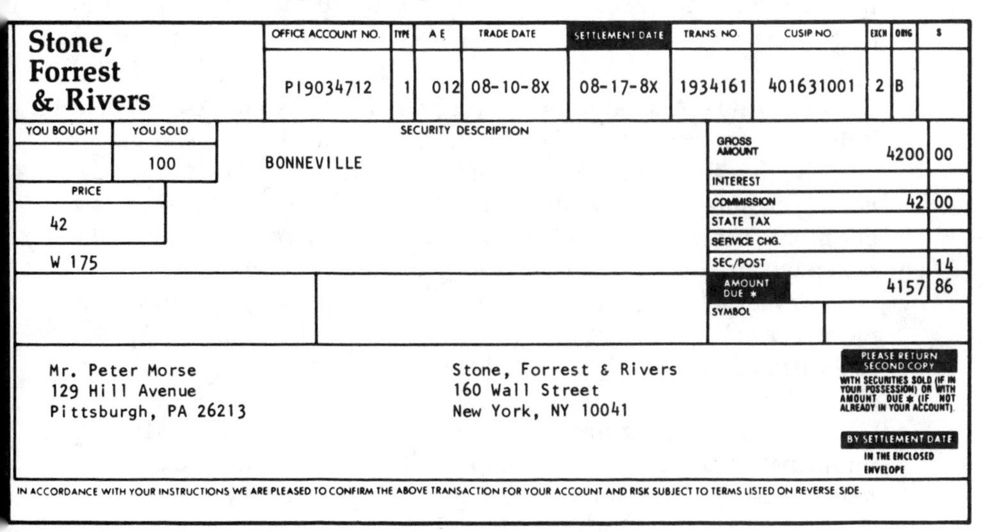

Stone, Forrest & Rivers

OFFICE ACCOUNT NO.	TYPE	A E	TRADE DATE	SETTLEMENT DATE	TRANS. NO.	CUSIP NO.	EXCH	ORIG	$
P19034712	1	012	08-10-8X	08-17-8X	1934161	401631001	2	B	

YOU BOUGHT	YOU SOLD	PRICE	SECURITY DESCRIPTION
	100	42	BONNEVILLE

W 175

GROSS AMOUNT	4200	00
INTEREST		
COMMISSION	42	00
STATE TAX		
SERVICE CHG.		
SEC/POST		14
AMOUNT DUE *	4157	86
SYMBOL		

Mr. Peter Morse
129 Hill Avenue
Pittsburgh, PA 26213

Stone, Forrest & Rivers
160 Wall Street
New York, NY 10041

PLEASE RETURN SECOND COPY WITH SECURITIES SOLD (IF IN YOUR POSSESSION) OR WITH AMOUNT DUE * (IF NOT ALREADY IN YOUR ACCOUNT). BY SETTLEMENT DATE IN THE ENCLOSED ENVELOPE

IN ACCORDANCE WITH YOUR INSTRUCTIONS WE ARE PLEASED TO CONFIRM THE ABOVE TRANSACTION FOR YOUR ACCOUNT AND RISK SUBJECT TO TERMS LISTED ON REVERSE SIDE.

Corporate bond interest is computed on a 360-day basis. Because of the transaction between purchase and seller, accrued interest belongs to the seller. It is always added to first money. Because commission belongs to the client's firm, it is added to cost in a purchase, but subtracted from the proceeds in a sale.

Example: The purchase transaction occurred on trade date May 9, with settlement on May 16.

First money:	
\$1,000 Continental 9% FA 2003 @ 92 =	\$920.00
Plus: Accrued interest	
(\$1,000 × .09 × 105/360)	26.25
Total contract money	\$946.25
Plus: Commission (\$5/bond, with minimum of \$30)	+ 30.00
	\$976.25

SF&R's client would pay \$976.25 for these bonds.

SF&R's P&S department must be careful in computing interest. Some bonds, such as income or adjustment bonds, may not carry accrued interest. Neither do bonds that are already in default; they trade *flat* (that is, without accrued interest).

P&S must also be aware of the payment periods on recently issued bonds. Many new bonds are not issued on their interest payment dates. So their first interest payment may be for less than six months (a *short coupon*) or for more than six months (a *long coupon*).

Example: An F&A bond pays interest every February and August first. If the bonds are issued on March 1, the first payment on August 1 is for only five months (a short coupon). If the bonds are issued in January, the issuing organization may not want to go through the expense of paying one month's interest; instead, it might pay seven month's interest on the next payment date on August 1 (a long coupon).

Paying a long or short coupon payment on the first interest payment date is based on the date of issuance, which is commonly known as the *dated date*. After the first period has passed, the bond reverts to its six-month cycle.

Instruments that trade at basis prices, such as T bills and many municipal securities, have to compute differently. SF&R's P&S would refer to basis books to arrive at the equivalent first money.

Example:

In a 100,000 commercial paper transaction, a client buys a 10% rate on Le Baron Loan Corp. 90-day paper.

The purchaser of this discounted instrument receives full face value if it is held to maturity. The difference between the value paid at the time of purchase and the value received at maturity is the interest earned on the money, and it translates into yield.

Full face value:

$$100{,}000 - \frac{90}{360} \times \frac{10}{100} \times \frac{100{,}000}{1}$$

Less: Discount (1×1×2,500)	$100,000
	– 2,500
Client pays	$ 97,500

While crude, this computation satisfies our purpose here. This client pays $97,500. At maturity, 90 days later, the client receives $100,000. The difference of $2,500, the interest, represents 90 days (a quarter-year) at 10%.

COMPARISON

Whether SF&R's clients have transacted as principals for the firm's trading accounts or as agents against other firms through SF&R, there must be an offset for every account buying or selling. The customer accounts, the trading accounts, and other accounts must all agree in quantity, security, and first money.

Options Comparison

Since SF&R trades options on behalf of their clients, the vast majority of their transactions are in listed options. Let's follow the listed option comparison process. (The comparison procedure for options is an intelligent and simple one.) Because listed options settle next day—that is, on the next business day—comparison takes place on trade dates. All option transactions are sent to the comparison facility of the exchange of execution for comparison.

Executed	*Comparison Facility*
Chicago Board Option Exchange	CBOE Facility
Amex & NYSE Options	Securities Industry Automation Corporation
Philadelphia Stock Exchange	Stock Clearing Corporation of Philadelphia
Pacific Stock Exchange	Pacific Clearing Corporation

Since SF&R is a member of the CBOE, the firm executes its options transactions on the CBOE and sends the trades to the exchange's facility for comparison on the night of trade date. Each customer-side transaction must have a street-side (an opposing broker), and the two sides must match in all aspects. Of some importance is the fact that SF&R records reveal whom we traded with. More important is that the opposing firm agrees with the details of the trade.

The trade data that SF&R submits for comparison contains the following information.

1. Its clearing member's number.
2. The opposing firm's clearing number.
3. Bought or sold.
4. The terms of the trade:
   a. Option description.
   b. Quantity.
   c. Price and or first money.
5. Trade date and settlement date.

Options trades require the additional information:

6. The principal behind the trade: customer, firm, or market maker/specialist.
7. Whether the transaction is establishing or terminating a position, that is, open or close.

For comparison, only the first five items are necessary. Items 6 and 7 are important in later processing.

The comparison facility takes input from all the clearing member firms. Once the data is collected, the clearing corporation performs a comparison routine. Each clearing firm then receives a report showing which trades compare and which do not. SF&R submits to the clearing facility trades that the opposing firm either doesn't know or doesn't agree with. In turn, opposing brokers submit trades that SF&R doesn't know or doesn't agree with.

SF&R receives these reports in the early evening of trade date. The results are verified against the customer-side positions and then against the actual floor reports. SF&R makes as many corrections as possible and resubmits the adjustments to the comparison facility. All the other firms are doing the same. When the correcting entries are received, the central facility performs another comparison match.

The final comparison reports are sent to the member firm later that evening.

ROTNS. Any trade that SF&R still needs to balance, but that was not compared, must be returned to the floor of execution for reconcilement. This procedure, known as *out trades* or ROTN takes place the day after the trade.

The ROTN form (Figure 36-3) informs the executing broker on the floor of execution of the problem in comparing the transaction. The form states the problem: a price difference, security difference, opposing broker name difference, or other differences. The two executing brokers meet, discuss, and resolve the ROTN, preferably before the market opens for the day's trading.

Once P&S receives the corrected data from the floor broker, it processes the trade. Some corrections affect customer transactions, while others affect the street-side entries. Still others do not affect SF&R's books at all, because the opposing firm has to make the corrections.

Corrections being made against customer positions are very expensive to process. The firm earns income when the original trade is processed. Changes to the original entry necessitate the processing of a cancel and a rebill (two separate entries)—for no additional revenue. The two entries follow the same operating cycle as the original transaction, but the client pays only one commission. So the two of the three entries are pure expense.

This is the procedure for questioned, or uncompared, trades.

FIGURE 36-3.

N.Y. STOCK EXCHANGE QUESTIONED OPTIONS TRADE

MAJOR BROKER CHANGE COPY

CODE	TRANS. NUMBER	TIME HR.	TIME MIN.	B/S	CONTRACTS	P PUT C CALL	OPTION SERIES SYMBOL	EXPIRATION MO.	EXPIRATION YR	STRIKE PRICE DOLLAR	STRIKE PRICE FRACTION	PREMIUM DOLLARS	PREMIUM FRACTION
	025207	02	53	S	2	C	NDX	MAY	85	215			15/16
C	025207												

CLEAR NO.	EXEC. BROKER I.D.	TRANS. (O) (C)	ACCT. F.C.S. P.N.	CERT	CONTRA CLEAR NO.	CONTRA BROKER NO.	TRADE DATE MO.	TRADE DATE DAY	OPTIONAL DATA	PRIM OCC CL. NO.	TRADER CODE	EXCH. I.D.
035	4074	O	C		590	4466	04	19	SQ 84			7
035												

THIS CONSTITUTES NOTICE THAT THE ABOVE TRADE INPUT WAS REJECTED FROM CLEARANCE PROCESSING AND MUST BE RESOLVED IN ACCORDANCE WITH OPTION RULE 764

BUY: OK DK — BUYING FIRM: OK DK — GIVE UP BROKER

SELL: OK DK — SELLING FIRM: OK DK — GIVE UP BROKER

TO: ______ (EXECUTING BROKER)

PAGE 3 OF 3 NYSE ______ OTHER SIDE (EXECUTING BROKER)

Option Clearing Corporation. Options, unlike stock or corporate and municipal bonds, go through a different type of comparison process. In the case of stocks or bonds, comparison occurs at a clearing corporation and settles in a depository. Listed options, however, compare at a computer facility of the exchange and, after comparison, are forwarded to Option Clearing Corporation for position and margining. Since listed options are in book entry form only (that is, there is no physical certificate), there isn't a need for a depository.

Listed options settle the next business day. That is, comparison is effected on trade date, and the trades are settled the next business day.

The exchange on which the particular option trades provides a facility for comparison. Chicago Board Option Exchange (CBOE) compares transactions of these members at their facility. Options executed on the AMEX or NYSE are compared using the facility of SIAC (Security Industry Automation Corporation). Options executed on the PHLX are compared at SCCP (Stock Clearing Corporation of Philadelphia). Trades executed on the Pacific Stock Exchange are compared through Pacific Clearing Corp., which really consists of the SIAC computers.

The comparison procedure, whether floor-driven or submitted from "upstairs," is the same as that described for equities, except the cycle is far shorter.

If comparison doesn't occur on trade date, the problem is returned to the floor for reconcilement the next morning. *All* option exchanges mandate that problems of the previous day be resolved *before* the opening of the day's business. This control is important: A new day's business doesn't begin until the previous day's work is cleared up. The respective brokers have until that afternoon to trade out of errors.

Trades returned to the CBOE floor for reconcilement are referred to as *ROTN (rejected option trade notices)*. On the floor of the AMEX, they are referred to as *DKs (don't knows)*, and on the NYSE the term *QOTNs (questionable option trade notices)* is used.

Since trades that are compared on trade date at the various exchange facilities are forwarded to Option Clearing Corporation (OCC) that night, trades that are reconciled the next morning (T+1) are not included in the various firm positions maintained at OCC. These reconciled transactions become part of the next day's transactions and therefore part of the next day's balances.

Option trades (and futures for that matter) have two cycles, or "lives." The first is the trade, which must be compared against the opposing firm; the second is the effect the trade has on an exercisable or assignable position. Remember that a holder, or owner, of an option has the privilege of exercising, whereas a writer, or seller, has the obligation to perform the terms of the contract, should the position be assigned.

When a client or the firm's proprietary account buys an option, the purchase may be to establish a holder's position, or to close out (trade out) of a previous written position. In a similar fashion, the seller of an option may be establishing a written position or closing out (trading out of) a previous owner's, or holder's, position.

A buyer of an option who wants to establish a position (that is, be an owner), is said to be *buying open*. To unwind, close out, or get out of a buy open position, the holder can exercise, or *sell closed* (sell to close). On the other side, where a position is established, a writer is said to be a *sell open* (selling to open a position). To unwind, close out, or get out of a written position, the writer can *buy close* (buy to close). A writer's position may be terminated by OCC by assigning an exercise.

Buy open	=	Sell close, Exercise
Buy close, Assignment	=	Sell open

Or

Bo	=	Sc, E
Bc, A	=	So

Because all options expire, expiration is not included in the equation (all unexercised positions in an expired option go "flat").

After trade comparison and position adjustment have occurred, all long (holder, buyers') positions are against Option Clearing Corporation, as are all sellers' (writers' or short) positions. In other words, OCC stands between all holders and writers. Exercises by holders of options are made against OCC, and OCC turns them around and makes assignment on a random basis. This feature permits option users to go into and out of positions with ease, with the contra parties to the trades not caring. In over-the-counter options, the buyers and sellers stay locked; to trade out of a position usually means that both sides of the original trade must agree to the close-out. Or, if one side trades out of the position, that side is said to go *long and short*, since the original contra party is not obligated to accept the new position.

Examples:

Listed option

1. Frei & Cook buys 1 call from Wellington & Co.
2. The trade compares.
3. Frei & Cook is a holder against OCC.
4. Wellington & Co. is a writer against OCC.

Frei & Cook sells the call to Bahl & Puck, who has no previous position.

1. The trade compares.
2. Bahl & Puck is a holder against OCC.
3. Wellington & Co. remains as a writer against OCC.
4. Frei & Cook is flat (i.e., has no position).

In the case of an over-the-counter option, which does not use the facility of a clearing corporation, the result would be different.

1. Frei & Cook buys a call from Wellington & Co.
2. The trade compares.
3. Frei & Cook owns a call, written by Wellington & Co.
4. Frei & Cook wants to close out position and contacts Wellington & Co. If Wellington & Co. is interested, it will buy the call back from Frei & Cook. Both go flat. If Wellington is not interested:

    1. Frei & Cook sells the call to Bahl & Puck.
    2. Frei & Cook remains long against Wellington & Co.
    3. Frei & Cook is now a writer against Bahl & Puck.

Option trades originate either with customers, a firm proprietary, a specialist, or a market-maker. As these four types of accounts represent distinctly different interests, their positions must be maintained separately and may not be commingled. This is true for both firm records and the firm's positions at OCC. To maintain control of the firm's internal and external records at OCC, trades being processed through the system carry specific designations so that they will be carried in the correct designated account.

Firms that enter transactions for their own account(s) and for their clients may code client accounts and may not code proprietary trades, since any trade not coded would automatically become a firm trading entry. Firms that enter trades for their clients have to code each client's transaction, because each position belongs to the individual client and may not be netted. For position purposes, clients who own options must be kept apart from clients who wrote options.

The firms that trade for themselves are given a lost of latitude on how their OCC reports are presented. A firm may want a *net* report, that is, all proprietary trading netted into one total position, or a *broad* report, with the total long and the total short. The firm may also request separate reports by trading account.

The daily position reports submitted by OCC to their members reflect the data that the corporation has received from the various comparison facilities. This data, in turn, represents the information received from and/or agreed to by the specific clearing firm.

Example: Stone, Forrest & Rivers is one of the clearing firms. It enters orders for and reports option executions to its clients, as well as trade options for its own proprietary accounts. Therefore, it receives two sets of reports each day: one for its client positions, and one for its proprietary positions. We will review the proprietary position first:

	Holders	*Writers*
Previous position		30
	3	
		5
	10	
		25
	50	
		5
	20	
Closing position	18	

All of the transactions under the word *Holders* are buys, whereas all the transactions under the word *Writers* are sales. As SF&R nets its proprietary trading, it doesn't matter if the trade is to buy open, buy closed, sell open, or sell closed. Buy transactions simply increase a holder's position or reduce written position, whereas sell transactions increase a written position or reduce holders. The result is always a net of either a holder's or writer's position.

Client positions are different. As each client's transaction affects that client's position, the effect of the transaction must be noted on the original ticket. This notation of effect on a position carries through to the OCC daily position report.

Example:

OPTION CALLS ZUP OCT 40—CUSTOMER, APRIL 25, 19XX

	Holders	*Writers*
Previous position	30	15
O		5
O	3	
C	10	
C		6
O	4	
E		2
A	5	
Closing position	29	5

SF&R client's position at the beginning of the day was holders 30 and writers 15 contracts. The activity for the day affecting holders consisted of the buy open of (3+4) contracts, the sell close of 6 contracts, and an exercise of 2 contracts. Transactions affecting writers consisted of a sell open of 5 contracts, a buy close of 10 contracts, and an assignment of 5 contracts.

Applying the activity to the opening position, we have 20 holders (30+3+4–6–2), writers 5 (15+5–10–5). The SF&R closing client's position for the day is holders 29, writers 5.

The premiums involved with all of the option transactions for SF&R's clients and their proprietary positions are also netted into one balance figure per category. This net is added or subtracted from the previous day's balances. For example, suppose that SF&R's customer's netted balance (a result of all activity in all option positions) was a debit and this day's balance was a debit. Then the two would be added together and SF&R would owe the difference. If, on the other hand, the daily balance was a credit, it would be applied to SF&R's debit, and OCC would owe SF&R the difference. Should SF&R be "running" a credit balance, then the reverse would be true.

In addition to balancing the daily position, SF&R must also post "margin" at OCC. This margin is different from client margin. In computing the margin, OCC takes into account what its exposure is compared to SF&R client's position and what its exposure is compared to SF&R proprietary trading. The two balances may *not* be netted. An example of this margin computation is that all client-*owned* positions are excluded since they do not pose any risk to OCC. Options that are written against security (by "covered" writers) are also excluded from client account margin at OCC because they don't pose any risk either.

When an option is exercised, it is exercised against OCC. OCC then turns the exercises around and assigns a writer, or writers, in that option series. The settlement of the exercise follows the usual path of the underlying issue.

Exercises of equity options result in the delivery of the underlying, usually 100 shares against payment in the United States. This is usually accomplished by delivering the issue through NSCC as part of the firm's settling trades. The exercise eventually becomes part of CNS and flows through to DTC. Exercises take five business days to settle; assignments, because they are delivered the next morning, have four days to settle. OCC's exercise and assignment is an overnight process. Due to the fact that the settlement cycle of an equity trade is longer than the period given in an assignment, the party being assigned is given a one-day grace period to honor the assignment.

Example: Monday, July 14, an account of SF&R exercises a call option on PIP at 50. The exercise is against OCC, which processes it that evening. On Tuesday morning, the firm of Overland and Underwater (O&U) is notified that an assignment has been made against their written proprietary position. (Any exercise can be assigned to any writer per option series.) O&U goes into the market on Tuesday and acquires 100 shares of PIP. That trade will settle the following Tuesday, July 22, a day after the settlement of the exercise was due: the July 14 trade date calls for a July 21 settlement—assuming the current settlement cycle is still T+5. (If, for example, settlement cycle were to be reduced to T+3, then trade day, July 14, will settle Thursday, July 17, with the assignment hitting on July 15, settlement on July 18).

Exercises of index or other cash-settling options settle next business day. Exercises on Monday, July 14, will be assigned Tuesday, July 15. At the same time that the assignment "hits" the writer, the account is charged the amount owed. In cash-settling options, the writer always pays.

Example 1: A call on the IND Index, with an exercise price of 350, is exercised when the IND index closed at 357. As each IND Index has a multiple of $100, the 7-point difference between exercise and index value is equal to $100. Therefore, the writer pays the holder $700 on the next business day.

Example 2: A put on the IND Index, with an exercise price of 360, is exercised when the IND Index is at 357. The writer will pay the holder the $300 difference ($360–357=3×$100=$300) on the next business day.

Currency options trade in the currency of denomination, but are exercisable in the underlying currency. The British pound contract, traded on the PHLX, is denominated in dollars, but, when exercised, the British pound sterling is the deliverable. Since the dollar-denominated contract is based on 31,250 GBP, exercise of the option requires payment of dollars for pounds. These exercises must be accomplished two days after exercise within the country whose currency is being traded. Any firm offering currency options as a product to its clients, or for its own proprietary interest, must have arrangements with an OCC-acceptable bank to transact the exchange of currency in that country.

Unlike other listed options, currency options have two expirations per month. They expire the Saturday before the third Wednesday or on the last Saturday of the month. Other listed options expire the Saturday after the third Friday of the expiration month.

Finally, as options expire on Saturdays, a discipline exists known as *ex by ex (exercise by exception)*. Under this rule, equity options that are in the money by 1/4 point or more for proprietary options, or 3/4 point or more for clients, will automatically be exercised at expiration if no counterinstructions are received. In the case of index option, the sums are .05 for proprietary positions and .25 for clients. The ex by ex rules avoid confusion as to what is to be done when an in the money option is about to expire, and no instructions have been received in the P&S area from stockbrokers representing their clients, or traders, at the firm.

Futures Comparison

Like options, futures are compared on trade date. But because the comparing facility also acts as the clearing corporation, no central clearing corporation exists. Of all the instruments traded, only listed options use a central facility.

Comparison takes place on the trade date. The comparison cycle for futures is similar to that of options, but the open contracts are maintained by the exchange's clearing corporation, not forwarded to a central point. All trades, which are executed on futures exchanges, are compared through the clearing corporation.

Equities Comparison

Listed equity transactions follow a longer comparison process than those for listed options. Transactions in listed options settle next business day, whereas equity transactions settle five business days later.

Example: Trades executed on Monday, May 21, settle the following Monday, May 28. Trades on Tuesday, May 22, settle the following Tuesday, May 29, and so on.

If a bank holiday falls on a weekday, then one day is added to the settlement cycle. In such cases, two trade days, which are affected by the holiday, settle on the same business day.

Example: For trades executed on May 24, settlement would normally be May 31. Because the Memorial Day holiday falls within the settlement cycle, settlement is actually June 1.

Equity trades must be compared through the clearing corporation representing the executing exchange.

Exchange	*Clearing Corporation*
New York Stock Exchange American Stock Exchange	National Securities Clearing Corporation (NSCC)
Pacific Stock Exchange	Pacific Clearing Corporation
Philadelphia Stock Exchange	Stock Clearing Corporation of Philadelphia
Midwest Stock Exchange	Midwest Clearing Corporation
Boston Stock Exchange	Boston Clearing Corporation

AN ILLUSTRATIVE COMPARISON (NEW YORK STOCK EXCHANGE)

For each day's trades, the P&S department and clearing corporation go through a series of trade comparisons, called *contracts*. Rarely are all the day's trades compared perfectly on the first contract. So the P&S and clearing personnel collaborate, with the clearing facility running trade comparisons and the P&S departments of the member firms straightening out uncompared or unsubmitted trades.

For each equity trading cycle on the NYSE, NSCC produces two sets of contract sheets:

1. A *regular way contract* produced on the night after trade date (T+1).
2. A *supplemental contract* produced the second night after trade (T+2).

Regular Way Contract

Example: Figure 36-4 is a regular way contract sheet for Stone, Forrest & Rivers. It contains trades submitted to National Securities Clearing Corporation for trades of Monday, April 4, and settlement on April 11. The top row contains:

- SF&R's clearing number and name.
- The trade date.
- The name of contract sheet.
- The settlement date.
- The name of the clearing corporation division.
- Trade number.

Trades are listed in alphabetical or CUSIP number order and arranged in three columns.

- *Compared trades:* Trades whose details are accepted by both the submitting firm (Stone, Forrest & Rivers) and the opposing (or contra) firm reporting of the trade.
- *Uncompared trades:* Transactions submitted by SF&R but not agreed to by the opposing firm in some or all of the comparison details.
- *Advisory transactions:* Trades that an opposing firm has submitted against Stone, Forrest & Rivers but that SF&R doesn't

FIGURE 36-4. *The regular way contract.*

CLEARING MEMBER	CM. NO.	TRADE DATE (MO DAY YR)	PURCHASE CONTRACT	SETTL. DATE (MO DAY YR)	National Securities Clearing Corporation
STONE, FORREST & RIVERS	035	04 04 8X	REGULAR WAY	04 11 8X	SCC-NYSE

COMPARED PURCHASES							UNCOMPARED PURCHASES					ADVISORY DATA				
SELLER	ACCT OF	QUANTITY	CONTRACT AMOUNT	SUMM DIFF	UNIT PRICE	SPEC CODE	ADJ CODE	SELLER	ACCT OF	QUANTITY	CONTRACT AMOUNT	SELLER	ACCT OF	QUANTITY	CONTRACT AMOUNT	CONTROL NO.
CNS	AJB	AMERICAN JELLY BEAN CUSIP: 003456106		000												
164 TOTAL		100 100	3,800.00 3,800.00		38.00000											0213892
CNS	POW	POWER COMPANY CUSIP: 642311105		000												
590 TOTAL		100 100	1,600.00 1,600.00		16.00000											02364137
					15.87500			590		100	1,587.50					01247231
					15.62500							590		100	1,562.50	02436483
CNS	RAM	RAMS SHOE INC. CUSIP: 723103103		000												
					24.00000							336		100	2,400.00	0213746
CNS	SOP	SWAMP OPTICAL LTD. CUSIP: 734026104		000												
031 TOTAL		100 100	5,450.00 5,450.00		54.50000											02940341
CNS	ZAP	ZAPPETCH CORP. CUSIP: 829462107		000												
					32.12500			305		100	3,212.50					04983411

BUY

SUBJECT TO THE BY-LAWS

APPROXIMATE

ADJUSTMENT CODES
A1 ADDED BY ADVISORY

D3 DELETE CONTRACT COMPARED ITEM OR ADVISORY

agree with in some detail or in its entirety. SF&R is given an "advisory" notice for these trades.

COMPARISON

After an order has been executed, two major functions occur:

- Comparison
- Confirmation

comparison and confirmation. *Comparison*, which will be discussed here, is the firm-to-firm verification of the trade, whereas *confirmation* (discussed later) involves firm-to-client notification of the transaction.

Principal Trades

Transactions executed "customer vs. trading account" are easily compared, since the firm itself is the "street sale." Should a discrepancy occur, the events need only be verified with the firm trader.

Market-Maker Trades

A variation of a principal trade takes place when the firm traders are market-makers or dealers, and they trade not only with the firm's customers but with other nonmarket-making firms. These are *market-maker trades*. These firms are buying or selling against your firm's trading accounts, either for themselves or for their customers. In this case, the street side (opposing firm) transaction must be compared to ensure that they are cognizant of the transactions.

Agency Transaction

In an *agency transaction*, your firm acts as a broker or agent. The firm itself buys or sells for its customers with another firm and charges the client commission for the service. In this case, the firm must compare the transaction with the opposing, or contra, firm to ensure that all of the details of the transaction are known and agreed to.

What Is Being Compared

Example: Stone, Forrest & Rivers (SF&R) purchases 100 shares of RAM at 46 from Spear, Fish & Hunt (SFH) for its client, Al Luminium. Since this is an agency transaction, SF&R's client, Al Luminium, will pay $4,600 plus commission. Because commission rates are not set by the industry, each firm maintains its own commission schedule. SF&R charges $75 for this type of transaction. The total cost to the client is $4,675. The commission charged is SF&R income, or revenue. The $4,600 (100 shares × $46) is what SF&R owes the contra firm, Spear, Fish & Hunt (SFH). Therefore, comparison between SF&R and SFH involves:

1. SFR bought 100 RAM @ 46 for $4,600 from SFH.
2. SFH sold 100 RAM @ 46 for $4,600 to SFR.

Whether Spear, Fish & Hunt has purchased the security for their client or for their own proprietary account is their business and doesn't concern SF&R.

Types of Comparison

Comparison can be effected many different ways. The procedures are usually set by the nature of the product and the market place in which it trades. It can range from a manual exchange of comparison notices on a trade-for-trade basis to a computerized comparison that locks in the details at the point of execution.

Trade for Trade. Some products, because of their comparatively low trading volume or substantial size, may compare on a *trade-for-trade basis.* This means that each transaction is compared between buying and selling firm on a trade-for-trade, or item-for-item, basis. Each transaction is compared individually.

In this method, buyer and seller exchange trade detail notices. After reviewing the trade detail, the contra party determines whether agreement to the terms exist. If so, the contra "stamps" the confirmation and returns it to the originator. Buyer and seller exchange these notices.

The term *stamps* means that a stamp containing the firm's

name and/or ID is affixed to the document and returned to the issuer. In most products, stamping means acceptance by the firm of the trade. In some products, the agreement can be rescinded by the phrase *stamped in error.*

If the contra broker does not agree with terms of the trade, a *DK* is affixed to the comparison. *DK* stands for *Don't Know.* This phrase *DK* is official notice that the contra firm does not agree with the terms of the trade. Upon receipt of the DK notice, the P&S employee of the originating firm takes the trade ticket to the trader or whoever consummated the trade for investigation.

The reason for a DK is manifold. The trader may have copied the wrong contra party name. The contra party may have forgotten to process the transaction. There may have been confusion over the security traded or the price. Or the trader may have thought a trade occurred when it really hadn't. Whatever the reason, the discrepancy must be resolved for the transaction to settle.

Systematized Comparison

In *systematized comparison,* the buying and selling brokers/dealers send their trade details to a central processing facility, known as a *clearing corporation.* The data received is processed, and the results appear on a document known as a *contract sheet(s).* This report informs the recipient as to whether the trade has been compared.

The three results that could occur are:

1. Submitter and contra side agree.
2. Contra party does not agree with submitter.
3. Contra firm submitted details that the primary submitter doesn't know.

(Remember, we are considering one firm's contract sheet.)

Stone, Forrest & Rivers is a participant in a clearing corporation. Each business day, they submit their trade details to the clearing corporation. That submission may be via "mag tape," "computer to computer," or by on-line entry via terminal. Some firms may still be submitting data in written form, which must be "keypunched" into the system.

The clearing corporation (such as National Security Clearing Corporation, Mortgage Backed Security Clearing Corp., or Stock Clearing Corporation of Philadelphia) accepts this data and runs matching programs. The results are published on computer-generated reports and distributed to the member firms. Stone, Forrest & Rivers receives its results, which contain:

1. *Compared*—SFR equals contra broker: SFR ≠ contra.
2. Uncompared—SFR input does not match contra firm: SFR ≠ contra.
3. *Advisory (or adjustment):* Opposing firm submitted data that SFR doesn't know: contra ≠ SFR.

Examples: Trades that SF&R and the contra firm agree with are called *compared.*

SFR bought 1,000 POW @ 86 from GRC.
GRC sold 1,000 POW @ 86 to SFR.

A trade that SF&R believes to have compared, but that the contra party does not agree with, is *uncompared.*

SF&R bought 1,000 POW @ 86 from GRC.
GRC sold 0.

A trade submitted against SFR that it doesn't know is referred to as an *advisory*, or *adjustment*.

SFR bought 0.
GRC sold 1,000 POW @ 86 to SFR.

To maintain control and sanity, most clearing corporations do not permit submitters to alter or change their submissions. However, the contra party named in the submission has the ability to accept the proposed trade. By this method, SF&R and the contra party can research trade differences. SF&R will verify its uncompared trades against its advisory transaction, and, where the contra broker dealer version of the trade may be correct, accept that version. If this situation exists, SF&R will submit an acceptance notice to the clearing corporation, a copy of which will go to the contra firm. Other trades appearing in the adjustment column will be checked against unexecuted orders to make sure that a transaction hasn't been overissued.

The contra firms perform the same function. Trades that

SF&R has submitted, and that the contra parties now agree with, will be accepted by the contra party. They will submit acceptance notices to the clearing corporation, a copy of which will go to SFR.

The acceptance notice used by National Security Clearing Corporation is known as an *advisory*. The form used to accomplish the same in listed options at the Chicago Board Option Exchange is referred to as an *adjustment* notice. Regardless of its name, the form received by the clearing corporation is processed in the next cycle, and the item appears on both brokers contract sheets as "compared."

Trades the SF&R wants, but for some reason cannot be compared, are returned to the point of execution for reconcilement. The broker or trader that had reported the execution must contact the contra party and resolve the discrepancy. The process of having the contracting parties resolve the discrepancies has different names in different market places. On the trading floor of the New York Stock Exchange, the process is referred to as *QT*, or *questioned trade*. The same process on the AMEX floor and over the counter is known as a *DK*, for *don't know*. On the CBOE, the process is referred to as a *ROTN*, for *rejected option trade notice*. Future exchanges refer to the process as *RTN*, for *rejected trade notices*, or simply *out trades*. Whatever it is called, the alleged parties to the trade must reconcile the differences.

Regardless of the outcome, a client's order that was entitled to be executed must be executed regardless of the cause of the discrepancy. Should a trade not have actually occurred, but the client was entitled to an execution, the broker or trader must "cover" the mistake and execute a transaction on behalf of the client. The client is entitled to receive the original execution price, or the cover price, whichever is better.

Floor Derived or Locked-in Executions

From the time a trade is agreed to, to the time it is compared, the executing parties are exposed to market risk. Depending on the product and/or the market place, this exposure could be minor or major; therefore, the industry has taken steps to expedite the comparison process.

On most future exchange floors, the trading day is divided into time periods. Trades executed in one time period must be compared by a later time period. There is usually one skipped period, after which the party failing to submit trade data for the "match" could be subject to fine. This strict regimentation is enforced by the exchanges.

Example: Wheat, Golden & Silver (WGS) executes future contracts for their clients during period 2. The contra firm, Korn & Bean (KB), has done the same for their client. Both firms should submit details of the trade during period 3, with the latest allowable time being period 4. If, for some reason, WGS or KB has not submitted the trade detail to the exchange for comparison, an exchange official will investigate the cause of the delay. If one of the firms is at fault, it could be fined.

Assuming all goes correctly, WGS will receive KB's version of the transaction, and KB will receive WGS's version at the same time. Any discrepancy will be addressed immediately. If all is correct, the trades are accepted, and comparison has occurred.

Another process that has minimized the exposure is through *on-line comparison*, or *locked-in trade*. Under this concept, firms enter their orders into an electronic trade routing system. The order arrives at its point of execution. When the market's value permits, the order is executed. Automatically the system, or the executing party, appends the contra firm's ID to the transaction, and a comparison, or match, occurs at that time.

Two such systems are NYSE's DOT and NASD's SOES. *DOT (Designated Order Turnaround)* accepts orders from member firms. The orders are routed to the specialist's post, where the security is trading. There it is stored by price. Market orders, of course, are executed immediately. Limit orders are "filled" on the buy side, highest price first, then on the sell side, lowest price first. When the price is reached, the order becomes executable.

Trades executed through DOT are executed against an omnibus account. The contra side to a DOT execution is *TOD*. The contra firm to the trade will be given the name DOT. Unless there has been a serious mistake in price, the order is deemed to be executed and compared. On the evening of trade date, the specialist reconciles the two omnibus accounts, DOT & TOD. As far as the member firms are concerned, however, they have compared transactions and have to go no further.

The NASD's *SOES* (operates in a similar fashion. Market-makers or dealers submit their quotes to NASD. Orders entering the system are routed to the best bid, or best offer, at that time and executed. The system captures the order, the firm entering order, the execution, and the dealer who is trading. All this data is captured, and comparison occurs.

At the writing of this section, each market place is studying, developing, and implementing quicker ways of affecting comparison.

Example: The contract sheet in Figure 36-4 reveals the following information:

1. SFR bought 100 shares of AJB from Clearing Firm 164. The contra firm knows the trade, and it is compared.
2. SFR bought 2×100 shares of POW from Clearing Firm 590. SFR knows 100 @ 16 and 100 @ $15\frac{7}{8}$. Clearing firm 590 knows 100 @ 16 and 100 @ $15\frac{5}{8}$. The report shows compared on the trade @ 16, but SF&R is uncompared on the other trade. SF&R's uncompared trade at $15\frac{7}{8}$ will appear as an advisory on 590's sell contract sheet, and its trade at $15\frac{5}{8}$ will appear on its uncompared column, but as an advisory on SF&R's contract. For every advisory trade, the firm with the advisory trade receives an advisory notice.
3. Clearing Firm 336 is claiming a trade of 100 shares RAM @ 24. SF&R did not submit such a trade.
4. SF&R, Clearing Firm 035, bought 100 shares SOP at $54\frac{1}{2}$ from Firm 031. The contra firm knows the trade.
5. SF&R is claiming a trade of 100 shares ZAP @ $32\frac{1}{8}$ from Firm 305. The contra firm, 305, does not know the trade.

SF&R's P&S department reviews the problem trades on the morning of T+2 (two days after trade date, April 6) against its own internal record.

SF&R has an *order match computer system,* which is used during the trading day. One of its features is to report executions to the customer and store the prices for later entry into NSCC. Without this "single" price system, SF&R's personnel would have to check their customer trades against the street side. That is, they would have to verify that the trades executed on behalf of their customers agree with the transactions entered into on the customer's behalf.

FIGURE 36-5. *Stock purchase advisory.*

NSCC National Securities Clearing Corporation

STOCK PURCHASE ADVISORY

1	2	3-12	13-16							
B	ACT	CONTROL NO.	PURCHASER	ACCT OF	SELLER	SECURITY SYMBOL	CUSIP NO. (ISSUER / ISSUE / CK)	SP	F	EX
2	1	0213746			336	RAM	723103 10 3			

DO NOT ERASE OR CHANGE PRINTED DATA

TRADE DATE (MO. DAY YR.)	QUANTITY	UNIT PRICE	CONTRACT AMOUNT	SETTL. DATE (MO. DAY YR.)	SPECIAL TRADE
04 04 xx	100	24.00	2400.00	04 11 xx	

The above uncompared item was submitted to NSCC by "SELLER" indicating you as purchaser.

INSTRUCTIONS TO NSCC

ADD THE ABOVE ITEM EXACTLY AS PRINTED TO OUR PURCHASE CONTRACT LIST

PURCHASER: TO ADD THE ABOVE ITEM
1. IMPRINT YOUR NAME & NUMBER STAMP ON COPIES 1 & 2.
2. RETURN COPIES 1 & 2 TO NSCC.
3. KEEP COPY 3 AS YOUR RECORD OF ADD.

SUBJECT TO THE BY-LAWS AND THE RULES OF NSCC.

SCL 7 REV. 11-80

Stone Forrest & Rivers 035
PURCHASER'S NAME & NUMBER STAMP

Example: Because the AJB trade compares, there isn't any need to check further. A review of POW shows a price difference. SF&R is claiming a price of 15 7/8. The opposing firm is claiming 15⅝. According to SF&R's records, the price of 15⅞ is correct. SF&R can do nothing more at this time.

Sometimes a trade is not submitted to clearing by either a buying or selling firm because of errors on the parts of both parties. Such a trade can be added by the selling firm. To do so, the seller submits a form, known as *add by seller,* to the clearing corporation. (See Figure 36-6.)

Supplemental Contract

Example: On the morning of T+3 (three days after trade), SF&R receives the T+2 supplemental contract. (See Figure 36-7.) A review of that contract shows that two trouble items from the regular way contract sheet have been rectified: (1) clearing firm 590's acknowledgment of SF&R's trades to buy 100 POW at 1587.50 and (2) SF&R's acknowledgment of clearing firm 336's sale of 100 RAM at 24.

One trouble item remains. SF&R is trying to purchase 100 Zappeth Corp. at 31⅛. SF&R shows the trade executed against clearing firm 305. SF&R sends a preprinted *questionable trade* (QT) form (Figure 36-8) to the executing broker that reported the trade. SF&R broker meets with the opposing broker and rectifies the problem. In this case, clearing firm 305

FIGURE 36-6. *Add-by seller form.*

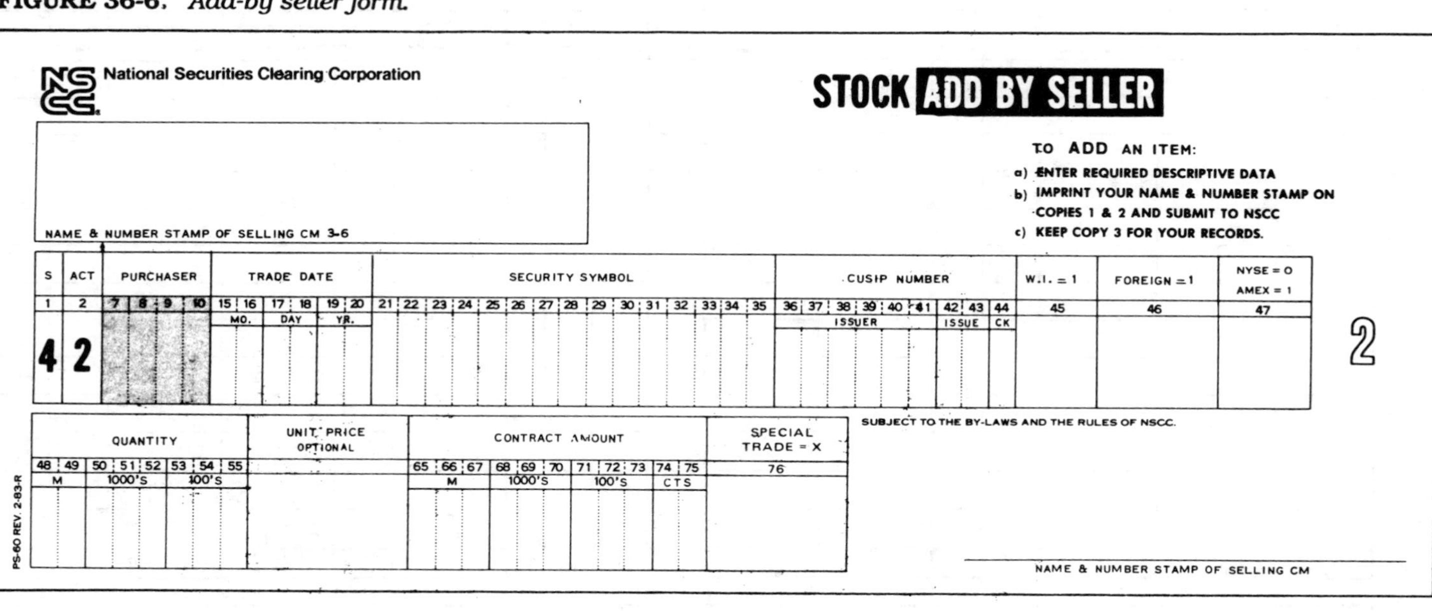

National Securities Clearing Corporation

STOCK ADD BY SELLER

NAME & NUMBER STAMP OF SELLING CM 3-6

TO ADD AN ITEM:

a) ENTER REQUIRED DESCRIPTIVE DATA
b) IMPRINT YOUR NAME & NUMBER STAMP ON COPIES 1 & 2 AND SUBMIT TO NSCC
c) KEEP COPY 3 FOR YOUR RECORDS.

S	ACT	PURCHASER	TRADE DATE	SECURITY SYMBOL	CUSIP NUMBER	W.I. = 1	FOREIGN = 1	NYSE = 0 AMEX = 1
1	2	7 8 9 10	15 16 17 18 19 20	21 22 23 24 25 26 27 28 29 30 31 32 33 34 35	36 37 38 39 40 41 42 43 44	45	46	47
			MO. DAY YR.		ISSUER ISSUE CK			
4	2							

2

QUANTITY	UNIT PRICE OPTIONAL	CONTRACT AMOUNT	SPECIAL TRADE = X
48 49 50 51 52 53 54 55		65 66 67 68 69 70 71 72 73 74 75	76
M 1000'S 100'S		M 1000'S 100'S CTS	

SUBJECT TO THE BY-LAWS AND THE RULES OF NSCC.

NAME & NUMBER STAMP OF SELLING CM

PS-60 REV. 2-83-R

FIGURE 36-7. *The supplemental contract.*

CLEARING MEMBER	CM. NO.	TRADE DATE MO DAY YR	PURCHASE CONTRACT	SETTL. DATE MO DAY YR	National Securities Clearing Corporation SCC-NYSE
STONE, FORREST & RIVERS	035	04 04 8X	SUPPLEMENTAL T + 2	04 11 8X	

COMPARED PURCHASES								UNCOMPARED PURCHASES					ADVISORY DATA				
SELLER	ACCT OF	QUANTITY	CONTRACT AMOUNT	SUMM DIFF	UNIT PRICE	SPEC CODE	ADJ CODE	SELLER	ACCT OF	QUANTITY	CONTRACT AMOUNT		SELLER	ACCT OF	QUANTITY	CONTRACT AMOUNT	CONTROL NO.
	3 3	300 300	10,850.00 10,850.00	CNS	TOTALS CARRIED FORWARD GRAND TOTAL CARRIED FORWARD												
CNS	* POW	POWER COMPANY CUSIP: 642311105		000													
590 TOTAL		100 200	1,587.50 3,187.50		15.87500		A1										
CNS	* RAM	RAMS SHOE INC. CUSIP: 723103103															
336 TOTAL		100 100	2,400.00 2,400.00		24.00000		A1										

B U Y

SUBJECT TO THE BY-LAWS AND THE RULES OF NSCC

SCL 10

ODD PENNY BREAKAGE

APPROXIMATE DECIMAL EQUIVALENT

ADJUSTMENT CODES
A1 ADDED BY ADVISORY
A2 SUPPLEMENTAL ADD BY SELLER
D3 DELETE CONTRACT COMPARED ITEM OR ADVISORY
D4 DELETE ADD BY SELLER
OL ODD LOT
A7 FAIL ADD BY SELLER
K STOCK FAIL DELETE

*DESIGNATES TRANSACTION OUT OF HI-LO PRICE RANGE.

FIGURE 36-8. *NYSE QT form.*

CONTRACT CONTROL NO.

INITIATING BROKER

EXECUTING BROKER

TRADE DATE			SETTLEMENT DATE		
MONTH	DAY	YEAR	MONTH	DAY	YEAR

SECURITY SYMBOL

QUANTITY	PRICE

BUY		CIRCLE ONE		SELL	
OK	DK	B	S	OK	DK

BUYING FIRM	PAIR OFF	SELLING FIRM
CLEARING NO.	CLEARING NO.	CLEARING NO.
EXEC BROKER	EXEC BROKER	EXEC BROKER

76 SPECIAL TRADE ☐ ERROR ACCOUNT / ADJUST. 70 YES ☐ NO ☐

SHARE DIFFERENCE

KNOWS	DK'S

PRICE DIFFERENCE

KNOWS	DK'S

REMARKS

FOR SIAC USE ONLY

71	72	73	74	75	77	78	79	80	
TD	SD	SYM	SH	PRC	CB TK RR	MB AK JR	NP OR NE		

FIRM

broker had reported the trade to the wrong clearing firm. That firm, of course, does not know the ZAP trade VS GRC 305. The 305 broker signs SF&R's QT and the trade is resolved. The signed QT is then processed.

Added Trades

Any trades that were not submitted until now can be turned in by either the selling or buying firm, on a form known as *clearing house comparison* (CHC). That night, the clearing house runs another comparison match, incorporating all CHCs, QTs, and/or DKs. On the following morning, the clearing corporation provides members with an *added trade contract*. This is a catch-all contract that contains all trades submitted as of T+4.

Added Trade Contract

On the morning of T+4, SF&R receives its added trade contract, which shows ZAP compared. (See Figure 36-9.)

The Amex comparison cycle for equity transactions is very similar to the NYSE procedure. The difference is that the Amex uses a "DK" (don't know) form instead of a QT.

Balancing the Customer-Side—As-of Trades

The preceding illustration focused on trade comparisons between contra firms. The P&S function also includes the continuous balancing of customer-side and street-side transactions. Particularly, P&S must be alert customer-side errors.

Sometimes the order gets "lost" while being transmitted to the point of execution, or the report of execution does not get back to operation for processing. These trades, known as *as-of trades*, are processed on one day but *as of* a previous day.

Another reason for as-of trades is an error at the point of execution:

- An order might be overlooked and not executed, in which case it must be executed right away. (The firm must absorb any loss to the client.)
- The order might be executed and reported at an incorrect price. The transaction must be cancelled and a new trade processed for the correct price.
- The transaction might be processed for the wrong security. If the error occurs in processing, it can be cancelled and rebilled. However, if the order is executed for the wrong security, the incorrect trade must be processed through the firm's error account and a correct trade made with appropriate price adjustments.

FIGURE 36-9. *The added trade contract.*

CLEARING MEMBER	CM. NO.	TRADE DATE (MO DAY YR)	PURCHASE CONTRACT	SETTL. DATE (MO DAY YR)	National Securities Clearing Corporation (NSCC)
STONE, FORREST & RIVERS	035	VARIOUS	ADDED TRADES A/T	04 11 8X	SCC-NYSE

COMPARED PURCHASES							UNCOMPARED PURCHASES					ADVISORY DATA				
SELLER	ACCT OF	QUANTITY	CONTRACT AMOUNT	SUMM DIFF	UNIT PRICE	SPEC CODE	ADJ CODE	SELLER	ACCT OF	QUANTITY	CONTRACT AMOUNT	SELLER	ACCT OF	QUANTITY	CONTRACT AMOUNT	CONTROL NO.
	5	500 50	14,837.50	CNS	TOTALS CARRIED FORWARD											
	5	500	14,837.50	GRAND TOTALS CARRIED FORWARD												
CNS	ZAP	ZAPPETH CORP. CUSIP: 829462107		000		Q										
305	100	3,212.50			32.12500											
	1	100	3,212.50		CNS A/T TOTAL											
	6	600	18,050.00		CNS FINAL CONTRACT TOTAL											

BUY

SUBJECT TO THE BY-LAWS AND THE RULES OF NSCC

SCL 10

ODD PENNY BREAKAGE

APPROXIMATE DECIMAL EQUIVALENT

ADJUSTMENT CODES
A1 ADDED BY ADVISORY
A2 SUPPLEMENTAL ADD BY SELLER
D3 DELETE CONTRACT COMPARED ITEM OR ADVISORY
D4 DELETE ADD BY SELLER
OL ODD LOT
A7 FAIL ADD BY SELLER
K STOCK FAIL DELETE

*DESIGNATES TRANSACTION OUT OF HI-LO PRICE RANGE.

FIGURE 36-10. *The don't know (DK) Notice.*

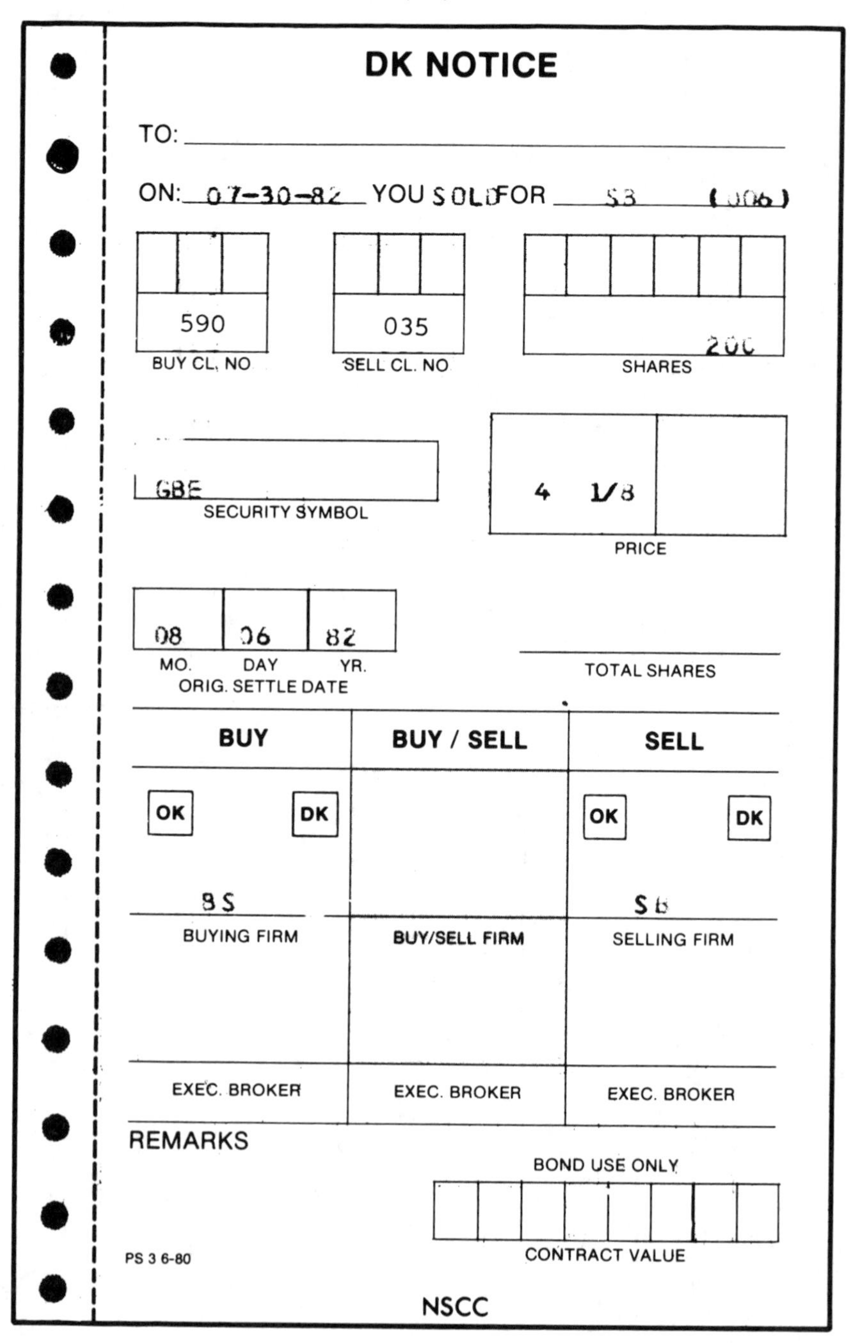

DK NOTICE

TO:

ON: 07-30-82 YOU SOLD FOR S3 (006)

590
BUY CL. NO

035
SELL CL. NO

200
SHARES

GBE
SECURITY SYMBOL

4 1/8
PRICE

08 06 82
MO. DAY YR.
ORIG. SETTLE DATE

TOTAL SHARES

BUY	BUY / SELL	SELL
OK DK		OK DK
BS		SB
BUYING FIRM	BUY/SELL FIRM	SELLING FIRM
EXEC. BROKER	EXEC. BROKER	EXEC. BROKER

REMARKS

BOND USE ONLY

CONTRACT VALUE

PS 3 6-80

NSCC

Over-the-Counter Trades Comparison

Over-the-counter trades that are compared through the clearing corporation follow the same procedures listed trades do. The only difference is that DKs and QTs are not used because there is no central execution point where brokers can meet to reconcile the transactions. In place of these forms, the advisory process lasts for two days (T+2 and T+3).

Certain types of security trades that are not compared through a clearing corporation must be compared on a trade-by-trade basis. For each such trade, SF&R's P&S department readies a *comparison ticket*, which has all details of trade, and sends it to the opposing broker. This procedure is called *sending the comparison*. The ticket can be sent either through a clearing corp's central receiving and delivery unit by runners, who go from firm to firm leaving the comparison at each location, or through the mail.

At the same time, contra firms are sending their comparisons, or *comps*, to SF&R, which the P&S personnel check against their trade blotters. (Needless to say, contra firms are also checking SF&R's comparisons.) If the terms of the trade on the comparison agree with those on the blotter, the P&S department workers *stamp* a copy of the comparison, that is, they affix the name "Stone, Forrest & Rivers" to the comp by means of a rubber stamp. Then they return one stamped copy to the contra broker. Stamped comparisons are important because they represent acceptance of the transactions.

On the other hand, if SF&R does not know the trade, the P&S member initials "DK" (don't know) on the comparison and returns it to the contra broker. DKs signify trouble items, which must be brought to the attention of SF&R traders. The trader who executed the problem transaction has to contact the opposing firm's trader and work out the problem.

Trades that are not compared through a clearing corporation are labor-intensive and time-consuming. Various industry groups are attempting to get more and more types of securities into the clearing corporation "fold."

Mortgage-Backed Securities

Most GNMAs, Freddie Macs, FNMAs, and Sally Maes settle once a month, usually the third Wednesday of the month. Comparison is accomplished on a trade-for-trade basis or through Mortgage-Backed Security Clearing Corporation (MBSCC).

Because these instruments pay interest and principal monthly, the amount of principal outstanding for a pool differs from month to month. To determine the outstanding principal in any month, the P&S uses a *factor table.* This table contains the factor that, if multiplied by the original value of the pool's certificate, gives the current month's principal. On this amount interest is then accrued.

When customers buy a certain type of GNMAs or other mortgage-backed securities, known as TBAs, they receive confirmations without "money." A *TBA* transaction settles at a later date. If the customer closes out or sells the position while the instrument is still in TBA form, P&S issues another confirmation "without" money, and the profit or loss is settled when the TBA becomes regular way. Any customer still maintaining a position when the TBA goes regular way receives a *cancel (CXL) confirmation* for the TBA and a regular way confirm containing the figuration necessary to settle the trade.

Mortgage-backed securities are traded either as regular or forwards. Regular transactions involve the exchange of established pools. Forwards, which also include TBAs, are traded "out" months at a time.

Regular Way Trades

Regular way trades are compared and settled between participants once the pool is identified. Comparison is usually by telex, SWIFT or fax. This form of comparison is used due to the amount of money involved on each trade and the resulting market exposure risk. Delivery is made by book entry or physical forwards and TBAs.

Forward or TBA interfirm transactions are processed through MBSCC (Mortgage-Backed Securities Clearing Corporation). MBSCC carries each firm's positions by type of instrument, coupon rate and delivery month of the forward or TBA transactions. The type we will assume—GNMA pass–through; coupon rate 8%, settlement date for forward trades.

Stone, Forrest & Rivers is a member of MBSCC; each day it submits its inter-firm forward transaction to MBSCC. Among the transactions are its GNMA 8% forward transactions due for settlement in March.

The transactions go through comparison with the other MBSCC members. Once the trades are agreed to, they become part of each members per issue "rolling balance." SFR has several different positions running concurrently. Each day, its trades are added or subtracted from its balance, and the money side adjusted for the amount of transactions. These rolling balances reflect the exposure each firm has to the industry. As these are forward transactions, the amount of money involved in the trade is not exchanged until final settlement.

On day one, SF&R bought $50,000,000 worth of GNMA 8% pass-through due for settlement in March. It has also sold $30,000,000 worth of the same issue on that day. All trades are compared, and therefore, SF&R's closing position is "long" $20,000,000 GNMA 8% forwards due for delivery in March.

The next days settling transaction reflects a not purchase balance of $10,000,000 GNMA 8% for March settlement. Therefore, SF&R's balance is now "long" $30,000,000 GNMA 8% March XXXX.

The next day SF&R bought $40,000,000 worth and sold $80,000,000 worth GNMA 8% forwards due March for a net trading balance of "short" $40,000,000 GNMA 8%. When this trade balance is added to SF&R's rolling balance, what will the new position be?

Net Balance

Day 1—$20,000,000 Long (bought more than it sold)
2—$30,000,000 Long (bought 10,000,000 more than it sold)
3—$10,000,000 Short (sold 40,000,000 more than it bought)

Its new position is short $10,000,000 worth of GNMA 8% forwards due for settlement in March.

The process continues until the actual settlement date when

MBSCC notifies the participants who have positions of their receive/delivery and monetary obligations.

As the trades have been netted intrafirm and the results added or subtracted from the firm's position at MBSCC, final settlement will most likely not occur with the same firms that were originally involved with the trade. Therefore, MBSCC, which has maintained these rolling balances, will issue SBO (Settlement Balance Order) instructions to its participants. As these are compared trades, each buy has a sell, and therefore, the resulting netting should leave a balanced position between firms that end up net buyers and those that end up net sellers.

SF&R is a participant in PTC (Participant Trust Company), as well as DTC (Depository Trust Company). It settles its GNMA pass-through transaction by giving PTC receive or delivery instructions, and settles its CMO-type transaction by giving DTC instructions.

Unlike most of the other issues we have examined, these products settle in *Same Day Funds* or SDF. Some of these other issues we have reviewed settle in NDF, or *Next Day Funds.* Another name for Same Day Funds is Fed Funds, whereas Next Day Funds are also referred to as Clearing House Funds.

Settlement of pass-through securities is different from that of other issues. Pass-through issues pay interest and principal periodically. Included in principal pay down is also the prepayments of debts. In the case of mortgage loans, some of those loans will become part of pools. Once in a pool, the monthly payments by the homeowners include a pay down of the mortgages. When people refinance their homes, or relocate and pay off the existing mortgage, the total pay downs of the loan also pass through to the pool owner. These pay downs are known as prepayments.

As the amount of principal in a pool is not constant, it is almost impossible to deliver the exact amount required by the trade. Therefore, at the writing of this chapter, the seller can deliver up to four pools per million dollars as long as they are over or under the million by 2%, and that none of the pools, three or less, total the lower threshold of $980,000 (2% × $1,000,000 = $20,000; $1,000,000 – $20,000 = $980,000). Because of the ability to mix and match pools, a firm can maximize profits or minimize losses. For example, using a made-up standard product, the following trades occurred.

Bought	*Sold*	*Profit*
$1,000,000 @ .96	$1,000,000 @ 96 1/8	$1,250,000
$1,000,000 @ 96 1/2	$1,000,000 @ 96 5/8	$1,250,000
$1,000,000 @ 96 3/4	$1,000,000 @ 96 7/8	$1,250,000
	Total Profit	$3,750,000

The pass-through received against the purchases were:

@ 96 —$1,020,000 principal
@ 96 1/2— $995,000 principal
@ 96 3/4— $980,000 principal

The Allocation

By allocating the deliveries "highest" principal in highest price out, we can maximize our profit—

Purchase Side	*– Sale Side*	*= Profit (Loss)*
1,020,000 principal × .96 = $979,200.00	vs. Sale 96 7/8 = $988,125.00	= $8,925.00
995,000 principal @ 96 1/2 = $960,175.00	vs. Sale 96 5/8 = $961,418.75	= $1,243.75
980,000 principal @ 96 3/4 = $948,150.00	vs. Sale 96 1/8 = $942,025.00	= (6,125.00)
	Total:	$4,043.75

By matching the highest principal amount received in against the highest price out, we were able to increase our profits from $3,750 to $4,043.75. The $293.75 may not appear to be worth the effort, but remember, it was only on three transactions. What if the firm had 3,000 trades involved in the settlement process? This method of settlement is known as *allocation*.

When-Issued (WI) Transactions

In the equity world, a similar practice occurs on *when-issued (WI) transactions*, which are transactions for buying and selling securities about to be issued, usually through a rights offering.

Such trades are entered into on a WI basis. When municipals are offered before the settlement date of the offering is established, they also trade in this manner.

Through or Ex the Clearing Corporation

Two expressions should not be confused because they have two different meanings. *Through the clearing corporation* can mean the use of either its computer facility's comparison routine or its centralized point of receipt and delivery. *Ex the clearing corporation* (or just *ex-clearing*) can also mean one of two things: (1) not through the computerized comparison facility but through the centralized point for receipt and delivery, or (2) away from the centralized location altogether.

Settlement

Special codes are also needed for the different settlement cycles, which depend on the type of security involved in the transaction.

There are four ways to settle a transaction:

1. Regular way.
2. Next day.
3. Cash.
4. Seller's and buyer's option.

Regular Way. Most securities settle five business days after the trade date. A trade taking place today must be paid for (if purchased) or delivered (if sold) five business days from the trade date. For example, a trade executed on May 11 settles on May 18. This kind of settlement, because it is the most common, is known as *regular way settlement.*

Next Business Day. Transactions in options, futures, and some government securities settle on the *next business day.* For example, a trade executed on Monday, January 3, settles on Tuesday, January 4. On the fourth, all parties make either payment or delivery (delivery may be either physically or by book entry). A transaction on Friday settles Monday (barring holidays).

Cash Settlement. Certain types of money market instruments, i.e. CD's, CP's & BA's settle on their trade date. In addition during certain times of the year, for special reasons, a transaction sometimes has to settle on the same day as the trade. This is known as a *cash settlement.*

Example: Due to tax law, a profitable trade might have to settle in the same year. Therefore, if December 31 is the last business day of the year, an individual who wants to close out a profitable position on that day, so that the gain applies to the current year, must enter into a cash transaction.

Seller's or Buyer's Option. Delivery may be delayed for up to sixty calendar days, when a client cannot take or make physical delivery for an extended period. A delayed delivery may be at either the seller's or buyer's option. The purpose and use of delayed deliveries vary from one client situation to another.

Example: While customer White is on a business trip for a month, he instructs his stockbroker to sell a security that White has in a safe at home. White *cannot* deliver the securities to the brokerage firm under a regular way trade.

But the broker may enter the sell order with the notation "Seller's 30," which informs all concerned that the settlement for this trade must be delayed 30 calendar days. The selling firm has to find a buyer who is willing to wait thirty days for receipt of the security. When a buyer is located and the execution price agreed upon, a trade is processed with the settlement date thirty days from the trade date.

The settlement cycle must be noted on the trade ticket as it is processed. Generally, regular way trades without notation, and all other transactions carry special coding. The P&S department uses such coding to make sure that the trades settle on the correct days.

"As-of" Trades

Sometimes a transaction is not processed on the trade date due to one or more processing difficulties. Yet it must still be recorded on the trade date. When such a trade undergoes processing, it is labelled as an *as-of* trade—"as of the day before" or "as of two days before" and so on.

Example: A trade executed on Monday, April 3, is not processed until Tuesday, April 4. It is processed with the notation "As of April 3," and the settlement is based on the April 3 date.

BOOKING AND CONFIRMATION

Every transaction has to be *booked*, that is, entered on the firm's records. If everyone performs his or her assignment diligently and accurately, the customer's transaction is correctly reflected on the confirmation and the trade cleared with the opposing broker.

If someone has made an error, then the P&S departments (in most firms) have to make a *trade correction*, a costly waste of the brokerage firm's resources.

A typical error is booking a transaction to the wrong account. Occasionally, a customer has more than one account with a firm.

Example: A client has one account for the husband, one for the wife, one for both as joint tenants with rights of survivorship, and one for each child under the Uniform Gift to Minors Act. The customer instructs the stockbroker to enter into a transaction for the wrong account. By the time the customer discovers the mistake, the trade is booked. The stockbroker must then give instructions to cancel (cxl) the trade from the wrong account and enter it in the correct one.

An employee of the P&S staff makes the appropriate entries. These entries, affecting most of the processing cycle, are almost as costly as three trades: (1) the original, (2) the cancellation, and (3) the correction. Yet the firm receives the commission on only one trade, the actual execution, and nothing on the other two. The firm can very easily lose money on the transaction. Combined with the additional costs of as-of trades, trade correction expenses can effect a firm's profitability. If the firm takes enough such losses, it can go *out of business*, leaving its *employees without jobs*.

Floor Brokerage Fees

Although the member firms' floor brokers are paid a salary to execute orders for their firm's customers, the other floor members (the specialists and two-dollar brokers) charge fees for this service. In so doing, they earn revenue for their firms, from which they pay their own expenses. Once a month, these fees are billed to the using firms, which must record each trade to make certain that the billings are correct. In most firms, this record-keeping, or *booking*, is performed by individuals in the P&S area.

SUMMARY

On a given day in the P&S area, executions are coded and the security identified. Trades are figured, processed, compared (reconciled), and booked. All of this is performed just to make certain that a client in New York, Chicago, Miami, San Francisco, Boise, or anywhere else has a valid transaction.

CHAPTER 37

Margin

All customer transactions pass through the margin function. Margin customers must comply with rules and regulations set forth by the Securities and Exchange Commission and the self-regulatory organizations, such as the New York Stock Exchange. Like the P&S and other operational areas, the margin department is always processing the transactions for many different trading days.

With the essentials of margin explained in Chapter 8, several questions arise:

- What happens if the market value of the stock rises?
- You can buy stock on margin but can you "sell" them on margin?
- Can you trade other securities, such as options, on margin?

REG T EXCESS

The market value of stocks, purchased on margin, may rise. When it does, the increased value is known as *excess equity*. It is "excess" because it is more than the equity required by Regulation T, or Reg T. It is *Reg T excess.*

Example: Assuming a margin rate of 60%, a customer buys 100 shares of DUD at 50. The client deposits $3,000 (60%) and borrows $2,000 (40%).

Equity + Loan value = Market value
$3,000 + $2,000 = $5,000

The market value of DUD increases to $100 per share and so the current market value of the 100 shares in the account is $10,000 ($100 × 100 shares). Since the customer borrows only $2,000 for the original purchase, the equity is $8,000.

Equity + Loan value	= Market value
Equity + $2,000	= $10,000
Equity	= $10,000 – $2,000
Equity	= $8,000

The client calls the Store, Forrest & Rivers stockbroker and asks if any more money can be borrowed. The stockbroker relays the question to SF&R's margin department, where an employee performs the following computation:

Current market value	$10,000
Times the loan value (40%)	.40
Loan value ($)	$ 4,000
Less debit balance (amount borrowed)	$ 2,000
Reg T excess	$ 2,000

The client may withdraw the $2,000 Reg T excess as cash.

BUYING POWER

A client may also apply Reg T excess in an account to a margin purchase. The excess equity is then said to have *buying power.* It represents the part of the purchase price that the client can put up instead of cash.

What, then, is the maximum purchase that the client can make on margin? To arrive at that amount, simply divide margin rate into the buying power dollar amount.

Example: The $2,000 excess can be applied by the client to a new trade. The excess equals 60% of what can be bought.

$$\text{Buying power} = \frac{\text{Reg T excess}}{\text{Margin rate}}$$

$$= \frac{\$2,000}{.60} = \$3,333.33$$

In other words, the current market value of any new purchase can be up to $3,333.34 without the client having to deposit more equity. Of that total value, $2,000 (60%) is equity applied from the client's excess equity, and $1,333.34 (40%) is a new loan from the brokerage firm. The client decides to buy $3,333.34 worth of ROS. The client can purchase $3,333.34 worth of marginable securities.

Current market value		$13,333.34
DUD	$10,000.00	
ROS	3,333.34	
Less Equity		8,000.00
DUD	$ 6,000	
ROS	2,000	
Debit balance		$ 5,333.34

The client has substituted excess loan value ($2,000) with securities. The debit balance of $5,333.34 is the equivalent of the loan value of 40% ($13,333.34 × .40). The equity of $8,000 is the equivalent of the margin rate ($13,333.34 × .60).

MINIMUM MAINTENANCE

If a rise in market value creates Reg T excess (equity), what effect does a decrease in value have? To answer that question, we must explain minimum maintenance.

Minimum maintenance margin is the minimum amount of equity that a customer must have in a margin account. The minimum is prescribed by the New York Stock Exchange or other exchanges' maintenance rules. As the market prices of securities fluctuate, they create changes in a margin account's equity. (Don't forget the formula: Equity plus Debit balance equals Market value.) If the market value goes up or down, while debit balance stays the same, then the equity *has* to change.) If the equity in an account falls below 25% of the market value or becomes 1/3 of the debit balance, the customer is asked to maintain the equity at either of these levels. The customer must somehow restore the level of the equity to satisfy these minimums.

A Working Illustration

Let's follow an account through several transactions, to see how a margin account "works."

With the margin rate at 50%, customer Perry (account CG401243) wants to open a margin account with the purchase of 100 shares of stock at 50. After the paperwork is completed and the trade settled, the account looks like this:

Long 100 PIP @ 50

Current market value	$5,000
Less: Equity (customer's cash)	–2,500
Debit balance (loan from firm)	$2,500

The stock rises to 80:

Current market value	$8,000
Less: Equity	–5,500
Debit balance	$2,500

On $8,000 worth of market value, Reg T permits SF&R to lend 50%, or $4,000, but SF&R has loaned the customer only $2,500. Now that the market value has gone up, so has the equity. So the customer may borrow $1,500 more. The margin employee informs the SF&R stockbroker in Chicago that the account has $1,500 excess. The computation is as follows:

Current market value (CMV)	$8,000
Loan value rate (LVR)	× 50%
Loan value (LV)	$4,000
Debit balance (DB)	–2,500
Reg T excess	$1,500

Perry can remove the $1,500 excess from the account—that is, borrow it—or apply it to the new purchase. If he removes it, the account is:

Long 100 PIP @ 80

Current market value	$8,000
Less: Equity	–4,000
Debit balance	$4,000

But Perry is interested in purchasing shares of WOW, which is trading at $30 per share, and he does not want to "put in" any more money. Perry's $1,500 from the loan value of PIP is used to buy WOW, and the firm lends the other 50% of the value of WOW. The customer can therefore purchase $3,000 worth of WOW.

Long 100 PIP at 80

Current market value PIP	$ 8,000
Plus: Current market value WOW	+ 3,000
Total current market value	$11,000
Equity	– 5,500
Debit balance	$ 5,500

Now our customer wants to purchase 100 ZAP at 70. SF&R's stockbroker informs Perry that there isn't any excess:

CMV	$11,000
Times	× 50%
Loan value	5,500
Debit balance	– 5,500
Excess equity	0

The client orders the purchase and, with no excess *equity*, must put up 50% of the value in five business days. Instead of sending SF&R a check for $3,500 (50% of $7,000), Perry deposits fully paid-for, marginable shares of MOM. With MOM selling at 17½, the customer sends 400 shares, for a market value of $7,000 ($17.50 × 400 shares). The loan value on $7,000 worth of stock is $3,500 (50%). Now SF&R may lend Perry $3,500 on MOM to cover his obligation on ZAP. The account is now as follows:

Long 400 MOM at 17½	$ 7,000
100 PIP at 80	8,000
100 WOW at 30	3,000
100 ZAP at 70	7,000
Total current market value	$25,000
Less: Equity	12,500
Debit balance	$12,500

The lending, step-by-step, took place as follows:

PIP	$ 2,500
PIP to acquire WOW	1,500
WOW	1,500
MOM to buy ZAP	3,500
ZAP	3,500
Debit balance	$12,500

The market value in the account falls from 25,000 to $23,000. The account is as follows:

Current market value	$23,000
Equity	–10,500
Debit balance	$12,500

Note how the $2,000 drop in market value is offset by the $2,000 drop in equity.

The customer wants to purchase 100 shares of POP at $20 per share. Despite the drop in market value, Perry can purchase POP just by depositing 50% of the *purchase price.* He does *not* have to bring the account up to 50%. With the purchase of 100 shares of POP at 20, the account has a margin value of $25,000, an equity of $11,500 and a debit balance of $13,500.

With the debit balance of $13,500, to what level can the equity fall before the client Perry is called for more money? Under the maintenance rules, the equity in the account cannot be less than one-third of the debit balance.

$$\frac{1}{3} \times \frac{\$13{,}500}{1} = \$4{,}500$$

Because debit balance plus equity equals market value, then $13,500 plus $4,500 = $18,000.

With the debit balance at $13,500, the equity cannot fall below $4,500; said another way, the market value cannot fall below $18,000.

Should the account drop in value below $18,000, the client would get called for additional funds.

SHORT SALE

Customer Nordin (account M1313412) from SF&R's Miami office believes that the value of BUM, currently at 80 per share, is about to fall—that is, she thinks it is overpriced. After making certain that Nordin has a margin account and that the stock is available for loan, SF&R's Miami broker enters an order to sell short 100 BUM at the market. The trade is made. Nordin must deposit 50% of the short sale value, or $4,000. When properly margined, the account is:

Short 100 BUM 80	$ 8,000
Equity (credit)	+ 4,000
Credit balance	$12,000

Because the customer has borrowed the stock through SF&R, 100% of the value must be frozen to protect the firm against the customer's inability to "buy back" the borrowed or sold stock. As the price of BUM fluctuates, SF&R is moving money between the customer's equity and the current market value of the stock. BUM rises to $85 per share. The account is as follows:

Short 100 BUM 85	$ 8,500
Equity	3,500
Credit	$12,000

If BUM continues to rise in price, the customer's equity is depleted. (Note how a rise in market value "hurts" a short position, whereas it enhances a long position.)

Once a short sale is made, two things may come into play as the market value of the stock fluctuates:

- *Mark to the market:* As the market value of borrowed stock goes up, the brokerage firm may request additional funds from the customer (short seller). Should the market value decline, the client may request funds from the firm. Either way, the account is marked to the market price on a daily basis.

- *Maintenance requirement:* To protect SF&R against unfavorable movements in price, self-regulatory agencies have established a minimum equity for a short position at which the customer is called for more money. In a short sale, the maintenance requirement is 30% of market value. Brokerage firms may require a higher minimum than the SROs requirement, but never less.

With BUM at 80 ($8,000), Nordin had to deposit 50% of the sale, or $4,000. The maintenance requirement is $2,400 ($8,000 × .30 = $2400) therefore the account has "surplus" over maintenance of $1,600 ($4,000 – $2,400).

When BUM rises to $81 per share, SF&R deducts $100 from the customer's equity and places it into frozen funds:

Short 100 BUM 81	$ 8,100
Equity	3,900
Credit	$12,000

At the same time, the maintenance increases from $2,400 to $2,430 ($8,100 × .30). The one-point move reduces the surplus of equity over maintenance by 130%, or in this case $130 (from $1,600 to $1,470).

	Was	*Is*
Equity	$4,000	$3,900
Maintenance	–2,400	–2,430
Excess equity	$1,600	$1,470

SF&R's margin department must not allow the equity to fall below the 30% minimum maintenance. To determine when a minimum maintenance call is necessary, the margin staff does a simple computation: They divide the surplus equity by the maintenance rate plus 100%, they see that they will have to call for additional money if BUM rises 12 3/8 points.

$$\text{Price rise to a maintenance call} = \frac{\text{Excess equity}}{\text{Maintenance rate} = 100\%}$$

$$= \frac{\$1{,}600}{30\% + 100\%} \text{ or } \frac{\$1{,}600}{.30 + .100}$$

$$= \frac{\$1{,}600}{1.30}$$

$$= \$1{,}230.77$$

This amount represents the dollar amount of a rise in market value for 100 shares of BUM. To arrive at the rise per share, the margin employee simply divides by 100 shares.

$$\text{Price rise per share} = \frac{\$1{,}230.77}{100 \text{ shares}}$$

$$= \$12.31\text{/share, or } 12\tfrac{3}{8}$$

In other words, if BUM trades at 92 3/8 (80 + 12 3/8), the equity in the account is close to the required minimum, and a maintenance call might have to go out to the customer.

Let's see why this is so. With BUM at 80, the maintenance requirement is $2,400 ($8,000 × .30). The customer has $4,000 in the account—plenty of equity. Should the value of 100 shares of BUM rise to $9,237.50 (92⅜), the maintenance requirement would be $2,771.25 ($9,237.50 × .30). The customer still has $4,000 in the account, so she still has plenty of equity, right?

Wrong. Since this is a *short* position, the rise in price *decreased* the equity in the account. The price rise in a short position is like a price decrease in a long position. As a result, you have to deduct the dollar value of the price from the equity:

Equity	$4,000.00
Less: Price rise	1,237.50
Reduced equity	$2,763.50

Nordin does not have enough equity to cover the minimum requirement—but just barely. The minimum required is $2,771.25, and her reduced equity is $2,763.50. A maintenance call must go out.

RESTRICTED ACCOUNTS

When the amount of equity is between Reg T excess and the minimum maintenance, the account is a *restricted account*. In other words, the account doesn't have Reg T excess, but the equity has not fallen far enough to oblige the client to deposit additional funds. Any new purchases necessitate initial margin or the current margin rate (for equities) of *the* purchase. Sales made in the account while it is restricted permit the client to withdraw 50% of proceeds.

SPECIAL MEMORANDUM ACCOUNT (SMA)

To record this release of 50%, as well as other money entries, the margin department uses a bookkeeping account called a *special memorandum account (SMA)*. When a sale of securities is made in a margin account, the security position is dropped from the account, and the money received is applied against the debit balance. After the sale has "cleared the books," the account does not reflect the sale. It would take a margin employee a good amount of time to determine if, first, a sale has taken place and, second, whether the releasable funds had been previously withdrawn. The SMA saves the margin department this waste of time by recording such events, which could have taken place but didn't.

Example An account sells $5,000 worth of stock in a restricted account. On settlement date, the client can withdraw 50% of the sale's proceeds, or $2,500. If the client doesn't withdraw the $2,500, it is posted to the SMA.

If at a latter date the client decides to withdraw the money, the margin department checks the SMA, sees the $2,500 entry, and approves the payment.

In addition to watching minimum maintenance and sending "house calls," margin employees use the SMA to determine what is permitted in the accounts. The SMA is essential to the working of the margin area.

ACTIVITY STATEMENT

To provide a record of an account's activity and ever changing status, the margin department issues periodic activity statements. Although the format of this statement may vary from firm to firm, the basic information remains the same.

Let's examine SF&R's statement. The account shown in Figure 37-1 is operated from SF&R's Chicago office. The account number is CG401243, the salesperson is C15, and the customer is Mr. Philip O'Dendren of 15 92nd Street, Dairy Falls, Illinois 60685.

On July 29, trade date, the customer purchased 500 shares of McNeil Corp. at 13½. With commission added, the settlement money is $6,917. This transaction was to close out a previous short position.

The account is long 1,000 shares of Universal Foods Corp. and short 500 Ametek, Inc. and 500 Oak Industries. The "Settlement Date Position" column shows the account to be long 1,000 shares of Universal Foods Corp. but short 500 shares of Ametek, Inc. and 500 shares of McNeil Corp. These McNeil Corp. shares remain in a short position because the July 29 trade had not settled when the activity sheets were produced. The share quantities for these positions therefore appear in the "Trade Date Position" column, not in the column headed "Settlement Date Position."

On the upper right-hand portion of the statement, in the first

FIGURE 37-1. *An SF&R account.*

ACCOUNT NUMBER	TYPE	A.E.	TAX IDENTIFICATION	FULL ACCOUNT NAME AND ADDRESS
CG-401124	2 MARGIN	C15	018-43-0119	Mr Philip O'Dendron 15 92nd Street Dairy Falls, ILL 60685

ACTIVE TYPES 123 9

PREVIOUS		PREVIOUS	
T.D BAL	2886222CR	S.D BAL	2886222CR
MKT VAL	19875	HOUSE SUR	39294
EQUITY	54357	NYSE SUR	40288
% EQUITY	10000	HOUSE CALL	
CASH AVAIL	3010722	NYSE CALL	
SMA BAL	30107	DAYS F.D CALL	
BUYING PWR	60214	TOTAL FED CALL	
SUPER REST			

PAGE NO	1
REPORT DATE	072282
LAST STATUS	071682
LAST CHANGE	072082

GENERAL ACCOUNT INFORMATION

HOLD PROCEEDS
TFR & HOLD STREET NAME
HOLD INCOME

ALTO JNL

MISCELLANEOUS TOTALS	
DAILY INT	
REG/SHRT VAL	
SHORT VALUE	22062
SMA CHG	2864
DEBIT RESTRICTION	

NEW ACCOUNT TOTALS			
T.D BAL	2886222CR	S.D BALANCE	2886222CR
MARKET VALUE	19750	HOUSE SURPLUS	41333
EQUITY	53977	NYSE SURPLUS	42321
% EQUITY	10000	HOUSE CALL	
CASH AVAIL	32071	NYSE CALL	
SMA BALANCE	32971	TODAY'S FED CALL	
BUYING PWR	65942	TOTAL FED CALL	

TRANS DATE	TRANS NO OR LAST ACTIVITY DATE	QUANTITY	PRICE OR TYPE OF UNIT	T R	AMOUNT	SMA	CUSIP	EXCH	SEC	SECURITY LOCATION: SEGREGATION	SAFEKEEPING	TRANSFER	TRADE DATE POSITION: LONG	S	SHORT	SECURITY POSITION	SETTLEMENT DATE POSITION	MARKET VALUE	CLOSING PRICE
	040582						031105109	1	1					S	500	AMETEK INC		12,812-	255
0729	201452	500	134	T	691700	*	582562104	1	1							MC NEIL CORP			134
																SHORT COVER			
	072382						671400109	1	1					S	500	OAK INDUSTRIES INC		9,250-	184
	041482						913538104	1	1	1000			1000			UNIVERSAL FOODS CORP	1000	19,750	196
																<			
					286447-	*										TODAYS EXCESS			

column of figures labeled "Previous," the "SMA Bal" line carries a figure of $30,107. Because the SMA is accumulated excess, the "Buying Power" (given a margin rate of 50%) is double the SMA, or $60,214.

Like many member firms, SF&R sets its in-house maintenance requirement at a higher level than that required by the New York Stock Exchange. Look at the next column of "Previous" (settlement date) line. "SF&R's House Sur." (surplus equity) is $39,294; on the following line the "NYSE Sur." is $40,288. SF&R will send out a house call for $994 "ahead of" the NYSE limit.

OPTION MARGIN

Stone, Forrest & Rivers' margin section daily reviews accounts that have option positions. Option positions are different from equity and debt positions in that the former represent an intent while the latter represents actual ownership of an issue.

Option margin is firm protection. If there isn't any risk to the firm, either real or perceived, there isn't any margin. Money due from a transaction must be paid for in full. If there is risk to the firm, a margin formula is then applied.

Example 1: Account BS0444291 owns 100 shares KID at 50. The client sells a call on KID and receives the premium. If the option is exercised against this account, the firm will deliver the client's security. (The owner of call has the privilege of "calling in," or buying, the underlying security. The seller, or writer, of a call option must deliver the underlying security, which in this example is KID, on exercise.) Since the firm is not exposed to any risk with this position, there isn't any margin applied to the option. This is known as a *covered option position.*

Example 2: Account BS0496842 is anticipating a drop in the price of ZAP. Since puts increase in value as the underlying issue's value falls, the client expects to profit from a decrease in ZAP's market value. If ZAP actually increases in value, the value of the puts will fall, and the options could expire worthless. In any event, the firm is not at risk because the client must pay for the purchase of the put options in full (10 puts × 100 shares × 3 = $3,000, plus commission).

Under Regulation T and NYSE rules, a firm cannot lend money on an option position because, when the option expires, the firm will be left with an unsecured loan. As a result, long option positions are not marginable.

Example 1: Another account, CG3492731, sells (writes) 10 calls POW Apr 60 at 2. POW is currently at $59 per share. The client believes that POW will fall in value; therefore the call premium will fall also (the call's market value rises with the underlying and falls with the underlying's value.) Since the client does not own 1,000 shares of POW, this option position is considered uncovered (naked), and margin must be charged. The margin is needed in case the market value of POW rises and the firm had responded to an exercise and covered the loss.

Let's assume POW rises to 70 by expiration. A call with a strike price of 60 would be worth 10 points, because the *owner* of the call option could call in a stock worth $70 per share and pay the option's strike price of $60 per share. Since the client, in this example, received only $2 per share ($200 per option), the firm would be at risk because the underlying stock rose against the client's position. The firm will collect margin from the client to cover the risk, and, as the market value continued to rise, more margin would be required.

The margin calculation for an uncovered equity option position is 20% of the underlying value, plus the premium, less the out-of-the-money sum, if any, with a minimum of 10% plus premium. In this example, the option(s) are out of money, since no one will "call in" (buy) stock at $60 (the strike price) when the security is trading at $59.

The margin calculation is:

1. Each option has 100 shares of stock underlying it.
2. The position is for 10 options.

			Or
20% of underlying value:			
$59 × 100 shares	=	$59,000	$ 5,900
× number of options		10	.10 (10%)
		$59,000	$ 5,900
× 20%		.20	+ 2,000
		$11,800	$ 7,900
Plus the premium:			
$2 × 100 × 10	=	2,000	
		$13,800	
Less the out-of-the-money amount:			
$1 × 100 × 10	=	(1,000)	
		$12,800	

Since the $12,800 is higher, it becomes the margin requirement.

Example 2: A/C BW106341 sells 5 puts WAM Jun 40 at 3. WAM is at 39. Is the WAM put options in, at, or out of the money? The margin calculation is:

20% of underlying value		
$39 × 100 shares per option × 5 options	=	$19,500
		× .20
		$ 3,900
Plus the premium:		
Premium $3 × 100 shares per option × 5 options		1,500
Less the out-of-the-money sum, if any (These options are in the money since anyone who had one "free" could buy the stock at $39 per share and "put" it out at $40, strike price)		0
Margin requirement		$54,000

Minimum computation: 10% plus premium

$19,500 × 10%	=	$1,950
Premium	=	1,500
		$3,450

Since $5,400 is the higher requirement, it is required to carry this position.

For margin purposes, spreads exist whenever a client is long *and* short (bought and sold) equal numbers of puts *or* calls on the same underlying, but with different expiration months and/or strike prices.

Examples: The following are spreads:

1. Long 1 call EEK Jun 40
   Short 1 call EEK Jun 45
2. Long 1 call EEK Jan 40
   Short 1 call EEK Feb 40
3. Long 1 put MIP Sep 30
   Short 1 put MIP Sep 25
4. Short 1 put TOP Apr 35
   Long 1 put TOP Mar 35

The following are not spreads:

1.	L	1	put	ZAP	Apr	40
	L	1	call	ZAP	Apr	40
2.	L	1	put	PIP	Oct	40
	S	1	put	POW	Oct	40
3.	L	1	call	RAP	Sep	35
	L	1	call	RAP	Oct	30

In a spread, one option (the more expensive one) is the *main option.* If the main option is long (bought), the other option acts to reduce the premium or cost.

Examples:

L 1 call PAM Nov 40
S 1 call PAM Nov 45

The lower strike price call, with the longest time remaining, always has the most value, because it will "go" into the money first.

Example: If the stock PAM is above 40 but less than 45, the 40 strike price is in the money; the 45 strike price call is out of the money.

Let's assume that the Nov 40 call is trading at 4 ($400 per option), and that the Nov 45 call is trading for 1½ ($150 per option). The client who believes that PAM would not rise above $45 per share could buy the 40 and sell the 45 for a "net" cost of 2½, or $250 per option ($400 for the 40, less $150 for the 45 = $250).

If, on the other hand, the more expensive option was the one that was sold, the other option in the spread acts as an insurance policy. For example:

S 1 Put PAT Nov 30
B 1 Put PAT Nov 25

In puts, the higher strike price option, with the longest time to go, has the most value, because it will go into the money first.

Example: Refer to the previous example. If the stock was between $25 and $30 per share, the Nov 30 put would be in the money, and the Nov 25 would be out of the money. In this position, the client would want the price of PAT to rise so that both options would expire out of the money.

Let's assume PAT was at $30 per share. The PAT Nov 30 option was trading at $4; the PAT Nov 25 option was trading at 1. If the client is correct, the market value of PAT stays at 30 or rises, both options expire worthless, and the client keeps $300 per spread ($400 for the 30, less $100 for the 25). If, however, the client is wrong, the price of PAT falls below 25; whatever the client lost on the S 1 put PAT Nov 30 when the stock went below 25 is made up by gains in the L 1 put PAT Nov 25. For instance, at expiration PAT is trading at 20, the Nov 30 is worth 10 points, and the Nov 25 is worth 5 points. The client would be facing a 5-point loss, less the 3 points of premium received for a real loss of 2 points. If the stock was at $15 per share at expiration, the 30 strike price put would be worth 15 points, and the 25 strike price put would be worth 10 points. The client would be losing $1,500 on the sale of the 30 put, but earning 1,000 on the buy of the 25 put, for a spread difference of $500. When the $300 premium, which was received on the original trade, is subtracted, the client is left with a $200 loss.

Margin charged on option positions, as already stated, is required when there is real or perceived risk to the firm. Due to the "perceived" part, any spread in which the sold option expires after the bought option is automatically charged margin based on an uncovered position from day one. The reason is that, at some later date, the long (bought) option will expire and the client will be left with a short (sold) uncovered option.

In spread positions where the long (bought) option expires on or after the short (sold) option and has the greater value, the client pays the difference (spread), because the firm doesn't have any risk, there isn't need for margin.

If, however, the long option expires on or after the short option with the short option as the main option, the margin requirement is the difference between strike price, or the calculation for an uncovered option, whichever is less.

Example:

S 1 call JAY Oct 40 = 6
B 1 call JAY Oct 45 = 3

JAY common stock is trading at 40.

Step 1: Calculate the difference between strike prices:

Long	45	strike price
Short	40	strike price
	5	point × 100 shares = $500

Step 2

Market value of 100 shares JAY	=	$4,000
× 20%		.20
		$ 800
Plus the premium		600
		$1,400
Less the out-of-the-money amount		0
		$1,400

Margin required is $500 (computation does not take into consideration the $300 premium received, and other expenses).

The final option position is a *straddle* or *combo,* either of which is defined as buys or sells of equal numbers of puts and calls, all having the same underlying. If both have the same series description, the position is a *straddle;* if the series description is different, it is known as a *combo.*

Example: The following are straddles:

1.	B	1	put	BOB	Jan	60
	B	1	call	BOB	Jan	60
2.	S	1	put	SAN	Jun	30
	S	1	call	SAN	Jun	30

The following are combos:

1.	B	1	put	SRA	Oct	35
	B	1	call	SRA	Oct	40
2.	S	1	put	MEL	Jul	50
	S	1	call	MEL	Oct	55

The following are not straddles or combos:

1.	S	1	put	LEE	Mar	15
	S	1	put	LEE	Mar	17½
2.	B	1	put	LAR	Nov	25
	B	1	call	LAR	Nov	25
3.	B	1	put	LAR	Oct	35
	S	1	call	LAR	Oct	55

In the case of straddle or combo, if the position is bought, the client pays the premiums in full, and no margin is charged as long as there is no risk to the firm. The client owns both positions.

If, however, the straddle or combo is sold, both positions are computed as uncovered options. The margin requirement is the requirement of the greater side, plus the in-the-money sum of the other side.

Example:

S 1 call LAR Oct 35 = 5
S 1 put LAR Oct 40 = 3
LAR is selling at 38

Call		*Put*	
100 LAR 38		100 LAR 38	
$3,800		$3,800	
× .20		× .20	
760		760	
500	Premium	300	Premium
$1,260		$1,060	
0	Less out-of-the-money amount	0	Less out-of-the-money amount
$1,260		$1,060	

The margin requirement is the "greater" side (the call), plus the in-the-money amount from the other side (put 2 points in the money).

$1,260	Margin requirement, call
+ 200	In-the-money amount, put
$1,460	Margin required for position

Note: Reviewed here is the margin required for equity options. The margin required for other products requires the application of different amounts and/or percentages. In any event, a firm's requirement may be higher or more restrictive.

FUTURE MARGIN

Future margin is based on a product (commodity, debt instrument, index, currency, metal) that is to be delivered at a later time. The buyer and seller of the future are really involved with a promise. The buyer is relying on the seller's "promise" to deliver; the seller is relying on the buyer's "promise" to pay upon receipt. Between the two parties are the clearing firms and clearing corporations that must make good for the terms of the contract.

Futures, like many other products, give the participant the ability not only to receive or deliver, but also to trade out of, or liquidate, positions. Between the time the position is opened to the time it is finally settled, the price on which the future product itself is based can change drastically.

Because the future is a "promise," the amount of margin

must be enough to protect all interested parties. Yet it must not be so high as to prevent participants from being able to benefit from the product.

Future margin is usually maintained between 3 and 5% of what is underlying the contract. This sum may be reflected as a fixed dollar sum or as a percentage. Index futures have the highest requirement of 10%. Again, as with all margin, regardless of product, the brokerage firm, commodity house, or other entity may charge higher rates.

Standard and Maintenance Margin

The gold contract is 100 troy ounces. If a particular gold future is trading at $350.00 per ounce, then a contract on gold at that price would have a value of $35,000. Assuming 5% margin, the margin per contract would be approximately $1,750. Therefore, the buyer and seller of a gold futures contract would be expected to deposit $1,750 for the contract. This is known as *standard margin.*

When the exchange on which the future trades establishes the standard margin, they also establish maintenance margin.

Example: Assume the maintenance margin for gold is 2%. This means that the amount of margin in a client's account may not be less than $700 ($35,000 × .02 = $700). We will keep margin at these rates throughout the following examples.

The 6-month gold future is trading on the New York Commodity Exchange (COMEX) at $350 per ounce when a client of SF&R decides to buy one contract. The client, Nat Lee, must deposit standard margin by the next business day. Nat would deposit $1,750.

Making to the Market

Another firm, Giant, Reckor & Crane has a client, Emile LeOlder, wanting to sell. Emile will also have to deposit $1,750 when the trade is made.

Nat	*Emile*
L1 gold 6-month @ $350.00	S1 gold 6-month @ $350.00
Standard margin $1,750	Standard margin $1,750

Assume that, at the end of the trading day, gold 6-month future contract closes at 350.50. Both firms would have to "mark" their client's account to the market. This means the money balances in the account must be altered to show the proper adjustment for profit or loss that resulted from that day's trading.

Since Nat took the contract on at $350.00, and the price is now $350.50, Nat's account is credited (given) the $50.00. Emile's account would reflect a decrease of 50 cents × 100 = $50.00. At the end of the day's trading, Nat has an $1,800 balance; Emile has $1,700.

This daily *mark to the market,* or "P&S-ing," is important, because it brings all of the positions in a given contract to the same price.

Just as these two illustrative accounts were adjusted to show the price difference, so would every other account that held positions in this contract, regardless of the price or time of commitment. All prices in this particular contract would be adjusted against the $350.50 close.

Example: Nat has a $50 profit at this point. If the position is "liquidated" or closed out, Nat would receive the $1,800 from the account. Having only put up $1,750, the $50 profit is reflected in the difference. If Emile, on the other hand, liquidates the position, Emile would receive a check for $1,700, reflecting the $50 loss. (Commission is ignored in these examples.)

Should the participants decide to maintain the positions until delivery, Nat is *contracted* to buy 100 troy ounces of gold for $35,000 (100 × $350), and Emile is contracted to deliver 100 troy ounces of gold and receive $35,000. As Nat already paid $1,750 (standard margin), Nat would owe the difference: $35,000 – 1,750 = $33,250. Upon payment of the $33,250, Nat has fulfilled the terms of the contract.

Emile has to deliver 100 troy ounces according to the terms of the contract. When this is accomplished, Emile will receive $35,000 plus the standard margin of $1,750, for a total of $36,750 (the $1,750 is Emile's money).

Delivery and Payment

Example: Gold is at $350.50 an ounce at the time of delivery. When the account is marked to the market, Nat would have had a profitable position, the account would have been credited $50.00 (50 cents × 100 troy ounces). The account would have contained $1,750 standard margin and $50 variation margin, for a total of $1,800. If gold is settling at $350.50 an ounce, SF&R (Nat's firm) would take Nat's standard margin, $1,750, plus the additional money Nat owes, $33,250, and the variation margin, $50, and purchase the gold for their client, Nat, for $35,050,00 or $350.50 per ounce. Nat's profit is now hidden in the fact that Nat paid $35,000 ($1,750 standard margin plus $33,250 additional deposit) for $35,000 worth of gold; the variation margin made up the difference.

Emile, on the other hand, received $36,750 when the gold was delivered. This sum, from Emile's point of view, is made up of the $1,750 standard margin and the $35,000. In reality, Emile's account was charged $50 variation margin when the gold rose from $350.00 to $350.50. Emile's firm, Giant, Reckor & Crane (GRC), has taken Emile's gold and delivered it as required by contract. (Actually, GRC has instructed Emile how and where to deliver it, but that's a different subject not to be discussed here.)

Upon delivery of the gold, $35,050 is received. This sum, plus Emile's remaining Standard Margin of $1,700 would total the money owed to Emile ($35,050 + $1,700 = $36,750).

Nat's Account		*Emile's Account*	
B1 gold 6 months @ $350		S1 gold 6 months @ $350	

Both deposit standard margin.

L1 gold 6 months @	$ 350	S1 Gold 6 months @	$ 350
Standard margin	$1,750	Standard margin	$1,750
	$1,750		$1,750

Gold rises to $350.50.

Long 1 gold 6 months @	$ 350	Short 1 gold 6 months @	$ 350
Standard margin	$1,750	Standard margin	$1,750
Variation margin	+ 50	Variation margin	- 50
	$1,800		$1,700

Standard margin accounts are adjusted to reflect current contract value.

If either party closes out the position at this market level, he or she would be trading at $350.50. Nat would have a $50 profit ($1,800 – $1750 = $50). Emile would have a $50 loss ($1,750 – $1,700 = $50).

If Nat is still "long" the position at the time of delivery, he would have to pay $35,000 in total. Having deposited $1,750, Nat would owe the difference ($33,250). The firm would take Nat's $35,000 and the variation margin of $50, and acquire the gold at 350.50 per ounce.

$ 1,750	Standard margin
33,250	Additional deposit
$35,000	Total cost to Nat
+ 50	Variation Margin
$35,050	Total cost for receipt of gold

Nat's contract stated that the cost to Nat for 100 troy ounces of gold would be $350.00 per ounce, and that is what it cost Nat.

If Emile is still short the position at the time of delivery, he would have to deliver the gold and receive $35,000 plus the standard margin that Emile had placed in the account, for a total of $36,750.

When Emile's gold is delivered, the firm will receive $35,050, the current value for gold. The firm takes the $35,050 plus whatever funds remain in the account, and delivers it to Emile.

Emile is contracted to deliver gold and receive		$35,000
Emile is to receive the standard margin deposit		+ 1,750
		$36,750
Emile will actually receive for the delivered gold		$35,050
Emile's deposit to standard margin	$1,750	
Less variation margin	- 50	
Remaining standard margin		+ 1,700
		$36,750

Emile's contract term has been satisfied.

Had the price of gold fallen instead, the adjustments for variation margin would be reversed. Both parties would still be contracting for $35,000 worth of gold, but Nat would be paying $35,000 for $34,950 worth of gold:

Standard margin	$ 1,750	
Variation margin	- 50	
	$ 1,700	
	$33,250	additional funds owed by Nat
	$34,950	

Paid by Nat = $35,000 ($1,750 + 33,250 = $35,000)
Value of gold = $34,950 (1,700 + 33,250 = $34,950)

Emile would receive $35,000 plus the standard margin of 1,750 deposited, for a total of $36,750. In reality:

Standard margin	$ 1,750
Variation margin	+ 50
	1,800
Actually received for the gold	34,950
	$36,750

Settling

Stone, Forrest & Rivers and Giant, Reckor & Crane are members of COMEX. Each day, when the "closing" or "settling" price of gold contracts is established, the firms adjust the variation margin for any of their client's holding these contracts. Even though all these positions represent compared transactions, after all the daily trading of the futures contract has been settled, open contract positions will still remain. For each contract owned, somewhere in the world is a contact sold, or short. Therefore, the two firms first adjust their clients who are long the contracts (who own the contracts) against those who are short (who owe the contract amount). Since the firm is most likely not perfectly offset, the difference between their clients' long and short positions is either a pay or a collect figure against the COMEX's clearing corporation. Again, because each long must have a short, the clearing corporation is acting as a pass-through in this process. As such, all future contracts of a given product, of a given month, will be adjusted to one unique price, and each month, within each product, has its own settlement price.

Future Comparison and Confirmation

Due to the fact that "futures" represent a commitment to settle a contract at a later date, the amount of margin that must be deposited by clients is extremely low, ranging from 3 to 10% depending on the product (member firms may charge more). Therefore, the P&S cycle utilized in futures occurs soon after trade.

Comparison

Comparison on futures exchanges occurs on trade date. Actually, trades are "matched" during the trading day in "periods" or "zones"; that is, the participant to a trade in one zone (an hour, for example) must submit the details of the transaction to the exchange by another zone (such as two hours later). If this is not accomplished and the participant knows the transaction as a valid trade, nonsubmitting participants can be fined or censured.

Under this system, all transactions should be matched before the brokers and traders leave the trading floor that day. Any discrepancies or other problems will be addressed the next morning before the opening of business.

Confirmation

Because future products settle the next business day, and due to the limited amount deposited by clients, trade confirmations are expedited. Clients who trade in this market respond to phone calls for additional funds, when needed, from their commodities future merchant (CFM). In addition, the use of telex and fax communications to relay the details of the trade is quite common.

THE ITEMS DUE LIST

Another margin area responsibility is to make certain that funds and securities are delivered and received in good order and on time. All activity in clients' accounts, regardless of types of issue traded, must be supervised by margin personnel.

In equities, the margin area maintains an *items due list*, which informs margin personnel of the monies or securities owed by clients. The margin personnel inform the account executives of these items, and the reps contact the clients to resolve problems.

EXTENSIONS

In a cash account, funds for equity purchases are due by the fifth, but no later than the seventh, business day; margin accounts must have the necessary funds by the fifth business day. Sales require the deposit of securities by the tenth business day after settlement date. Should a client fail to meet these requirements for a valid reason, the firm files for extension.

Specifically, the margin personnel file for extensions of time with self-regulatory organizations when a client has a good reason for tardiness. Clients are permitted five extensions in a chronological year. After that, their accounts are restricted and market action is taken to satisfy the client's deficiency. If the reason for tardiness is not acceptable to the firm, the firm may choose not to file for extension and take the appropriate market action.

SUMMARY

On any particular date, like other operation areas, the margin department, works on may different days' trades. The next section discusses the handling of funds and securities—the daily routine of the cashier's area.

CHAPTER 38

Cashiering

The cashiering function manages the firm's most critical assets, securities and cash. Specifically, this department must move securities as efficiently as possible so as to minimize the firm's need to borrow and maximize profit potentials.

In SF&R the cashier's areas of responsibility are:

- Receive and deliver.
- Vault.
- Stock loan/stock borrow.
- Bank loan.
- Transfer.
- Reorganization.

These sections of the department work jointly to use the firm's securities and other resources as effectively as possible.

The cashier's department becomes involved with operations:

- On the day before settlement.
- On settlement day.
- In the post-settlement period.

RECEIVE AND DELIVER

The Day Before Settlement

The length of a *settlement cycle,* (that is, the number of days between trade and settlement dates) varies according to the instruments being traded. Obviously, the shorter this cycle, the less time SF&R has to prepare for settlement. In commercial paper transactions, which settle on the same day as trade, processing time is minimal. Yet the trade must be entered into the system, figured and verified. Then receive and delivery instructions have to be prepared and delivery made—all on the trade date.

Generally, SF&R's cashiering staff prepare for settlement on the morning prior to settlement date. On that morning, trade blotters, arriving in the cashier's areas, inform the personnel there of pending settlements. This information is vital to the work of the Receive and Deliver and vault sections.

Securities may be vaulted on the firm's premises, at depositories, or at a custodial bank. Where the securities are retained depends on the nature of the firm's business, on the volume of transactions in a type of security, and on the coverage of the firm's insurance policies. For example, because commercial paper is available in large denominations and is usually in bearer form, SF&R maintains its inventory and customer's positions at a bank. The bank, acting as an extension of the firm's cashiering area, therefore executes receive, deliver, and maturity instructions issued by SF&R's commercial paper personnel.

Transactions in corporate securities follow the five-business-day settlement cycle. So these trades enter the cashiering area on the day before settlement. By this time, most of these transactions have been compared through the clearing corporations and are being readied for settlement.

Continuous Net Settlement (CNS)

The National Securities Clearing Corporation provides its participants with a report known as the *projection report*. It informs the cashiers departments of remaining settlement positions due that day and the net settlement positions for the next day. All day long, receives and deliveries are posted to the projection report.

At the end of the day, receives or deliveries that have not been completed are "rolled" into tomorrow's settling positions.

Since the security positions on this report are part of continuous net settlement, one day's uncompleted delivery or receive position is simply netted into the next day's positions.

Example: Today SF&R is due to deliver 100 shares of ZAP, but, for one reason or another, it does not make delivery; the next day, SF&R is due to receive 100 shares of ZAP. Instead, the 100-share receipt is used to offset the undelivered 100 shares of the day before. The two positions cancel each other out.

In the CNS, open "fail" items are updated daily. In a given security, a firm can have only one fail to receive or one fail to deliver at a time or be flat. This system eliminates multiple fails that non-CNS securities experience.

Depository Trust Company (DTC)

As a participant of Depository Trust Company (DTC), SF&R settles most of its stock and bond transactions through this service firm.

Tomorrow's settlement depository-located securities begins tonight:

1. The firm adds today's open receives and delivers to tomorrow's settling position.
2. Then it informs the clearing corporation as to which securities can be used for settlement and which cannot. Those that cannot be used are part of SF&Rs *exemption* position and instruction.
3. The firm also requests *priorities* to receive issues that may be needed for particular purposes.

Exemptions are used by firms to control positions. A *level 1 exemption* freezes a security position up to the limit established by the exemption. A *level 2 exemption* also freezes positions but allows certain security movements to be excluded from the exemption. Level 3 has no restriction.

Example: The use of exemptions is very important to the security and cash management of SF&R. SF&R must maintain 15,000 shares of Marnee Corp. against customer's "seg" positions. All of its shares of Marnee are on deposit at DTC. Therefore SF&R gives a level 1 exemption for 15,000 shares, which means NSCC and DTC interfaces cannot move any Marnee shares from its depository position until, by one means or another, the position has accumulated more than 15,000 shares.

On the night before settlement, the clearing corporation sends an updated receive and delivery computer tape to the depository. The tape contains all its member firms updated receive and delivery positions, exemptions, and priorities.

At the depository, the tape is passed against the security positions that Stone, Forrest & Rivers is maintaining at the depository. (Of course, the same is done for all member firms.) Bookkeeping entries record the movement of securities from delivering firms to receiving firms. Because all such movements, both receives and delivers, are made by bookkeeping entries, the total number of shares per security on deposit remains the same. No physical movement of securities has transpired. The total number of shares owned by a particular firm, however, may change. The net result of this night time processing is reported to the clearing corporation, which prepares the next morning's projection report. The depository's night cycle is known as *PDQ*.

During settlement day, bookkeeping movements taking place between the clearing Corporation and the depository continue. Participating firms deposit or withdraw physical securities. These day time cycles are known as *mainline activities*. Cleaned up receivers and deliverers are posted to the projected report by SF&R's personnel. On the night of settlement, the cashier's staff begin the next day's settlement routine.

Netted Balance Orders

Some securities are not eligible for CNS processing. For such securities, the National Securities Clearing Corporation issues netted *receive balance orders* (RBOs) or *deliver balance orders* (DBOs). These balance orders are instructions for settlement. They may be "cleaned up" either through the physical receive or delivery of securities or through instructions to the depository to receive or deliver the securities.

SF&R's cashiering area, in control of both physical and

depository security locations, determines which form of delivery to use in settling. The cashiering area receives securities against RBOs and delivers securities against DBOs.

Trade-for-Trade Settlement

A trade-for-trade cycle does not afford SF&R, or any other firm, the advantages of continuous net settlement or netted balance orders. Each transaction must be settled on its own. The securities, usually physical, must be pulled from the vault, prepared for delivery, and sent to the buying firm. The cashiering employees receive and deliver securities throughout the day by this trade-for-trade method.

An Illustrative Comparison

Example: The following compared buys and sells of TIP cover a two-day period. For simplicity, each trade is for 100 shares.

	SF&R	*Contra (Street-Side)*
Day 1	B 100 TIP @ 42	Firm A
	B 100 TIP @ 42	Firm B
	S 100 TIP @ 43	Firm A
Day 2	S 100 TIP @ 43	Firm C
	S 100 TIP @ 43	Firm B
	B 100 TIP @ 42	Firm D

On a trade-for-trade basis, SF&R has to receive or deliver securities against each trade. On Day 1, the firm buys 100 @ 42 from Firm A and sells 100 @ 43 to the same firm. The only difference between the two trades is in the prices. Even if the prices were the same, SF&R has to exchange securities and checks with Firm A. They do so, and that transaction is settled.

Firm B, however, fails to deliver the stock to SF&R on Day 1; it becomes a fail to receive. On Day 2, SF&R's delivery of stock to Firm B would still leave Day 1's fail to receive open. If SF&R is unable to deliver to B on Day 2, then SF&R's records on Day 3 would show a fail to receive at 42 from Day 1, as well as a fail to deliver at 42 from Day 2.

Eventually the fails are "cleaned up" (settled). In the meantime, for a $100 difference, both SF&R and Firm B have to maintain and monitor the fails.

Even without the complicating presence of fails, the trade-for-trade system can be cumbersome. Settling Day 1's trades of TIP necessitates two receives and one delivery. Day 2's trades necessitates two deliveries and one receive.

Given today's trading volume, this type of settlement would be a nightmare. Balance orders facilitate settlements. Because all the trades are compared, each buyer has a seller. In a given security's trades, only the execution prices vary. With price variations on a comparable basis, all the trades are the same. NSCC deals with price variations by adjusting each trader per security against the settlement price. NSCC charges firms that benefit on the trade and credits firms that are disadvantaged.

Example: Let's use the same trades as in the previous example. On Day 1, NSCC establishes the settlement price at 43. (Each clearing corp formulates the settlement price in a way that is agreed to by the clearing corporation's participants.) SF&R has purchased 2 × 100 shares at 42. The clearing corporation instructs SF&R to pay 43. The clearing corporation credits SF&R with $200 (2 × $100), obtains the $200 from the sellers at $42, and instructs the seller to receive $43 per share. So, upon receipt of the 100 shares, SF&R theoretically pays $4,200 plus $100 to the clearing corporation, for a total of $43 per share.

With all the day's prices adjusted to 43, all trades of TIP are now the same. Because SF&R bought 200 and sold 100, it is given a balance order to receive 100 of TIP at 43 from a firm that netted to a delivery position.

Adjusting the settlement price for each security enables NSCC to net all trades in the security to one receive or payment. As you can see, RBOs and DBOs greatly reduced the number of receives and deliveries made by the industry. Yet receives or deliveries not made on settlement dates still became fails. A system known either as net-by-net or as continuous net settlement (CNS) eased the "fail" crunch. With NSCC's receive and delivery instructions and DTC's holding security positions for the firm, receives and delivers could be made by book entry. As an added benefit, a fail could contain the same information as a trade: name of firm, bought or sold, quantity, security, price, first money, and opposing firm's ID. So fails could be included in the next day's settling trades.

Example: On Day 2, SF&R is supposed to DELIVER 100 shares of TIP. In a CNS system, Day 1's fail to receive is netted with Day 2's settlement. As a result, SF&R is *flat*, that is, it does not have to receive or deliver.

Thus, as SF&R completes the streetside obligation for its many trades, the settlement cycle draws to a close. Some settlement cycles require physical delivery; others are made through depositories, and still others through a custodial bank. Each form of settlement demands its own form of monetary settlement:

- To settle through CNS, SF&R either pays one check to the clearing corporation or receives one check from it for all the transactions settled that day.
- To settle through netted balance orders, SF&R issues one check for each security named on the balance order. For example, if Stone, Forrest & Rivers receives ten securities through balance orders, SF&R has to issue ten checks. Correspondingly, it receives a check for each security delivered.
- To settle on a trade-for-trade basis, SF&R draws or receives a check for each settling transaction.

The cashier's department is responsible for all settlements against the clearing corporation. In addition, the cashier's area controls the receive and delivery money made on the night of T + 4 (the PDQ system) and the remaining receives and delivers made through DTC on T + 5 (the mainline system).

Most transactions settle in five days and settle in clearing house funds (*next-day money*). Options and futures, which are next-day settlers, also settle this way. Securities that settle same day, such as commercial paper, make use of Fed funds (*same-day money*). The method of payment is important to SF&R because the cashier's area is responsible for moving money, specifically that enough money is available in the correct bank when needed.

CUSTOMER-SIDE SETTLEMENT

While settling streetside transactions, SF&R also receives checks from its customers and issues checks to them. Some of these checks are trade-related, others are not.

Customers' checks received as payment for purchases must be "booked" accurately and promptly. If they are not, the margin department may send customers erroneous calls for money. This kind of mistake only angers clients.

When SF&R issues checks to a customer who has sold securities, the cashier's area must be sure that the delivery of the security is a good one. SF&R cannot pay on a bad delivery because the "bad" security is nonnegotiable. Securities may be rendered nonnegotiable for several reasons. Securities registered in an individual's name need only a stock/bond power, properly executed by the client, to make the certificate negotiable. If the security is registered in the name of a deceased person or a corporation, many additional papers are needed.

SF&R cannot use such securities for delivery or transfer to the purchaser until it is made negotiable. SF&R is left "holding the bag": Having paid the client good funds, the firm cannot collect from the purchaser until it gets the securities into deliverable form. Accepting a bad delivery is therefore a very costly mistake to the firm.

DELIVERY

Delivery Versus Payment (DVP)

Some of SF&R's accounts are *delivery versus payment (DVP)*, also known as *cash on delivery* (COD) or *cash on receipt (COR)*. In this type of account, the client pays for purchases upon receipt of the securities and gets paid for sales upon their delivery. Usually institutions, such as banks or insurance companies, use this type of account. Because large numbers of shares or bonds are involved in these transactions, SF&R tries to gather all of the certificates necessary on purchases so that delivery to the account's custodian can be made as promptly as possible.

The ID System

Several of the depositories offer an institutional client settlement service to satisfy the need to make third-party settlements. Institutions, such as pension funds, insurance companies, and corporations, utilize the facility of a custodian bank to settle transactions and to maintain their securities positions. These custodial banks act on instructions received from their clients to receive and deliver securities against payment. It is the custodial bank, the third party, with whom the brokerage firm must settle institutional transactions.

Example: Natcar Corp. maintains a pension plan for its clients. The plan is carried as an account at Stone, Forrest & Rivers, a brokerage firm, and at Rachael National Bank, a custodial bank. When Natcar's pension group decides to change their holdings, to invest more money into the pension plan, or to sell securities to generate cash necessary to pay out pension benefits, they contact their broker at SFR to discuss the various alternatives, and then give orders to buy or sell, or buy and sell, different securities. SFR executes these orders and reports the results to Natcar.

Natcar must now inform their custodial bank of the transactions, so that they, the custodian bank, will know to receive or deliver securities, and the amount of money involved in the transaction(s).

To facilitate this process, SFR has "standing instructions" on the customer account files for Natcar. The instructions are to receive and deliver versus payment with Rachael National Bank. Trades executed by SFR for Natcar will be processed through a central facilitator, *Institutional Delivery System.*

Before there was an Institutional Delivery System, brokerage firms would call their client's custodial bank prior to settlement to ensure that the bank knew the trade. If they didn't perform this verification, the firm would risk losing money due to overnight interest costs incurred when the securities involved in the delivery were DK'd (don't know). It is important to remember that very few security movements in a brokerage environment are free. Most involve a payment of money somewhere. For example, when you purchase stock through your firm, if they are selling the issue to you from their inventory, then they have paid for the security and must finance the position until you pay for it. When they purchase it for you from another firm, your firm has probably paid for the purchase on settlement date. When you pay for the purchase, your check offsets the funds used to settle the transaction with the opposing firm.

With the advent of the depositories and, with it, book entry settlement, it became possible to verify and settle client-side transactions as easily as it was to settle street-side (or brokerage-firm-side) transactions.

After the execution of the transaction, SFR, an institutional broker, informs Natcar of the results. This information is later sent to the depository for redistribution to the custodial banks. During this period, the institution and the custodial bank discuss the details of the trade. When the custodial bank, Rachael National Bank, receives notification of the transactions from the ID System, it reviews the terms with the client's institutions. If all is in agreement, they will send an affirmation of the trade to the depository, who then redistributes it to SFR.

On settlement date, SFR and Rachel National Bank will receive or deliver versus payment, both operating on behalf of Natcar. All entries will be made by book entry, with the transaction money being netted with other settlements occurring that day.

Let's review the steps:

Step 1. Natcar, the client, and SFR (the broker) enter into a transaction by which SFR is to purchase 10,000 shares of Emily Frocks Ltd.

Step 2. SFR goes into the market place and buys 10,000 shares of Emily Frocks from Benson, another brokerage firm. The cost is $42 per share, or $420,000.

Step 3. SFR compares the transaction with Benson through the National Securities Clearing Corporation (NSCC).

Step 4. SFR notifies Natcar and Rachael National Bank of the transaction.

Step 5. Rachael National Bank affirms the transaction.

Step 6. On settlement date, Benson delivers 10,000 shares of Emily Frocks to Stone, Forrest & Rivers through Depository Trust Company by book entry.

Step 7. SFR delivers the securities through the ID system to Rachael National Bank for the account of Natcar.

Step 8. Upon notification of receipt, Rachael National Bank releases $420,000 to SFR.

Step 9. SFR is debited and Benson is credited the $420,000.

Note: This is a simplistic explanation of what occurs. There are many brokerage firms settling many transactions with many custodian banks. In addition, some of these steps occur simultaneously.

What happens, however, if Rachael National Bank somehow does not know the transaction? When they receive notification of the trade from SFR via DTC's ID system, they verify their instructions and then notify DTC that they don't know (DK) the trade. This information is forwarded to SFR's P&S area.

Once the DK notification has been received, SFR's P&S personnel contact the registered representative who "covers" the Natcar account, advising him or her of the problem. The DK could occur for several reasons:

1. The registered representative copied an incorrect account number and the transaction is not for Natcar.
2. Natcar has changed its delivery instructions, and Rachael National Bank is not its custodial bank any longer.
3. Natcar neglected to affirm the transaction with Rachael National Bank.
4. SFR forgot to advise Natcar of the trade.
5. The terms of the trade are different from what was originally reported.

Regardless of the cause, SFR must reconcile the problem or it will be involved in an error. The 10,000 shares was purchased from Benson, another brokerage firm, who in turn probably sold it for their client. They will be looking for payment.

The registered representative reconciles the problem, and the process gets under way again. (*Note:* The settlement process occurred without the physical movement of securities.)

The contra party may also be acting on behalf of an institutional client. For example, suppose that Benson was acting for an institutional client who clears through its custodial bank, Wennan National Bank. Wennan National Bank is a participant at the Philadelphia Depository Trust Company, more commonly known as Philadep. On settlement date:

1. Wennan National Bank instructs Philadep to deliver 10,000 shares of Emily Frocks to Benson Brokerage at DTC.
2. Philadep makes a bookkeeping entry taking the shares from

Wennan National Bank and placing them in DTC's omnibus account for Benson Brokerage.

3. DTC takes the stock, again by bookkeeping entry, from its account at Philadep and gives it to Benson Brokerage.
4. For settlement, it takes the shares from Benson Brokerage account and gives it to Stone, Forrest & Rivers (SFR).
5. Then, on instruction from SFR, it removes the shares from SFR's account and gives it to Rachael National bank for the account of Natcar, the new owner.

Note: All of these entries occur without the movement of physical securities.

What happens to the $420,000 (10,000 shares at 42) needed for settlement? They become part of each entity's settlement figures, netted along with their other transactions into a one-check settlement for the day.

VAULTING

Over the years, the methods for vaulting securities have changed. Today, as a result, vaulting procedures differ according to the type of security. For example, listed options are certificateless; so vaulting is unnecessary. Most corporate securities are eligible for depository vaulting. Munis are becoming DTC-eligible, but most are physical in bearer form. Like any multiproduct firm, SF&R must be set up to handle the vaulting of different securities.

Segregated (Seg) Securities

According to Regulation T, two conditions exist where securities must be locked up and cannot be commingled with the firm's own securities:

1. Customer's fully-paid-for securities.
2. Securities in a customer's margin account with a value over 140% of the account's debit balance.

FIGURE 38-1. *500 shares of AT&T are being placed in the vault ("Box In").*

BOX IN

DATE 7/28

BY

KEY CODE		
2	0	C
1	2	3

OFFICE			ACCT. NUMBER						T
9	7	0	0	0	0	1	0	8	1
4	5	6	7	8	9	10	11	12	13

QUANTITY							
					5	0	0
14	15	16	17	18	19	20	21

OFF
48

CUSIP NUMBER								
1	9	3	0	4	7	0	0	1
69	70	71	72	73	74	75	76	77

C/C
1
78

SECURITY: AT&T

CERTIFICATE: MARK TYME

NUMBERS: C149371-5

SBHU 375

FROM: BS191349

The firm must have these securities segregated from all others. They must be in an isolated location, and they may not be used for loan, short sales, or hypothecation. These securities are commonly nicknamed *seg*, short for "segregated."

BANK LOAN

By signing a margin agreement, a client gives SF&R permission to use securities valued up to 140% of the account's debit balance to borrow money from banks. The borrowed money is used to pay for the purchase in the client's account.

Example: A client buys $10,000 worth of stock. With the margin rate at 50%, the client gives SF&R a check for $5,000, and SF&R lends the client the remaining $5,000. Both SF&R's $5,000 and the client's $5,000 are used to pay for the purchase. Because the banks will not lend dollar for dollar, SF&R sends the customer's securities valued at $7,000 (140% of the debit balance of $5,000) to the bank. Upon receipt of the securities, the bank lends SF&R the $5,000 on loan to the client.

Let's see how this works.

Example: Customer CG401243 buys 100 PIP @ 50. The firm hypothecates (pledges) securities to obtain the $2,500 being loaned by the client. To obtain this money, SF&R deposits $3,500 worth of PIP at the lending bank ($2,500 × 1.40%). At $50 per share, 70 shares of PIP are hypothecated ($3,500 divided by $50). The remaining 30 shares are locked up in "seg." When PIP rises to $80 a share, SF&R's bank loan section ensures that only $3,500 worth—about 44 shares—of PIP is at the bank. The remaining 56 shares are "locked up."

When the customer wants to borrow the additional $1,500, SF&R sends 26 shares, or $2,100 worth, of PIP to the bank to borrow the needed $1,500. With the customer's debit at $4,000, SF&R has hypothecated 70 shares, or $5,600, of PIP @ 80 ($4,000 × 1.40 = $5,600). The proceeds can be used to buy $3,000 worth of WOW (100 shares @ 30). Thus the customer borrows $1,500 from SF&R on the value of WOW. To make that loan, SF&R pledges $2,100 ($1,500 × 1.40) to the bank. The loan arrangements are now as follows:

70 shares of PIP @ 80 =	$5,600
70 shares of WOW @ 30 =	2,100
Total value	$7,700
Customer's debit	$5,500
	× 1.40
	$7,700

The client has two securities in position with a combined value of $11,000. The first can lend up to 140% of the debit balance, which is $7,700 in this case ($5,500 × 1.40). SF&R can use any combination of the two securities to secure the needed funds, as long as $3,300 worth of PIP and/or WOW, in any combination, are locked up in seg.

Since SF&R's customer has signed a lending agreement (in addition to the margin agreement) the firm can obtain loans from other sources of funds. SF&R's stock loan/stock borrow section maintains contacts with other firms that lend SF&R money against loaned securities. The cash that SF&R receives is then used to support the debit balances.

Because the value of securities changes from day to day and because securities' positions in customer accounts vary daily, SF&R's vault personnel receive "seg" reports every day. These employees make sure that SF&R has enough securities to satisfy seg requirements before they can "pull" securities for other purposes.

Free, or nonseg, securities may also be used to cover short sales of other clients, and to "clean up" fails. To maintain such flexibility in security usage, the firm's policy is to require any client signing a margin agreement to also sign a lending agreement.

This task is complicated by the fact that SF&R, like many brokerage firms, maintains some securities at central depositories and must keep enough securities at the depositories to satisfy "seg" requirements, while keeping securities available for delivery. A further requirement is that securities maintained by custodian banks, operating on behalf of SF&R, fall under the same "seg" rules as securities maintained in SF&R's vault. Cashiering's receive and deliver section issues instructions to these banks. So the bank and the firm must work closely together to control positions, receives, delivers, transfers, and any movement of securities.

Registration of Securities in Street Name

Most securities are kept in the registered form known as "street name." This means that they are registered in acceptable delivery form for the firm's use. The beneficial owner, however, is the customer, who is entitled to *all* the privileges and rights of ownership. Such registered securities are usually vaulted in street name, that is, maintained in the name of the brokerage firm or depository.

Some clients keep their fully paid-for securities on SF&R's premises but registered in their own names. These securities are said to be registered in "name of," or maintained in, safekeeping. Although SF&R provides vaulting services, the clients receive dividends, proxy information, and all other information from the issuing company. When these clients sell the securities, the firm has to make certain that these particular securities are used for delivery. If SF&R were to use street name stock in error, the clients are left with the misconception that the securities were sold yet wonder why dividend checks and other mailings are still being sent to them.

TRANSFER

Registering certificates is the function of the transfer section, which instructs the firm's transfer agent on the action to be taken.

Securities are actually transferred by *transfer agents,* which are usually banks that maintain the ownership books for the issuing entity (such as corporations). Securities are sent to such banks for transfer or cancelled, and instructions are requested for new securities issued in their place. Any mistake, such as the misspelling of a client's name, means that the newly issued security has to be returned to the transfer agent for reissue.

There are two types of transfer: regular and legal.

Regular Transfer

When negotiable securities are received by SF&R's cashiering area and require transfer, they are sent immediately to the transfer section for processing. When nonnegotiable securities are received from clients, they are sent to the vault, while notices are sent to the branch office servicing the client describing the document(s) needed. A file is maintained until the document is received, and the security is then routed for transfer.

Securities returned from transfer are in either the client's name or street name (SF&R's, the depository's or the custodian bank's).

Legal Transfers

Some transfers, known as *legal transfers*, require special handling. Legal transfers are necessary in the case of corporate-owned, estate, or certain fiduciary transfers. Corporate-owned securities require not only the usual paperwork, but also a corporate resolution and copies of the corporate charter or bylaws. Transfers on behalf of an estate require copies of death certificates, an affidavit of domicile, tax waivers, and other special documents. Each of the required forms must be completed and filed, together with the other required documents, to effect transfer.

Legal transfers require extra diligence on the part of the staff because additional paperwork is needed, such as affidavits of domicile, corporate resolutions, tax waivers, trust agreements, and probable documents. To complicate matters, some types of legal transfer require accompanying documents with expiration dates. If the transfer section needs additional paperwork on a legal transfer, they must request and get it before the other documents expire. Otherwise, the expired papers must, in turn, be requested—and the cycle continues.

Individual Versus Standing Instructions

Whether the physical transfer of certificates originates from the firm or from a depository, it is effected by either "individual" or "standing" instructions. *Individual instructions* must be initiated each time a transfer for a particular customer is needed. *Standing instructions* establish ongoing procedures, which can therefore be automated. Each time standing instructions can be applied to a transaction, you can standardize the transfer process and thereby eliminate some of the manual steps involved in individual instructions.

The Transfer Agent

When a security is "pulled" from the vault, fanfold (or multipart) forms are produced for the transfer. The certificate and accompanying forms are forwarded to the transfer agent, who is selected by the issuing entity. When the firm delivers the certificate to the transfer agent, it obtains a receipt, or *window ticket*. Upon receipt of the certificate, the transfer agent cancels it, issues a new certificate, registers the new certificate in accordance with the instructions, and returns it to the firm. When the certificates are ready, the firm surrenders the window ticket and receives the newly registered certificate.

The transfer agent also keeps records of outstanding certificates by certificate numbers. Each issue has its own series of num-

FIGURE 38-2. *A window ticket.*

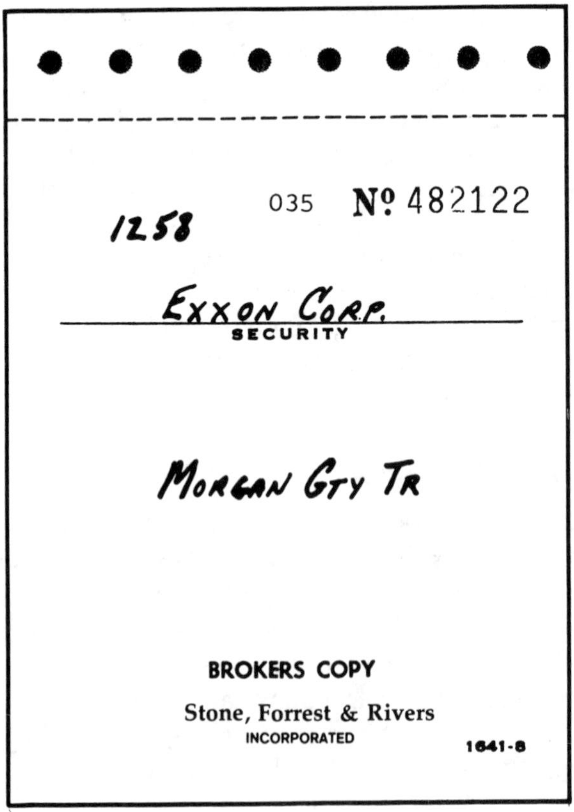

035 Nº 482122

1258

Exxon Corp.

SECURITY

Morgan Gty Tr

BROKERS COPY

Stone, Forrest & Rivers

INCORPORATED

1641-8

bers and each registration its own unique number. Each number is used only once, and accuracy is (by the firm as well as by the transfer agent) important for dividend processing and for searching stock record problems. (Records may be microfilmed.)

Some of the depositories offer transfer service. Upon instructions from the firm, the depository places securities with a transfer agent, which then follows the usual transfer procedure. Upon receipt of the newly registered certificate, the depository then delivers them to the requesting firm.

REORGANIZATIONS, TENDERS, AND SPIN-OFFS

Reorganizations are generally mergers in which the security of one company is surrendered for that of another. Company A merges with Company B to form Company C. Stockholders of Companies A and B may exchange their shares for stock in Company C.

Example: Company A merges with Company B to form Company C. The *reorganizations section*, or *reorg*, is responsible for obtaining the necessary physical shares, representing the recorded ownership of the brokerage firm's customers, and submitting them for the new shares. The new company's stock must be allocated among the stockholders of the merged companies in the proportion of their ownership. This task often involves computing full and fractional shares, because each customer *must* receive the amount deserved. Any error in the processing of the security could cost the brokerage firm money to correct.

Tender offers are similar to reorgs except that one firm makes an offer, usually in cash, for a certain number of shares of another company. Tender offers are usually made at prices higher than the current market price of the security. Stock owners may or may not want to accept the tender offer, and the company making the tender may accept all or part of the shares tendered.

In the event of a tender offer, the reorg section must, as part of its daily routine:

1. Secure enough securities to satisfy the instructions of the firm's customer.
2. Submit the securities to the tender agent within the allotted time.

FIGURE 38-3. *Instructions to the transfer agent.*

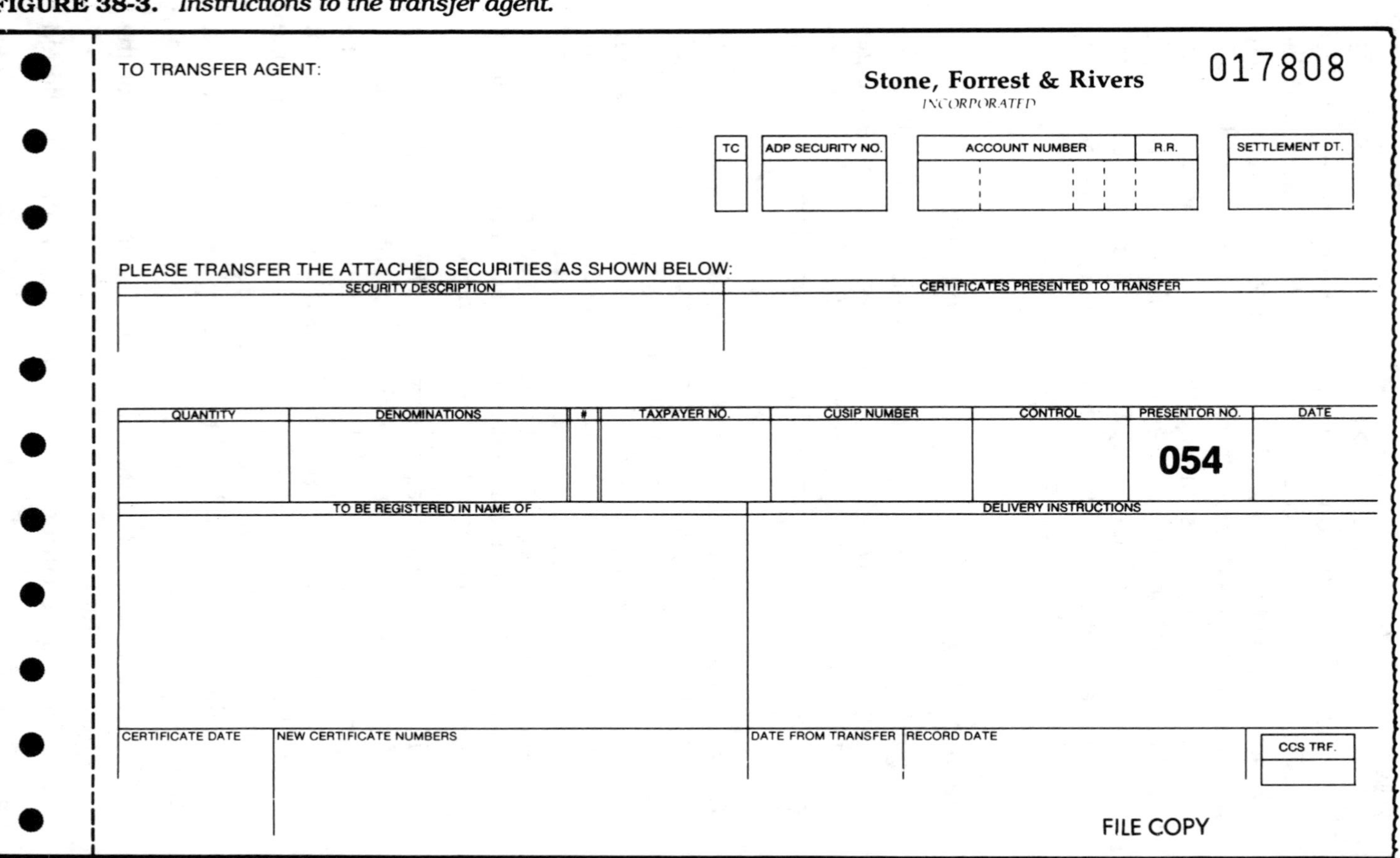

TO TRANSFER AGENT:

Stone, Forrest & Rivers
INCORPORATED

017808

TC	ADP SECURITY NO.	ACCOUNT NUMBER	R.R.	SETTLEMENT DT.

PLEASE TRANSFER THE ATTACHED SECURITIES AS SHOWN BELOW:

SECURITY DESCRIPTION	CERTIFICATES PRESENTED TO TRANSFER

QUANTITY	DENOMINATIONS	#	TAXPAYER NO.	CUSIP NUMBER	CONTROL	PRESENTOR NO.	DATE
						054	

TO BE REGISTERED IN NAME OF	DELIVERY INSTRUCTIONS

CERTIFICATE DATE	NEW CERTIFICATE NUMBERS	DATE FROM TRANSFER	RECORD DATE	CCS TRF.

FILE COPY

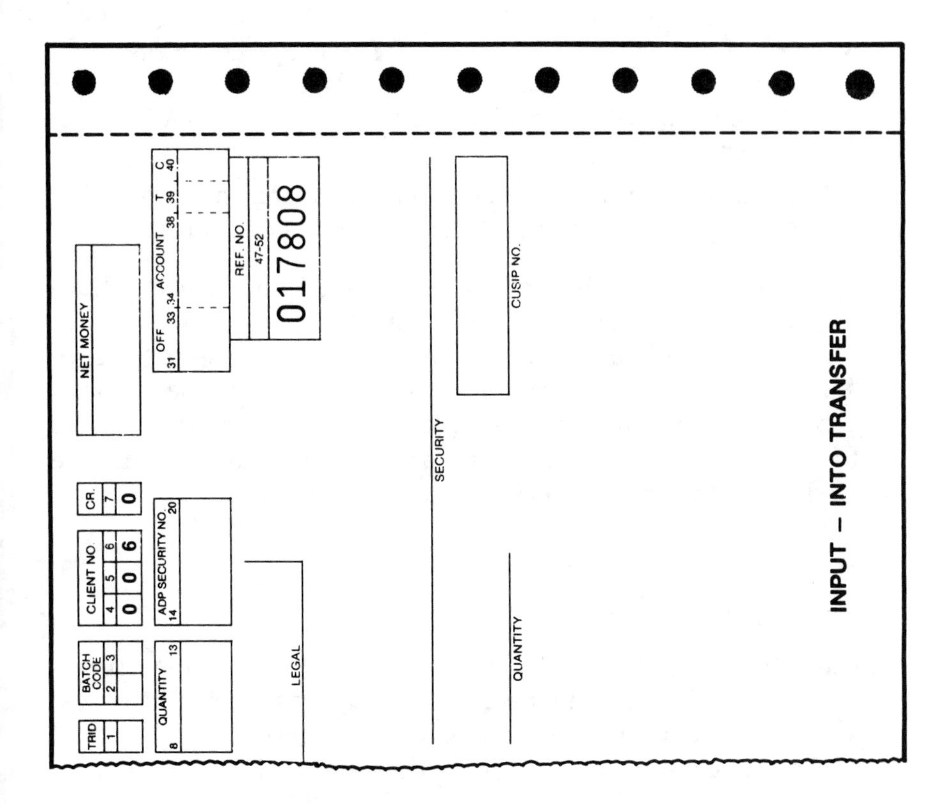

TRID 1

BATCH CODE 2 3

CLIENT NO. 4 5 6 — 0 0 6

CR. 7 — 0

NET MONEY

QUANTITY 8 13

ADP SECURITY NO. 14 20

OFF ACCOUNT T C — 31 33 34 38 39 40

REF. NO. 47-52 — 017808

LEGAL

SECURITY

CUSIP NO.

QUANTITY

INPUT – INTO TRANSFER

3. Allocate the cash received among the participating customers.
4. Balance out, to a zero position, the shares submitted, the shares tendered, and the cash received per account.

All this usually has to be accomplished during heavy trading markets and changeable tender offers.

In a *spin-off,* a company separates, or "spins-off," a subsidiary. The so-called *parent company* may spin off one or many subsidiaries in different share ratios. In so doing, it issues shares to its current security holders, and these securities must be credited to the appropriate customers' accounts.

SUMMARY

Cashiering supervises the movement of the brokerage firm's money, doing everything necessary to use it as efficiently as possible. Correspondingly, the stock record department, the subject of the next chapter, supervises the flow of securities.

CHAPTER 39

Accounting

To understand brokerage accounting, you must first understand accounting in general. While most of us are trained to make entries affecting securities or futures products, what escapes our attention is that the cash, or money, side of the entry drives the security entry and determines whether it is a debit or credit.

This is further disguised by the simple fact that, whenever we see an "accounting" of our own finances, we are actually seeing it through the "eyes" of someone else. For example, when we deposit money into our checking account, the bank *credits* our accounts. The bank credits our accounts because "our" accounts are a liability to the bank; they owe us that money. Actually, "your" bank account is not "yours." It is the bank's account, which they have assigned for you to use. It is their account, presented in the format of their account number structure to which your name and other information are affixed. This is no different than your firm's clients' accounts. It is your firm's account number to which the client's name, address, and so on are assigned.

To prove this, when you call your bank or any other entity that you have an account with, you usually give your name, to which they ask, "And what is your *account* number?" That question serves two purposes: First, it gets them away from the embarrassment of not knowing who you are; second, it is easier for you to know the account number than it is for them to research it.

THE ACCOUNTING PROCESS

Debits and Credits

To understand the mechanics of accounting, remember that all movements in a company are recorded by entries and that every entry has two sides: a debit and a credit. Debits and credits must always be, in total, equal and offsetting. To be complete, each entry must therefore have equal and offsetting debits and credits.

In addition, all accounts fall into one of five categories: revenue, expense, assets, liabilities, or net worth. Entries are made to adjust accounts to reflect movements among these five categories.

For the accounting system to work, a starting point is needed to which all agree and adhere, and against which all other entries are determined. Many years ago, it was determined that cash is an asset and that all assets are to have debit balances. Assets could have just as easily been credits, but the determination was made that assets were to be debits. This assumption is the foundation for accounting as we know it.

If cash is an asset, and if assets are always debits, then you can figure out the effect it has on cash.

Example: Lee Nolium begins working. At the end of the first week, she is paid a salary of $500. Since cash is an asset, assets are debits, we know that one side of the entry must be a debit to cash of $500. The other entry must account for where it came from: Salary is revenue, and therefore must be a credit. Lee deposits her paycheck into "her" bank account. The bank credits "her" account, which is a liability to them, since they owe Lee the money, and they debit their asset account called cash.

Debit	*Credit*
Asset cash $500	Revenue salary $500

Banks Books

Debit	*Credit*
Asset cash $500	Client account $500

**Note:* Accounts payable is the bank's account that was assigned to Lee.

Profit and Loss Statement and Balance Sheet

It would be appropriate at this point to define the five account categories:

Asset: Something owned by, or owed to, the recording entity.

Liability: Something owed by the entity.

Net worth: The difference between assets and liabilities (aka Stockholders' equity).

Revenue: Income generated from the efforts of the recording firm.

Expenses: Costs incurred in securing revenue.

Example: At the end of month, which contained four pay periods (some months contain five), Lee Nolium received $2,000 in salary. She paid rent of $600, taxes of $500, utilities $250, transportation to and from work $100, and $300 for food and meals. From an accounting standpoint, Lee had the following "profit and loss" profile:

Lee's Profit and Loss Statement

Revenue: Salaries		$2,000
Expenses:		
Rent	600	
Taxes	500	
Utilities	250	
Transportation	100	
Food	300	
Total expenses		1,750
Net profit		$ 250

Since Lee deposited her pay into her checking account and paid each bill as it came in, she should have $250 remaining in her checking account. The remaining $250 in cash is offset by the $250 net profit. It would be appropriate to move the result of operations, the $250 profit, into net worth. As Lee has no liabilities, her final money position is:

Lee's Balance Sheet

Debit		Credit	
Asset: Cash	$250	Liability	0
		Net Worth	250
	$250		$250

Based on what we know, Lee has a net worth of $250.

In accounting, the preceding presentation showing revenue and expense is called the Profit and Loss Statement, or Income Statement. The second presentation, known as the Balance Sheet, shows that assets equal liability plus net worth.

Journal Ledger

For the month, Lee would have made the following journal entries (if she maintained a journal ledger):

Journal Entries

Date	*Entry*	*Debit*	*Credit*	*Ledger Entry*
1/5	Cash [checking account]	$500		(1)
	Salary		$500	(1)
	To record salary received			
1/5	Food expense	75		(2)
	Cash [checking account]		75	(2)
	Bought food, check #1001			
1/5	Tax expense	125		(3)
	Cash [checking account]		125	(3)
	Paid income taxes, check #1002			
1/5	Transportation expense	25		(4)
	Cash [checking account]		25	(4)
	Bought weekly train ticket, check #1003			
1/12	Cash [checking account]	$500		(5)
	Salary		$500	(5)
	To record salary received			
1/12	Food expense	75		(6)
	Cash		75	(6)
	Bought food, check #1004			
1/12	Tax expense	125		(7)
	Cash		125	(7)
	Paid taxes, check #1005	125		
1/12	Transportation expense	25		(8)
	Cash		25	(8)
	Bought weekly ticket, check #1006			
1/19	Cash [checking account]	$500		(9)
	Salary		$500	(9)
	To record salary received			
1/19	Food expense	75		(10)
	Cash [checking account]		75	(10)
	Bought food, check #1007			
1/19	Tax expense	125		(11)
	Cash [checking account]		125	(11)
	Paid income taxes, #1008			

Date	*Entry*	*Debit*	*Credit*	*Ledger Entry*
1/19	Transportation expense	25		(12)
	Cash [checking account]		25	(12)
	Bought weekly train ticket, check #1009			
1/26	Cash	$500		(13)
	Salary		$500	(13)
	To record salary received			
1/26	Food expense	75		(14)
	Cash		75	(14)
	Bought food, check #1010			
1/26	Tax expense	125		(15)
	Cash		125	(15)
	Paid taxes, check #1011			
1/26	Transportation expense	25		(16)
	Cash		25	(16)
	Bought weekly ticket, check #1012			
1/26	Utilities expense	250		(17)
	Cash		250	(17)
	Paid utility bill, check #1013			
1/26	Rent expense	600		(18)
	Cash		600	(18)
	Paid rent, check #1014			

All of Lee's financial entries for January are recorded on the journal. Note that each entry affected an account and the balance within each account.

Ledger Accounts

The next step is to "post" the journal entries to their respective ledger accounts (which will be displayed at "T" accounts).

In T accounts, entries to the left are debits, entries to the right are credits.

Cash (Debit)	*Cash* (Credit)	*Salary* (Debit)	*Salary* (Credit)	*Rent Expense* (Debit)	*Rent Expense* (Credit)
1 500	75 (2)		500 (1)	(18) 600	
	125 (3)		500 (5)		
	25 (4)		500 (9)		
5 500	75 (6)		500 (13)		
	125 (7)				
	25 (8)				
9 500	25 (10)				
	125 (11)				
	25 (12)				

13	500	75	(14)
		125	(15)
		25	(16)
		250	(17)
		600	(18)

Food Expense

(2)	75	
(6)	75	
(10)	75	
(14)	75	

Tax Expense

(3)	125	
(7)	125	
(11)	125	
(15)	125	

Transportation Expense

(4)	25	
(8)	25	
(12)	25	
(16)	25	

Utility Expense

(17)	250	

Net Worth

The next step is to close or balance out each account. For example: Cash Account

Cash

Debit	Credit
500	
	75
	125
	25
500	
	75
	125
	25
500	
	75
	125
	25
500	
	75
	125
	25
	250
	600
2,000	1,750
−1,750	
250	Debit

If each debit has an equal and offsetting credit, then the results of the preceding entries should be in balance.

Debit		=	*Credit*	
Cash	$ 250		Salary	2,000
Rent	600			
Food	300			
Tax	500			
Transportation	100			
Utilities	250			
	$2,000	=		$2,000

Trial Balance

The last step is commonly known as a *trial balance* which tests that all posted entries are in balance.

From the trial balance, we can now extract the Balance Sheet and Profit and Loss Statement, presented earlier.

Lee's Balance Sheet

Debit		*Credit*	
Asset: Cash	$250	Liability	0
		Net worth	250
	$250		$250

Lee's Profit and Loss Statement

Revenue: Salaries		$2,000
Expenses:		
Rent	600	
Taxes	500	
Utilities	250	
Transportation	100	
Food	300	
Total expenses		$1,750
Net profit		$ 250

INTRODUCTION TO BROKERAGE ACCOUNTING

Example: Al Luminium, a client of SF&R, buys 100 ZAP at 47 for $4,770. Al's confirmation reads:

First money $4,700, Commission $70, Net money $4,770

First Money	Commission	Net Money
$4,700	$70	$4,770

Because SF&R acted in the capacity as a broker in the transaction, it purchased the security from another firm. It owes that firm $4,700 when the stock is received. If the stock is not received by settlement date, the position will become a fail to receive.

In essence, a fail to receive is an accounts payable. This is part of brokerage accounting that becomes confusing. While we are trained to focus on the security, in name and account position, it is the *value* of the issue, both present and future, that is of concern.

For booking purposes, even though the other firm owes SF&R stock, the entry is booked from the money standpoint. Likewise, while SF&R owes Al stock, Al owes SF&R money; so the entry is posted as a debit, an asset, an Account Receivable. To understand brokerage accounting, you must understand the money side of the entry.

Example Client Sandy Beach buys 1,000 EU at $16 per share. The trade is an agency transaction, since SF&R bought the stock for Sandy from Meadows & Pond, another broker dealer. Beach's account would reflect the following position (commission and taxes are omitted):

Security			*Money*		
Debit	*Credit*	*Description*	*Debit*	*Credit*	*Balance*
1,000		Water Log's, Inc.	16,000		16,000 Db

If the stock is not received from Meadows & Pond, a fail to receive will be set up. It will look like this:

Security			*Money*		
Debit	*Credit*	*Description*	*Debit*	*Credit*	*Balance*
1,000		Water Log's, Inc.		16,000	16,000 Cr

Note: Both entries are equal and opposite.

Beach pays for the purchase:

Security			*Money*		
Debit	*Credit*	*Description*	*Debit*	*Credit*	*Balance*
		Check received		16,000	0

Offset entry on firm books—cash account:

Security					
Debit	*Credit*	*Description*	*Debit*	*Credit*	*Balance*
		Check vs. Beach A/C	16,000		16,000 Db

In other words, the cash portion of the Accounts Receivable (aka Beach's Account) was "cleaned up." The firm's Cash Account was debited and now reflects the balance.

As to the street side, Meadows & Pond delivers the 1,000 shares and SF&R pays them $16,000. The entries are as follows:

Security			*Money*		
Debit	Credit	Description	Debit	Credit	Balance
1,000		Water Logs, Inc.	16,000		0
(Clean up fail to receive)					
1,000		Water Logs, Inc.			
(Entry putting security in vault)					
				16,000	0
(Payment of cash)					

All of these entries would occur in the respective accounts:

Sandy Beach	=	LO984321
Fail to receive	=	NFR5000
Vault	=	NYV5000
Cash	=	6666USD

As such, the entries would appear as follows:

Account #	*Security*				*Money*		
	Debit (Long)	Credit (Short)	Balance	Description	Debit	Credit	Balance
L098431	1,000		1,000 Db.	Water Logs, Inc.	$16,000		16,000 Db.
NFR5000		1,000	1,000 Cr.	Water Logs, Inc.		$16,000	16,000 Cr.
L0984321				Check received		16,000	0
6666USD				CHVVSLO984321	16,000		16,000 Db.
NFR5000	1,000		0	Water Logs, Inc.	16,000		0
6666USD						16,000	0
NYV5000		1,000	1,000 Cr.	Water Logs, Inc.			

If you review the entries, you will notice that the Fail to Receive Account and Cash Account balanced out to zero. However "A/C L094321" is long 1,000 shares (Db) versus SFR's Vault NYV5000 1,000 Cr. If we deliver the stock to the client, these two accounts would go flat also.

When a client or the firm's trading account first buys a security, the account is debited. The term used is *long*—they are "long" the issue. Since the purchase requires payment, the cash, or money, side of the transaction is debited, since it is an Account Receivable, which is an asset. When the stock becomes part of the firm's possessions, the location account, where the position is maintained, is credited to offset the long position.

The account, which is the location account for the client's or trading account's long position (debit) is a credit. Where is security maintained? It is maintained in:

1. Vault.
2. Transfer.
3. Stock loan.
4. Depository.
5. Custodial bank.
6. Bank loan.

Stock going into any of these six positions is credited. Therefore, these position accounts either have credit balances, or they are flat (that is, have no balance).

When a client or the trading account first sells, the account is credited. The client or trading account is said to be *short*. The money position is also credited, because the money is owed by the firm. The sale represents an accounts payable, therefore a liability, and therefore a credit. If the short position is a bona fide short sale, as opposed to a sale where the client hadn't delivered the owned stock by settlement date of the trade, the security sold must be borrowed. Since the security position is a credit, the offset (that is, the account from which the security was borrowed) must be a debit. Therefore stock can be borrowed from the following accounts:

Stock borrowed
Client
Proprietary

The difference between this example and the previous one is that while this one is concerned with an established "position," the former is concerned with location. In the case of a short sale, there isn't any location, since the security is delivered to the buyer to satisfy the sale obligation.

REPORTING

Focus Report

Like all brokerage firms, SF&R has to file certain information with the government and self-regulatory bodies. Perhaps the most familiar of such reports is the *Financial and Operational Combined Uniform Single (Focus) Report.* This report demonstrates the firm's financial ability to carry on its business. The report discounts all nonliquid assets by 100%. (That is, ignores their value completely.) Then it reduces the value of other assets according to the amount of prudent risk they represent. Liabilities are carried at full exposure; only those that are 100% covered are excluded. Total liabilities are then divided by total assets. The ratio resulting from this test dramatizes the firm's strength in the face of adversity. Under this rigid test, liabilities usually exceed assets. Ratios of 4 to 1 to 8 to 1 are normal. The various self-regulatory organizations monitor firms and grow suspicious of those whose ratios reach 10 to 1 or 12 to 1. The rule is that a firm's ratio may not exceed 15 to 1. At this point, a firm usually goes out of business anyway.

The 15c3-3 Report

The *15c3-3 report* protects customers by isolating all clients' exposure to the firm and vice versa. If the total customers' credit balances exceed their debit balances, SF&R has to deposit cash in a bank account. If total customer debit exceeds credit, the deposit is not necessary.

SUMMARY

SF&R's accounting department is a multifaceted department, whose responsibilities extend to many areas: First, it must reconcile the daily cash positions. Second, it must receive and issue checks for services rendered and received. Third, it is required to complete reports.

CHAPTER 40

Stock Record

The stock record department is responsible for keeping track of the movement of all securities into, out of, and within the brokerage firm. To perform this task, the stock record applies accounting methods to security movement. Every debit must have a corresponding credit and vice versa. Entries made on one day appear on the record the next business day.

With stock record in hand, an employee of this department looks for entries that don't "balance." Due to the vast number of entries "hitting" the stock record, one side of an entry very possibly might appear, while the other side does not. SF&R's stock record personnel must track down each out-of-balance condition and make the appropriate correcting entries.

In addition, a good stock record person can "see" illogical entries when reading the record. To the novice, the record is just a set of numbers signifying security movements. To a stock record person, however, each series of numbers tells a story. This story can be read and corrective action taken, even though an out-of-balance condition may not exist.

THE NUMBERING SYSTEM

Like many firms, SF&R uses a system that consists of three sets of numbers:

1. On the client side, a unique number identifies the particular account and its servicing branch.
2. On the street side, a numbered set of accounts is used to record the movement of securities through various locations, such as the vault, transfer, fail to receive, or fail to deliver.
3. A third set of numbers is used for SF&R trading or inventory accounts.

Example: On the customer side, SF&R identifies each branch location by an abbreviation. The Boston office's symbol is BN, whereas Detroit is signified by DT, San Francisco by by SF, and so on.

The account itself is identified by a unique, six-digit number. An account in the Boston branch might be BN104566. The first digit after the branch code identifies the division that the branch belongs to. SF&R has nine sales divisions: 1-New England, 2-Mid-Atlantic, 3-South Atlantic, 4-Northern Mideast, 5-Southern Midwest, 6-North Pacific, 7-Central Pacific, 8-South Pacific, and 9-nondomestic branches. Because Boston belongs to the New England group, its account numbers always begin with BN1, whereas Chicago is CG4, and Los Angeles is LA8.

For its street-side operations, SF&R's divisional and branch-level cashiering areas have a second numbering system. The vault in New York is coded NYB5, whereas the vault in Chicago is CGB5. New york Transfer into firm name is NYT10000 and transfer into customer name is NYT2. Note that the first digit in the street-side system indicates location, not the sales division.

Finally, trading accounts are identified by their locations. "Zero" as the first digit means "trading desk." OTC equity transactions coming from the trading desk in New York are labeled NY0), and the Dallas equities trading desk is DL0. The Dallas municipal bond trading desk is DL03, and so on.

With this stock account system, SF&R's stock record department can easily read the record.

Example The firm buys 50M Chicago High School District's FA8%-2005 for its Chicago inventory account. The trading desk quickly resells 5M of them to a Detroit client. On settlement date, the bonds are received from the selling firm and placed in the Chicago vault. The stock record shows the following entries under the heading "Chicago High School District's FA8%2005-CUSIP#936454210."

Account	*Price or Entry*	*Debit (Long)*	*Credit (Short)*	*Position*
DT401312	97.5	5,000		5,000
CG030000	97.0	50,000		
CG030000	97.5		5,000	45,000
CGB50000	Receive		50,000	50,000 Cr.

The stock record also carries the opening and closing positions per account, as well as segregation, transfer, and other such designations.

The next day's stock record shows the following movements:

Account	*Price or Entry*	*Debit (Long)*	*Credit (Short)*	*Position*
DT4013129	Deliver		5,000	0
CG030000	97.8		45,000	0
SF793421	97.8	45,000		45,000
CGB50000	Deliver	5,000		45,000 Cr.

In other words, the bonds were delivered to the Detroit client and SF&R's CG trading department sold 45M bonds to a client at the San Francisco office.

THE DAILY AND MAIN STOCK RECORDS

The stock record is usually maintained in security order, and accounts appear within each security. SF&R's version is the *activity run*, sometimes referred to as *the daily*. (See Figure 40-1.) The only accounts appearing on the daily record are those that "moved" on that day. The *weekly* or *main stock record* shows all accounts for which a position exists on a given day; it is a stock balance sheet.

Example: The main stock record for Milwaukee Paper Co. is as follows:

Account	*Long*	*Short*	*Account*	*Long*	*Short*
BN172143	200		BU306244		100
DL506432	400		DL534321	200	
DN572345	100		CGB50000		200
NYB500000		600			

FIGURE 40-1. *Daily activity run.*

Stone, Forrest & Rivers

DAILY STOCK RECORD ACTIVITY

DYNAFLOW TECHNOLOGY INC 164341001

Account	Action	Pre Psn	Debit	Credit	Clo Psn	
AL101432	31-1/4		100		100	
BA134471	REC		100		100	
BS154371	31-1/2	5,500		3,000	2,500	
BS121171	DEL	200		200		
HT142723	31-1/2			200	200Cr	
NYB50000		7,483Cr		200	7,683Cr	2,800Cr
NYT1000		3,400Cr	200		3,200Cr	
NYFD0001			3,200		3,200	

FIGURE 40-1. *(cont.)*

Stone, Forrest & Rivers

DAILY STOCK RECORD ACTIVITY

GIANT, RECKER & CRANE 230916001

Account	Action	Pre Psn	Debit	Credit	Clo Psn	
CG416192	18-1/4	300	200		500	
DL526131	18-1/2	200	1,000		1,200	
OM500131	REC		200		200	
OM501621	REC		200		200	
SL516241	COR	500Cr	500			
SL512641	COR	500		500		
DT500000		62,483		1,200	63,683	
NYB50000		5,832		400	6,232	

FIGURE 40-2. *Weekly (main) stock record.*

Stone, Forrest & Rivers

STOCK RECORD POSITION RUN

DYNAFLOW TECHNOLOGY INC 164341001

Account	Debit	Credit	Account	Debit	Credit
BA113471	100		CG449711	100	
BS107131	175		CG452712	725	
BS124913		100	DN5011472	425	
BS13472	100		DN505272	300	
BS154371	2,500		DN510011	400	
NY227471	300		SF723311	75	
NY247872	5,000		SF726512	25	
AL204321	200		SF727131	550	
AL125831		100	LA810161	300	
PH20721	400		CGB50000		300
PI20943	200		DTC50000		8,625
DC249312		100	LAB50000		100
DC274322	100		LAT10000		200
DC375322	300		NYB50000		2,600
AT300471	200		NYT10000		300
MI301972	500		PSD50000		575
MI302432	100		SFB50000		75

The stock record department is not the only user of the full stock record. Someone auditing the vaults could verify having 200 shares in the Chicago box and 600 shares in the New York box. The dividend department also uses the stock record "take-off" to verify the registration of securities physical positions against the stock record's positions. They then debit and credit the affected accounts on the dividend payable date.

Example If today were a record date for a dividend, accounts BN172143, DL506432, DL534321, and DN572345 are credited with the dividend, and account BU306244 is charged on the payable date. The two vault or box positions are not affected.

BALANCING THE STOCK RECORD

This record *must at all times accurately reflect* SF&R's obligations or liabilities, as well as its assets. The record's integrity is vital to SF&R's continued business. So SF&R's stock record personnel must "balance" the record every day.

In the balancing procedure, SF&R personnel look for *breaks*, which are unbalanced entries. As you might expect, the stock record department uses a numbered system: ZZZMMDDY. The letters ZZZ refer to a break account, MM to month, DD to daily, and Y to year.

Example ZZZ11156 means that the break (ZZZ) occurred on November 15, 1986.

The break account always replaced the missing entry or net of missing entries.

Example The following position appears on the record 0742731 United Zorak Corp.

Account	*Long*	*Short*
DL526431	100	
SA304291	100	
NYB50000		100
ZZZ11256		100

The Dallas Texas and Savannah Georgia offices each received 100 shares for clients. Yet only 100 shares "show" going into the New York box. The break account has locked in the error. SF&R's stock record personnel research the discrepancy by reviewing the many blotters and other source documents afforded them. In reviewing the various documents, they find that the stock for the Dallas client was not "booked" into the Dallas box. The correction entry is:

Account	*Debit*	*Credit*
ZZZ11256	100	
DLB50000		100

The entry is made on a stock record journal, which "hits" the record's next day's work. As a result of the entry, the break account goes *flat*, or *zero balance*, and the Dallas box reflects its position of 100 shares. An obvious break is thus corrected.

With their ability to "read" the report, however, the stock record personnel notice another error. Stock received for a Savannah client should not have been booked to NYB without first being placed in the SA box. After researching this "abnormal" movement, they determined that the entry was "booked" incorrectly, and so a journal entry is made:

Account	*Debit*	*Credit*
NYB50000	100	
SAB50000		100

OTHER USES OF THE STOCK RECORD

On the stock record appear *memo fields*, such as segregation, safekeeping, and the like. These memo fields are used by different areas of the cashier's department to locate and use securities for deliveries, loans, and other purposes.

Example: The record shows shares "locked up" in seg with no actual security position. The firm could have stock in the name of a client who has previously sold the security, by using some other shares for delivery? If so, if the stock in seg is negotiable, SF&R can transfer it into the name of the firm and, upon its return from transfer, substitute it for erroneously used security. If, in fact, the customer's stock was (correctly) used for delivery, then the error was made in not adjusting the memo field; the memo field has to be changed.

SUMMARY

The importance of the stock record department cannot *ever* be overstated. With its ability to keep the record factual and in balance, it is the ultimate preserve of order.

CHAPTER 41

Dividend

When the board of directors of a corporation declare dividends to its registered stock owners, the dividend department of the brokerage firm must make certain that the proper persons get the dividend. The corporation pays dividends to the *holders of record,* that is, the persons in whose names the stock is registered. The problem is securities are not always registered in the proper street name or the names of the beneficial owners, who are entitled to the dividends. Securities may be registered in:

1. The name of the actual (beneficial) owner.
2. In the name of a nominee, such as a depository or fiduciary.
3. In street name or firm's name.
4. In the name of another (former) owner.
5. In a nominee name representing the former owner.

BALANCING THE STOCK RECORD

Vaulted Securities

To get the dividends paid to the right people, every certificate in the firm must be accounted for. When a dividend has its record date, the dividend department obtains a printout or *takeoff,* of the affected security's positions throughout the firm—long or short in accounts, on loan, in seg, in the vault, and so on. The printout is a version of the stock record, giving the security's name, the number of shares long or short, the account number, and the rate or amount of the dividend.

With this report in hand, the SF&R dividend personnel begin to verify the registration of the certificates in the firm against their positions. SF&R maintains securities in its own vault and at depositories. The first step is to compare the physical count of the shares actually there with the number shown on the printout. Once these two numbers are matched, the dividend staff must verify registration of the securities. Securities registered in SF&R's nominee name or that of the depository are easy to record; the staff knows that SF&R will get the dividend sum for these shares from the paying corporation. A harder task is to verify the shares registered in clients' names. The question is whether these clients still own the shares being held in their names.

Why wouldn't these clients still own the securities? SF&R permits clients to keep fully paid-for securities registered in their names and address but deposited in the firm's vaults. These stockholders receive all dividends and proxy information directly from the issuer. When these owners sell the stock, the firm must make certain that the certificates in the vault are used. Sometimes, however, the dividend department discovers that a client is not long (does not own the stock) over the record date, while the vault is still housing stock registered in the client's name. In such a case, the corporation is going to pay the dividend to the wrong person. The dividend personnel have to instruct the firm to transfer the stock into SF&R's name and charge the client's account for (1) the amount owed and (2) for the amount of the dividend. (The customer will receive the dividend directly from the paying agent.)

Securities in Fails

Next step in balancing the record is to review all the fails to receive and fails to deliver. When a fail-to-receive item is open over the record date, the dividend department prepares a claim against the firm that owes SF&R the dividend. In the case of a fail to deliver, SF&R awaits a claim from the other firm.

Securities in Transfer

The dividend department also reviews items in transfer. When securities are transferred into good names in time for the record date, the related dividends are accounted for correctly. However, when items miss transfer, SF&R's dividend department must issue the appropriate claims and/or adjustments.

Securities Involved in As-of Trades

When an as-of trade is processed before the settlement date, it should be recorded on the proper settlement date. No further action is required to get the dividend paid to the proper person. But when an as-of trade adjustment is made *after* the settlement date, it is not part of the record takeoff, and adjustments must be made to account for the dividend.

The Balanced Takeoff

With all questions resolved and accounted for, SF&R should have a balanced takeoff. On the dividend payable date, SF&R receives a check or money transfer from the dividend disbursing agent (DDA) of the corporation for the dividend owed on all shares registered in SF&R's name. At the same time, the depositories receive checks for dividends on all the shares they are holding in their name on behalf of the participating firms. The depositories, in turn, credit the firms for the appropriate dividend amounts.

Claims for dividends are issued and received. Those received are reviewed for accuracy against SF&R's records.

Finally, all the accounts on SF&R's records for the dividend-paying security is either debited or credited the amount due. If the balancing procedure has been done correctly, then debits equal credits and the record is in balance.

THE CASH DIVIDEND CYCLE

The Record Date

Cash dividends are paid on a per share basis. The corporation's board of directors declare the dividends to record holders of the *record date* for payment on another date called the *payable date.*

Example: On April 1, the board of directors of Zip Co. declare a 25-cent-per-share dividend to stockholders of record on the night of April 15. The payable date chosen is May 1.

To be eligible for the cash dividend, a purchaser must buy the stock no later than the fifth business day before record date. Any stock purchased after that day, on a regular way basis, is not entitled to the dividend.

Ex-Dividend Date

The first day that a new purchaser is not entitled to the cash dividend is called the *ex-dividend date,* which is four business days before record date. This date is of importance for several reasons.

1. A purchaser on this day does not receive the dividend.
2. Open GTC buy limit orders and sell stop orders are reduced by the next higher fraction. For instance, for a 20-cent dividend, the limit or stop is reduced a 1/4 point; for a 45-cent dividend, a 1/2 point; for a 50-cent dividend, a 1/2 point, and so on.
3. All other influences on the market being (theoretically) equal, the stock will open for trading at a price less the dividend. For example, if the stock paying a 10-cent dividend closes at 40, if opens at 39⅞ on the ex-dividend date.

STOCK DIVIDENDS

Dividends of Less Than 25%

Stock dividends for less than 25% are handled in the same fashion as cash dividends.

Example: WIP Ltd. decides to declare a 10% stock dividend. Each holder of record receives one share for each ten shares held. The stock is distributed on the payable date. If the stock dividend does not equal a full share, then either cash, or scrip, for less than one full share is issued.

Dividends for More Than 25%

On stock dividends for more than 25% and stock splits, the ex-dividend date is the day after payable date. Because the market price is reduced by the amount of the dividend on the ex-dividend date, a split or dividend of over 25% could drastically reduce the value of stock on loan or securities carried on margin. The value lost can create regulatory complications even if it is only temporary.

Due Bills

From the fourth business day before the record date until (and including) the payable date, all trades in a stock-dividend-paying security carry *due bills,* which are IOUs for the stock to be issued on the payable date.

Example: On a two-for-one split, the ex-dividend date is the day after the payable date. An SF&R client, Mr. Compton, buys 100 shares of RIP at 50, so that it settles before record date. But delivery of the stock to SF&R occurs after the record date. SF&R pays $5,000 to the delivering firm (100 shares × $50) and demands a due bill for the additional 100 shares that will result from the split.

On the day following the payable date for RIP's two-for-one split, Mr. Compton's shares are worth only $25 each. Now SF&R has to claim the second 100 shares, the firm can do with the due bill. SF&R now surrenders the due bill and receives the second hundred for Mr. Compton's account.

- Compton buys 100 RIP @ 50 $5,000
- Compton receives 100 RIP @ 50 $5,000
- Value of Compton's stock after split 100 RIP @ 25 $2,500
- Compton's account after due bill is satisfied 200 RIP @ 25 $5,000

BONDS

Bonds may be owned in either registered or bearer form. Specifically, they may be:

1. *Fully registered*—principal is owned by and interest is paid to only the registered owner.
2. *Registered as to principal only*—ownership of principal is registered but interest is paid in coupon form.
3. *Bearer form*—ownership is unrecorded on the certificate, and interest is in coupon form. (That is, the bearer cuts off the bond one coupon for each interest payment as it comes due.)

Bonds that are *fully registered*, whether in beneficial or nominee form, require the same balancing procedure as for stock dividends. The positions reflected on the takeoff are verified against physical holdings. Similarly, the dividend department receives interest checks from the agent of the issuing entity, and makes sure that this sum equals the amount applied against the client's accounts.

If in coupon form, the bond certificates must be secured and the coupon is removed, a procedure popularly known as *clipping coupons*. The "clipped" coupons are surrendered to the paying bank, and the interest received is distributed among the bondholders' accounts.

Accounting for Accrued Interest

Bonds pay interest, usually every six months. When bond trades settle, the buyer pays the seller for any interest accrued to the seller. The work of the bond interest area is therefore simplified. When an interest payment check is received at SF&R, all the bond interest department has to do is credit the appropriate long accounts and debit the short accounts. It need not be concerned with the length of time that a client has owned the bonds.

DISPOSITION OF DIVIDEND/INTEREST PAYMENTS

Credits made to clients' accounts are generally disbursed in accordance with the clients' wishes and SF&R's policy. Dividends and/or interest payments to clients can remain in their accounts or be disbursed monthly and sometimes weekly.

When dividend or interest amounts are debited to an account, the client may make good for the debit by depositing a check for sum owed, let it become part of a margin debit balance or have it deducted from proceeds.

SUMMARY

The dividend department is responsible for ensuring that dividend and interest payments get into the hands of the rightful participants. To accomplish this task, it must keep track of who owns the stocks and bonds in the SF&R vault, at the depository, at banks, or out on loan.

CHAPTER 42

Proxy

When SF&R holds a security that is registered in a client's name, the issuing company sends all information directly to the client. But when SF&R holds a security in nominee name on behalf of a client, it is obliged to forward to the client all information disseminated by the issuing company. Because the corporation doesn't know the actual (beneficial) owner, it sends all financial statements, proxies, and other materials to SF&R, which must, in turn, send the materials to the true owners.

The proxy department handles this assignment. Although the name is "proxy department," the work entails all communications from the issuer: annual and semiannual reports, dividend announcements, corporate management changes, and *any* written communication from the corporation to its shareholders.

THE FORWARDING PROCEDURE

Upon receipt of a communication, the proxy department must secure enough copies to forward them to all the beneficial owners. First, the department obtains a copy of SF&R's master stock record to determine the number of accounts involved.

Then, it goes back to the issuing company or its agent and requests the number of copies needed. Upon receipt of the copies, the department forwards them to the actual clients.

Example: While just about all companies send annual reports to their shareholders, some companies send semiannual or even quarterly reports. In all cases, the proxy department must secure a current holders list from the firm's records, prepare name and address labels, and mail the documents to the clients.

Proxies

Proxies follow the same procedure. Because most shareholders are unable to attend the corporation's annual meeting, they exercise their voting privileges through proxies. By entering their votes on proxies, shareholders are assured a say in the matters proposed at the annual shareholders meeting.

Example: Park Avenue Limited is having their annual stockholders meeting in Flint, Michigan. Notices of the meeting are placed in the newspapers and proxy material prepared. Along with the actual proxy, the company publishes a colorful and informative year-end brochure. The document contains a summary of the company's profit and loss statement and balance sheet. It also describes the products, plants, and other holdings of Park Avenue Limited. Color pictures enhance the brochure's appearance, while bringing a feeling of belonging to the shareholder.

SF&R has Park Avenue stock registered in its name on behalf of many of its customers. Upon receipt of the proxies and a brochure, it checks the stock records, which reveals 72,863 shares owned by 104 SF&R clients. The number of shares owned by any one account ranges from 1,000 shares to one. The proxy department then sends to the company for enough copies of the brochure to be mailed to all its clients. Each customer, regardless of the number of shares owned, must receive a copy of the year-end brochures, as well as a proxy for shares held.

SF&R's EDP department produces two sets of labels for the proxy staff: One set contains the client's account number, name, and address; these "gum" (self-stick) labels are affixed to the envelope. The second type of label contains the same information, plus the *number of shares owned;* this label is affixed to the proxy and mailed to the client. A return envelope is included in the package. When the document, proxy, and envelopes are prepared, everything is mailed to the client.

Upon receiving the document, the client completes the proxy and mails it back to SF&R. Proxies have to be received by the *cut-off date,* which is a day that gives SF&R enough time to get the votes in to Park Avenue Limited in time to be counted. Proxies that are not received in time are not voted. Those that do come in on time are voted in accordance with the client's instructions.

SF&R can vote only 72,853 shares. The proxies returned and voted by SF&R, on behalf of its clients, cannot exceed this number. (Remember, Park Avenue Limited does not know SF&R's customers—only SF&R.)

SUMMARY

Consider the number of corporations whose common stocks trade in public markets daily every day. How many yearly reports do you think are issued annually? Consider, also, all investors (clients) involved in the marketplace daily. For each corporation whose stock is registered in SF&R's name, annual reports, proxies, and other materials must be channeled to *every* customer who owns the company's stock. The SF&R proxy department must process all of this material. You can only begin to appreciate the workload handled by the proxy department.

CHAPTER 43

New Accounts (Name and Address)

SF&R account executives earn their livelihoods by generating commissions. To sustain and enhance their incomes, brokers are constantly trying to open new accounts and generate new business. As each account is opened, various forms must be completed and forwarded to the new account, or name and address, department. This department verifies the completeness of the document and requests additional information when needed. Every day, the SF&R name and address department is involved in opening new accounts, changing addresses or other data, and securing papers required to operate an account. It is a full-time job.

OPENING ACCOUNTS

Cash Account

An account executive in SF&R's Atlanta office opens a new cash account. The stockholder completes the name and address form (Figure 43-1) from information given by the client. This form includes the client's:

1. Full name.
2. Home address and telephone number.

FIGURE 43-1. *SF&R's new account information form.*

SF&R Incorporated

New Account Information (Confidential)

ACCOUNT NUMBER

Branch | Account | Type | Ck. | RR

RR REGISTERED IN STATE OF CUSTOMERS RESIDENCE ☐ YES ☐ NO

ACCOUNT TITLE (in full as it should appear on billings; if JT Acct. specify JT/WROS or Ten. in common)

NAME ______

ADDRESS ______

CITY ______ STATE ______ ZIP ______

SOCIAL SECURITY OR TAX IDENTIFICATION # ______

RESIDENT OF N.Y. STATE ☐ YES ☐ NO

CITIZENSHIP (Country) ______ AGE ______

DIVIDENDS ☐ PAY MONTHLY ☐ HOLD

INSTRUCTIONS (SEE EXPLANATION ON BACK) CHECK ONE

☐ HOLD SECURITIES IN FIRM NAME AND HOLD FUNDS (3/7)

☐ TRANSFER AND MAIL SECURITIES AS BILLED REMIT FUNDS (1/8)

☐ SETTLE TRADES C.O.D. THROUGH CLIENT'S AGENT (5/6) ☐ SAME AS ABOVE
AGENTS NAME, ADDRESS, DEPARTMENT, CLIENT'S IDENTIFICATION NUMBER

______

☐ FOLLOW SPECIAL INSTRUCTIONS ON BACK (Check appropriate instructions)

☐ ALTERNATE NAME – DUPLICATE STATEMENTS, CONFIRMATION, ALTERNATE TRANSFER NAME, ALTERNATE DIVIDEND PAYEE (SEE BACK)

*INSTITUTIONAL A/C FILL IN SHADED AREAS ONLY

INITIAL TRANSACTION	AMOUNT OF DEPOSIT $	TRF of A/C ☐	FORMER BROKER

TYPE OF ACCOUNT

- ☐ CASH
- ☐ MARGIN
- ☐ EMPLOYEE RELATED
- ☐ DISCRETIONARY
- ☐ OPTION (PROSPECTUS FURNISHED ______) DATE

PAPERS NEEDED

- ☐ JOINT ACCT. AGREEMENT
- ☐ MARGIN AGREEMENT
- ☐ TRUST AGREEMENT
- ☐ ESTATE PAPERS
- ☐ CORPORATE RESOLUTION
- ☐ PARTNERSHIP AGREEMENT
- ☐ N.Y. NON-RESIDENT WAIVER
- ☐ FIRST PARTY TRADING AUTHORITY
- ☐ THIRD PARTY TRADING AUTHORITY
- ☐ OPTION AGREEMENT
- ☐ INVESTMENT CLUB AGREEMENT
- ☐ INVESTMENT ADVISOR
- ☐ OTHER

EMPLOYER NAME and ADDRESS (IF UNEMPLOYED, SOURCE OF INCOME)	OCCUPATION/POSITION OR TYPE OF BUSINESS BUSINESS PHONE
HOME ADDRESS (IF NOT ALREADY GIVEN)	HOME PHONE
NAME OF BANK REFERENCE (IF BRANCH BANK INCLUDE LOCATION)	TYPE OF BANK ACCOUNT ☐ CHECKING ☐ SAVINGS ☐ COMMERCIAL ☐ OTHER

IS THIS ACCOUNT TO BE OPERATED BY ANY OTHER PERSON THAN THE OWNER? ☐ NO ☐ YES, NAME ______ A/C # ______

RELATION TO CUSTOMER ______ OCCUPATION ______

ADDRESS ______ EMPLOYER ______

EXPERIENCE OF PERSON HOLDING THIRD PARTY TRADING AUTHORITY if APPLICABLE

DOES CLIENT OWN ANY UNREGISTERED STOCK? ☐ NO ☐ YES, COMPANY

DOES CLIENT OR MEMBER OF IMMEDIATE FAMILY HAVE ANY DIRECT OR INDIRECT CONTROL RELATIONSHIP WITH A PUBLICLY OWNED COMPANY? ☐ NO ☐ YES, COMPANY

HOW WAS ACCOUNT ACQUIRED? ☐ SOLICITED ☐ CALL IN ☐ AD LEAD ☐ RE-OPENED ☐ PERSONALLY KNOWN TO RR ______ YEARS

REFERRED BY

MARITAL STATUS ☐ M ☐ S SPOUSE'S NAME ______ AGE OF DEPENDENTS ______

SPOUSE'S EMPLOYER ______

APPROXIMATE NET WORTH $	ANNUAL INCOME $	APPROX. TAX BRACKET %	AMOUNT LIFE INSURANCE $

CUSTOMER'S MAIN INVESTMENT OBJECTIVES ☐ SAFETY OF PRINCIPAL ☐ INCOME ☐ LONG TERM GROWTH ☐ TRADING PROFITS

ADDITIONAL INFORMATION FOR CLIENTS INTENDING TO WRITE UNCOVERED OPTIONS

DOES CLIENT HAVE ANY PREVIOUS EXPERIENCE IN OPTION/COMMODITY TRADING? ☐ NO ☐ YES HOW LONG? ☐ CALLS ☐ PUTS ☐ SPREADS ☐ COMMODITY

HAVE YOU DISCUSSED TO CLIENT'S UNDERSTANDING THE RISK OF WRITING UNCOVERED OPTIONS? ☐ NO ☐ YES

ESTIMATED LIQUID NET WORTH CASH $ SECURITIES $ OTHER $

OTHER RELEVANT FINANCIAL INFORMATION.

DOES CLIENT MAKE HIS OWN INVESTMENT DECISIONS? ☐ NO ☐ YES ☐ OCCASIONALLY

THE ABOVE IS CORRECT TO THE BEST OF MY KNOWLEDGE AND BELIEF (SIGN FULL NAME)

DATE ______ SIGNED ______ REGISTERED REPRESENTATIVE DATE ______ SIGNED ______ OFFICER/ROP

ORIGINAL

3. Business name, address, and telephone number.
4. Bank name, branch, and account number at which the client conducts business.
5. Social security number.
6. Investment objectives, such as income, growth, safety, or the like.
7. Any other information, such as whether the client is of legal age to conduct business.

Upon being informed of the new customer by the broker, the branch office staff assign a new account number, AT300123, and copies it onto the client's order.

With the name and address completed, the customer is permitted to carry on business in a cash account. All purchases must be paid for in full by the fifth business day, but no later than the seventh business day. In the case of sales, the client must present deliverable securities by the tenth day after sale.

In addition, the customer has to instruct the account executive on how to handle all transactions, such as, for purchases, "Hold security in street (SF&R's) name." "Transfer into the client's name and ship the certificates to the home address," or "Transfer the security into the client's name and hold the certificate at SF&R for safekeeping." In the case of sales, the instruction might be. "Pay proceeds" or "Hold funds in account." These instructions are important to SF&R because they enable the firm to process securities according to the customers' wishes.

Margin Account

A stockholder in the Dallas office opens a new account for a customer who wishes to make purchases on margin. The branch operations personnel assign a new number, DL543124, and the account executive completes the name and address form. In addition, the client is given another document to sign, which contains three statements: (1) a margin agreement, (2) a lending agreement, and (3) a truth in lending disclosures.

The Margin Agreement. The *margin agreement* states the terms under which the account is to be operated. Commonly, this form lays out four terms (among others):

1. Purchases must be paid for by the fifth business day.
2. Interest is charged on any debit balance in the account.
3. SF&R has the right to take action in the account should the client fail to perform.
4. The firm may *hypothecate* the securities, that is, use the securities as collateral to borrow money from a bank and thereby secure the debit balance.

The Lending Agreement. The *lending agreement* gives the firm permission to use marginable securities in a way other than hypothecation. In the interest of obtaining funds for margin accounts at the lowest rates possible, this agreement permits the firm to pursue money at costs that are lower than what a bank charges. For example, the loanable securities in a client's account can be delivered against another account's short sale.

The Truth in Lending Agreement. The *truth in lending agreement* informs clients as to how the firm computes interest costs on their debit balances: the interest rate charged, the formula used, and any other information deemed pertinent by the federal Truth in Lending Law.

Joint Account

A married couple in SF&R's Boston office wants to open a joint account. They must sign a *joint account agreement* in addition to the other new account agreements.

One form of a joint account is with *rights of survivorship* (JTROS), in which, upon the death of one of the two participants, all rights go to the survivor.

Tenants in common, another type of joint account, differs from JTROS. Upon the death of one of the participants, the deceased person's share goes into the deceased person's estate and not to the survivor.

An Account for Children

A customer of SF&R's New York office wants to open accounts for his children, who are all under eighteen years of age. The accounts are opened, one for each child, under the Uniform Gift to

FIGURE 43-2a. *SF&R's margin agreement (front).*

Stone, Forrest & Rivers
INCORPORATED

Customer Margin Agreement / Loan Consent

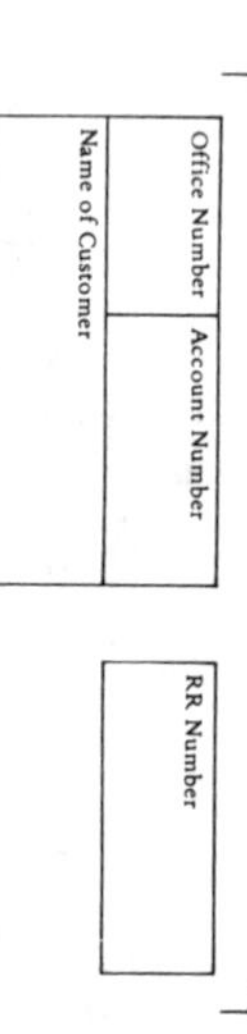

Gentlemen:

In consideration of your accepting and carrying for the undersigned one or more accounts (whether designated by name, number or otherwise) the undersigned hereby consents and agrees that:

1. Applicable Rules and Statutes

All transactions under this agreement shall be subject to the constitution, rules, regulations, customs and usage of the exchange or market, and its clearing house, if any, where the transactions are executed by you or your agents, applicable provisions of the federal securities laws, and the rules and regulations of the United States Securities and Exchange Commission, and the Board of Governors of the Federal Reserve System.

2. Liens

Any and all monies, securities, or property belonging to the undersigned or in which the undersigned may have an interest held by you or carried in any of my accounts (either individually or jointly with others) shall be subject to a general lien for the discharge of all of the undersigned's debts and obligations to you, wherever or however arising and without regard to whether or not you have made advances with respect to such property, and irrespective of the number of such accounts you shall have the right to transfer, and you are hereby authorized to sell and/or purchase any and all property in any such accounts without notice to satisfy such general line. You shall have the right to transfer monies, securities, and other property so held by you from or to any other of the accounts of the undersigned whenever in your judgment you consider such a transfer necessary for your protection. In enforcing your lien, you shall have the discretion to determine which securities and property are to be sold and which contracts are to be closed.

3. Authority to Pledge

Any or all securities or any other property, now or hereafter held by you, or carried by you for the undersigned (either individually or jointly with others), or deposited to secure the same, may from time to time and without notice to me, be carried in your general loans and may be pledged, repledged, hypothecated or re-hypothecated, separately or in common with other securities or any other property, for the sum due to you thereon or for a greater sum, and without retaining in your possession and control for delivery a like amount of similar securities.

4. Authority to Borrow

In case of the sale of any security or other property by you at the direction of the undersigned and your inability to deliver the same to the purchaser by reason of failure of the undersigned to supply you therewith, then and in such event, the undersigned authorizes you to borrow any security or other property necessary to make delivery thereof, and the undersigned hereby agrees to be responsible for any loss which you may sustain thereby and any premiums which you may be required to pay thereof, and for any loss which you may sustain by reason for your inability to borrow the security or other property sold.

5. Maintenance of Margin

The undersigned will at all times maintain margins for said accounts, as required by you from time to time.

6. Payment of Indebtedness upon Demand

The undersigned shall at all times be liable for the payment upon demand of any debit balance or other obligations owing in any of the accounts of the undersigned with you and the undersigned shall be liable to you for any deficiency remaining in any such accounts in the event of the liquidation thereof, in whole or in part, by you or by the undersigned; and, the undersigned shall make payment of such obligations and indebtedness upon demand.

The reasonable costs and expenses of collection of the debit balance and any unpaid deficiency in the accounts of the undersigned with you, including, but not limited to, attorney's fees, incurred and payable or paid by you shall be payable to you by the undersigned.

7. Designation of Orders

It is understood and agreed that the undersigned, when placing with you any sell order for short account, will designate it as such and hereby authorizes you to mark such order as being "short," and when placing with you any order for long account, will designate it as such and hereby authorizes you to mark such orders as being "long." Any sell order which the undersigned shall designate as being for long account as above provided, is for securities then owned by the undersigned and, if such securities are not then deliverable by you from any account of the undersigned, the placing of such order shall constitute a representation by the undersigned that it is impracticable for him then to deliver such securities to you but that he will deliver them as soon as it is possible for him to do so. It is understood that such delivery is due on or before the settlement date of the transaction.

8. Capacity

In all transactions between you and the undersigned, the undersigned understands that you are acting as the brokers of the undersigned, except when you disclose to the undersigned in the confirmation that you are acting as dealers for your own account or as brokers for some other person.

9. Presumption of Receipt of Communications

Communications may be sent to the undersigned at the address of the undersigned or at such other address as the undersigned may hereafter give you in writing, and all communications so sent, whether by mail, telegraph, messenger or otherwise, shall be deemed given to the undersigned personally, whether actually received or not.

10. Reports and Statements

Reports of executions of orders and statements of the account of the undersigned shall be conclusive if not objected to in writing, the former within five (5) days, the latter within ten (10) days, of the date on which such material was forwarded by you or your agents to the undersigned, by mail or otherwise.

11. Free Credit Balances

It is understood and agreed that any free credit balance in any account in which I have an interest is maintained in such account solely for the purpose of investment or reinvestment in securities or other investment instruments.

12. Margin Interest Charges

The undersigned acknowledges receipt of Truth-in-Lending Disclosure Statement. It is understood that interest will be charged on debit balances in accordance with the methods and procedures described in this statement or in any amendment or revision thereto which may be provided to me. Unless otherwise noted hereon, or unless I am provided notice to the contrary in accordance with the relevant provisions of this agreement, the following schedule shall set forth the maximum charges to be made on debit balances in the undersigned's accounts:

Average Debit Balance for Interest Period	Interest Charge Above Broker Call Loan Rate
$ 0–15,000	2.0%
15,001–50,000	1.5%
50,001–and over	1.0%

13. Agreement to Arbitrate Controversies

It is agreed that any controversy between us arising out of your business or this agreement shall be submitted to arbitration conducted under the provisions of the Constitution and Rules of the Board of Governors of the New York Stock Exchange or pursuant to the Code of Arbitration of the National Association of Securities Dealers, as the undersigned may elect.

FIGURE 43-2b. *Margin agreement (back).*

Arbitration must be commenced upon service of either a written demand for arbitration or a written notice of intention to arbitrate, therein electing the arbitration tribunal. In the event the undersigned does not make such designation within five (5) days of such demand or notice, then the undersigned authorizes you to do so on behalf of the undersigned.

14. Extraordinary Events

You shall not be liable for any loss caused directly or indirectly by government restrictions, exchange or market rulings, suspension of trading, war, strikes or other conditions beyond your control.

15. Representation as to Capacity to Enter into Agreement

The undersigned, if an individual, represents that the undersigned is of full age, that the undersigned is not an employee of any exchange, or of any corporation of which any exchange owns a majority of the capital stock, or of a member of any exchange, or of a member firm or member corporation registered on any exchange or of a bank, trust company, insurance company or of any corporation, firm or individual engaged in the business of dealing either as broker or as principal in securities, bills of exchange, bankers' acceptances or commercial paper or other forms of credit securities or instruments. The undersigned further represents that no one except the undersigned has an interest in the account or accounts of the undersigned with you.

16. Joint and Several Liability

If the undersigned shall consist of more than one individual, their obligations under this agreement shall be joint and several.

17. Rights under Agreement

Your failure to insist at any time upon strict compliance with this agreement or with any of its terms or any continued course of such conduct on your part shall in no event constitute or be considered a waiver by you of any of your rights or privileges. The undersigned hereby expressly agrees that you shall not be bound by any representation or agreement heretofore or hereafter made by any of your employees or agents which in any way purports to modify, affect or diminish your rights under this agreement, and that no representation or advice by you or your employees or agents regarding the purchase or sale by the undersigned of any securities, or other property bought or sold on the undersigned's order or carried or held in any manner for the undersigned's account shall be deemed to be a representation with respect to the future value or performance of such securities, or other property.

18. Continuity of Agreement

This agreement shall inure to the benefit of your successors and assigns, by merger, consolidation or otherwise, and you may transfer the account of the undersigned to any such successors or assigns.

This agreement and all the terms thereof shall be binding upon the undersigned's heirs, executors, administrators, personal representatives and assigns. In the event of the undersigned's death, incompetency, or disability, whether or not executors, administrators, committee or conservators of my estate and property shall have qualified or been appointed, you may cancel any open orders for the purchase or sale of any property, you may place orders for the sale of the property which you may be carrying for me and for which payment has not been made or buy any property of which my accounts may be short, or any part thereof, under the same terms and conditions as hereinabove stated, as though the undersigned were alive and competent without prior notice to the undersigned's heirs, executors, administrators, personal representatives, assigns, committee or conservators, without prior demand or call of any kind upon them or any of them.

19. Headings are Descriptive

The heading of each provision hereof is for descriptive purposes only and shall not be deemed to modify or qualify any of the rights or obligations set forth in each provision.

20. Separability

If any provision or condition of this agreement shall be held to be invalid or unenforceable by any court, or regulatory or self-regulatory agency or body, such invalidity or unenforceability shall attach only to such provision or condition. The validity of the remaining provisions and conditions shall not be affected thereby and this agreement shall be carried out as if such invalid or unenforceable provision or condition were not contained herein.

21. Written Authority Required for Waiver or Modification

Except as herein otherwise expressly provided, no provision of this agreement shall in any respect be waived, altered, modified or amended unless such waiver, alteration, modification or amendment is committed to writing and signed by an officer of your organization.

22. The Laws of the State of New York Govern

This agreement and its enforcement shall be governed by the laws of the State of New York, shall cover individually and collectively all accounts which the undersigned may open or reopen with you, and shall inure to the benefit of your successors and assigns whether by merger, consolidation or otherwise, and you may transfer the accounts of the undersigned to your successors and assigns.

23. Acknowledgement of Receipt of Agreement

The undersigned has read this agreement in its entirety before signing, and acknowledges receipt of a copy of this agreement.

Dated ______________________________

INDIVIDUAL OR JOINT ACCOUNT SIGNATURE

____

____

(Second Party, If Joint Account)

PARTNERSHIP SIGNATURE

____

(Name of Partnership)

By ______________________________

(A Partner)

CORPORATION SIGNATURE

____

(Name of Corporation)

By ______________________________

Title ______________________________

Lending Agreement

You are hereby specifically authorized to lend to yourselves, as principal or otherwise, or to others, any securities held by you on margin for any accounts of the undersigned or as collateral therefore, either separately or with other securities.

This agreement shall inure to the benefit of your successors and assigns, by merger, consolidation or otherwise, and you may transfer the account of the undersigned to any such successors or assigns.

Dated ______________________________

INDIVIDUAL OR JOINT ACCOUNT SIGNATURE

____

____

(Second Party, If Joint Account)

PARTNERSHIP SIGNATURE

____

(Name of Partnership)

By ______________________________

(A Partner)

CORPORATION SIGNATURE

____

(Name of Corporation)

By ______________________________

Title ______________________________

FIGURE 43-3a. *SF&R's joint account (front).*

Stone, Forrest & Rivers
INCORPORATED

Joint Account Agreement

Gentlemen:

In consideration of your carrying a joint account for the undersigned, the undersigned jointly and severally agree that each of them shall have authority on behalf of the joint account to buy, sell (including short sales), and otherwise deal in, through you as brokers, stocks, bonds and other securities, on margin or otherwise; to receive on behalf of the joint account demands, notices, confirmations, reports, statements of account and communications of every kind; to receive on behalf of the joint account money, securities and property of every kind and to dispose of same; to make on behalf of the joint account agreements relating to any of the foregoing matters and to terminate or modify same or waive any of the provisions thereof; and generally to deal with you on behalf of the joint account as fully and completely as if he alone were interested in said accounts, all without notice to the other or others interested in said account. You are authorized to follow the instructions of any of the undersigned in every respect concerning the said joint account with you and to make deliveries to any of the undersigned, or upon his instructions, of any or all securities in the said joint account, and to make payments to any of the undersigned, or upon his order, of any or all monies at any time or from time to time in the said joint account as he may order and direct, even if such deliveries and/or payments shall be made to him personally, and not for the joint account of the undersigned. In the event of any such deliveries of securities or payments of monies to any of the undersigned as aforesaid, you shall be under no duty or obligation to inquire into the purpose or propriety of any such demand for delivery of securities or payment of monies, and you shall not be bound to see to the application or disposition of the said securities and/or monies so delivered or paid to any of the undersigned or upon his order. The authority hereby conferred shall remain in force until written notice of the revocation addressed to you is delivered at your main office.

The liability of the undersigned with respect to said account shall be joint and several. The undersigned further agree jointly and severally that all property you may at any time be holding or carrying for any one or more of the undersigned shall be subject to a lien in your favor for the discharge of the obligations of the joint account to you, such lien to be in addition to and not in substitution of the rights and remedies you otherwise would have.

It is further agreed that in the event of the death of either or any of the undersigned, the survivor or survivors shall immediately give you written notice thereof, and you may, before or after receiving such notice, take such proceeding, require such papers and inheritance or estate tax waivers, retain such portion of and/or restrict transactions in the account as you may deem advisable to protect you against any tax, liability, penalty or loss under any present or future laws or otherwise. The estate of any of the undersigned who shall have died shall be liable and each survivor shall continue liable jointly and severally, to you for any net debit balance or loss in said account in any way resulting from the completion of transactions initiated prior to the receipt by you of the written notice of the death of the decedent or incurred in the liquidation of the account or the adjustment of the interests of the respective parties.

FIGURE 43-3b. *Joint account (back).*

In the event of the death of either or any of the undersigned the interests in the account as of the close of business on the date of the death of the decedent (or on the next following business day if the date of death is not a business day), shall be as follows:

______________________ or his or her estate ______________%
Name of Participant

______________________ or his or her estate ______________%
Name of Participant

______________________ or his or her estate ______________%
Name of Participant

but any taxes, costs, expenses or other charges becoming a lien against or being payable out of the account as the result of the death of the decedent, or through the exercise by his or her estate or representatives of any rights in the account shall, so far as possible, be deducted from the interest of the estate of such decedent. This provision shall not release the decedent's estate from the liability provided for in the next preceding paragraph.

The undersigned request you to open the joint account under the following designation:

____

Subject to the provisions hereof, all notices or communications for the undersigned in respect of the joint account are to be directed to

Name ____

Address ____

City ______________________ State ______________________ Zip __________

Dated, ______________________ Very truly yours,

______________________ ______________________
(City) *(State)*

____

____

____

FIGURE 43-4a. *SF&R's power of attorney (front).*

Stone, Forrest & Rivers
INCORPORATED

Trading Authorization Limited
Purchases and Sales of Securit
Power of Attorney—Third Pa

Gentlemen:

The undersigned hereby authorizes____________________
(whose signature appears below) as his agent and attorney in fact with full discretion, power and authority to sell (including short sales), purchase, exchange, convert, tender, trade or otherwise acquire or dispose of stocks, bonds and any other securities including the purchases and/or sale of option contracts (exchange traded or over-the-counter, puts, calls, etc.) to open new option positions or close existing positions, to exercise option contracts and to sell option contracts as either a covered or uncovered writer, and/or contracts relating to the same on margin or otherwise in accordance with yo terms and conditions for the undersigned's account and risk in the undersigned's name and number on your books. The undersigned hereby agrees to indemnify and hold you harmless from and to pay you promptly on demand any and all losses arising therefrom or debit balance due thereon.

In all of the above described transactions you are authorized to follow the instructions of ____________________ ____________________ in every respect concerning the undersigned's account with you; and he is authorized to act for the undersigned and in the undersigned's behalf in the same manner and with the sam force and effect as the undersigned might or could do with respect to the aforementioned transaction as well as with resp to all other things necessary or incidental to the furtherance or conduct of such purchases, sales or transactions.

The undersigned hereby ratifies and confirms any and all transactions with you heretofore or hereafter made by the aforesaid agent or for the undersigned's account.

In connection with this trading authorization which I have executed appointing____________________ ____________________ my agent and attorney in fact, I wish to state that, while my primary interest is in the creation of long-term capital gains, I am prepared to take short-term profits or losses, in the event of the above described option transactions. I recognize that due to the sho term nature of options, my agent or attorney in fact may be trading options to a greater degree than stocks and/or bonds, in that connection I understand I will be charged a commission each time a trade is effected. I further understand that option trading has a number of inherent risks connected therewith and I am full prepared financially to undertake such risks.

I further understand that my agent and attorney in fact as named herein may be buying and selling securities for his own account and/or acting as agent and attorney in fact for other persons in such trans actions. I understand that the same security will not always be bought or sold for the same price for eac account. You are directed to follow the instructions of my agent and attorney in fact as named herein, who shall be solely responsible for suitability of investments, timing of purchases and sales and all relate matters.

This authorization and indemnity is in addition to (and in no way limits or restricts) any rights which you may have under any other agreements between the undersigned and your Firm.

This agreement shall be interpreted under the laws of the State of Illinois.

FIGURE 43-4b. *Power of attorney (back).*

This authorization and indemnity is also a continuing one and shall remain in full force and effect until revoked by the undersigned by a written notice addressed to you and delivered to your office at 55 Water Street, New York, New York, 10041, but such revocation shall not affect any liability in any way resulting from transactions initiated irrespective of any charges or changes at any time in the personnel thereof for any cause whatsoever, and of the assigns of your present Firm o any successor Firm.

Very truly yours,

____

____

Off.______ Acc. No.______________ RR ______

____
Dated

____
City, State

____
Signature of Authorized Agent

FIGURE 43-5a. *SF&R's corporate account form (front).*

Stone, Forrest & Rivers **Corporation Account**
INCORPORATED

(Authorizing Trading in Securities and Permitting Margin Transactions and Short Sales)

To:

Gentlemen:

The undersigned Corporation, by .... its President, pursuant to the resolutions, a copy of which, certified by the Secretary, is annexed hereto, hereby authorizes you to open an account in the name of said Corporation; and the undersigned represents that no one other than the undersigned has any interest in such account. This agreement shall incure to the benefit of your present firm and its successors and assigns in business, irrespective of any change or changes of any kind in the personnel thereof for any cause whatsoever. This authorization shall continue in force until revoked by the undersigned corporation by written notice addressed to you and delivered at your office.

Dated, ...

....
(City) (State)

Very truly yours,

....

By ....
President

I, , being the Secretary of , hereby certify that the annexed resolutions were duly adopted at a meeting of the Board of Directors of said Corporation, duly held on the .... day of ...., at which a quorum of said Board of Directors was present and acting throughout and that no action has been taken to rescind or amend said resolutions and that the same are now in full force and effect.

I further certify that each of the following has been duly elected and is now legally holding the office set opposite his name:

, President
, Vice-President
, Treasurer
, Secretary

I further certify that the said Corporation is duly organized and existing and has the power to take the action called for by the resolutions annexed hereto.

IN WITNESS WHEREOF, I have hereunto affixed my hand this .... day of ...., 19 ....

....
Secretary

FIGURE 43-5b. *Corporate account form (back).*

CERTIFIED COPY OF CERTAIN RESOLUTIONS ADOPTED BY THE BOARD OF DIRECTORS WHEREBY THE ESTABLISHMENT AND MAINTENANCE OF TRADING ACCOUNTS HAVE BEEN AUTHORIZED

RESOLVED–

FIRST: That the President or any Vice President of this Corporation, or   or   be and they hereby are, and each of them hereby is, authorized and empowered, for and on behalf of this Corporation ("Corporation"), to establish and maintain one or more accounts with A. G. Becker Incorporated ("Brokers") for the purpose of purchasing, investing in, or otherwise acquiring, selling, possessing, transferring, exchanging, pledging, or otherwise disposing of, or turning to account of, or realizing upon, and generally dealing in and with any and all forms of securities including, but not by way of limitation, shares, stocks, bonds, debentures, notes, scrip, participating certificates, rights to subscribe, options, warrants, certificates of deposit, mortgages, choses in action, evidences of indebtedness, commercial paper, certificates of indebtedness and certificates of interest of any and every kind and nature whatsoever, secured or unsecured, whether represented by trust, participating and/or other certificates or otherwise. Such authorization shall include the opening of margin accounts and making of short sales.*

The fullest authority at all times with respect to any such commitment or with respect to any transaction deemed by any of the said officers and/or agents to be proper in connection therewith is hereby conferred, including authority (without limiting the generality of the foregoing) to give written or oral instructions to the Brokers with respect to said transactions; to borrow money and securities from or through the Brokers, and to secure repayment thereof with the property of the Corporation; to bind and obligate the Corporation to and for the carrying out of any contract, arrangement, or transaction, which shall be entered into by any such officer and/or agent for and on behalf of the Corporation with or through the Brokers; to pay in cash or by checks and/or drafts drawn upon the funds of the Corporation such sums as may be necessary in connection with any of the said accounts; to deliver securities to and deposit funds, with Brokers; to order the transfer or delivery of securities or funds to any other person whatsoever, and/or to order the transfer of record of any securities to any name selected by any of the said officers or agents; to affix the corporate seal to any documents or agreements, or otherwise; to endorse any securities in order to pass title thereto; to direct the sale or exercise of any rights with respect to any securities; to sign for the Corporation all releases, powers of attorney and/or other documents in connection with any such account, and to agree to any terms or conditions to control any such account; to direct the Brokers to surrender any securities to the proper agent or party for the purpose of effecting any exchange or conversion, or for the purpose of deposit with any protective or similar committee, or otherwise; to accept delivery of any securities; to appoint any other person or persons to do any and all things which any of the said officers and/or agents is hereby empowered to do, and generally to do and take all action necessary in connection with the account, or considered desirable by such officer and/or agent with respect thereto.

SECOND: That the Brokers may deal with any and all of the persons directly or indirectly by the foregoing resolution empowered, as though they were dealing with the Corporation directly.

THIRD: That the Secretary of the Corporation be and he is hereby authorized, empowered and directed to certify, under the seal of the Corporation, or otherwise, to the Brokers:

(a) a true copy of these resolutions;
(b) specimen signatures of each and every person by these resolutions empowered;
(c) a certificate (which, if required by the Brokers, shall be supported by an opinion of the general counsel of the Corporation, or other counsel satisfactory to the Brokers) that the Corporation is duly organized and existing, that its charter empowers it to transact the business by these resolutions defined, and that no limitation has been imposed upon such powers by the By-Laws or otherwise.

FOURTH: That the Brokers may rely upon any certification given in accordance with these resolutions, as continuing fully effective unless and until the Brokers shall receive due written notice of a change in or the rescission of the authority so evidenced, and the dispatch or receipt of any other form of notice shall not constitute a waiver of this provision, nor shall the fact that any person hereby empowered ceases to be an officer of the Corporation or becomes an officer under some other title, in any way affects the powers hereby conferred. The failure to supply any specimen signature shall not invalidate any transaction if the transaction is in accordance with authority actually granted.

FIFTH: That in the event of any change in the office or powers of persons hereby empowered, the Secretary shall certify such changes to the Brokers in writing in the manner hereinabove provided, which notification, when received, shall be adequate both to terminate the powers of the persons theretofore authorized, and to empower the persons thereby substituted.

SIXTH: That the foregoing resolutions and the certificates actually furnished to the Brokers by the Secretary of the Corporation pursuant thereto, be and they hereby are made irrevocable until written notice of the revocation thereof shall have been received by the Brokers.

*Note: If any portion of the first paragraph is not applicable please strike out the inapplicable part.

Minors Act, which protects the minors from the misuse of their funds by adults. Once money or a security is placed in this type of account, it belongs to the minor. The custodian of the account must make sure that the account is managed in accordance with accepted practices and within the so-called "prudent man" guidelines. In other words, investment can be made only in securities of the highest quality. Speculative or high-risk securities may not be purchased, and the account may not be used as a "trading" vehicle.

Opening an Account with Power of Attorney

A group of clients of the St. Louis office wants to permit another person (a third party) to operate accounts on their behalf. Each customer must sign a "power of attorney" form, which can be either limited or full. A *limited power of attorney* can entitle the third party only to buy and sell in the account. A *full power of attorney* empowers the person to deposit and withdraw securities or cash, as well as enter orders in the account.

In addition, a new account form must be completed for the person holding the power of attorney. The same type information is needed for the third party as is needed for the beneficial owner of the account.

Other Accounts

There are other types of accounts—trust accounts, corporate accounts, pension, partnerships, and estates. The new accounts department is responsible for the followup that makes sure the accounts are opened properly.

MAINTAINING ACCOUNTS

Ongoing accounts must be continuously monitored. Customers change their addresses, names, phone numbers, and places of business periodically. SF&R's new accounts department receives notification of these changes from the branch system. Their responsibility is to ensure that the changes are made promptly and accurately.

Example: Customer Rafferty, who maintains a cash account, suddenly decides to write (sell) call options against stock that she owns. Once the options are sold, SF&R requires that she must receive:

1. An Option Clearing Corporation prospectus.
2. An option agreement.
3. A margin agreement.
4. A lending agreement.
5. A truth in lending notice.

To assist in making certain that all accounts are operating in accordance with the rules, the name and address department periodically receives a computer run that compares types of accounts with positions against the coded records of the accounts. Customers' names and addresses are maintained on computer file, along with codes denoting which forms are on file. The computer run, by means of these codes, compares the customer account's position against the forms needed to maintain that position. Discrepancies must be researched and, as needed, the account's stockbrokers are notified and corrected forms sent to the customer.

Any client who refuses to complete the required forms are turned over to the SF&R compliance department. This department contacts the customer and then takes appropriate action.

SUMMARY

The name and address function, also know as "new accounts," is concerned primarily with obtaining and maintaining the documentation necessary for each account of the firm.

PART V

THE BANK-BROKERAGE FIRM RELATIONSHIP

CHAPTER 44

The Commercial Bank as a Source of Financing

Stone, Forrest & Rivers uses many of the services provided by commercial banks. SF&R turns to commercial banks:

- To assist in the financing of its margin accounts and inventory positions.
- To augment its cashiering operation in the settlement of trades in government and money market instruments.
- To obtain same-day money via the bank's Fed wire.

MARGIN DEBIT BALANCES

Some of SF&R's large retail clientele maintain margin accounts, whose debit balances require financing. One of SF&R's sources for the funds necessary to carry these debit balances is the commercial bank.

Example: Customer Blackwell purchases $10,000 worth of securities and deposits the required $5,000. SF&R lends the other $5,000, thereby creating a debit balance.

Current market value	$10,000
Equity	5,000
Debit balance	$ 5,000

The $5,000 that SF&R pays to the seller on behalf of Blackwell constitutes a real loan. The seller of the securities doesn't care how Blackwell pays for them. All the seller cares about is receiving $10,000 upon settlement of the trades.

To have the funds for such a loan, SF&R borrows from commercial banks and pledges the customers securities as collateral.

Two forms, completed by the client, enable SF&R to arrange this kind of financing. The *margin agreement* allows SF&R to hypothecate (or pledge) customers' securities at a commercial bank to obtain funds on a loan basis. The *lending agreement* permits SF&R to obtain funds from other means, such as stock loan. We are concerned only with hypothecation in this section.

SF&R may use security valued at 140% of the customer's debit balance. The remaining securities in customers' accounts must be locked up in seg and may not be used for loan purposes.

The commercial banks conducting business with SF&R will not, however, lend a dollar for every dollar of the pledged security's market value. Federal Regulation T permits lending up to 140% of the customer's debit balance to secure sufficient funds.

Example: SF&R takes $7,000 (140% × $5,000) worth of Blackwells securities to Banker's First Continental, a commercial bank, to obtain the $5,000 loan.

MONITORING THE VALUE OF PLEDGED SECURITIES

Each day, members of SF&R cashiering staff and Banker's First Continental's staff verify the security positions pledged at the bank. SF&R's staff ensures that enough of the right stock is pledged.

How much is "enough"? Each business day, two unrelated factors affect the dollar amount worth of securities maintained on loan: Market *price movement* and *trading activity.*

Market Price Movement

The value of the security is pledged as collateral against the loan, not the shares themselves. As market prices rise, SF&R must call securities from loan; as they fall, additional securities must be pledged.

Banker's First Continental does not want to find its loans uncollateralized due to a move in market prices. So it always has the value of securities hypothecated to ensure that the loan is covered.

The bank's daily routine includes tests of the marketability of the pledged securities. The rule of thumb for measuring marketability is that, the less liquid a security, the greater the "haircut" imposed by the bank. The *haircut* is the percentage taken off the market value of the security for loan purposes.

Example: If the haircut is 30%, $10,000 worth of stock brings only $7,000 on loan. If the haircut is 50%, $10,000 worth of stock brings only $5,000 on loan. Banker's First Continental performs this test because the market value of a security is meaningful only if there is enough depth in the marketplace to absorb the securities, should the bank have to liquidate them.

TRADING ACTIVITY

As customers buy and sell securities in their margin accounts, the number of securities and issues pledged change. SF&R's cashiering personnel get a daily seg listing, which tells them what can be loaned and what may not.

Banker's First Continental's staff has no idea as to what trades took place at SF&R. All they can do is continuously compare the value of the securities, both received for pledge and removed from pledge, with the total value of the outstanding loans. If the brokerage firm is reducing the overall loans, the bank must make certain that the funds are, in fact, returned before the securities are removed from pledge. If the firm is increasing its loans, the bank must ensure that enough securities are pledged.

Securities used against loans are retained in SF&R's name but in negotiable form. The securities belong to SF&R's customers and are only pledged with the bank. When customers' bonds are pledged, the interest belongs to the customers, not to the bank.

SF&R pays the bank interest on the loans, and it obtains

these funds by charging the debit balances in customers' margin accounts.

INVENTORY ACCOUNTS

As a market in OTC common stock, corporate bonds, and municipal bonds, SF&R maintains an inventory in each of these types of securities. SF&R must therefore finance these positions on a day-to-day basis and procures much of its inventory financing from Banker's First Continental. As in margin financing, SF&R pledges securities as collateral for the loan.

The amount of securities pledged depends on the trading accounts' settled position, not on the inventory as of the trade date. This point is important because there are three different answers to the question, "What's your position?" Traders respond in terms of their current trading position. They do not consider whether trades are pending settlement date or whether previous day's trades have, in fact, been settled. Somebody looking at a stock record position answers in terms of the settlement day position, which includes fails to receive and fails to deliver. The third answer, which concerns SF&R and Banker's First Continental, is the *settled position* that is, securities that SF&R has paid for and is still carrying.

Because SF&R owns the securities in trading accounts, it can use 100% of them to obtain loans. Still, Banker's First Continental does not lend dollar for dollar on these securities. The haircut imposed depends on the type of security and/or the financial strength of the security's issuer.

POSITIVE CARRY

When SF&R pledges bonds as collateral for a loan, it must weigh the interest it receives on the bonds *(interest earned)* against the interest it pays or the loan *(interest expense)*. When the interest dollars received on the bond are higher than the interest charged by the bank, SF&R is said to have a *positive carry*. Normally, the difference between interest earned and interest expense is negative, that is, the expense is greater than earnings.

LINES OF CREDIT

Based on SF&R's financial strength, Banker's First Continental has extended the firm a line of credit. SF&R keeps its inventory position within the limits of its credit line.

The credit line also plays a role in SF&R's relationship with Option Clearing Corporation of which it is a member. Against its open option positions, SF&R must prove financial capability of covering its commitments. SF&R's line of credit with Banker's First Continental (BFC) is large enough to cover the open commitments. The line of credit becomes necessary if the firm were unable to meet its obligations. For this continuous promise by BFC, SF&R pays the bank a fee of between ½ to ¾ of a percent annually on the size of the credit line, even if it is not used.

FORMS OF COLLATERAL

Brokerage firms may secure a loan with a bank in several ways:

1. By physically delivering stock to the bank.
2. By book entry "delivery" through the service of a depository.
3. By means of an account of pledge (AP).

Physical Delivery

Firms that maintain securities on their premises and that do not use any automated service must send their securities to the bank to secure the loan. These securities are delivered to the bank each evening and picked up each morning by the firm's runners. Upon receipt and verification of the securities, BFC credits the firm the appropriate loan amount.

The amount of money that can be loaned on securities depends on their type and quality. Banks lend a brokerage firm up to 70% of an equity's market value and up to 95% of a U.S. Treasury's value.

Book Entry "Delivery"

Securities can be moved, by means of book entry at the depository. The firm notifies the depository of the securities to be pledged. The depository isolates, by means of computer programs, (book entry), the security on behalf of the lending bank. The bank then advances the firm the money.

Account of Pledge (AP)

Certain states have banking laws that permit banks to lend money to a brokerage firm when it notifies the bank that the security has been segregated in the firm's vault. The firm, in effect, gives an *account of pledge (AP)*. In the case of an AP, the bank's auditors have the right to "see" the pledged securities.

SUMMARY

The method of hypothecating customer's securities or financing inventories depends on several factors: the firm's relationship with the bank, the state's banking law, and the services offered by the firm's depository.

Regardless of the method, the bank's personnel must verify the value of the securities, maintaining and regularly updating loan ability rates or percentages on securities.

CHAPTER 45

The Commercial Bank As Underwriter

Municipal securities are brought to market through competitive underwritings, in which banks participate. BFC (you guessed it) is one such bank.

The state wants to issue municipal securities to raise money for a project. BFC wants to manage the underwriting. So it contacts other banks and brokerage firms that may be interested in joining the underwriting group. Interested firms and banks meet with BFC to discuss the considerations that go into preparing their bid. The group reviews their options, and then each participant submits what it considers to be the best bid. BFC, as the manager, reviews the bids submitted and attempts to strike a median bid.

The bid from BFC's group is submitted, along with those of other competing underwriting managers, to the municipal agency requesting the financing. The municipality reviews the bids and selects the one that best fits its needs by offering the most financing for the least cost. (The bids are usually open to public inspection).

In this particular case, BFC wins the bid and the underwriting begins. SF&R is part of BFC's group, as are other firms. In addition to the underwriters, bonds are allocated to other firms that will assist in distribution and that make up the *selling group*. The entire group now begins to distribute the new issue.

Settlement

Munis that BFC sells its customers are sent from the syndicate area to figuration. The bonds are usually traded in basis points and figured with accrued interest (as of the dated date). They are then processed through the customer's account. Five business days later, the client is expected to pay for the acquisitions.

Vaulting

Usually, the certificates are placed in BFC vaults and segregated.

Some municipal bonds are eligible for inclusion in the Depository Trust Company (DTC) system. The distribution of DTC-eligible bonds among the participants and then again among the participants' clients is simplified. Deliveries for selling group participants, for clients, or for agents of clients of the selling group firms, as long as they are DTC members, is accomplished by book entry. Physical deliveries are necessary only for non-DTC members.

As the selling group's customer pays for the bonds, the firm deducts its selling concession and pays BFC the remainder. Upon receipt of the proceeds, BFC releases the bonds to the firm, either physically or via book entry. (Actually, the firms pay BFC on settlement date whether or not all of their customers have paid.)

CHAPTER 46

The Commercial Bank as Issuer of Commercial Loans and Paper

Corporations may obtain short-term funds by arranging commercial loans. The financially strongest corporations have the highest ratings. As a result, they qualify for loans at the *prime rate,* which is the lowest interest rate at which a bank will lend money to a corporation. A corporation that does not qualify for the prime rate has to pay higher interest rates to obtain funds.

A corporation, however, may not borrow at the prime rate indefinitely, for two reasons.

First, the amount it can borrow depends day by day on the funds that the bank has available for loan. Commercial banks may lend funds from deposits maintained by its many customers, while part of the deposits, known as the *reserve requirement* (at 12%), must be segregated. The remainder can be used for loans. The nonloanable part of the deposits constitute the Federal Reserve requirement, commonly known as *Fed funds.* These become loanable when the requirement falls below the reserve actually deposited. If a bank has lent as much as it is permitted, a corporation may not borrow more, no matter what its rating. The corporation may turn to other banks for additional loans.

Second, whether a corporation can take out a loan depends on the total amount of loans that the corporation has outstanding. As a corporation borrows more and more without offsetting assets or revenue, its ability to repay the loans may become suspect, until it may no longer be permitted to borrow at the prime rate. As a commercial bank, BFC has many corporations as customers. Corporations turn to many banks for commercial loans.

The rest of this chapter is concerned with BFC's selling and issuing various types of money market instruments. BFC processes these transactions as would a brokerage firm: Trades must be figured and then booked to customers and/or the bank's accounts. The trading cycle culminates with settlement, with the receipt or delivery and offsetting payment.

COMMERCIAL PAPER

Lending corporations and the financing divisions of corporations have a continuous need for funds. One of the ways to raise monies is by issuing commercial paper. Issuing corporations continuously monitor the flow of money against their needs. They borrow only what they need, depending on the availability of money and near-term interest rate projections.

BFC is involved in commercial paper in two ways: (1) It issues commercial paper on the instructions of a client corporation, and (2) it obtains commercial paper for its own clients.

Issuing Commercial Paper

The first step in the issuance of commercial paper occurs when a company in need of short-term funds contacts a bank or commercial paper dealer. (Corporations offer paper to dealers at a slightly higher rate than they do to banks. This permits the dealer to mark up the paper (that is, lower the yield) in reselling it in the market. The mark-up compensates the dealer for processing the trades as well as for taking market risk.) The bank or dealer then contacts a commercial-paper-issuing corporation. The time of the loan, the amount available, and the terms of interest to be paid are negotiated. Upon agreement, the issuing corporation instructs its bank to print and release the paper.

BFC is the issuing bank for several major corporations. Upon receiving notification, BFC *cuts* (or issues) the paper. The issuance is processed through a BFC computer facility, and, around noon, the paper is delivered to the commercial paper buyer. The money involved in the issuance is settled via the Fed wire on the trade date.

BFC records the issuance of the new debt in the company's account. Upon settlement or receipt of the funds via the Fed wire, BFC credits the funds received to the company's account.

Acquiring Commercial Paper

BFC also acquires commercial paper for its customers. BFC and its client discusses the amount of money available, as well as the time it will be lendible. BFC then calls various corporations and negotiates the terms of the loan. The corporation giving the most favorable terms receives the loan. BFC then issues the paper and places it in its vaults.

The BFC client who purchases commercial paper is notified of the purchase by phone and again by written confirmation. Its account is debited (long) the paper, and its money balances are reduced. The issuing corporation's account, on the other hand, is credited the paper, and its money balances are increased (credited).

Because the money moves between a BFC customer's and BFC-affiliated corporation, the transaction is accomplished intra-firm. So the money and commercial paper are moved between accounts and settlement effected all on trade date.

Vaulting

Some commercial paper purchasers are custodial customers of BFC. After receiving the paper from the issuing corporation's agent issuer, BFC sends the paper to the vaulting section. Through the Fed wire, BFC settles the cash owed on the paper between the custodial client and the corporation agent. BFC pays the money in accordance with the client's written instructions.

In BFC's vault, the commercial paper belonging to various customers is stored until it nears maturity.

Retiring the Paper

Approximately five days before the paper is due for collection, BFC personnel begin to prepare it for retirement. The paper is pulled from the vault and verified against the position reports.

Paper to be retired at BFC is sent from the vault to the commercial paper division of BFC. On the maturity date, all paper in the hands of BFC's commercial paper division is cancelled. The corporations whose paper is being retired are charged for the amounts of the loans plus interest owed. The accounts of BFC customers are credited for the interest sum.

Paper that must be surrendered for payment at another bank is sent to the bank for redemption. Paper being retired interbank is paid for on the date of maturity if the retiring bank has the paper on hand. Sometimes, especially with paper redeemable out of town, something goes wrong and the paper is not presented on time. The redeeming bank may accept a due bill from the bank or from a correspondent of the bank sending the paper. If the paper or due bill is not presented on maturity, the corporation has free use of the money, because interest is no longer paid.

CERTIFICATES OF DEPOSIT (CDs)

Banker's First Continental issues several types of CDs.

- *Nonnegotiable*—These CDs of smaller denominations, can be redeemed only at the bank.
- *Negotiable*—CDs of larger denominations can be traded in the secondary market.
- *Euro*—European branches of BFC issue Euro CDs, which represent dollars invested abroad. In Europe, these CDs are regarded in the same manner as when an American branch of a foreign bank issues its own CDs (Yankee CDs) here in the United States.

CDs, like commercial paper, are issued by the bank for same-day settlement. When issued intrabank, CDs are processed through BFCs computer system and settled in the same manner as commercial paper. Sales involving parties outside the bank require settlement via the Fed wire.

The physical CD is processed as is commercial paper. Purchases are processed through BFC's computer system and invoices produced. BFC's staff ensures the accuracy of the invoices and releases the CD upon payment.

The CD certificates are delivered either to the purchaser, to an agent of the purchaser, or to the BFC vault in the case of its own customers. Upon maturity, the CD instrument is surrendered for payment or for reinvestment (that is, for *rollover*) into a new CD.

CHAPTER 47

The Commercial Bank's Role in International Trade

BANKER'S ACCEPTANCES (BAs)

To span the gap, between shipment of goods and payment for them in international trade, a *banker's acceptance* is used. BFC issues BAs on behalf of its corporate clients that import goods, as well as on behalf of its investing clients that have an interest in acquiring instruments of this nature.

Example: One of BFC corporate clients, Giant, Reckor & Crane (GRC), imports goods from Europe. A manufacturer located in Sweden receives the order from GRC and faces the following problems:

1. Why should the manufacturer go without compensation while the goods are in transit?
2. What if GRC cannot pay for the goods when they arrive?
3. What happens if the goods are lost or damaged in transit?

The last question is the easiest to answer. The goods in transit are insured against loss or damage. But what about the first two questions?

GRC goes to its representative at BFC and arranges for a letter of credit to cover the cost of the purchase. The letter is sent to the manufacturer's agent bank in Sweden. Upon receipt, the manufacturer sends the bill of lading, invoice, and other documentation back to BFC.

If the bill of lading is "stamped" by GRC, it becomes a *trade acceptance.* When BFC stamps the bill, it becomes a *banker's acceptance.*

Upon acceptance of the bill, BFC transmits funds to the manufacturer's agent bank. GRC has in reality financed the incoming inventory and pays BFC interest on the loan.

In another section of BFC, a client is looking to invest money for a short period. The client does not want to run the risk of market fluctuations and is considering only short-term instruments. Besides CDs, CPs, T bills, a banker's acceptance is available. The client selects GRC's BA, which is then credited to the client's account; the funds are taken from the client's account and credited to BFC.

At the end of the BA's life, the procedure is reversed: The BA is retired, and the customer's account is credited the amount borrowed plus accrued interest owed by GRC.

CHAPTER 48

The Commercial Bank and Cashiering Services

USING THE FED WIRE

SF&R trades many securities that require Fed fund (same-day-money) settlement. Whereas brokerage firms do not have access to the Fed wire, commercial banks that are Federal Reserve System members do. Since BFC is such a bank, it receives and delivers cash movements on behalf of SF&R, SF&R trades that settle via Fed funds (primarily trades in Treasury instruments, such as GNMAs and Freddie MAcs). Because these instruments usually trade in large sizes and SF&R maintains millions of dollars worth of them for its customers, the firm uses the bank as a custodian for these securities and as an extension of its cashiering operation for receive and deliver.

Banker's First Continental offers its brokerage firm customers a netting and clearing service for government trades. BFC settles trades in two ways: First, trades between firms that are customers of BFC, are considered intrabank settlements and need not go through the Fed wire. The bank's netting service reduces the number of receives and delivers that each participating firm has to make on a given day. Second, trades not entered into with a BFC participant are settled on a trade-on-trade basis through the Fed wire.

A Typical Day

Each morning SF&R sends BFC its pending settling trades, including the day's settling trades and previous day's settling trades that were not satisfied (fails).

BFC receives "receive or deliver" instructions from its customer firms. The instructions contain the description of the instrument, the quantity, and the amount of money involved. The data is fed into BFC's computer system. Trades involving BFC participants are paired off and netted. SF&R is informed of the quantity received or delivered and the money involved. The bank simply debits or credits SF&R's accounts accordingly. Trades that do not involve participants are settled via the Fed wire. Based on SF&R's instructions, the bank receives or delivers against payment across the Fed wire. SF&R receives notification of both kinds of settlements so that it may note the movements on their internal records.

SF&R also maintains a communication network with the bank to facilitate same-day trades, inventory control, and money management.

Some of the larger firms communicate with BFC via computer terminals. These on-line systems permit the firm and bank to communicate during the day. As the bank processes entries, it also records them on the firm's records by means of entries made into the terminals. At the other end of the communications network, the firm's cashiering department, as they occur, monitors daily movements. By recording and monitoring receives and delivers as they occur, the firm manages its securities movements with great proficiency.

During the course of the day, SF&R monitors BFC activity for other reasons to ensure that it has enough funds to meet its obligations at BFC. At the end of the day's processing, BFC returns items that have not been settled.

Institutional Delivery (ID) System

Some customers, namely institutions and large retail clients, maintain their security positions at banks. Trades executed by brokerage firms on behalf of these customers may be settled either as *receiver versus payment (RVP)* or *delivery versus payment*

(DVP). In either type of settlement, the customer gives the brokerage firm's stockbroker buy/sell instructions and then, when notified of execution, gives the custodian bank's representative receive or deliver instruction. The bank acts merely as custodian for the customer.

Because a dual set of instructions is needed, many problems occur in the settlement of these trades. Sometimes the bank does not recognize the trade because the client neglected to inform the people there. Or the brokerage firm sends the security to the wrong department at the bank or even, in some cases, to the wrong bank. In turn, the banks, given instructions from the client, look to receive or deliver the stock on the wrong day, or it expects the trade from another firm. And so on. A better method was needed to tie together customer, brokerage firm, and bank.

Procedures centering around a depository, such as Depository Trust Company (DTC), reduce these problems. DTC instituted the *institutional delivery (ID)* system, which allows for open communication between the brokerage firm and the agent bank *prior to settlement.*

Both SF&R and BFC participate in the ID system. SF&R's new account department maintains—in addition to the usual information, such as name, address, occupation, and so on—records of delivery instructions. Included in the delivery instructions is the bank's name, the responsible area within the bank, and the bank's *financial institution number system (FINS)* number.

When an SF&R customer enters into a trade, SF&R sends copies of the transactions to DTC for entry into the ID system. Specifically, on the first or second day after the trade date, SF&R forwards to Depository Trust Company such details of the trade as quantity, description, price, settlement money, trade date, settlement date, and the like. Upon receipt of trades, DTC's computer network rearranges (sorts) the received data into custodian bank order. DTC then notifies the corresponding bank, in this case BFC, of the pending transaction.

Affirmations. BFC's staff verifies the terms received from SF&R via the ID systems against the instructions received from the customer. If the terms of the trade are agreed to, the bank *affirms* the trade. An *affirmation,* which includes the method of settlement, constitutes acceptance of the trade. BFC'S R&D section may choose to settle via book entry at DTC or physically via the "bank's window."

The "affirmations" are returned to DTC, which, in turn, notifies the respective brokerage firms of the acceptances. SF&R's cashiering personnel verify the affirmations against the items originally sent to DTC for inclusion in the ID system.

Setting Up Receives and Delivers. For approved trades, the cashier's department begins to set up the delivery or receive.

For *receives from banks* (customer-sold securities), SF&R makes certain that the street-side (contra broker) is correct and in place. Upon receipt of the security from BFC, SF&R "turns it around," and delivers the security to the contra broker, and pays the customer. SF&R must then complete the sale by delivering the security to the contra broker for it to get paid. If it does not complete delivery, SF&R is left with the securities and a paid-out check. In all probability, SF&R has to finance this undelivered (fail to deliver) item, and financing incurs an expense in the form of interest. Because SF&R cannot regain this money from other sources, the financing is an expense that erodes SF&R's profitability.

SF&R has the same problem when a customer purchases stock and uses a bank as a custodian. After affirmation, SF&R must wait until the selling firm delivers the security. Upon receipt of the securities, SF&R turns the securities around and delivers them to the bank for payment. If SF&R cannot complete this part of the cycle, it is holding paid-for securities for which it has not yet paid. Again, it must finance these securities until delivery can be made. And again, financing presents a real expense to the firm.

Don't Knows (DK s). Sometimes the bank does not recognize the trades submitted by DTC; these are *don't knows (DKs).* This type of trade constitutes a problem at SF&R. The firm must begin to research the problem, including calling the stockbroker to verify that the delivery instructions are correct. The broker may even have to call the customer to make certain that the delivery instructions are correct. If the customer concurs with the instruction, then the customer has to call the bank to find out where the order went wrong.

SUMMARY

Whatever the problem—be it SF&R's, the bank's, or the customer's—a lot of time and effort is wasted before the problem is resolved. Both BFC and SF&R incur unnecessary expense, and both share in the consequences of an unhappy customer.

CHAPTER 49

The Commercial Bank as Dividend Disbursing Agent (DDA)

Banker's First Continental is the dividend disbursing agent for several corporations, among which is Cavalari International Corp. Cavalari has both common and preferred stocks outstanding as well as some long-term corporate debt. BFC is the paying agent for all of Cavalari's securities.

COMMON STOCK

When Cavalari's board of directors declare a dividend on the company's common stock, they also establish the record date, the payable date, and the amount of the dividend per share. Knowing, of course, how many shares are outstanding. Cavalari deposits the appropriate sum in its dividend payable account at BFC. The funds must be *good* (that is, cleared) on payable date for BFC to issue the dividend payments.

BFC, who is also the registrar for Cavalari stock, maintains the records of registered holders. (Remember that the "registered" holder may be either the beneficial or nominee.) BFC processes transfers of a security's ownership up to the evening of the record date. At that point, it "closes its books."

Whoever is registered on the night of record is paid the

dividend. If a brokerage firm—acting on its own behalf or that of a client, institution, individual, or any other party—does not have the stock properly registered by the night of record date, then it does not receive the dividend from BFC. The firm has *missed transfer,* and it must claim the dividend from the party who received it. The brokerage firm can get this information from the certificate or by contacting BFC, who upon submission of proper identification by the claimant, can give the name and address of the dividend's recipient.

On payable date, BFC issues dividend payments to the registered holders. One check is issued, as are money transfers, for each registration in accordance with the total position of each registered holder.

Example: Cavalari Corp. has 9,000,000 shares of common stock outstanding. Its board authorizes a 50 cents per share dividend, therefore deposits $4,500,000 in its account at BFC. The bank, having the names and addresses of the shares' registered owners, issues checks to holders totalling $4,500,000.

Depository Trust Company has 125,800 shares of Cavalari Corp. on deposit. The stock is registered in the nominee name of DTC, "CEDE." Assuming a 50-cents-per-share dividend, BFC pay DTC $62,900 ($.50 × 125,800 shares). DTC then apportions the dividend, by position, among its depositors.

In turn, depositors apportion the dividend by position to the beneficial owners. One DTC depositor, Stone, Forest & Rivers, has 41,275 shares registered in DTC's name and is paid $20,637.50 ($.50 × 41,275 shares). SF&R apportions the dividend payment among its clients' accounts according to the security's position on their books. If any of "SF&R's" shares either for the beneficial owner or the organization is not properly registered, SF&R will claim the dividend.

PREFERRED STOCK

Preferred stock follows the same basic procedure as common. Since, however, preferred dividends are set at the time of issuance and payments are usually set at quarterly intervals, Cavalari, being a healthy company, simply authorizes payment of the dividends when due. Companies that are not so well financed may not authorize the dividend.

BONDS

Since Cavalari's corporate bonds are in registered form, the names and addresses of the registered holders are maintained by BFC. Cavalari Corp., accumulates funds for interest payments in the company's interest payment account at the bank. On payment date, BFC issues payments to the registered owners.

For bonds, the record date is the night before payable. To facilitate record keeping, however, BFC and other paying agents close their books approximately one week before payable date. So, to be entitled to the interest payment from the agent, the bonds must be in for transfer before this "cutoff" date. The industry therefore looks at this last day to "make transfer" as the record date.

Neither Cavalari nor BFC is concerned with who bought or who sold bonds during the interest period. On payment date, BFC pays a full six months' worth of interest to the registered owner. As in the case of equity securities, bonds that are not registered in time oblige either the bond owner or the agency acting in the owner's behalf to claim the interest.

BFC is also the paying agent for the municipality (city). The municipality's bonds are in *bearer form,* that is, they are not registered and carry coupons, which are detached as payments become due. The dated coupons are clipped from the bond, as payments come due, and surrendered to the bank.

The coupon represents payment of six-months' interest. Unlike registered bond payments, which are made automatically to holders, bearer bond payments are made only when owners surrender the coupons. Failure to surrender the coupons when they are due gives the municipality, in effect, free money because no interest is paid on the uncollected interest.

TRANSFER AGENT

Banker's First Continental acts as the transfer agent for some of the firms with which it conducts business, and Cavalari International is one of them. As transfer agent, the bank is responsible for the timely and accurate recording of security ownership. Every share of outstanding stock must be accounted for, as well as every dollar of debt in the form of bonds. BFC therefore maintains registration in two files, each of which must be in balance at all times.

Each business day, stock is turned over to BFC for reregistration. The certificates to be cancelled are verified against the files to ensure authenticity. Once the validity of the certificate is established, the following steps are taken:

1. New certificates are issued in accordance with the transfer instruction.
2. The certificate numbers of the new stock are recorded in both the numerical and registration files.
3. New registration is recorded on both files.
4. The old certificate numbers are recorded with the new registration, along with the date of cancellation.
5. The old certificate number and registration are cancelled, and the new certificate number and date of issuance are noted next to cancellation notation.

BFC can now locate:

- What certificate was issued against one that cancelled.
- What certificate was cancelled by one that was issued.
- The dates of cancellations of the old and of the issuance of the new.

With the entries verified once, the entries are verified again the next morning. The total shares cancelled must equal the total shares issued.

BFC ships the new securities in accordance with the delivery instructions on the transfer form. The instructions may call for delivery to an individual, to a brokerage firm, to a bank, or to depository.

Fast Automatic Stock Transfer (FAST)

Depository Trust Company, in cooperation with various transfer agents, maintains a service known as Fast Automatic Stock Transfer (FAST) service. DTC maintains at the transfer agent's bank, a *Jumbo certificate,* which represents most or all of the shares of a given security on deposit at DTC. When one of the participants requests a transfer of the security through DTC, the Depository notifies the agent to issue the certificate against the Jumbo certificate. The bank reduces the size of the Jumbo certificate (cancels the old one and issues a new, smaller one) and then issues the requested shares.

Because DTC does not have to pull certificates from its vault and surrender them to the transfer agent, the transfer is expedited. The FAST system can save about two days over the conventional transfer process.

SUMMARY

In many ways, bank processing is similar to the procedures used by brokerage firms. Trades must be figured and recorded. Positions must be verified. Securities and funds must be moved daily inter- and intrabank.

In others, the two procedures differ. The banks have access to the Fed wire for settlement, may issue short-term debt instruments, and lend money. Brokerage firms may do none of these things.

CHAPTER 50

The Commercial Bank as Customer of the Brokerage Firm

Banker's First Continental manages portfolios, in a fiduciary capacity, for trusts, pension funds, and other institutional accounts. As a manager, BFC must buy and sell securities in accordance with the fund's objective.

THE PORTFOLIO MANAGERS

The portfolio managers at BFC adhere to its customer's terms at all times. For example, in the case of a pension fund, BFC managers invest money on a regular basis as participants make their contributions. Yet retired participants can usually receive either a one-time lump-sum payment or periodic withdrawals over a predetermined period. This flow of cash into and out of the fund requires portfolio adjustments—that is, the buying and selling of securities.

The portfolio managers at BFC adjust securities positions for other reasons. An acquired security may have reached its objective—or failed to reach its objective. Another company's stock may appear to be a better investment, or one of the companies in the portfolio may have reduced its dividend payment. Any one of a myriad of reasons may require adjustments in a portfolio.

USE OF BROKERAGE FIRMS

BFC uses various brokerage firms to execute its orders. The brokerage firms are given code numbers for the accounts, such as Banker's First Continental Trust #013472, and the address of the BFC branch that services the account. In-house, BFC maintains its accounts by name and number.

EXECUTING ORDERS

The portfolio manager writes the order ticket and forwards it to BFC's order desk. From there, a trader phones the orders to a representative at the selected brokerage firm—in this case, one of SF&R's institutional brokers.

When the order is executed, the bank's trader and SF&R's broker review the terms of the trade and all other charges, such as the amount of commission.

If the trader and broker agree, the trader forwards the trade to its figuration area for computation. BFC's accounts are charged a service fee on a per-trade or per month basis, or even on the basis of some combination of both. Depending on the agreement between BFC and the customer, the bank's figuration department applies the appropriate fees. The transaction, along with the completed figuration, continues through the processing cycle.

On, usually, the day after trade date, both the customer and bank's R&D section receive confirmations of the trade. For purchases, the customer is expected to have the proceeds available in the account by settlement date.

SF&R, through the ID system, notifies BFC's R&D of the pending trade. The R&D section matches the ID notice against the instructions received from BFC's trade processing system. If all is in order, the trade is affirmed.

By the day before settlement, BFC's R&D section has either affirmed or DK'd the transaction.

In the case of a *buy*, R&D must pay and select the method of settlement, that is, either DTC or physical delivery. *Sell* trades work in reverse. Upon affirmation of a sell transaction. BFC notifies the brokerage firm how delivery is to be effected. The firm must then set up to receive the securities accordingly.

SUMMARY

When a bank buys and sells securities for their institutional clients, it does so through brokerage firms. The ID system enables banks and firms, together, to efficiently execute the portfolio manager's buy and sells.

PART VI

FOREIGN MARKETS

CHAPTER 51

International Settlement

"The world is shrinking" is more than an old cliche. As it does, international boundaries, which in the past kept firms national, seem to be disappearing. Business flows in all directions. Not only are United States firms opening sales offices in other countries, they are also forming subsidiaries and other entities that will trade in those local market places. Likewise, many foreign countries are developing U.S.-based operations. For example, for the first time, not all U.S. government dealer firms are U.S.-based.

This portion of the book will address some of our foreign markets. We will be discussing their trading markets and settlement systems.

UNITED KINGDOM

In 1986, trading on the London Stock Exchange (LSE, aka International Stock Exchange) moved "upstairs," and computerized trading began. Known as SEAQ, the trading system operates among brokers and market makers, or dealers. SEAQ provides a facility for trading not only ordinary and preferred shares, but also corporate debt securities, (bonds) and U.K. government issues.

The SEAQ market is displayed on television-type monitors, with traders and brokers entering into transactions called *bargains*. Depending on LSE-established criteria, issues trade in any one of three SEAQ levels. Each of the three levels offers a different degree of information about a particular issue's trading history.

Upon acceptance of a bid or offer, a trade occurs. The acceptance is captured at the point of execution and is sent to the next step in the process known as *checking*. Checking is a batch process occurring on the night of trade date at the LSE facility. The results of the "checking" process are known to the participants on trade date plus one (T+1). Reports are distributed to participants displaying the activity that has been recorded.

From the checking process, trades flow from the LSE (SEAQ) into settlement, currently in the form of a system known as *Talisman*. This process is to be changed in the near future by a newer and more efficient process known as *Taurus*. Talisman is a trade-for-trade settlement system. Monies, however, can be settled on a net basis through the London Stock Exchange.

As of the writing of this section, UK equities settle on a fortnight basis. Trades that take place during weeks 1 and 2 flow into a settlement preparation week (week 3), with actual settlement occurring the Monday of week 4.

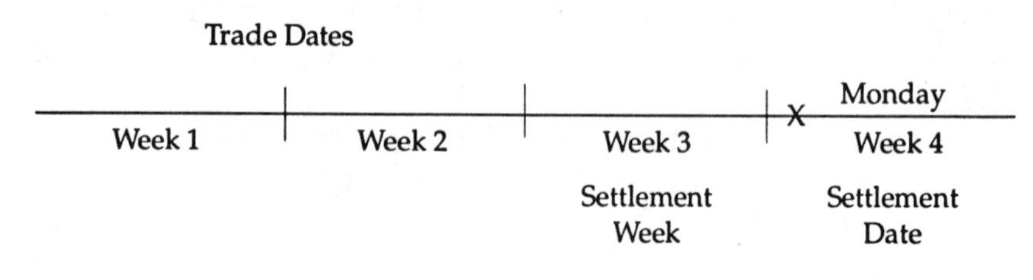

The trades of weeks 3 and 4 are passed through settlement week 5, with actual settlement occurring Monday of week 6, and so on. The planned replacement for Talisman, Taurus, will have many enhancements, one of which is the ability to eventually have a T+3 settlement cycle. The first step will be to have equity trades migrate from a fortnight settlement cycle to a T+10 (trade date plus 10). Corporate debt stock, however, currently settles through Talisman on a T+5 (trade date plus 5) basis.

U.K. government issues, known as *gilts*, are settled next day (T+1), with the Central Gilt Office (CGO). The CGO operates a computer-based system for the settling and recordkeeping of transactions. In this certificateless environment, changes in ownership are accomplished by book entry.

An interesting facet of gilts is their "negative" interest. Debt instruments in the United States have "positive" interest, that is, the buyer always pays the seller accrued interest. As the bond nears its payment period, transfer agents "close" their books to clean up any pending reregistrations. For trades settling during this period, the securities will not be transferred out of the seller's name into the buyer's name. Therefore, the buyer will pay the seller the accrued interest, and then the buyer's firm will have to make "claim" on the seller's firm for the period's interest when it is paid. However with more and more securities being maintained at a depository in street name, the problem of paying double interest to the seller is dissipating and no longer entails the quantity or work it once did.

Example: Assume that a bond has interest computed on a 360-day basis, paying interest every six months (180 days), and that it is registered in the name of the seller or of the firm representing the seller. One week before the payable date, the transfer agent "closes" the books and the registration of the bond cannot be changed during this period. A buyer acquiring the bond with 178 days of accrued interest would include the interest amount owed with the settlement of the trade. Two days later (at 180 days), the seller or seller's firm would receive the full six months' interest from the issuing agent, since the seller is still the registered owner. The buyer's firm would claim the six months' interest from the seller's firm and give it to the buyer. The net between what the buyer paid (178 days) and what the buyer received (180 days) is what accrued to the buyer during the period (that is, 2 days: 180 – 178 = 2 days).

British Gilts have avoided this problem by employing negative interest. From the time the instrument cannot be reregistered until the time it is payable, the seller pays the buyer the interest that is to accrue to the buyer. In the above example, the seller would have paid the buyer the two days interest. When the seller receives the six months' interest from the issuer, the seller would be left with interest actually owed: 180 days' interest received, less 2 days interest paid to the buyer, equals 178 days owed to the seller.

GERMANY

Of seven exchanges in Germany, the Frankfurt Stock Exchange is the largest. As on other exchanges, securities are fitted into three trading classes. The securities of the largest, most active, and best capitalized companies trade in a market known as the *Amtlicher Handel.* Securities trading in this range are assigned to *Kursmaklers.* A Kursmakler is not a market-maker, but is responsible for the maintenance of a fair and orderly market, and for setting the price at which round lots and odd lots (less than 50 shares) are filled.

Freimaklers, who are also members of the exchanges, are floor traders who trade for their own accounts. They provide, when needed, the difference between supply and demand when the *Kursmakler* sets the price.

As stated earlier, securities are assigned to *Kursmaklers.* Unlike the markets that have continuous trading, the Kursmakler bunches incoming orders. These orders are received from member banks, since broker/dealers do not exist in Germany. The banks gather their clients' orders and forward them to the *Kursmakler,* or broker, for execution.

When the *Kursmakler* has accumulated orders, a pairing off process begins. All buy and sell market orders, all buy limit orders above the determined set price, all sell limit orders below the set price, as well as all buy and sell limit orders at the determined set price, must be executed. The *Kursmakler* tries to pair off the buy and sell interests as best as possible, with assistance of the *Freimaklers* (who buy or sell the difference). Once the price is set, all orders that qualify for executions are "filled." The collective process then begins again.

Lesser known companies qualify for listing and trading in the Geregelter Market. The market operates with brokers and *Freimaklers. Kursmaklers* do not participate in this market.

The third market, known as *Freiverkehr,* trades foreign shares and those of small capitalized firms. It is the least regulated of the German exchange market.

Prices and quotes for daily transactions are transmitted over a system called *BOSS (Boerson Order Service System).* The system can also route orders to the *Kursmaklers* for execution.

Over-the-counter transactions, along with those futures and options listed for trading on the Deutsche Terminborse (DTB), are traded on a computer-based system known as *IBIS (Interbank Information System)* and *DTB.* It is similar to other computer-based systems used in other countries.

Trades executed through these different market places are forwarded to Kassenverein for settling. Trades are settled on T+2 by means of a method known as *chaining.* Under the chaining concept, receives and delivers are set up in chronological order. Securities are delivered against payment. The firm receiving the payment goes on to receive against payment securities owed to it, then delivers securities against payment, and so on. Hence the name "chaining."

The German markets also maintain ties for cross-border settlement. This is accomplished through Auslandskassenverein. Among the interfaces that exist are those with France's Sicovam, Italy's Moante Titoli, Cedel, and Euroclear.

FRANCE

As with most other countries, France has an on-line trading system, called *CAC.* Trades executed through this system are locked-in trades that are compared by the *ISB (Inter Sociétés de Bourse*). Because these transactions are locked in, comparison is actually effected on trade date. Trades occurring away from CAC are compared on T+1.

In France, cash trades settle on T+3. Regular way trades settle once a month, at the end of the month. This monthly process includes the trades from the 15th of one month through the 15th of the next. The settlement cycle for these issues, therefore, is 15 to 45 days.

The French settlement process consists of two parts: Relit

and Sicovam. Relit is involved with trade comparison between members as well as between members and banks.

Trade comparison between members is accomplished by CAC feeding into ISB on the night of trade date. The accepted trades are then offset by the *Société des Borse Francaises* (SBF), which guarantees settlement. It will replace a defaulting firm, and has access to security lending to complete settlement.

Member firm trades are netted and eventually flow into *Denouement* for final settlement. Denouement is part of SICOVAM, which is the French Central Depository.

ITALY

The major exchange of Italy is the Milan Stock Exchange, on which nine active trading pits exist. Trading is by open outcry, and settlement is on a monthly basis.

The exchange operates under the Ministry of Treasury and the *CONSOB (Commissione Nazionale per le Societe e la Borsa)*. The CONSOB actually supervises the securities business.

In this market, ownership is evidenced by ordinary and preferred shares. Debt markets are dominated by government issues. CCT, a form of government bond, has variable coupons, whereas BTP, another version, has fixed coupons.

A junior market, *Mercato Ristretta*, also exists for trading the shares of firms of lesser capitalization.

Settlement date for shares executed on the main exchange is monthly, whereas securities traded on Mercato Ristretta settle in 10 business days.

After being compared, trades flow through to the Italian Depository, Monte Titoli S.p.A., which settles the transaction on a book entry basis.

JAPAN

There are eight exchanges in Japan, of which the Tokyo Stock Exchange (TSE) is the biggest. There are three classifications of members on the Tokyo Stock Exchange: regular members, special members and Saitori members.

The *regular members* can buy or sell securities for their clients or for their own proprietary accounts. *Special members* act as brokers in trying to execute orders that could not be completed on other exchanges. *Saitori members* act as brokers for transactions on the TSE, and as such, they cannot have general public customers and cannot trade for their own accounts. The Japanese markets are order-driven, and not market-maker-driven, since regular members will react to Saitori requests for market making when off-floor orders are not sufficient to permit trade completion.

Trades executed on the Japanese exchanges settle on T+3. Comparison occurs directly after the trade and flows into a netting process within JSCC (Japan Securities Clearing Corporation).

The TSE has two order routing systems. One, known as *FORES (Floor Order Routing and Execution System)*, deposits small orders from the member firm to the Saitori for execution via a display book. The other system *CORES* (*Computer Assisted Order Routing and Execution System*), is used for the more inactive issues, and it will automatically execute orders if the other side is found.

Trades executed through FORES or CORES are immediately transmitted to members. Members verify the notice against their internal records. On T+1, members who have found discrepancies report them to the exchange for correction. On T+2, preparation for settlement occurs; T+3 results in netting.

After the netting process has been completed, book entry delivery and receipt instructions are given by JSCC to Japan's depository JASDEC (Japan Security Depository Center).

Trades in Japanese government bonds do not settle in such a regimented process. The length of time between trade date and settlement can be as much as 15 days or as little as 6, with many trade dates flowing into one settlement date.

Another interesting feature of Japanese government bonds is that interest is computed on an actual/365-day basis, without any regard for leap year. The computation for accrued interest also uses the "factor" method.

HONG KONG

Trades executed on the Stock Exchange of Hong Kong (SEHK) enter into the Central Clearing and Settlement System (CCASS).

At the writing of this text, CCASS is a trade-for-trade settlement system operated by Hong Kong Securities Clearing Co. Ltd. (HKSCC). However, unlike any other clearing entities, HKSCC does not guarantee settlement of trades.

The Stock Exchange of Hong Kong has moved from T+1 (trade date plus 1) settlement cycle to a T+2 cycle, and has no intention of complying with the general recommendation of a universal T+3 settlement cycle. Settlement of trades may be DVP (delivery versus payment) or free.

CEDEL AND EUROCLEAR

The two major international settlement facilities in Europe are Cedel and Euroclear. While they originated for different purposes, the needs of the market place have moved these two into the same arena. In 1980, an "electronic bridge" went into operation between these two facilities, allowing book entry settlement between each other's members.

Trade comparison at these facilities occurs four times a day. Buyers submit input instructions, and sellers submit delivery instructions. The system to effect comparison is known as ACE, which was developed by ISMA (International Securities Market Association, formerly AIBO). Cedel and Euroclear comparison can occur as early as trade date, although T+1 is common.

The ACE system, with its four matches per day, can be used to direct matched data into settlement. Trades that do not match are maintained by the clearing entities and are repeatedly reported until a match occurs or until the transactions are cancelled.

Matched trade settlement is effected by DVP (delivery versus payment), with security movement and the agreed-to currency denomination being used in the settlement process. Once effected, settlement is final.

Cedel and Euroclear do not maintain depositories. Instead, they utilize the local depositories of the countries of issuance. They also maintain settlement links with the clearing entities of the issuing countries. Therefore, members of Cedel or Euroclear can settle "cross-border" trades without being members of the countries' individual clearing entities.

To settle transactions, both clearing entities participate in the "chaining" process with deliveries versus payments and receipts versus payments being made in sequence. An added feature is the availability of security loan to expedite settlement. Should a participant not be able to complete a delivery, and should the participant be an active participant in the loan program, the securities needed will automatically be provided, if available. Later in the chaining process, should the needed shares be delivered to the borrowing firm, the loan will be returned.

Cedel and Euroclear also provide Forex transactions for their participants. This allows settlement of any transaction in any currency agreed to at the time of trade.

INTERNATIONAL BOND INTEREST CALCULATIONS

In the United States, bond interest is computed using different bases. For example, corporate and most municipal bonds have accrued interest calculated on a 360-day basis, with each month having 30 days. U.S. Treasury bills have interest computed on an actual/360-day basis and the interest on U.S. Treasury bonds and notes is computed at a base of actual/actual. We further differentiate the methods of calculating instruments that use 30/360 into two different categories, those that carry a 31st settlement date as 30 days for the month, and those that assume it to represent 29 days.

Example: Let's look at the 30/360 differences. Assume a bond has an interest payment period of "MS," or March and September 1. A trade is made that settles July 31. Since interest accrues up to, but not including, settlement date, 30 days of accrued interest to the month of July would appear to make sense, since it is the day before the 31st. A trade settling August 1, would also accrue 30 days' interest, since no month can have more than 30 days in the 30/360 scenario. The other way to look at the same picture is to say that as no month can have more than 30 days in the calculation, the 31st is the same as the 30th, and therefore only 29 days should have accrued for that month. This would mean that a trade settling August 1 would be 30 days; in contrast, one settling on the 31st would only count for 29 days.

Here is the calculation for a March and September bond trade settling July 31:

Method 1: 30/360		*Method 2:* 30/360E	
March	30	March	30
April	30	April	30
May	30	May	30
June	30	June	30
July	30	July	29
	150 days		149 days

What if the same bond trade settled August 1?

Method 1: 30/360		*Method 2:* 30/360E	
March	30	March	30
April	30	April	30
May	30	May	30
June	30	June	30
July	30	July	30
	150 days		150 days

As we enter the global world, we find other methods of calculation.

British government bonds, gilts, compute interest on an actual/actual basis, paid semiannually. This is identical to the method used for U.S. Treasuries. What differentiates these bonds from those of the U.S. Treasury is the employment of negative interest. If the settlement date of a transaction falls within the last 37 days before a payment date, the seller pays the buyer the interest that would have accrued to the buyer by the payment date. The seller then receives the full period's interest from the issuer's agent. The difference between what the seller receives from the agent and what the seller paid the buyer, is what has been earned by the seller for the period the bonds were owned.

Example: A gilt with a payment cycle of FA is transacted, with a settlement of July 21. The six-month period involved contains 181 days in a nonleap year. For a trade settling July 21, 170 of the 181 days' interest would be owed to the seller. The difference, 11 days, is what the buyer is entitled to receive. Therefore, when this trade is computed, the seller would pay the buyer 11 days' interest, and on August 1 the seller would receive 181 days' interest.

The difference between the two payments is the 170 days actually owed to the seller. U.S. Treasury bonds do not employ a negative interest method. Therefore, the buyer would pay the seller 170 days' interest; if the buyer (firm) was unable, for whatever reason, to get the instruments properly registered, it would have to "make claim" for the 181 days' interest that the seller would have also received as the registered owner.

Another interesting bond is the Japanese government bond. The bonds have accrued interest calculated on an actual/365-day basis, regardless of whether or not it is a leap year. In addition, the computation includes the use of a "factor." Under this concept, a "factor" must be determined by taking the number of days accrued and dividing them by 365, then multiplying the result by the coupon rate. The computation of the factor is taken to seven decimal places. The resulting factor is then multiplied by the face amount and divided by 100.

Example: Let's assume 25 days of a 1,000,000 JPY bond with a coupon rate of 5%:

$$\text{Accrued interest} = \frac{25}{360} \times 5 = .3424655 \text{ (the factor)}$$

$$.3424655 \times 1{,}000{,}000 \div 100 = 3{,}424.66 \text{ JPY}$$

Unlike many other instruments, Japanese government bonds do not settle in fixed cycles. Settlement date can be anywhere from 6 to 15 days after trade date. In other words, many trade dates will have the same settlement date.

US Treasury bonds, U.K. gilts, and Japanese government bonds pay interest semiannually. French government bonds, OATS and BTANS, and German government issues pay interest annually. Therefore, an owner of the semiannual payer has the opportunity to have earned more than the owner of an annual payer, due to the compounding effect of reinvesting the six-month payment by the recepient at the current interest rate.

Glossary

Accrued Interest. The amount of interest that the buyer owes the seller on transactions involving fixed income securities, such as most bond and notes.

Add by Seller. Form submitted by the selling firm (two days after trade date) to compare trades *not* previously submitted to National Securities Clearing Corporation (NSCC).

Added Trade Contract. The last in a series of contract reports rendered by NSCC. It contains the totals of previously compared trades from the regular way contract, supplemental contract sheets, and the trades compared through QT, DK, and CHC processing.

ADR. *See* American Depository Receipt.

Advisory Processing. Procedure by which the opposing firm's version of a trade is accepted by the named firm. Advisory notices accompany regular way contract reports received from NSCC.

Agency Transaction. A trade in which the firm operates as a broker, that is, it executes trades as an agent and charges a commission for the service.

All or None. A phrase used in certain underwritings and on some orders. In an underwriting, it is an instruction by corporation to a stand-by underwriter to take *all* of the forthcoming issue *or none*. On large-quantity orders, it is an instruction to fill *all* of the order or *none* of it.

American Depository Receipt (ADR). A share of stock that is issued by an American bank and that is backed by foreign securities on deposit.

American Stock Exchange (AMEX). Located at 86 Trinity Place, New York, New York, a major stock and option exchange.

Amortization. An accounting term indicating the apportionment of an incurred expense over the life of an asset. For example, if a three-year magazine subscription (an expense) is paid in year one, it should be "amortized" (or "spread out") over the three-year life of the subscription (the asset).

Annual Report. A formal presentation of the corporation's financial statements that is sent to this registered stockholders. If shares are registered in nominee name (in the care of the brokerage firm), the proxy department has to obtain copies of the report and mail them to the beneficial owners (clients).

Arbitrage. A strategy by which an industry professional trades in two offsetting positions for profit. Arbitrage is brought into play when disparities appear in the prices of the same or equivalent securities. For example, RAP preferred is convertible into five shares of common, The common is trading at 15 1/8 per share and the preferred is trading at 75. The arbitrageur would buy the preferred at 75, convert to five times the number of common, and sell the equivalent number of common at 75 5/8.

Asked. The offer side of a quote or the selling price. A quote represents the highest bid and lowest asked (offer) available in the marketplace at a given point in time.

As-of. A term used to describe any trade processed not on the actual trade date, but "as of" the actual trade date.

Asset. Anything owned by the corporation.

Average. Also known as an index, a mathematical computation that indicates the value of a number of securities as a group. The three most popular averages are the Dow Jones Industrial Average (DJI), Standard & Poors (S & P) 500, and the New York Stock Exchange Composite. The average, which may be market-weighted, share-weighted, or price-weighted, indicates performance.

Balance Sheet. An accounting statement reflecting the firm's financial condition in terms of assets, liabilities, and net worth (ownership). In a Balance sheet, Assets = Liabilities + Net Worth.

BAN. *See* Bond Anticipation Note.

Banker Acceptance. A discounted debt instrument used in international trade to expedite payment of goods in transit between exporting and importing countries.

Basis Price. A method of pricing municipal bonds, T bills, and certain other instruments. It is an expression of yield to maturity.

Bear. Someone who thinks that the value of the market or of a security will fall.

Bearer Form. Unrecorded security ownership. The individual "bearing" the instrument is assumed to be the owner.

Bearer Instrument. Any instrument (security) in bearer form.

Bear Market. A market in which prices are generally declining.

Beneficial Owner. The owner of a security who is entitled to all the benefits associated with ownership; customers' securities are often registered not in the name of the customer, but rather in the name of the brokerage firm or the central depository. Even so, the customer remains the real or beneficial owner.

Best-Efforts Underwriting. An offering of new stock in which the underwriter makes a "best effort" to place the issue but is not responsible for unsold portions.

Bid. The buy side of a quote. A quote is comprised of the highest *bid* (price at which someone is willing to buy) and lowest asked (price at which someone is willing to sell).

Big Board. A popular name for the New York Stock Exchange.

Blotter. Another name for a listing used in operations. A "blotter" usually carries trades and customer account numbers, segregated by point of execution.

Blotter Code. A system by which trades are identified by type and place of execution. The code enables firms to "balance" customer-street-side trades.

Blue Chip. A term used to describe the common stocks of corporations with the strongest of reputations. (In poker, the blue chip is usually assigned the highest money value.)

Blue Sky Rules. Security rules of the various states. If a new issue is being sold interstate and has a value of more than $1,500,000, it must be approved for sale in each state. This process is known as "blue skying."

Bond. A debt instrument; a security that represents the debt of a corporation, a municipality, the Federal government, or any other entity. A bond is usually long-term in nature—10 to 30 years.

Bond Anticipation Note (BAN). A short-term-term municipal debt instrument.

Book-Value. A Value computed by subtracting the total liabilities from the value of all assets on the balance sheet, then dividing by the number of common shares. This is an accounting term that has no relation to the securities market value.

Boston Stock Exchange (BSE). An equities exchange in Boston, Massachussetts.

Box. Another name for vault; where securities are maintained at the firm.

Breakpoint. A purchase of shares in an open-end investment company mutual fund that is large enough to entitle the buyer to a lower sales charge. A series of breakpoints is established by the fund, at each of which the charge is reduced.

British Pound Sterling. Aka GBP—currency of Great Britain.

Broker. (1) An individual who buys or sells securities for customers (a stockbroker).

(2) On an exchange, one who executes public orders on an agency basis (a floor broker or commission house broker).

(3) As a slang term, a firm that executes orders for others (a brokerage firm).

Broker's Call Rate. The rate that banks charge brokerage firms for the financing of margin accounts and inventory positions.

Brokerage Firm. A partnership or corporation that is in business to provide security services for a general marketplace.

BSE. *See* Boston Stock Exchange.

Bull. Someone who thinks that the value of the market or of a security will rise.

Bull Market. A market in which prices are generally rising.

Business District Conduct Committee. Part of the NASD that investigates, reviews, and renders a verdict on customer complaints or other industry improprieties.

Buy Close. An option transaction that reduces or eliminates a written position.

Buy Open. An option transaction that establishes or increases a "holder" or owners position.

Buying Power. In a margin account, the maximum dollar amount of securities that the client can purchase or sell short without having to deposit additional funds.

Call (Option). An option that permits the owner to buy a contracted amount of underlying security at a set price (strike or exercise price) for a predetermined period of time (up to the expiration date).

Callable. A securities feature that allows the issuer to retire the issue when desired. Should the issue be called, the issuer usually pays a premium.

Capital Gain. A trading profit. Trading gains that occur in six months or less are short-term capital gains; those that occur in periods longer than six months are long-term capital gains. Short-term and long-term capital gains are treated differently for tax purposes.

Capital Loss. A trading loss. Losses are long-or-short-term as are gains. *See* Capital Gain.

Capitalization. The total dollar value of all common stock, preferred stock, and bonds issued by a corporation.

Capital Stock. The common and preferred stock of a company.

Cash Account. A customer account in which all securities purchased must be paid for in full by the fifth business day, but no later than the seventh business day after trade.

Cash Dividend. Dividends that corporations pay, on a per-share basis, to stockholders from their earnings.

Cash Sale. A trade that settles on trade date and that is used in equities at the end of the year for tax purposes.

CBOE. *See* Chicago Board Option Exchange.

CBT. *See* Chicago Board of Trade.

CD. Canadian dollar—currency of Canada.

CEDEL. One of two major clearing entities in Europe.

Certificate. The physical document evidencing ownership (a share of stock) or debt (a bond).

Certificate of Deposit (CD). A short-term debt instrument issued by banks. CDs of large denominations are negotiable and can be traded in the secondary market.

CFTC. *See* Commodities Future Trading Commission.

Chaining. A method of settlement used by European clearing entities where shares and funds flow back and forth during the settlement cycle. Trading is "cleaned up" (settled) in date order and size within date. There isn't any netting.

Checking. Method of trade comparison used on the London Stock Exchange.

CHF. Swiss franc—currency of Switzerland.

Clearing Corporations. A central receiving and distribution center operated for its members, who are made up of various brokerage firms. Many offer automated systems that expedite comparison procedures. Among these are NSCC (National Securities Clearing Corp.) and OCC (Options Clearing Corporation).

Clearing House Comparison (CHC). A form used to submit traders to NSCC that have missed the normal entry methods. Such trades enter the system on the third business day of the trade cycle.

Chicago Board Option Exchange (CBOE). Listed option trading was originated by this marketplace on April 26, 1973.

Chicago Board of Trade (CBT). A major commodity exchange located at 141 East Jackson Boulevard, Chicago, Illinois.

Chicago Mercantile Exchange. A major commodity exchange in Chicago, Illinois.

Close End Fund. A fund whose offering of shares is closed. That is, once the initial offering is completed, the fund stops offering and acquiring its shares. The value of the shares is then determined by supply and demand, rather than by calculation of net asset value.

CME. *See* Chicago Mercantile Exchanges.

CMO. *See* Collateralized Mortgage Obligation.

CNS. *See* Continuous Net Settlement.

Collateral. An asset pledged to support a loan.

Collateralized Mortgage Obligation—CMO. A form of Asset Backed Securities that are securitized and issued in time sequences or tranches.

Collateral Trust Bond. A debt instrument issued by one corporation and backed by the securities of another corporation.

Combination Order. In listed options trading, an order to simultaneously buy or sell a put and a call, each having the same underlying security but different series designations.

COMEX. A commodity exchange located at 4 World Trade Center, New York, New York.

Commercial Paper. A short-term debt instrument issued by corporations.

Its rate of interest is set at issuance and can be realized only if held to maturity.

Commission. (1) The amount charged by a firm on an agency transaction. (2) The method by which account executives are compensated.

Commission House Broker. A floor broker who is employed by a brokerage house to execute orders on the exchange floor for the firm and its customers.

Commodities Future Trading Commission (CFTC). Responsible for the enforcement of rules and regulations of the futures industry.

Commodity Swap. An exchange between two parties, usually future for physical.

Common Stock. A security, issued in shares, that represents ownership of a corporation. Common stockholders may vote for the management and receive dividends after all other obligations of the corporation are satisfied.

Comparison. The process by which two contra brokerage firms in a trade agree to the terms of the transaction. Comparison can be either through a clearing corporation or on a trade-for-trade basis (that is, ex the clearing corporation).

Confirmation. A trade invoice, issued to customers of brokerage firms, that serves as written notice of the trade, giving price, security description, settlement money, trade and settlement dates, plus other pertinent information.

Continuous Net Settlement (CNS). The process by which a previous day's fail positions are included in the next day's settling positions.

Convertible Issue (Bond). A security's feature that permits the issue holder to convert into another issue, usually common stock. This privilege can be used only once. The preferred stock- or bondholder can convert from that issue to another, but not back.

Cooling-Off-Period. The period, usually 20 days, between the filing of the registration statement on a new issue with the SEC and the effective date of the offering.

Corporate Bond. A debt instrument issued by a corporation. It is usually fixed income, that is, it carries a fixed rate of interest. From issuance, the life of a bond may be as long as 30 years.

Credit Balance. The funds available to a client in a cash or margin account. In a short sale, this balance represents the customer's liability.

Cumulative Preferred. A preferred stock feature that entitles the holder to the later payment of dividends that were not paid when due. The dividends are, in this sense, "cumulative." The dividends accumulate and must be paid (along with present dividends) before common stockholders may receive any dividends.

Curb Exchange. An archaic name for the American Stock Exchange (Amex).

Currency Swap. The exchange of currencies between two parties. This is usually accomplished through borrowing by respective parties in their respective homeland and then swapping loans.

CUSIP. The Committee on Uniform Security Identification Procedure, an interindustry security coding service. Each type of security has its own unique CUSIP number.

Dated Date. The first day that interest starts to accrue on newly issued bonds.

Day Order. An order that, if not executed on the day it is entered, expires at the close of that day's trading.

Day Trade. The buying and selling of the same security on the same day.

DBO. *See* Delivery Balance Order.

Dealer. A firm that functions as a market maker and that, as such, positions the security to buy and sell versus the public and/or brokerage community.

Debenture Bond. A debt that is issued by a corporation and that is backed or secured by nothing but the good name of the issuing company.

Debit Balance. The amount of loan in a margin account.

Deed of Trust. *See* Indenture.

Delete of Compared. A form, as well as a process, used to delete trades that were compared by mistake through NSCC.

Delivery Balance Order (DBO). An order issued by the clearing corporation to any firm that, after the day's trades are netted, has a delivery or sale position remaining. The order defines what is to be delivered to whom.

Demand As-of. A form used in the NSCC OTC comparison system. Its purpose is to give a firm that is DKing a trade a last chance to accept the trade. After the DKing firm has turned down the demand as-of, the submitting firm is no longer obligated to accept the trade and can take other action.

Depository. A central location for keeping securities on deposit.

Depository Trust Company (DTC). A corporation, owned by banks and brokerage firms, that holds securities, arranges for their receipt and delivery, and arranges for the payments in settlement.

Depreciation. An account in which a firm writes off the declining value of machinery and equipment over the earning life of the equipment.

Designated Order Turnaround (DOT). An order routing and execution reporting system of the NYSE. Orders up to 599 shares may be entered by member firms through this system.

Differential. The fraction of a point added to the purchase price of, or subtracted from the sale price of, odd lot orders. The charge represents compensation to the dealer/specialist for executing the odd lot order.

Director. A corporate board member elected by the stockholders.

Discretionary Account. A client account in which the account executive is permitted to buy and sell securities for the client *without* the client's prior permission. The opening of such an account requires the special permission of the firm's management.

Discretionary Order. An order entered by the account executive for a discretionary account. The account executive decides on the security, quantity, and price.

Dividend. A portion of a corporation's assets paid to stockholders on a per-share basis. Preferred stock is supposed to pay a regular and prescribed dividend amount. Common stock pays varying amounts when declared.

DK. *See* Don't Know.

Dollar Cost Averaging. An investment method used in mutual funds by which clients invest the same dollar amount periodically. Because mutual funds permit the buying of fractional shares, all of the investor's payment is used in the acquisition of fund shares.

Do Not Increase (DNI). An instruction that informs order handling personnel not to increase the quantity of shares specified on the order in the event of a stock dividend. DNI is placed on buy limit, sell stop, and stop limit GTC orders.

Do Not Reduce (DNR). An instruction that informs the order handling personnel not to reduce the price of the order by the amount of dividends, if and when paid by the corporation. DNR is placed on buy limit, sell stop, and sell stop limit GTC orders.

Don't Know (DK). A term used throughout the industry meaning "unknown item." On the AMEX, the term applies to equity transactions that cannot be compared by the morning of trade date plus three business days. It is also used over-the-counter for comparison purposes.

DOT. *See* Designated Order Turnaround.

Double Taxation. Corporations pay taxes on revenue before paying dividends. The dividends, in the hands of the stockholder, are taxed again as ordinary income. Hence "double" taxation.

Downstairs Trader. A trader who operates on the floor of an exchange and who "trades" positions against the public market. *See also* Upstairs Trader.

Downtick. A listed equity trade whose price is lower than that of the last different sale.

DM. Deutsche mark—the currency of Germany.

DNI. *See* Do Not Increase.

DNR. *See* Do not Reduce.

DTC. *See* Depository Trust Company.

Due Bill. An IOU used primarily in the settlement of trades involved in dividend and split situations, when the security is unavailable for delivery.

Due Diligence Meeting. The last meeting between corporate officials and underwriters prior to the issuance of the security. At the meeting, the content of the prospectus is discussed, and relevant parts of the underwriting are put into place.

Earnings Report. A corporate financial statement that reports and nets out all earning and expenses to a profit or loss. It is therefore sometimes referred to as the profit and loss (P&L) statement.

Effective Date. The first date after the cooling-off period of a new issue that the security can be offered.

Equipment Trust Bonds. Debt instruments that are issued by some corporations and that are backed by "rolling stock" (such as airplanes or locomotives and freight cars).

Equity. The portion in an account that reflects the customer's ownership interest.

Escrow Receipt. A guarantee of delivery issued by a qualified bank to a clearing corporation, such as OCC, on behalf of the bank's customer. The member brokerage firm acts as a conduit for this document.

Euroclear. One of two major clearing entities in Europe.

Ex by Ex. A process by which "in the money" options about to expire are automatically exercised unless instructions are received to the contrary.

Ex-Dividend Date. The first day on which the purchaser of the security is not entitled to the dividend. It is also the day that price of the security drops to the next highest fraction of the dividend amount.

Exercise Price. *See* Strike Price.

Expense. Costs incurred in trying to obtain revenue.

Expiration Month. The month in which an option or futures contract ceases to exist (expires).

Face Value. The debt (or loan) amount that appears on the face of the certificate and that the issuer must pay at maturity.

Factor Table. A table used to compute the outstanding principal on Pass-Throughs—Ginnie Maes, Freddie Macs, and Fannie Maes.

Fail. A transaction that is not settled on the appropriate day.

Fail to Deliver. An unfulfilled commitment by a selling firm to deliver a security if the parties to the trade are unable to settle on the settlement date.

Fail to Receive. An unfulfilled commitment by a purchasing firm to receive a security that is not settled on settlement date.

Fast Automatic Stock Transfer (Fast). A service offered by DTC.

Fed Funds. Same-day money transfers between member banks of the Federal Reserve System by means of the Fed wire. These transfers are draw downs and loans of reserve deposits.

FF. French franc—currency of France.

Figuration. The computation of trades in the P&S department.

Fill or Kill (FOK). An order that requires execution of the entire quantity immediately. If not, the order is cancelled.

Fiscal Year. The twelve-month period during which a business maintains its financial records. Since this cycle does not have to coincide with the calendar year, it is known as the fiscal year.

Flat. A bond trading without accrued interest is said to be trading "flat."

Floor Broker. An exchange member who, as such, is permitted to conduct business on the exchange floor.

FOK. *See* Fill-or-Kill.

Foreign Exchange. *See* FOREX.

FOREX. Foreign Exchange is the trading of currencies against each other.

Forward. Basically an over the counter future. Whereas the terms of a futures product are fixed, the terms of a forward are generally negotiable making each contract nonfundable.

Free Stock. Loanable securities, that is, securities that can be used for loan or hypothecation. The securities are firm-owned shares or stock in a margin account that represents the debit balance.

Future. A contract that sets the price at the time of the transaction at which a delivery will be made at a later date.

Futures Contract. A long-term contract on an underlying instrument, such as a grain, precious metal, index, or interest rate instrument, by which the buyer and seller lock in a price for later delivery.

FX. *See* Forex.

GBP. Great British Pounds—currency of Great Britain.

General Obligation (GO) Bond. A muni bond whose issuer's ability to pay back principal and interest is based only on its full taxing power.

Gilts. Government Bonds of Great Britain.

GNMA. *See* Government National Mortgage Association.

GO. *See* General Obligation Bond.

Good-til-Cancelled (open) Order (GTC). An order that does not expire at the end of the day it is entered. Instead, it remains in force until it is either executed or cancelled.

Government National Mortgage Association (GNMA). A government corporation that provides primary mortgages through bond issuances. Its securities are called Ginnie Maes.

Growth Stock. Stock of a company in a new industry or of a company participating in an emerging industry.

GTC. *See* Good-til-Cancelled (open) Order.

Hypothecation. A brokerage firm's pledging of margin securities at a bank to secure the funds necessary to carry an account's debit balance.

ID System. *See* Institutional Delivery System.

Immediate-or-Cancel (IOC). An instruction on an order that requires as many lots as can be filled immediately and the rest cancelled.

Income Bonds. Bonds issued when the ability of the issuing company to pay interest is questioned. They are speculative instruments that pay high rates of interest.

Indenture. The terms of a corporate bond. Also known as deed of trust, it appears on the face of the bond certificate.

Industrial Revenue (ID Revenue, ID Revs, or industrial Rev) Bond. A form of muni bond whose issuer's ability to pay interest and principal is based on revenue earned from an industrial complex.

Institutional Delivery System. A service by Depository Trust Company (DTC) by which Broker/Dealers confirm and settle trades electronically.

Interest Rate Swaps. An exchange of interest rate payments between two parties. For example, fixed payment loan responsibilities for a floating rate.

Investment Banker. See Underwriter.

Issue. (1) The process by which a new security is brought to market. (2) Any security.

Kassenverein. Clearing and settlement facility for transactions occurring in Germany.

Legal Transfer. A type of transfer that requires legal documentation, in addition to the normal forms. Usually, in the name of a deceased person, a trust, or other third party.

Liability. Any claim against the corporation, including accounts payable, salaries payable, and bonds.

Limit Order. An order that sets the highest price the customer is willing to be paid or the lowest price acceptable. Buy orders may be executed at or below the limit price, but never higher. Sell orders may be executed at or above the limit price, but never lower.

Limited Tax Bond. A muni bond whose ability to pay back principal and interest is based on special tax.

Liquidation. (1) Closing out a position. (2) An action taken by the margin department when a client hasn't paid for a purchase.

Liquidity. The characteristic of a market that enables investors to buy and sell securities easily.

Listed Stock. Stock that has qualified for trading on an exchange.

Load. The sales charge on the purchase of the shares of some open-end mutual funds.

Loan Value. The amount of money, expressed as a percentage of market value, that the customer may borrow from the firm.

Long Position. (1) In a customer's account, securities that are either fully paid for (a cash account) or partially paid for (a margin account). (2) Any position on the firm's security records that has a debit balance.

LSE. London Stock Exchange.

Management Company. The group of individuals responsible for managing a mutual fund's portfolio.

Margin Account. An account in which the firm lends the customer money on purchases or securities on short sales. Customers must have enough equity in the account to pay for purchases by the fifth business day after trade or meet obligations that may be incurred immediately.

Margin Department. The operations department responsible for ensuring that customers' accounts are maintained in accordance with margin rules and regulations.

Mark-Down. The charge subtracted by a firm, acting as principal, from the price on a sell transaction.

Mark-to-Market. Process by which security position values are brought up to their current value. The customer may request the excess equity, or the firm may call for the deposit of additional funds. Either request is a "mark" to the market.

Mark-Up. The charge imposed by a firm, acting as principal, on a buy transaction.

Market Maker. Another term for dealer or specialist. In the interest of maintaining orderly trading, a market maker stands ready to trade against the public and therefore to make a market in an issue.

Market Order. An order to be executed at the current market price. Buy market orders accept the current offer, and sell market orders accept the current bid.

Maturity. The date on which a loan becomes due and payable—when bonds and other debt instruments must be repaid.

MBSCC. See Mortgage Backed Security Clearing Corp.

MCC. See Midwest Clearing Corporation.

Member. An individual who owns a membership (a seat) on an exchange.

Member Firm. A partnership or corporation that owns a membership on an exchange.

Merger. The combination of two or more companies into one through the exchange of stock.

Midwest Clearing Corporation (MCC). The clearing corporation of the Midwest Stock Exchange.

Minimum Maintenance. Established by the exchanges' margin rules, the level to which the equity in an account may fall before the client must deposit additional equity. It is expressed as a percentage relationship between debit balance and equity or between market value and equity.

Money Market Fund. A type of mutual fund that specializes in securities of the money market, such as T bills and commercial paper.

Money Market Instruments. Short-term debt instruments (such as U.S. Treasury bills, commercial paper, and banker's acceptances) that reflect current interest rates and that, because of their short life, do not respond to interest rate changes as longer-term instruments do.

Mortgage Backed Securities Clearing Corp. Responsible for comparing and clearing forward and TBA trades in Mortgage Backed Securities.

Mortgage Banker. An agent that facilitates the development of mortgage money by selling either whole mortgages or pooled mortgages into the market place.

Mortgage Bond. A debt instrument issued by a corporation and secured by real estate owned by the corporation (such as factories or office buildings).

MSRB. See Municipal Securities Rule Making Board.

Muni. Slang for municipal bond.

Municipal Bond. A long-term debt instrument issued by a state or local government. It usually carries a fixed rate of interest, which is paid semi-annually.

Municipal Note. A short-term debt instrument of a state or local government. Most popular are revenue, bond, and tax anticipation notes.

Municipal Securities Rule Making Board (MSRB). Establishes rules and regulations to be followed in the trading, dealings and customer relationships concerned in municipal securities.

Mutual Fund. A pooling of many investors' money for specific investment purposes. The fund is managed by a management company, which is responsible to adhering to the purpose of the fund.

National Association of Security Dealers (NASD). A self-regulating authority whose jurisdiction includes the over-the-counter market.

National Association of Security Dealers Automated Quotation Service (NASDAQ). A communication network used to store and access quotations for qualified over-the-counter securities.

National Securities Clearing Corporation (NSCC). A major clearing corporation offering many services to the brokerage community, including comparison of NYSE, AMEX, and over-the-counter transactions

Negative Interest. A process by which the seller pays the buyer interest that will accrue to the buyer by record date. Employed as bond nears its payment period.

Negotiable. A feature of a security that enables the owner to transfer ownership or title. A non-negotiable instrument has no value.

Net Asset Value (NAV). The dollar value of an open-end fund divided by the number outstanding fund shares. In an open-end fund quote, the NAV is the bid side, the offer side is the sales charges.

Net-by-Net. Originated at the Pacific Clearing Corp. (PCC), a method of merging fail positions into settling trades. This process greatly reduced the number of fails open on firms' books.

Net Worth. Part of the Balance sheet presentation. Assets – Liabilities = Net Worth. It is what belongs to the entity after liabilities are subtracted from assets.

New York Futures Exchange (NYFE). A commodities market located at 30 Broad Street, New York, New York, specializing in index futures.

New York Stock Exchange (NYSE). Located at 11 Wall Street, New York, New York, a primary market for buying and selling the securities of major corporations.

1933 Act. *See* Truth in Security Act.

1934 Act. *See* Securities and Exchange Act.

No-Load Fund. An open-end fund that does not impose a sales charge on customers who buy their shares.

Not Held (NH). An indication on an order that the execution does not depend on time; the broker or trader should take whatever time is necessary to ensure a good execution.

Notional. The amount of principal involved in a SWAP.

OBO. *See* Order Book Official.

OCC. *See* Options Clearing Corporation.

Odd Lot. A quantity of securities that is smaller than the standard unit of trading.

Open-End-Fund. A mutual fund that makes a continuous offering of its shares and stands ready to buy its shares upon surrender by the shareholders. The share value is determined by net asset value of the fund.

Option. A contract that entitles the buyer to buy (call) or sell (put) a predetermined quantity of an underlying security for a specific period of time at a preestablished price.

Option Class. The group of options, put or call, with the same underlying security.

Option Series. The group of options having the same strike price, expiration date, and unit of trading on the same underlying stock.

Options Clearing Corporation (OCC). A clearing corporation owned jointly by the exchanges dealing in listed options. OCC is the central or main clearing corporation for listed options. Options traded on any SEC-regulated exchange can be settled through OCC.

Order Book Official (OBO). An employee of certain exchanges who executes limit orders on behalf of the membership.

Order Room. An operations department responsible for monitoring pending orders, recording executions, maintaining customers' GTC orders, and resolving uncompared trades.

Ordinary Shares. In most other countries, their term for common stock.

Over-the-Counter Market. Comprised of a network of telephone and telecommunication systems over which unlisted securities and other issues trade. It is primarily a dealers' market.

Pacific Clearing Corporation (PCC). The clearing corporation of the Pacific Stock Exchange.

Pacific Stock Exchange (PSE). This exchange operates in San Francisco and Los Angeles.

Par. Face value.

Par Value. A value that a corporation assigns to its security for bookkeeping purposes.

P&S Department. *See* Purchase and Sales department.

Participant Trust Company. The depository for GNMA pass-through securities.

Participating Preferred. Preferred stock whose holders may "participate" with the common shareholders in any dividends paid over and above those normally paid to common and preferred stockholders.

Pass-Through Security. Instrument representing an interest in a pool of mortgages. Pass-throughs pay interest and principal on a monthly basis.

Penny Stocks. Extremely low-priced securities that trade over the counter.

Philadelphia Stock Exchange (PHLX). An equities and options exchange located in Philadelphia.

Point. A price movement of one full increment. For example, a stock rises one point when its price goes from 23 to 24.

Portfolio. The different securities owned in an account of a client. The more different securities are in the account, the larger the portfolio.

Pre-emptive Right. A right, sometimes required by the issuer's corporate charter, by which current owners must be given the opportunity to maintain their percentage ownership if additional shares of the same class are issued. Additional shares of the soon-to-be issued security is offered to current owners in proportion to their holdings before the issue can be offered to others. Usually one right is issued for each outstanding share. The rights a predeterminded cash amount are used to subscribe to the additional shares.

Preferred Stock. Stock that represents ownership in the issuing corporation and that has prior claim on dividends. In the case of bankruptcy, preferred stock has a claim on assets ahead of common stockholders. The expected dividend is part of the issue's description.

Preliminary Prospectus. See Red Herring.

Primary Market. (1) The initial offering of certain debt issues. (2) The main exchanges for equity trading.

Principal. A brokerage firm when it acts as a dealer and marks up a purchase price or marks down a sale price when reporting the execution.

Prospectus. A document that explains the terms of a new security offering—the officers, the outside public accounting firms, the legal opinion, and so on. It must be given to any customer who purchases new corporate and certain muni issues.

Proxy. A form and a process for voting via the mail, permitting stockholders to vote on key corporate issues without having to attend the actual meeting.

Proxy Fight. An attempt by a dissident group to take over the management of a corporation. The group sends proxies electing them to the board; the current management sends proxies favoring them. The shareholders cast their votes by selecting one proxy or the other.

PSE. See Pacific Stock Exchange.

PTC. See Participant Trust Company.

Public Offering Date. The first day the new issue is offered to the public, on or shortly after the effective date.

Put. An option that permits the owner to sell a standard amount of an underlying security at a set price for a predetermined period.

Questionable Trade (QT). A form used when an NYSE-originated trade cannot be compared by the morning of the trade date plus three.

Quote. The highest bid and lowest offer on a given security at a particular time.

RAN. *See* Revenue Anticipation Notes.

Receive Balance Order (RBO). An order issued by the clearing corporation to any firm with a long (or buy) position remaining after the day's compared trades have been netted. It states what will be delivered, what must be paid, and who is to deliver.

Receiver's Certificate. A certificate issued when a company is in financial trouble. Its purpose is to provide the company with funds to complete processing cycles so that more money can be obtained through its liquidation.

Record Date. The day that an individual must be the owner of record to be entitled to an upcoming dividend.

Red Herring. The preliminary prospectus. The name comes from the advisory that is printed on the face of the prospectus in red ink.

Redemption. The retiring of a debt instrument by paying cash.

Refunding. The retiring of a debt instrument by issuing a new debt instrument.

Registered Form. The recording of a security's ownership on the issuer's central ledger. Anyone delivering the security must prove that he or she is, in fact, the person to whom the security is registered.

Registered to Principal Only. A feature of a bond whose ownership is recorded on a central ledger and whose interest payments are made only when coupons are detached and cashed in. Payments are not automatically sent to the owner.

Registered Trader. A member of an exchange who is responsible for adding "liquidity" to the marketplace by purchasing or selling assigned securities from his or her inventory. Also known as competitive market makers or option principal members.

Registrar. A commercial bank or trust company that controls the issuance of securities.

Registration Statement. Document filed with the Securities and Exchange Commission (SEC) explaining an impending issue and pertinent data about the issuer. Based on the information provided, the SEC either permits or prevents the issue from being offered.

Reg T Excess. In a margin account, the amount by which the loan value exceeds the debit balance.

Regular Way Contract. The first contract sheet received from NSCC that contains compared, uncompared, and advisory data.

Regular Way Delivery. A type of settlement calling for delivery on the fifth business day after trade dates for stocks, corporate bonds, municipals. For government bonds and options, delivery is the first business day after trade.

Regulation A. A regulation governing the issuance of new securities.

Regulation T (Reg T). A federal regulation that governs the lending of money by brokerage firms to its customers.

Regulation U (Reg U). A federal regulation that governs the lending of money on securities by banks to their customers.

Rejected Option Trade Notice (ROTN). A procedure and form by which uncompared listed option trade is returned to broker who executed it for reconcilement.

Repurchase Agreement (Repo). An agreement used to finance certain government and money market inventory positions. The brokerage firm sells securities to the financing organization, with the agreement that the firm will repurchase them in the short-term future.

Restricted Account. As defined by Regulation T, a margin account in which the debit balance exceeds the loan value.

Revenue. Income earned or received by the entity.

Revenue Anticipation Note (RAN). A short-term debt instrument that is issued by municipalities and that is to be paid off by future (anticipated) revenue.

Revenue Bond. A muni bond whose issuer's ability to pay interest and principal is based on revenue earned from a specific project.

Right. *See* Pre-emptive Rights.

Risk Arbitrage. The simultaneous purchase and sale of different securities in anticipation of a merger or tender offer.

Round Lot. A standard trading unit. In common stocks, 100 shares make up a round lot. A round lot of bonds in the over-the-counter market is 5 bonds.

Rules of Fair Practice. Part of the NASD rules that govern the dealings of firms with the public.

SCCP. *See* Stock Clearing Corporation of Philadelphia.

SEAQ. London Stock Exchange's computerized trading system.

Secondary Market. The market in which securities are traded after the initial (or primary) offering. Gauged by the number of issues traded, the over-the-counter market is the largest secondary market.

Securities and Exchange Act (The 1934 Act). The Act governing the lending of money by brokerage firms (Reg T), including the short-sale (uptick) rule, and requirements regarding insiders or control led persons.

Securities and Exchange Commission (SEC). The federal agency responsible for the enforcement of laws governing the securities industry.

Securities Industry Automated Corporation (SIAC). The computer facility and trade processing company for NYSE, AMEX, NSCC, and PCC.

Segregation. The isolation of securities that the firm may not use for hypothecation or loan. The securities, which must be "locked up" by the firm, represent fully paid-for securities or the portion of a margin account in excess of loanable securities.

Sell Close. An option transaction that reduces or eliminates a holder's position.

Sell Open. An option transaction that establishes increases a writer's position.

Selling Against the Box. A short sale in which the client is also long the security. The tactic is used to "box" a profit or loss for application at another time.

Serial Bonds. An issue of bonds that matures over a period of years.

Settled Inventory. The portion of a trader's position that the firm has paid for and maintains. This is the portion that must be financed.

Settlement Date. The day when a transaction is to be completed. On this day, the buyer is to pay and the seller is to deliver.

Settlement Date Inventory. The total of all positions in a security on settlement date, including vault, transfer, fails, and elsewhere.

Short Account. Account in which the customer has sold securities not owned or does not intend to deliver against sale. Before a customer may sell short, a margin account must be opened.

Short Exempt. A phrase used to describe a short sale that is exempt from the short sale rules. For example, buying a convertible preferred, submitting conversion instructions, and selling the common stock before the stock is received.

Short Position. (1) A position in a customer's account in which the customer either owes the firm securities or has some other obligation to meet. (2) Any position on the firm's security records having a credit balance.

Short Sale. The sale of securities that are not owned or that are not intended for delivery. The short seller "borrows" the stock to make delivery with the intent to buy it back at a later date at a lower price.

SIAC. *See* Securities Industry Automated Corporation.

Size. The number of shares available in a quote. For example, if the quote and size on a stock is 9 1/4—1/2 3 x 5, it means that the bid is 9 1/4, the offer is 9 1/2, 300 shares are bid, and 500 shares are offered.

Specialist. A member of certain SEC-regulated exchanges who *must* make a market in assigned securities. Specialists also act as two-dollar brokers in executing orders entrusted to them.

Spread. (1) A long and short option position in either puts or calls on the same underlying stock but in a different series. (2) The difference between the bid and offer sides of a quote. (3) In underwriting, the difference between what the issuer receives from the underwriter and what underwriter sells the security for to the public on the offering.

Standard Margin. A term used in futures products which specifies the minimum amount a client must deposit per contract bought or sold.

Stock. A Security that represents ownership in a corporation and that is issued in "shares."

Stock/Bond Power. A form used as substitute for endorsement of a certificate. When completed and attached to the certificate, the security can be processed for delivery or transfer.

Stock Clearing Corporation of Philadelphia (SCCP). The clearing corporation of the Philadelphia Stock Exchange.

Stock Dividends. A dividend paid by corporations from retained earnings in the form of stock. The corporation declares the dividend as a percentage of shares outstanding.

Stock Loan/Borrow. Part of the cashiering function, this operation's department is responsible for lending excess seg stock and obtaining stock when needed by the firm.

Stock Record. A ledger on which all security movements and positions are recorded. The record is usually in two formats: One shows movements of the security the previous day, and the other shows the current security positions.

Stock Splits. The exchange of existing shares of stock for more newly issued shares from the same corporation. Since the number of shares outstanding increase, the price per share goes down. Splits do not increase or decrease the capitalization of the company, just redistribute it over more shares. The effect is the adjustment to the trading price.

Stop Order. A memorandum order that becomes a market order when the price is reached or passed. Buy stops are entered above the current market price; sell stops are entered below it.

Stop Limit Order. This order is similar to a stop order, but it becomes a limit order instead of a market order. Buy stop limit orders are entered above the current market; sell stops are extended below it.

Straddle. Simultaneous long or short positions of puts and calls having the same underlying security and same series designation.

Street Name. A form of registration in which securities are registered in the name of a brokerage firm, bank, or depository; it is acceptable as good delivery.

Side. The opposing, or contra, firm's side of trades. For example, customer agency transactions consummated on an exchange must be offset and balanced against the "opposing firm" or street side reports.

Strike (Exercise) Price. The price at which an option can be exercised. For example, the owner of a call ABC April 40 can call in (buy) 100 shares of ABC at 40; the strike price is 40.

Supplement Contract. A contract issued by the clearing corporation that includes total of the regular way contract, adjustments made through advisories, and adds by seller processing.

SWAPS. The exchange between two parties of currency, interest payments of commodities.

Syndicate. The group that is formed to conduct an underwriting and that includes the underwriting manager and other underwriters.

Takeover. The acquisition of control over a corporation by another company, which normally ousts the current management. The takeover can occur by means of a proxy fight or the acquisition of a controlling quantity of common stock.

Tape. A broadcasting facility which disseminates listed trades in order of their occurrences.

Tax Anticipation Note (TAN). A municipal note issued in anticipation of revenues from a future tax.

Tax Exempt Bonds. Municipal securities (whose interest is free from federal income tax).

TBA. To be announced. A forward type trade sold by a Mortgage Banker consisting of a pool of mortgages being formed. The unique pool number that will be assigned to this pool has not been announced.

Tender Offer. The offer made by one company or individual for shares of another company. The offer may be in the form of cash or securities.

Trade Date. The day a trade occurs.

Trade Date Inventory. A term used by trading departments to mean the total of all positions of a security at the start of the trading day.

Trade-for-Trade-Settlement. A form of settlement in which the buying clearing firm settles a trade directly with the selling firm. It excludes the use of any netting, CNS, or clearing system.

Tranche. Part of CMO issue with a fixed maturity date. A pool of debt is sectioned and sold with different maturities. Each "maturity" is a tranche.

Transfer. The process by which securities are reregistered to new owners. The old securities are cancelled and new ones issued to the new registrants.

Transfer Agent. A commercial bank that retains the names and addresses of registered securities owners and that reregisters traded securities to the names of the new owners.

Trial Balance. An accounting procedure whereby all cash balances are brought forward to determine that all cash entries were properly posted.

Truth in Security Act (1933 Act). A federal regulation governing the issuance of new corporate securities. This Act also covers certain municipal securities and mutual funds.

Two-Dollar Broker. An exchange member who executes orders from other member firms and charges a fee for each execution.

Underlying. (1) The security behind an option (2) The commodity underlying a futures contract.

Underwriter (Investment Banker). In a municipal underwriting, a brokerage firm or bank that acts as a conduit by taking the new issue from the municipality and reselling it. In a corporate offering, the underwriter must be a brokerage firm.

Underwriting. The process by which investment bankers bring new issues to the market.

Underwriting Manager. (1) In a negotiated underwriting, the investment banker whose client is the corporation wanting to bring out a new issue. (2) In a competitive underwriting, the lead firm in a group that is competing with other group(s) for a new issue.

Uniform Practice Code. Part of the NASD rules that govern the dealing of firms with each other.

Unit. At issuance, a "package" of securities, such as a bond and warrant, which become separable at a later date.

U.S. Treasury Bill (T Bill). The shortest-term instrument issued by the federal government. The maturities of these discounted issues do not exceed one year at issuance, with three-month (90-day) or six-month (180-day) paper being very common.

U.S. Treasury Bond (T Bond). The longest-term debt of the federal government, issued in coupon form for period of 10 to 30 years.

U.S. Treasury Notes (T Notes). An intermediate debt instrument of the federal government, issued in coupon or interest rate form and usually for 1 to 10 years.

Uptick. A listed equity trade at a price that is higher than that of the last sale.

Variation Margin. Daily mark to the market on clients' future contract positions.

Warrant. A security that allows the owner to purchase the issuing corporation's stock for a certain price over a stated period. That period could be 10 or 20 years, and the price of the conversion is much higher than the current price of stock issue. A warrant is usually issued with another security, such as one warranty plus one bond, both of which form one *unit*.

When Issued (WI). A phrase applied to securities that are about to be issued and whose settlement date is not set. Usually common stock issued under a rights offering trades "WI." Also, government bills auctioned on Tuesday but settled on Thursday trade in this manner.

Yen. Japanese yen—currency of Japan.

Yield. The rate of return on an investment. There are as many computations as there are different yields, such as current yield and yield-to-maturity.

Index

Accounting, 377-87
balance sheet, 379-80, 383; brokerage accounting, 383-86; debits/credits, 378; 15c3-3 report, 387; focus report, 387; journal ledger, 380-81; ledger accounts, 381-83; profit and loss statement, 379-80, 383; reporting, 387; trial balance, 383
Account maintenance, margin department, 84
Accruals, 104
Accrued interest:
bonds, 66-68
accounting for, 402
corporate bonds, 178-79
Activity statement, margin, 339-41
Add by seller, 314
Added trade contracts, 305, 317-18
Adds, 271
Adjustable rate bonds, 184
Adjustable rate preferred stock, 170
Adjusted trial balance, 104-5
Adjustments for dividends, 269-70
Affirmations, 441
Agency transaction, 27, 307-8
Agents, 34
All-or-none, 19
All-or-none (AON) orders, 60, 268
American Stock Exchange (AMEX), 36, 46, 68, 128, 272, 281
Amex option switching system (AMOS), 281; DKs (don't knows), 297; hand-signal system, 46; post-execution reporting (PERS), 281; specialists, 40
Amex option switching system (AMOS), 281
Arbitrage, 189-90
Arbitrage firms, 94
Arbitrageurs, 169, 189
As-of trades, 318, 327-28
and securities, 399
Asset-backed securities, 213-21, 254, 322
collateralized mortgage obligations (CMOs), 218-20; modified pass-throughs, 216-18; mortgage banker, role of, 215; real estate mortgage investment conduits (REMICs), 220; standbys/calls, 220-21; TBA (to be announced), 215-16
Assets, 105
At the market shares, 43
Auction, U.S. Government securities, 209
Auction market, 42, 161
Automation, exchanges, 281
"Away from" orders, 40

Bad delivery, 91
Balance blotters, 69
Balanced takeoff, 399
Balanced trades, 68
Balance sheet, 105-6, 379-80, 383
Balloon maturity, 202
Bankers' acceptances (BAs), 150-51, 226-27, 254, 436-37
trading, 227; use importing, 226-27
Bank loans, 92-93
commercial banks, 93
Banks, 145-52
bankers' acceptances (BAs), 150-51, 226-27, 254, 436-37; cashiering, 151-52; commercial loans/paper, 149-50; loans, 145-48; reserve requirements, 227; underwritings, 148-49
Basic order information, 57
Basis pricing, 30-32, 203-5
current yield, 30-31; municipal securities, 30-32; nominal yield, 30; over-the-counter (OTC) market, 30-32; U.S. government securities, 30-32; yield to maturity, 31
Bearer bonds, 91, 402, 445
Bearer certificates, 182
Beneficial owners, 92, 161-62
Best efforts underwriting, 19
Bidding procedure, competitive underwriting, 20-21
Bid (purchase) price, 32
Bids, 12
Block trading firms, 47-48
Blotter code, 289
Blue List, 28
Blue skying the issue, 11
Bond anticipation notes (BANs), 206-7
Bond interest calculations, 461-63
Bond price, corporate bonds, 176-80
Bond room, NYSE, 281
Bonds, 7, 17, 20, 36, 156, 172-85, 445
accrued interest, 66-68
accounting for, 402
dividends, 401-2; yield, 30-31, 177-78
Bond security, corporate bonds, 181-82
Bond units, municipal securities, 233-34
Booking, purchase and sales (P&S), 72, 328-29
BOSS (Boerson Order Service System), 456
Boston Stock Exchange (BSE), 36, 281
Bounced stock, 91
Breakpoints, 232-33
Brokerage accounting, 383-86
Brokerage firm margin requirements, futures, 242-43
Brokerage firms, 148, 160-61
choosing, 7; commission, 27; manufacturing phase in, 54; organization of, 53-54
Brokers, 34

AMEX, 46; CBOE, 47; futures, 242; over-the-counter (OTC) market, 34
Broker's call rate, 93
Bundes bonds, 253
Business Conduct Committee, NASD, 27
Business ownership:
corporation, 5-6; partnership, 4-5; proprietorship, 4
Buy-backs, 94
Buying open, 298
Buying power, 80-81, 331-32
Buy stop orders, 59

CAC system, 475
Callable bonds, 181
Callable preferred stock, 167
Call options, 236
Calls, 220-21
Cancel (CXL) confirmation, 322
Cash account purchases, 74-75
Cash accounts, 75, 120-23, 406-8
margin purchases vs., 74-75
Cash contracts, 244
Cash dividend cycle, 399-400
Cash dividends, 111-12, 113
common stock, 160; ex-dividend date (ex-date), 114, 400; record date, 399-400
Cash flow summary, 143
Cashiering, 89-95
banks, 151-52
bank loan, 368-70
customer-side settlement, 361-62; defined, 89; delivery, 362-66
delivery vs. payment (DVP), 362; ID system, 362-66
good deliverable form, 91; hypothecation, 92-93; receive and deliver, 90-91, 356-61;
continuous net settlement (CNS), 356-57; Depository Trust Company (DTC), 357-58; illustrative comparison, 359-61; netted balance orders, 358-59; trade-for-trade settlement, 359
reorganizations, 95, 373; spin-offs, 376; stock loan, 94; tender offers, 373-76; transfer, 94-95, 370-73
individual vs. standing instructions, 371; legal transfer, 371; regular transfer, 370-71; transfer agent, 372-73
vaulting, 92, 366-68
segregated (seg) securities, 366-68
Cashiering services, commercial banks, 438-42
Cash settlement, 327
Cash-settling options, 302-3
Cedel, 460-61
Central Clearing and Settlement System (CCASS), 459
Certificate:
common stock, 158-59; preferred stock, 164-65; rights, 190-93; warrants, 190-93
Certificates of deposit (CDs), 228-29, 255, 434-35
defined, 228; delivery, 435; interest, 229; issuance of, 434; trading, 229; types of, 229, 434
Chicago Board of Options Exchange (CBOE), 36, 47, 68, 235, 282-83, 297
Chicago Board of Trade (CBT), 36, 285
Chicago Mercantile Exchange (CME), 36, 285
Children's accounts, 409-18
prudent man guidelines, 130, 418
Clearing corporation margin requirements, futures, 242-43
Clearing facilities, 69-70
Clearing house comparison (CHC), 317-18
Clearing house funds, 151
Clipping coupons, 402
Closed-end funds, 231-32
Closed-end mortgage bonds, 181-82
Close-outs, margin department, 85-86
Closing activities, order room, 271
Codes, 65
Collateral:
commercial banks, 427-28
account of pledge (AP), 428; book entry delivery, 427-28; physical delivery, 427
Collateralized mortgage obligations (CMOs), 218-20
planned amortized certificate (PAC), 219; residual, 220; tranches, 218-20
Z tranches, 219
Collateral loans, 93, 225
Collateral trust bonds, 182
Combination orders, 60
Combos, 346
COMEX, 284, 351, 352
Commercial banks, 145
banker's acceptances (BAs), 436-37; brokerage firms, use of, 449; cashiering services, 438-42; collateral, 427-28
account of pledge (AP), 428; book entry delivery, 427-28; physical delivery, 427
as customers of brokerage firms, 448-50; as dividend disbursing agent (DDA), 443-47; international trade, role in, 436-37; inventory accounts, 426; as issuer of commercial paper/loans, 431-35; lines of credit, 426-27; loans from, 93; margin debt balances, 423-24; market price movement, 424-25; order execution, 449; pledged securities, monitoring value of, 424-25; portfolio managers, 448; positive carry, 426; as source of financing, 423-28; trading activity, 425; as underwriters, 429-30
settlement, 430; vaulting, 430
Commercial loans, 149, 172
Commercial paper, 149-50, 172, 222-25, 254, 432-33
acquiring, 433; certificates, handling, 224; defined, 222-23; financing, 225; issuance, 223; issuing, 432-33; maturity,

Commercial paper *(cont.)*
225; retiring, 434; settlement, 223-24; trading, 223; vaulting, 433
Commission, 22, 27
Commission house brokers, 37, 281
Commodities future merchant (CFM), 353
Commodity futures (commods), 36
Common stock, 7, 17, 155, 157-62, 443-44
cash dividends, 160; certificate, 158-59; dividends, 160; as investment vehicle, 162; over-the-counter (OTC) market, 161; trading, 161-62; underwriting, 160-61; voting, 157-60
Community property state, forms required by, 125
Comparison (reconcilement), 68-70, 293-304, 307-29; equities comparison, 304; futures comparison, 303-4; manual procedure, 69; options comparison, 293-303; over-the-counter trades comparison, 321
Comparison tickets, 321
Competitive underwriting, 20-21, 206-7
bidding procedure, 20-21; negotiated agreements compared to, 21
Compliance, 128-32
customer complaints, 131; registered principals, responsibilities; of, 130-31; registration requirements, 128-29; reporting, 131; stockbrokers and customer accounts, 129-30
Computer systems, 135-40
computer languages, 137-38; data, 137; defined, 136; executive programs, 136; hardware, 136-37; logic, 136; processing programs, 136; routines, 137-38; software, 137; subroutines, 137-38; types of, 138-40
mainframes, 138-39; microcomputers, 140; minicomputers, 139-40
Concession, 22
Confirmation, purchase and sales (P&S), 328-29
CONSOB (Commissione Nazionale per le; Societe a la Borsa), 458
Continuous net settlement (CNS), 356-57, 360-61
Contract sheets, 69, 309-10
Conversion, bonds, 181
Conversion rate, 168
Convertible bonds, 181
Convertible preferred stock, 168-69
Cooling-off period, 11-12
Corporate bonds, 172-85, 254
accrued interest, 178-79; bond price, 176-80; bond security, 181-82; collateral trust bonds, 182; coupon rate, 177; debenture bonds, 182; equipment trust bonds, 182; features, 183-85; adjustable rate bonds, 184; callable, 183-84; convertible, 184; sinking fund, 185; zero-coupon bonds, 184; hedging, 173-76; income bonds, 183; indenture, 180; interest payments, 176-79; interest rate, 173, 179-80; leverage, 173; mortgage bonds, 181-82; ratings, 180; receiver's certificate, 183; registration, 182-83; retiring, 181; trading of, 176
Corporate registrar, 113, 162
Corporate resolution, 125
Corporate securities, 16-19, 155-62
bonds, 7, 17, 20, 36, 156, 172-85; common stock, 7, 17, 155, 157-62; notes, 172-85; preferred stock, 17, 155, 163-71; shareholders, 156; state of incorporation, 16, 155
Corporations, 5-6
Coupon bonds, 91
Coupon rate, 177
Coupons, 200-201
Covered option position, 341
Credit balance, 78
Credits/debits, 378
Cum rights, 189
Cumulative preferred stock, 169-70
Currency, 251-54, 255
Currency options, 303
Current market value, 78-79
Current yield, 30-31
bonds, 177-78
CUSIP number, 289
Custodial agreements, 125
Customer configurations, EDP, 142
Customer's confirmation, 70-72
Customer-side settlement, 361-62

Daily activity run, 390-92
Daily cash record, 96, 101-8
accounts, establishing, 101-3; dual-entry bookkeeping, 103-4; uses of, 104-8;
adjusted trial balance, 104-5; balance sheet, 105-6; illustrative case, 106-8; profit and loss (P&L) statements, 105; trial balance, 104
Daily trading limits, futures, 244
Data entry, EDP, 142
Data processing manager, 140-41
Dated date, 292
Day orders, 264
Dealers, 27, 34
over-the-counter (OTC) market, 34
Dealer's broker, 205-6, 280
Debenture bonds, 182
Debit balance, 78-79, 123
defined, 76
Debits/credits, 378
Declaration date, 110
Deed of trust, 180
Deliver balance orders (DBOs), 358-59, 360
Delivery, 362-66
cashiering, 362-66
delivery versus payment (DVP), 362; ID system, 362-66
certificates of deposit (CDs), 435; futures, 244, 349-51; securities, 86
Delivery versus payment (DVP), 362, 440, 460

Depository Trust Company (DTC), 357-58, 440-41, 446-47
Deutsche Terminborse (DTB), 456-57
Direct placement, 223
Direct solicitation, mutual funds, 23
Dirty stock, 91
Discount form, commercial paper, 150
Dividend and Interest Compliance Act (1983), 124
Dividend department, 397-402
Dividend disbursing agent (DDA), 113, 114, 162, 399
Dividend rate, preferred stock, 167
Dividends, 109-16
  balanced takeoff, 399; bonds, 401-2; cash dividends, 111-12, 113, 399-400; common stock, 160; defined, 109; dividend cycle, 109-11
    declaration date, 110; payable date, 111, 114; record date, 110, 113-14
  dividend department, duties of, 113-15; ex-dividend date, 111-12, 114-15
    cash dividend, 114; due bills, 115; stock dividends over 25%, 114-15; stock splits, 114-15
  interest, 115-16; preferred stock, 166; and securities in transfer, 399; source of, 109; stock dividends, 112, 400-1
    due bills, 401; less than 25%, 400; more than 25%, 400-1
  stock record, balancing, 397-99; stock splits, 112-13; vaulted securities, 397-98
DKs (don't knows), 297, 321, 442
DNR (do not reduce), 111, 270
Dollar rate, 166
Domestic CDs, 229
Do not increase (DNI) instruction, 270
Do not reduce (DNR), 111, 270
DOT (designated order turnaround) system, 46, 281, 312
Dual-entry bookkeeping, 103-4
Dually listed securities, 36
Due bills, 115, 401
Due diligence meeting, 11-12
Dumping an issue, 12-13
Dutch auction, 22

Earnings report, 105
Effective date, 12
Electronic accounting machines (EAMs), 136
Electronic data processing (EDP), 133-44
  balancing, 142; cash flow summary, 143; computer systems, 135-40; customer configurations, 142; data entry, 142; data processing manager, 140-41; figuration, 142; in-house computer function, 140-41; margin calculations, 142-43; P&S listing, 142; processing sequence, 142-43; reports produced, 133-35
    daily, 133-34; weekly, 134
  service bureaus, 141; stock records, 143
Equipment trust bonds, 182
Equities comparison, 304
Equity, 78-79
  defined, 76
Equity options, 237
Euroclear, 460-61
Eurodollar CDs, 229, 434
Ex by ex (exercise by exception), 303
Exception report, 87
Excess, 80-81
Excess equity, 330-31
Exchanges, 35-48, 161, 280-85
  automation, 281; futures, 284-85; types of, 35-36
Ex-dividend date (ex-date), 111-12, 114-15, 116, 400
  cash dividends, 114, 400
Execution report, 61
Expiration date, options, 235
Extensions, 85, 353
Ex the clearing corporation, 326

Factor tables, 217-18, 322
Family of funds, 23
Farmers Home Administration (FmHA), 213-15
Fast Automatic Stock Transfer (FAST); service, 446-47
Federal Home Loan Mortgage Corporation; (FHLMC) (Freddie Mac), 219, 322
Federal Housing Authority (FHA), 213-15
Federal National Mortgage Association; (FNMA/Fannie Mae), 22, 322
Federal Reserve Board (Fed), 21-22, 75-76, 208-9
  book entry system, 211; Regulation T (Reg T), 77-78
Fed funds, 151, 431
Fed wire, 151, 224, 438-40
Fiduciary accounts, 130
15c3-3 report, 387
Figuration, purchase and sales (P&S), 66-68, 142, 289-93
Fill-or-kill (FOK) orders, 60, 268
Final prospectus, 8, 10
Financial and Operational Combined Uniform Single (Focus) Report, 387
Financial institution number system (FINS); number, 440
Finder, defined, 94
Firm quotes, 29, 277
First money, 278
Fixed income securities, 166
Floor brokerage fees, 328-29
Floor-derived executions, 311-14
Focus report, 387
Ford Credit Corporation (FCC), 149
Foreign currency options, 239
Foreign exchange (forex market/FX market), 251
Formal offering, mutual funds, 23
France, settlement, 457-58
Frankfurt Stock Exchange, 456-57
Free (non-seg) securities, 369
Free stock, 93

Freimaklers, 456
Freiverkehr, 456
Full power of attorney, 124, 418
Fully registered bonds, 182-83, 401-2
Futures, 241-44, 254, 255, 347-53
  brokers, 242; comparison, 303-4; daily trading limits, 244; delivery, 244, 349-51; exchanges, 284-85; futures contract: origin of, 241; value of, 241-42
  long position, 242; margin, 242-43, 347-53
    brokerage firm margin requirements, 242-43; clearing corporation margin requirements, 242-43; comparison, 352-53; confirmation, 352-53; delivery, 349-51; maintenance margin, 348; making to the market, 348-49; settlement, 351-52; standard margin, 243, 348; variation margin, 243
  rejected trade notices (RTN), 242; settlement, 242; short position, 242; traders, 242
Futures comparison, 303-4

General obligation bonds, 206
General partners, 5
General Motors Acceptance Corporation (GMAC), 149
German Bundes bonds, 253
Germany, settlement, 456-57
Good deliverable form, 91
Good-til-canceled (GTC) orders, 131, 264-65, 269-70, 271; confirmation of, 61
Government agency securities, 22
Government dealers, 21
Government National Mortgage Asociation (GNMA), 213, 322
GTC (good-til-canceled) orders, 264-65; confirmation of, 61
Guaranteed coupon, 217

Hand-signal system, 46
Hardware, computer, 136
Hedging, 173-76
Hong Kong, settlement, 459-60
Hot issue, 12
Housing and Urban Development (HUD), 213
Hypothecation, 92-93

IBIS (Interbank Information System), 457
Immediate-or-cancel (IOC) orders, 268
Income bonds, 183
Income statements, 105
Index options, 238-39, 302
Indications of interest, 8
Individual cash accounts, 120-23
Individual instructions, 371
Individual proprietorship, 4
Industrial revenue bonds, 206
In-house computer function, 140-41
Initial public offering (IPO), 7
Inside quotes, 278
Institutional (block) sale, 47-48
Institutional Delivery System (ID system), 362-66, 440-42
Intercurrency swaps, 248-49
Interest:
  certificates of deposit (CDs), 229; dividends, 115-16
Interest payments, corporate bonds, 176-79
Interest rate, corporate bonds, 173, 179-80
Interest-rate swaps, 246-48
Intermarket trading system, 281
International settlement, 453-63
  bond interest calculations, 461-63; Cedel/Euroclear, 460-61; France, 457-58; Germany, 456-57; Hong Kong, 459-60; Italy, 458; Japan, 458-59; United Kingdom, 453-55
Inventory accounts, commercial banks, 426
Investment habits, 10
ISB (Inter Societes de Bourse), 457
Italy, settlement, 458

Japan, settlement, 458-59
Joint accounts, 123-24, 409
Joint tenants with rights of survivorship; (JTROS), 123, 409
Journal ledger, 380-81
Jumbo certificate, 446-47

Known pool, 217
Know your customer rule, 129
Kursmakler, 456

Layoff/laying off the new issue, 19
LEAPS, 237
Ledger accounts, 104, 381-83
Legal transfers, 371
Lending agreement, 123, 409
Leverage, 173
Liabilities, 105
Limited partners, 5
Limited power of attorney, 124, 418
Limited tax bonds, 206
Limit orders, 40, 59, 263-64, 312
Lines of credit, commercial banks, 426-27
Liquidity, over-the-counter (OTC) market, 25-26
Listed options, 236-37, 282-84
  customer orders, 284; firm orders, 284; floor, 282; market makers, 284; open/close, 284; order execution, 282-84; rotation, 282
Listed securities, 35, 161
Load funds, 232-33
Loans, 145-48
  inventory positions, 145-47; margin loans, 147-48
Loan value, 79-80; defined, 76
Locked-in executions, 311-14
Locked-in trade, 312

Logic, computer, 136
London Stock Exchange (LSE), 453-55
gilts, 454-55; Talisman system, 454; Taurus system, 454
Long coupon, 292

Mainframes, 138-39
Mainline activities, 358
Maintenance call, 82
Maintenance margin, futures, 348
Making markets, 40, 161
Manager, syndicate group, 195
Manufacturing firm:
administration/support, 53; manufacturing/production, 52-53; marketing, 51-52; sales, 52
Margin, 73-88, 330-54
activity statement, 339-41; buying power, 80-81, 331-32; cash account vs. margin purchases, 74-75; current market value, 78-79; debit balance, 78-79; equity, 78-79; excess, 80-81; extensions, 353; futures, 242-43, 347-53; loan value, 79-80; margin accounts, 76-77; margin department, 73, 84-86
account maintenance, 84; clearance for issuance of checks, 84; close-outs, 85-86; delivery of securities, 86; extensions, 85; items due, 84-85; typical day in, 86-88
margin rate, 76, 77; minimum maintenance, 81-82, 332-35, 336
working illustration, 333-35
option margin, 341-47; Regulation T (Reg T), 77-78;
excess, 330-31
restricted accounts, 82-83, 238; short sale, 335-38; special miscellaneous (memorandum) account (SMA), 83, 338-39
Margin accounts, 76-77
opening, 123, 408-9
Margin agreement, 123, 408-9
Margin calculations, 142-43
Margin (credit) department, 73-88
Margin debt balances, commercial banks, 423-24
Margin department, 73, 84-86
Margin loans, 147-48
Mark-down, 278
Market contracts, 244
Market makers:
CBOE, 47; over-the-counter (OTC) market, 27-28
Market-maker trades, 307
agency transaction, 307-8; systematized comparisons, 309-11; trade-for-trade comparisons, 308-9
Market orders, 59, 312
Mark to the market, 336, 349
Mark-up, 278; over-the-counter (OTC) market, 27-28
Master file, customer, 122
Maturity, commercial paper, 225
Member banks, 151
Memory, computer, 136
Message switch programs, 138
Microcomputers, 140
Microfilm, 122
Midwest Stock Exchange (MSE), 36, 281
Minicomputers, 139-40
Minimum maintenance requirement, 81-82, 147, 332-35, 336
Missed transfer, 444
Modified pass-throughs, 216-18
Money managers, 93
Money market funds, 234
Money market instruments, 227
Mortgage Backed Security Clearing Corp. (MBSCC), 310, 322-24
Mortgage banker, role of, 215
Mortgage bonds, 181-82
Multitraded securities, 281-82
Municipal bonds (munis)/notes, 194-207, 254
balloon maturity, 202; basis pricing, 203-5; bond anticipation notes (BANs), 206-7; competitive underwriting, 206-7; coupons, 200-1; dealer's broker, 205-6, 280; general obligation bonds, 206; illustration of, 196-99; industrial revenue bonds, 206; limited tax bonds, 206; offering of, 195-202; and OTC market, 279; project notes (PNs), 206; revenue anticipation notes (RANs), 206-7; revenue bonds, 206; secondary market, 203; tax anticipation notes (TANs), 206-7; tax rates, effect of, 202; trading, 202-3; types of, 206-7
Municipal securities, 19-21
basis pricing, 30-32; bond units, 233-34
Mutual funds, 22-23, 230-34, 255
closed-end funds, 231-32; defined, 22, 230; getting shares to market, 23; load funds, 232-33; money market funds, 234; net asset value vs. market value, 231-32; no-load funds, 233; open-end funds, 231; purpose of, 230

National Association of Securities Dealers (NASD), 13, 26-27, 29, 128, 129, 130
SOES, 312-13
National Association of Security Dealers Automated Quotations (NASDAQ), 29, 276-77
levels, 276
National Securities Clearing Corporation; (NSCC), 69-70, 309-10, 356, 358, 360
National stock exchanges, 36
Negotiable CDs, 434
Negotiated underwriting, 7, 161, 166
Negotiated underwriting, example of, 13-15
Net asset value (NAV), 231; market value vs., 231-32
Net balance, 323-25
Netted balance orders, 358-59
Net worth, 105

New accounts, 120-27, 406-19
cash accounts, 120-23, 406-8; children's accounts, 409-18; joint accounts, 123-24, 409; maintaining, 418-19; margin accounts, 123, 408-9; new account forms, 121-22; power of attorney accounts, 124, 418; recordkeeping, 125-26
New issues, 18
New trades, order room, 270-71
New York Futures Exchange (NYFE), 286
New York Stock Exchange (NYSE), 36, 37-46, 68, 128, 130, 272, 280-81; auction market, 42; bond room, 281; clearing the floor, 44; commission house brokers, 37, 281; crowds, 41-42; display book, 46; DOT (designated order turnaround) system, 46, 281, 312; floor of, 38; illustrative comparison, 305-7; making markets, 40; memberships, prices of, 37; order execution, 40-41
parity, 44; precedence, 43-44; priority, 42-43; QOTNs (questionable option trade notices), 297; registered floor traders, 41, 281; round lots, 42-43; Rules 431-432, 77; seats on, 37; specialists, 40, 280-81; specialist's book, 40, 44-46; telephone booths, 41; trading language, 42; trading posts, 41-42; two-dollar brokers, 37-40, 281
Next business day, 326
Next-day money, 361
Night processing staff, order room, 259-60
No-load funds, 233
Nominal yield, 30
Nominee name, 92
Nominee registration, 162
Noncallable preferred stock, 167
Noncumulative preferred stock, 169
Non-negotiable CDs, 434
Notes, 20, 172-85
Not-held (NH) orders, 268
Nothing done (ND) response, 271
Notionals, 246

Odd lots, 161, 272
Offer (sale) price, 32
"Off" orders, 40
OKTP (OK to pay), 84
Old issues, 18
One cancels other (OCO) orders, 60
On-line comparison, 312
Open-ended mortgage bonds, 181
Open-end funds, 231
Option Clearing Corporation (OCC), 239-40, 295-303
Option exchange, 36
Option margin, 341-47
Options, 235-40, 255
call options, 236; covered option position, 341; defined, 235; equity options, 237; expiration date, 235; foreign currency options, 239; index options, 238-39; listed vs. OTC options, 236-37; on currency, 253-54; Option Clearing Corporation (OCC), 239-40; owner/holder, 235; put options, 236; reject option trade notice (ROTN), 239; settlement, 239-40; strike price, 235, 236; trading, 236-39; Treasury bills, 237-38; Treasury bonds, 238; Treasury notes, 238; underlying security, 235; writer, 235
Options comparison, 293-303
Option Clearing Corporation (OCC), 295-303; ROTNs, 295
Order book officials (OBOs), CBOE, 47, 282-83
Order department tasks, 60-63; GTC orders, confirming, 61; pending orders, organization of, 61-63; reconcilements, 60-61
Order execution:
commercial banks, 449; NYSE, 40-41
parity, 44; precedence, 43-44; priority, 42-43
Order match computer system, 313
Order room, 55-63, 259-73
adds, 271; adjustments for dividends, 269-70; basic order information, 57; closing activities, 271; do not increase (DNI) instruction, 270; do not reduce (DNR) instruction, 270; new trades, 270-71; night processing staff, 259-60; nothing done (ND) response, 271; odd-lot orders, 272; order form, 260-62; outs, 271; over-the-counter (OTC) market, 275; problem trades, resolving, 268-69; time instructions, 264-65; types of orders, 57-60, 262-68
all-or-none (AON), 268; day orders, 264; fill-or-kill (FOK) orders, 268; good-til-canceled (GTC) orders, 264-65, 269-70, 271; immediate-or-cancel (IOC) orders, 268; limit orders, 40, 59, 263-64; market orders, 59, 262-63; not-held (NH) orders, 268; short sales, 265; stop limit orders, 60, 267; stop orders, 59, 266-67
Outs, 271
Out trades, 295, 311
Over-the-counter (OTC) market, 25-34, 274-87
basis pricing, 30-32; Blue List, 28; bonds in, 279-80; brokers/dealers, 34; common stock, 161; flexibility of, 274-75; inventory, 276; liquidity, 25-26; listed options, 282-84
customer orders, 284; firm orders, 284; floor, 282; market makers, 284; open/close, 284; order execution, 282-84; rotation, 282
market makers, 27-28; market makers' inventories, 32-34; mark-up, 27-28; National Association of Securities Dealers (NASD), 26-27; National Association of Security Dealers Automated Quotations (NASDAQ), 276-77; nature of, 26-

27; and order room, 275; OTC options, 282; Pink Sheets, 28; quotations, 28-30
firm quotes, 29; subject (nominal) quotes, 30; types of, 277-78; work-out quotes, 30
Over-the-counter trades comparison, 321

Pacific Clearing Corp., 297
Pacific Stock Exchange (PSE), 36, 281, 297
Parent company, 376
Parity, 168
Participating preferred stock, 170
Partnership agreements, 5
Partnerships, 4-5
Payable date, dividends, 111, 399-400
PDQ system, 358, 361
Pending orders:
defined, 61; organization of, 61-63
Pending tape, 142
Philadelphia Stock Exchange (PHLX), 36, 281
Pink Sheets, 28
Planned amortized certificate (PAC), 219
Pledged securities, commercial banks, 424-25
Plus interest form, commercial paper, 150
Portfolio managers, 448
Positive carry, 426
Post-execution reporting (PERS), 281; AMEX, 281
Posting journal entries, 381-83
Pot, 14
Power of attorney accounts, 124, 418
Preemptive rights, 17-18, 188
Preferred stock, 17, 155, 163-71, 444
certificate, 164-65; defined, 163; dividends, 166; underwriting, 166-70
adjustable rate preferreds, 170; callable feature, 167; convertible feature, 168-69; cumulative preferreds, 169-70; dividend rate, 167; noncallable preferreds, 167; noncumulative preferreds, 169; participating preferreds, 170; putable preferreds, 170; self-liquidating preferreds, 170
Preliminary prospectus, 8, 9
Premium, 12, 204
Primary dealers, U.S. Government securities, 209
Prime lending rate, 149
Principal, 20, 27, 34, 64
Principal trades, 307
Priority prorata, 46
Privately held corporations, 6
Private sector, 16
Problem trades, resolving, 268-69
Profit and loss (P&L) statements, 105, 379-80, 383
Programs, computer, 136
Projection report, 356, 358
Project notes (PNs), 206
Proprietor, 4
Proprietorship, 4
Proxies, 117-19; forwarding procedure, 403-5
Proxy fight, 119
Prudent man guidelines, 130, 418
Publicly held corporations, 6
Public offering, 160
Public offering date, 12
Purchase and sales (P&S), 64-72
accrued interest, 66-68; added trades/added trade contracts, 317-18; as-of trades, 318, 327-28; blotter code, 289; booking, 72, 328-29; clearing facilities, 69-70; codes, 65; comparison (reconcilement), 68-70, 293-304, 307-29
equities comparison, 304; futures comparison, 303-4; manual procedure, 69; options comparison, 293-303; over-the-counter trades comparison, 321
confirmation, 328-29; CUSIP, 289; customer's confirmation, 70-72; figuration, 66-68, 289-93; floor brokerage fees, 328-29; floor-derived/locked-in executions, 311-14; market-maker trades, 307
agency transaction, 307-8; systematized comparisons, 309-11; trade-for-trade comparisons, 308-9
mortgage-backed securities, 322; net balance, 323-25; principal trades, 307; recording, 64-65, 288; regular-way trades, 322-23; settlement, 326-27
cash settlement, 327; next business day, 326; regular way, 326; seller's/buyer's options, 327
supplemental contracts, 314-17; through/ex the clearing corporation, 326; trade number, 289
when-issued (WI) transactions, 325-26
Pure auction, 22
Putable preferred stock, 170
Put options, 236

QOTNs (questionable option trade notices), 297
Quasi-fiduciary accounts, 130
Questionable trade (QT) form, 314, 316, 321
Quotations:
firm quotes, 29; inside quotes, 278; over-the-counter (OTC) market, 28-30; subject (nominal) quotes, 30; types of, 277-78; work-out quotes, 30

Ratings, corporate bonds, 180
Real estate mortgage investment conduits (REMICs), 220
Receive and deliver, 90-91, 356-61
continuous net settlement (CNS), 356-57; Depository Trust Company (DTC), 357-58; illustrative comparison, 359-61; netted balance orders, 358-59; trade-for-trade settlement, 359

Receive balance orders (RBOs), 358, 360
Receiver's certificate, 183
Receiver versus payment (RVP), 440
Reconcilement, 68-70
See also Comparison (reconcilement)
Record date, 110, 399-400
cash dividends, 399-400
Recording, purchase and sales (P&S), 64-65, 288
Redemption, bonds, 181
Red herring, 8
Refunding, bonds, 181
Regional exchanges, 36
Registered floor traders, NYSE, 41, 281
Registered issues, 161-62
Registered representatives, 128-29
Registered securities, 86
Registered to principal only bonds, 182, 401
Registration, corporate bonds, 182-83
Registration statement, 8
Regular transfer, 370-71
Regular way contracts, 305
Regular-way settlement, 326
Regular-way trades, 322-23
Regulation T (Reg T), 77-78, 147
excess, 330-31
Rejected trade notices (RTN), 242, 311
Reject option trade notice (ROTN), 239, 295, 311
Reorganizations, 95, 373
Reporting, 387
Repurchase agreements (repos), 94
Reserve requirements, banks, 227
Residual, 220
Restricted accounts, 82-83, 238
Retained earnings, 107-8
Retiring:
commercial paper, 434; corporate bonds, 181
Revenue anticipation notes (RANs), 206-7
Revenue bonds, 206
Reverse splits, 112
Rights, 186-90, 254
certificate, 190-93; cum rights, 189; as securities, 18; theoretical value of, 188
Round lots, 42-43, 161, 272
Rule of thumb formula, yield to maturity, 31, 203-4
Rules 431-432, 77
Rules of Fair Practice, NASD, 26
Running an inventory, 32

Same Day Funds (SDF), 324
Same-day money, 361
SCCP (Stock Clearing Corporation of Philadelphia), 297
SEAQ, 453-54
Seats, NYSE, 37
Secondary market, municipal bonds, 203
Securities:
and as-of trades, 399; distributing, 12; in fails, 398; issuance by corporation, 16-19; issuance by municipalities, 19-21; issuance by the public, 23; mutual funds, 22-23; rights as, 18; in transfer, 399; U.S. Government securities, 21-22
Securities and Exchange Commission (SEC), 8-11, 21, 330
Segregated (seg) securities, 93, 147-48, 366-68
Self-liquidating preferred stock, 170
Self-regulatory organizations (SROs), 128
Selling group, 11
Selling open, 298
Sell stop orders, 59
Sending the comparison, 321
Service bureaus, 141
Settled positions, 146
Settlement:
commercial banks, 430; commercial paper, 223-24; futures, 242, 351-52; options, 239-40; purchase and sales (P&S), 326-27
cash settlement, 327; next business day, 326; regular way, 326; seller's/buyer's options, 327
U.S. Government securities, 211
Settlement blotters, 69
Settlement date positions, 146
Shareholders, 156
Shopping an order, 30
Short coupon, 292
Short position, 242
Short sales, 265
and margin, 335-38
SIAC (Security Industry Automation Corporation), 297
SICOCAM (French Central Depository), 458
Signature cards, customers, 122
Silent partners, 5
Sinking fund, 181, 185
Software, computer, 136
Sole proprietorship, 4
Specialists, 40
AMEX, 46; NYSE, 40, 280-81
Specialist's book, 40, 44-46
Special miscellaneous (memorandum) account (SMA), 83, 338-39
Spin-offs, 376
Spot contracts, 244
Spread, 14
Spread orders, 60
Stabilizing the market, 12-13
Stamps, 308-9
Standard margin, futures, 243, 348
Standbys, 220-21
Standby underwriting, 18-19
Standing instructions, 371
State of incorporation, 16, 155
Stock, 6, 254
Stockbrokers, 128-29
Stock Clearing Corporation of Philadelpha, 310
Stock dividends, 112, 400-1
common stock, 160; due bills, 401; less than 25%, 400; more than 25%, 400-401

Stock Exchange of Hong Kong (SEHK), 459-60
Stock exchanges, *See* Exchanges
Stock loan, 94
Stock record, 96-100, 143, 388-96
account numbering/coding, 98-99
numbering system, 389-90
audits, 99-100; balancing, 394-95, 397-99; breaks, 98, 394; daily activity run, 390-92; memo fields, 395; weekly stock record, 390, 393
Stock splits, 112-13, 114-15
Stop limit orders, 60, 267
Stop orders, 59, 266-67
Straddle orders, 60
Straddles, 346
Street name, 162
registration of securities in, 370
Street-side positions, 113
Strike price, options, 235, 236
Strips, 211
Subject (nominal) quotes, 30, 277
Subscription price, 17-18
Subscription rights, *See* Rights
Supplemental contracts, 305, 314-17
Swaps, 245-50, 255
brokers, 246; intercurrency swaps, 248-49; interest-rate swaps, 246-48; notionals, 246; rate, 246
Syndicate group, 7-11
manager, 195
Systematized comparisons, 309-11

Tax anticipation notes (TANs), 206-7
TBAs/forwards, 215-16
TBA (to be announced), 215-16, 322
Telephone booths, NYSE, 41
Tenant by the entirety, 123
Tenants in common, 123-24, 409
Tender offers, 373-76
Term, 20
Through the clearing corporation, 326
Time instructions, 264-65
Tokyo Stock Exchange (TSE), 458-59
order routing systems, 459; regular members, 458; saitori members, 458-59
Trade-for-trade comparisons, 308-9
Trade-for-trade settlement, 359
Trade number, 289
Traders, 27
futures, 242
Trading:
bankers' acceptances (BAs), 227; certificates of deposit (CDs), 229; commercial paper, 223; common stock, 161-62; corporate bonds, 176; municipal bonds, 202-3; options, 236-39; U.S. Government securities, 211
Trading activity, commercial banks, 425
Trading language, NYSE, 42
Trading positions, 146
Trading posts, NYSE, 41-42
Tranches, 218-20
Transfer:
cashiering, 94-95, 370-73
individual vs. standing instructions, 371; legal transfer, 371; regular transfer, 370-71; transfer agent, 372-73
Transfer agents, 94-95, 113, 162, 372-73, 445-47
instructions to, 372, 374-75
Treasury bills (T bills), 209, 210
options written on, 237-38
Treasury bonds (T bonds), 209, 211
options written on, 238
Treasury notes (T notes), 209, 211
options written on, 238
Treasury securities, 21-22
Treasury strips, 211
Trial balance, 104, 383
Trust agreements, 125
Truth in lending agreement, 409
Two-dollar brokers, 37-40, 46, 281

Uncollateralized loans, 93
Underlying security, options, 235
Underwriting group, *See* Syndicate group
Underwriting procedure, 7-13
cooling-off period, 11-12; distributing the security, 12; investment banker, choosing, 7; stabilizing the market, 12-13; syndicate, 7-11
Underwritings, 16-24
all-or-none, 19; banks, 148-49
corporate issues, 148; municipals, 148-49
best efforts underwriting, 19; common stock, 160-61; corporate securities, 155-62; preferred stock, 166-70; securities, reasons for, 3-6; standby underwriting, 18-19
Uniform Practice Code, NASD, 26
United Kingdom, settlement, 453-55
U.S. Government securities, 21-22, 254
auction, 209; basis pricing, 30-32; Federal Reserve Board (Fed), 21-22, 75-76, 208-9; government agency securities, 22; primary dealers, 209; settlement, 211; trading, 211; Treasury securities, 21-22, 254
Treasury bills (T bills), 209, 210; Treasury bonds (T bonds), 209, 211; Treasury notes (T notes), 209, 211; Treasury strips, 211

Variation margin, futures, 243
Vaulted securities, 397-98
Vaulting, 92, 366-68
commercial banks, 430; commercial paper, 433; segregated (seg) securities, 366-68
Veterans Administration (VA), 213-15
Voting, common stock, 157-60

Warrants, 190-93, 254
certificate, 190-93; defined, 190; illustration of, 191-92
Weak issues, 12

Weekly stock record, 390, 393
When-issued (WI) transactions, 325-26
Window ticket, 372
Winning the bid, 20
Wire houses, 98
Wires, 135
Work-out quotes, 30
Writer, options, 235

Yankee CDs, 229, 434
Yield, bonds, 30-31, 177-78
Yield to maturity, 31

Zero-coupon bonds, 184
Z tranches, 219